DIS ⌖ Y0-DYT-406

JUL – 8 2025

Asheville-Buncombe
Technical Community College
Learning Resources Center
340 Victoria Road
Asheville, NC 28801

Transition to democracy

Edited by
The International Institute for Democracy

03-1759

Council of Europe Publishing

DISCARDED

Cover design: Graphic Design Workshop, Council of Europe
Council of Europe Publishing
F-67075 Strasbourg Cedex

ISBN 92-871-3356-5
© Council of Europe, 1997
Printed in Germany

Acknowledgement

The International Institute for Democracy is grateful to the European Commission for Democracy through Law for having put at our disposal the translations into English of a number of the constitutions included in this volume.

Asheville-Buncombe
Technical Community College
Learning Resources Center
340 Victoria Road
Asheville, NC 28801

Contents

Introduction

The International Institute for Democracy has decided to present in this new volume the texts of thirteen Constitutions of member states of the Commonwealth of Independent States, former republics of the Union of Soviet Socialist Republics (USSR)[1]. It was deemed appropriate to add the Mongolian Constitution, although Mongolia is not part of the CIS, because it used to have close ties with the USSR. Furthermore, some of these states have already joined the Council of Europe, and others aspire to membership.

In the aftermath of the collapse of the Union, each of these republics, many of them virtually created during the Soviet period, acquired all the attributes which symbolise the independent state, i. e. a flag, a national anthem, an emblem, but also the main one, a constitution to organise state power within society. Belarus is an exception in that it adopted two constitutions, the first passed by the Supreme Soviet in March 1994, the second, mainly intended to strengthen the powers of the President, adopted in a referendum in November 1996. It thus seems logical to reproduce both constitutions in their entirety.

The approval by referendum on 12 December 1993 of the Constitution of the Russian Federation[2] effectively opened up a new political, legal, economic and social era for Russia. Unlike the Soviet Constitutions of the past, the 1993 text enshrines a pluralist, democratic form of government based upon the republic, sovereignty of the people and the separation of powers. Where democratic principles are concerned, Article 1 of the Constitution lays down that "the Russian Federation/Russia is a democratic federative law-based state with a republican form of administration". The Constitution also states that the "multinational people of the Russian Federation is the bearer of sovereignty and the sole source of power within the Russian Federation" and that a "referendum and free elections are the highest direct expression of people's power" (Articles 3 (1) and 3 (3)). Citizens have the right to vote and to stand for election (Article 32 (2)). The principle of the separation of powers is laid down in Article 10 of the Constitution, which differs completely from the old Soviet Constitution of 1977, under which the organisation and activities of the Soviet state conformed to the principle of democratic centralism (under Article 3 of the 1977 Constitution). Lastly, political pluralism and a multi-party system are solemnly recognised in Article 13 (3), which thus differs from previous Constitutions through the dropping of the principle of the

---

1. The Constitution of Tajikistan is not included in this volume, as no official version in English was available at the time of going to press.

2. 58.4% of the votes cast were in favour and 41.6% against, turnout being 54.8%.

communist party's monopoly on representation. The inalienable and indefeasible rights of people and citizens, together with people's freedoms, are guaranteed in accordance with the universally recognised rules of international law (Article 17 (1) and 17 (2)).

The 1993 Constitution sets up a state governed by the rule of law and based on compliance with the Constitution (Article 15 (1)). The guardian of observance of the Constitution is the Constitutional Court. Article 2 of the Constitution in fact states that "the individual and his rights and freedoms are the highest value" and that "recognition, observance and protection of rights and freedoms of man and citizen is an obligation of the state". Individuals are regarded as individual entities and may therefore enjoy the rights and freedoms enshrined in all 47 articles of Chapter 2. The state is made responsible for creating the conditions for dignity of the individual and for fostering the free development of individuals.

In contrast to Soviet Constitutions of the past, the Russian Constitution does not require citizens to fulfil fundamental obligations and duties. Respect for their rights is guaranteed through the action of the Constitutional Court, comprising 19 judges, which, as well as settling disputes between federal organs and "subjects" relating to powers, verifying the constitutionality of legislation, of normative enactments of the President and of international treaties (Article 125 (2)), and interpreting the federal Constitution (Article 125 (5)), examines complaints about the "violation of constitutional rights and freedoms of citizens". The Russian Constitution draws in this context on the system of direct applications for rulings by Germany's Federal Constitutional Court (Article 93 (4a) of the Basic Law of 23 May 1949).

The Constitution is nevertheless marked by a strong presidential domination to the detriment of parliament, the powers of which are very much reduced. The President has significant powers, enabling him to dominate every aspect of institutional life. He simultaneously holds all the prerogatives of both the French and the American Presidents. Elected by direct universal suffrage for a four-year term, he is at one and the same time head of state and head of the executive. As head of state he is "the guarantor of the Constitution of the Russian Federation and of the rights and freedoms of man and citizen" (Article 80 (2)) and "determines the basic guidelines of the state's domestic and foreign policy" (Article 80 (3)). He also plays a large part in the functioning of the executive. The government is subject to his authority, the ministers responsible for maintaining order are directly subordinate to him, and he has significant powers of appointment. Inter alia, he appoints and removes from office, on proposals from the Prime Minister (Chairman of the Government), the Deputy Prime Ministers and the federal ministers.

The President and government are also allowed to intervene in the legislative and regulatory procedure. The President's power to introduce legislation is recognised, but, in particular, he has the right to veto legislation, a veto which can only be overridden by the Federal Assembly by a two-thirds majority. What is more, under Article 90 of the Constitution, the President may issue edicts and resolutions, which may not contravene the Constitution or federal laws. The Government of the Russian Federation issues decrees and orders "on the basis of and in implementation of the Constitution of the Russian Federation, federal laws and normative edicts of the President" (Article 115 (1)). However, on account of both the inefficiency of the legislature and the government's subordination to the President, the President may easily supplant both the Federal Assembly and the government.

Elected for a four-year term, the State Duma (lower house of parliament) and the Council of the Federation (upper house) form the Russian Federal Assembly. While the Federal Assembly does have considerable powers, it is unable to play the role of counterweight that it should have, so great are the President's prerogatives. The State Duma has legislative and budgetary powers; it is also able to initiate the procedure for removing the President of the Federation, to resolve the question of confidence in the government (Article 103 (1)) and to give its consent to the appointment of the Prime Minister by the President (Article 103 (1) (a)). It may also express lack of confidence in the government through a vote of censure requiring an absolute majority of Duma members. In the event of a no confidence vote, the President of the Federation has either to announce the dismissal of the government or to express disagreement with the State Duma's decision. Should the State Duma pass a no confidence vote again within three months, the President of the Federation may either dismiss the government or dissolve the Duma. Similarly, the Prime Minister may decide to ask the State Duma to express its confidence in the government, and if the Duma passes a no confidence vote against the government, the President either dismisses the government or dissolves the chamber within seven days.

It will hardly come as a surprise that such an institutional imbalance also exists in the constitutions of the other republics of the former USSR. Not being homogeneous nations, these republics first faced the need to create, or to strengthen existing, national sentiment, in order to ensure their political stability. This is why the constitutions adopted in 1992 by Turkmenistan, in December 1992 by Uzbekistan and in May 1993 by the Republic of Kyrghyzstan declare the language of the dominant ethnic group to be the official language. Furthermore, none of the constitutional texts of Kazakhstan, Uzbekistan, the Republic of Kyrghyzstan, Georgia and Ukraine recognise dual nationality. As for Turkmenistan, it took the risk of discomfiting the other republics and recognised dual nationality.

These republics' constitutions also include a very solemn affirmation of the principles of pluralist democracy. They all declare the people to be sovereign and the sole source of power. They grant individual rights to citizens, but the arrangements for guaranteeing these rights are not really effective. Some constitutions provide for more rights than others. Azerbaijan, for instance, a state which declares that the supreme aim of the state shall be to ensure human and civil rights and freedoms (Article 12 of the Constitution), gives a relatively long list of these rights. In contrast, Turkmenistan's Constitution lists fewer such rights, on the pretext that political stability has to be safeguarded and order maintained in the country. Sometimes, in wording reminiscent of the past, these rights are accompanied by obligations incumbent on citizens (see, for example, Articles 47 to 52 of the Uzbekistan Constitution).

The constitutions also advocate the separation of powers and a multi-party system. The separation of powers is taken to mean a simple division of executive, legislative and judicial bodies, but never a separation of functions. Some constitutions even, while affirming the separation of powers, go so far as to give the President the power to appoint judges, examples being those of Turkmenistan (Article 102) and Uzbekistan (Article 93 (11)); this hardly meets the requirements of the principle so dear to Montesquieu. Political pluralism is enshrined in the constitutions, but, particularly in the central Asian republics, it is thwarted by the continuing dominance of each republic's social and political life by clans, tribes, villages and families, impeding the play of political forces along the lines followed in the traditional democracies.

In fact, the opposition is usually sidelined or even suppressed. And it is very often an increase in the numbers of government parties which creates an illusion of democracy. Where the opposition has been able to take power, it has been overthrown immediately. One example of this is the Popular Front in Azerbaijan, which took power in 1992, only to lose it again shortly afterwards, in 1993. Another is the coalition between Muslims, democrats and nationalists in Tajikistan. Where the opposition has been able to take power, it has done so thanks to an internal crisis: very severe nationalist tensions in Tajikistan, and the war against the Armenians in the case of Azerbaijan.

The constitutions set up atypical forms of government which cannot be described as parliamentary or presidential. They are always marked by an overriding presidential influence. The constitutions of Turkmenistan and Belarus, for instance, describe the form of government that they introduce as a "presidential republic", a form which, in these specific cases, is also intensified by the personality cult attached to the elected Presidents. Only the President of Kyrghyzstan, Askar Akayev, who was elected to office in 1991 and re-elected in December 1995, has refused to rely on a strong presidential system.

As in Russia, the Presidents are simultaneously heads of state and heads of government, giving them significant powers. As heads of state they decide on the nation's policy, both domestic and foreign, and represent their states in foreign relations. They head governments, the members of which are in principle appointed by them, in some cases subject to parliamentary approval. They also have the power to introduce legislation and are allowed to request a second reading of legislation in parliament. In most cases, they have the power to veto any law not to their liking, a veto which can be overridden only by a two-thirds majority or more. They may also issue decrees which have the force of law, enabling them to make good any inefficiency of the legislature, and they hold full powers in the event of an emergency. Obviously they also have the power to dissolve parliament.

There is always a single or two-chamber parliament, its main functions being to pass legislation and the budget and to monitor the activities of the government. Some parliaments can pass votes of no confidence in the government or vote on the criminal liability of the President. Truth to tell, parliaments disguise the authoritarianism which exists in this form of government. Sometimes the very existence of a parliament strengthens the illusion that political decisions are not taken solely by the President, but with the people's wisdom, by which the president's initiatives are transformed into real domestic and foreign policy.

Are these constitutions not, as some people have claimed, just formal documents intended for the future? The adoption of new constitutions has already made it possible to break away from the practices which tied a country's fate to a single person or a single political party. Proper use of these constitutions should make it possible to take a decisive step forward in the quest for democracy.

General chronology
of the Soviet Union

1988

December 1: The Supreme Soviet amends the 1977 Constitution, establishing a new parliament and replacing the USSR Supreme Soviet by the Congress of People's Deputies. Of the 2 250 deputies, 750 will be elected by 32 official "social organisations" and 1 500 deputies by popular vote, of which 750 by single-member *territorial* constituencies and 750 by single-member *national-territorial* constituencies, organised to represent the Soviet Union's ethnic groups. From among its own members the congress will elect a bicameral 542-member Supreme Soviet.

1989

March 26: First round of Congress elections is held and 1 225 of the 1 500 seats are filled by direct constituency elections.

April 9: In 76 constituencies, where in March no candidate had polled the necessary absolute majority of votes, a second round of elections is held between the two best-placed candidates

April 25: The Communist Party Central Committee approves the retirement of 74 of its full members and 24 of candidate members, representing the conservative opposition to the reform plans.

May 14: A fresh round of Congress elections is held in 199 constituencies (where the process of nominating and selecting candidates had to begin all over again). The general election resulted in a defeat for a number of senior officials. Boris Yeltsin won 89.44% of the votes in the Moscow national-territorial constituency.

May 25: The Congress elects Mikhail Gorbachev as Chairman of the USSR Supreme Soviet, i.e. State President, by 2 123 votes against 87 votes and 11 abstentions.

May 26: Election of the new Supreme Soviet.

May 29: The Congress elects Anatoly Lukyanov as First Deputy Chairman of the Supreme Soviet by 1 934 votes to 179 with 137 abstentions.

June 7: The Supreme Soviet re-elects Nikolai Ryzhkov as Prime Minister.

July 27-28: 300 radical deputies establish an independent group within the Congress, under collective leadership of Boris Yeltsin, Andrei Sakharov, Yury Afanasyev, Gavriil Popov and Yury Palm.

October 24: The Supreme Soviet passes, by 254 votes to 85 with 36 abstentions, an amendment to the constitutional reforms adopted in 1988, providing for the abolishing of reserved seats for the CPSU and social organisations in the USSR Congress of People's Deputies.

December 12: The Congress debates on repealing Article 6 of the Soviet Constitution, a clause confirming the Communist Party of the Soviet Union

(CPSU) as the "leading and guiding force in soviet society and the nucleus of its political system", resulting in 839 votes to 1 138 with 56 abstentions.

1990

February 5: At a meeting of the CP central committee Gorbachev announces a new draft party policy, embodying the renouncement of the CPSU constitutionally guaranteed monopoly of power, clearing the way for a multiparty system.

February 7: The draft party policy is adopted with only Boris Yeltsin's vote against, arguing that the reforms do not go far enough.

March 13: The Congress votes, with 1 771 votes to 164 and 74 abstentions, to amend article 6 of the 1977 USSR constitution, abolishing the CPSU guaranteed monopoly of political power. It approves by 1 817 votes to 133 with 61 abstentions the creation of the post of President of the USSR.

March 15: The Congress elects Mikhail Gorbachev, by 1 329 votes to 495 with 54 invalid votes, as President of the USSR and swears him in immediately afterwards.

April 3: The Supreme Soviet passes a new law on "procedures for resolving matters connected with a union republic's secession from the USSR". A republic may secede subject to a referendum.

June 23: The Moldovan Supreme Soviet adopts a declaration, proclaiming the sovereignty of the Moldovan state.

July 12: Boris Yeltsin resigns his party membership.

August 23: The Armenian Supreme Soviet adopts a declaration, proclaiming that the Republic of Armenia is a sovereign state.

October 24: The Supreme Soviet adopts a law, reaffirming the supremacy of All-union Republican Laws, within the Union's competence.

December 20: Edward Shevardnadze, Foreign Minister since 1985, announces his resignation.

December 24: The Congress adopts by 1 605 votes to 54 with 86 abstentions a resolution approving a draft of the Union Treaty, providing for the distribution of power and republican rights within the USSR.

1991

January 14: The Supreme Soviet approves the nomination of Valentin Pavlov as Prime Minister.

March 17: An all-union referendum is held on the preservation of the USSR. Armenia, Georgia, Moldova and the Baltic States boycott the referendum. General turnout 80%. The results by each of the participating republics were:

Azerbaijan 93.3% in favour, 5.8% against, turnout 75.1%; Byelorussia 82.7% in favour, 16.1% against, turnout 83.3%; Kazakhstan 94.1% in favour, 5% against, turnout 88.2%; Kyrghyzstan 94.6% in favour, 4% against, turnout 92.9%; the Russian Federative Republic 71.3% in favour, 26.4% against, turnout 75.4%; Tadjikistan 96.2% in favour, 3.1% against, turnout 94.4%; Turkmenistan 97.9% in favour, 1.7% against, turnout 97.7%; Ukraine 70.2% in favour, 28% against, turnout 83.5%; Uzbekistan 93.7% in favour, 5.2% against, turnout 95.4%.

April 9: The Georgian Supreme Soviet adopts unanimously a formal declaration of "the restoration of state independence" and calls for negotiations with Soviet authorities on the issue of secession.

April 23: The President signs an agreement with the nine "referendum-participating" Presidents, aiming to achieve stable relations between the central and republican governments. It sets out a timetable for major political changes, starting with the signing of the new Union Treaty. No longer than six months after signature of the Treaty a new Union Constitution would be promulgated, followed by elections to the Congress of People's Deputies.

August 19: Attempted *coup d'état* in Moscow.

August 21: Gorbachev is reinstated as President.

August 24: Gorbachev resigns as the general secretary of the CP. The CP suspends its activities and dissolves the Central Committee.

September 5: The Congress adopts by 1 682 votes to 43 with 63 abstentions a draft law on a "Union of Sovereign States", which can be joined on a voluntary basis.

September 6: Estonia, Latvia and Lithuania officially leave the USSR to become independent states.

November 14: The leaders of all 12 republics, except Moldova and Armenia, reach an agreement on the formation of a "Union of Sovereign States", without the need of drafting a new constitution.

November 19: Edward Shevardnadze (first appointed in 1985) is reappointed as Minister for Foreign Affairs.

December 8: The Russian Federative Republic, Belarus and Ukraine sign the Minsk Agreement, establishing a Commonwealth of Independent States (CIS).

December 10: The original signatories' Supreme Soviet ratify the CIS declaration.

December 12: Kazakhstan, Kyrghyzstan, Tadjikistan, Turkmenistan and Uzbekistan sign the Alma Ata Agreement thus joining the CIS.

December 21: The CIS formally replaces the Soviet Union, grouping eleven republics with the exception of Georgia. The Russian Federative Republic takes over many of the former Union functions, including its seat in the UN Security Council. The post of President of the USSR is abolished.

December 25: Mikhail Gorbachev resigns.

December 26: The Soviet of the Republic and the Soviet of the Union issue a declaration on their own abolition.

Armenia

Chronology

1989

September 22: The Armenian Supreme Soviet appeals for help to the USSR Supreme Soviet in order to resolve the conflict on the status of Nagorno-Karabakh, the predominantly Armenian enclave in Azerbaijan, between Azerbaijan and Armenia.

September 25: President Mikhail Gorbachev issues an ultimatum to the leaders of Azerbaijan and Armenia to negotiate the lifting of several blockades, strikes and demonstrations with the aim for Azerbaijan autonomy and restoration of full Azerbaijan control over Nagorno-Karabakh.

November 4-7: The constituent congress of the Armenian National Movement is held in Yerevan and the 900 delegates adopt a programme which includes calls for "genuine sovereignty" for Armenian people, economic independence, reconstruction of the regions devastated by an earthquake, and for a political solution to the Nagorno-Karabakh question.

November 28: The USSR Supreme Soviet votes to end direct rule from Moscow over Nagorno-Karabakh. It is decided with only four votes against and 20 abstentions, to give the Azerbaijani authorities two months to pass new legislation guaranteeing full and real autonomy to Nagorno-Karabakh and establishing new government bodies for the enclave.

December 1: Armenia declares the enclave Nagorno-Karabakh to be a part of a "unified Armenian republic".

1990

April 6: Vladimir Movsisian is appointed as first secretary of the Armenian Communist Party (ACP), replacing Suren Arutiunian.

August 4: The Armenian Supreme Soviet elects Levon Ter-Petrossian as President of Armenia, defeating Vladimir Movsisian by 140 votes to 80.

August 13: Vazguen Manukyan, Ter-Petrossian's nominee, is elected as Prime Minister.

August 23: The Supreme Soviet adopts, by 183 votes to 2, a declaration on Armenia's "independent statehood", proclaiming that the Republic of Armenia is a sovereign state. It will form its own army and police and have the right to control its own natural resources, banks, economic policy and foreign relations. All Armenians living abroad have the right to citizenship. The declaration claims for Armenia inviolable borders which includes Nagorno-Karabakh. The red, blue and orange tricolour flag is restored to official use.

August 29: The Supreme Soviet declares a state of emergency and orders the ANA (Armenian National Army) to disband following the shooting of a parliamentarian Viktor Aivanzian, at the ANA headquarters.

November 30: Stepan Pogosian replaces Vladimir Movsisian as first secretary of the ACP.

1991

March 17: The parliament of Armenia refuses to participate in the all-union referendum on the preservation of the Soviet Union on the basis of fears that the new Union Treaty will enshrine neighbouring Azerbaijan rights to the disputed Nagorno-Karabakh region.

May 14: Stepan Pogosyan resigns as first secretary of the ACP.

June 1: Aram Sarkisian is elected as first secretary of the ACP. It is proposed to hold direct presidential elections.

August 19: Attempted *coup d'état* in Moscow.

September 7: The Communist Party votes to cease its activities, in order to radically reorganise.

September 21: A referendum is held on the independence of Armenia from the Soviet Union. On a 95.5% turnout, 94.39% vote in favour of secession.

September 23: The Supreme Council declares the country independent.

September 25: Prime Minister Vazgen Manukian resigns complaining of slander.

October 16: Presidential elections by universal suffrage bring back the incumbent, Levon Ter-Petrossian, to office with 83% of the votes.

December 8: The Russian Federative Republic, Belarus and Ukraine sign the Minsk Agreement, establishing a Commonwealth of Independent States (CIS).

December 12: Armenia signs the Alma Ata Agreement thus joining the CIS.

December 21: The CIS formally replaces the Soviet Union, grouping eleven republics with the exception of Georgia. The Russian Federative Republic takes over many of the former Union functions, including its seat in the UN Security Council.

December: A new government structure is formed on Presidential orders, consisting of 21 ministries and nine state directorates. The 185-seat Armenian Supreme Council is the highest legislative body. The president is directly elected.

1992

February 28: Withdrawal of CIS troops in Nagorno-Karabakh and on Armenia-Azerbaijan border.

March 2: President Levon Ter-Petrossian declares that Armenia has no territorial claims on Nagorno-Karabakh.

March 15: An agreement between Armenia and Azerbaijan envisaging a ceasefire and the lifting of economic sanctions is signed in Teheran.

May 15: At the CIS summit in Tashkent (Uzbekistan), Armenia, Russia, Kazakhstan, Kyrghyzstan, Tadjikistan and Uzbekistan sign a five-year collective security agreement providing for a collective response to aggression against any of its signatories.

August 10: President Levon Ter-Petrossian appeals to the signatories of the CIS collective security treaty to "carry out their obligations" in coming to Armenia's aid.

August 17: Opposition forces demand President Levon Ter-Petrossian to recognise the independence of the Nagorno-Karabakh republic or to resign. Parliament emergency session fails to reach agreement on holding a referendum to decide whether Ter-Petrossian should resign.

1993

February 2: President Levon Ter-Petrossian signs a decree dismissing Prime Minister Khosrov Haroutunian for an alleged "gross violation of etiquette" in criticising the government's draft budget and economic plan for 1993.

February 5: A large anti-government rally, organised by the National Self-Determination Association (NSD) opposition parties, takes place in Yerevan. They demand the resignation of Ter-Petrossian and the Armenian Supreme Council and the convening of a Constitutional Assembly to oversee early elections and the adoption of a new Constitution.

February 12: Hrand Bagratian is appointed as Prime Minister.

February 16: A new government is appointed in which opposition parties are included.

November 22: Armenia introduces its own national currency, the dram.

1994

July 27: The Defence Ministers of Azerbaijan and Armenia and the military leader of the disputed Armenian enclave (Nagorno-Karabakh) sign a ceasefire agreement.

December 29: The opposition "Dashnak" party (Armenian Revolutionary Federation (ARF)) is suspended by a decree of President Levon Ter-Petrossian.

1995

March 7: Armenia and Azerbaijan reach an agreement over the operation of the ceasefire originally announced in May 1994.

April 4: The President signs the electoral law, providing for the four-year election of members to the 190-seat National Assembly. 150 deputies are elected by majority system, with at least 25% of the votes cast, and 40 deputies are elected by proportional representation with a threshold of 5%.

June 22: Opposition parties, including the National Progress Party and the Constitutional Assembly (a bloc which comprises 10 parties), organise a demonstration protesting against their being barred from participating in the legislative elections of 5 July.

July 5: The first parliamentary elections since the independence of the country are held. 42.66% of the votes go to the Republican Bloc (Pan-Armenian National Movement), 16.88% to the Shaminar Women's Party and 12.10% to the Communist Party (55% turnout).

July 24: Hrand Bagratian is re-appointed as Prime Minister.

July 29: Second round of the general elections is held in the constituencies where no candidates secured an absolute majority in the first round. Republican Bloc (incl. HHSh) gains 42.66% and 119 seats; Shamiram Woman's Party gains 16.88% and 8 seats; Communist Party gains 12.1% and 7 seats; National Democratic Union gains 7.51% and 5 seats; National Self-Determination Union gains 5.57% and 3 seats; Armenian Liberal Democratic Party gains 2.52% and 1 seat; Armenian Revolutionary Federation 2.00% and 1 seat; Independents win 45 seats; 1 seat remains vacant. A referendum to approve the new constitution is held simultaneously: 828 370 votes in favour, 349 721 against; 39 440 ballots were invalid.

1996

January 26: The Parliamentary Assembly of the Council of Europe grants to the National Assembly of the Republic of Armenia special guest status.

March 5: A trial of 31 members of the opposition Dashnaktsutyun party opens at the Supreme Court in Yerevan. The accused including party leader Vagan Ovanesyan are charged with having planned a coup for 29 July 1995.

March 7: Armenia applies for membership of the Council of Europe.

September 22: Presidential elections are held. Incumbent President Levon Ter-Petrossian (Pan-Armenian National Movement) returns for a second five-year term in office in elections. He takes 51.75% (55% according to BBC World News Broadcasts) of the vote, easily defeating his main rival, Vazgen Manukian of the oppositional National Democratic Union (NDU) who wins 41.29% (38%). Communist Sergei Baladian comes a distant third with slightly over 6 %. The turnout in the ballot is 61%.

September 25-26: The publication of the results of the election leads to a mass demonstration organised by the opposition in Yerevan, in the course of which a group of persons invade the Parliament building and assault the President and first Vice-President of the National Assembly. This is followed by arrests, a stormy session of Parliament, the lifting of eight opposition members' parliamentary immunity, the closure of the opposition parties' headquarters and the declaration of a state of emergency.

October 3: The Organisation for Security and Co-operation in Europe (OSCE) reports doubts on the validity of the presidential elections; controversy over outcome continues.

November 4: Armen Sarkissian, member of the Pan-Armenian National Movement and former State Minister, is named as Prime Minister to replace Hrand Bagratian.

November 9: President Ter-Petrossian announces a major government reshuffle including the reorganisation of some ministries.

Constitution of the Republic of Armenia

YEREVAN – 1996

The Armenian people,
taking as a basis the fundamental principles of Armenian statehood and national goals set forth in the Declaration on Independence of Armenia; having fulfilled the sacred behest of its freedom-loving ancestors for the restoration of a sovereign state;
devoted to the strengthening and prosperity of the Mother country;
in order to ensure the freedom, general welfare and civil solidarity of generations, and to assure faithfulness to common human values;
does adopt the Constitution of the Republic of Armenia.

Chapter 1 – Provisions of Constitutional Order

Article 1
The Republic of Armenia is a sovereign, democratic, social, rule of law state.

Article 2
Power in the Republic of Armenia belongs to the people.
The people exercise their power through free elections, referendums, through bodies of state and local self-government, and public officers as prescribed by the Constitution.
The usurpation of power by any organisation or individual is a crime.

Article 3
Presidential elections, elections to the National Assembly and bodies of local self-government of the Republic, and referendums are held on the basis of universal, equal and direct suffrage by ballot.

Article 4
The state shall ensure the protection of human rights and freedoms on the basis of the Constitution and laws, in accordance with principles and norms of international law.

Article 5
State power shall be exercised in accordance with the Constitution and laws on the basis of the principle of the separation of legislative, executive and

judicial powers. State bodies and officials are authorised to carry out actions for which they are empowered by legislation.

Article 6
The supremacy of law shall be guaranteed in the Republic of Armenia. The Constitution of the Republic has supreme legal force, and its norms operate directly.
Laws, as well as other legal acts in contravention of the Constitution, shall not have legal force. Laws shall be implemented solely after promulgation. Legal acts related to human rights, freedoms and duties that are not promulgated shall not have legal force.
International treaties, concluded on behalf of the Republic of Armenia, shall apply after ratification. Ratified international treaties are a constituent part of the legal system of the Republic. In case other norms are established in them than are prescribed by laws, the norms of the treaties shall apply.

Article 7
A multi-party political system is recognised in the Republic of Armenia.
Parties shall be set up freely and promote the shaping and expression of the political will of people. The activities of political parties shall not contravene the Constitution and laws, and their structure and practice shall not contravene the principles of democracy. Political parties shall ensure the openness of their financial activities.

Article 8
The right of property is recognised and protected in the Republic of Armenia. The property owner shall use and dispose of the property at his/her discretion.
Exercise of the right to property shall not damage the environment or violate the rights and lawful interests of other persons, society or the state.
The state shall guarantee the free development and equal legal protection of all forms of property, freedom of economic activity, and free economic competition.

Article 9
The Republic of Armenia shall pursue its foreign policy on the basis of the norms of international law, with the aim of establishing good-neighbourly and mutually beneficial relations with all nations.

Article 10
The state shall ensure the protection and re-creation of the environment and the reasonable utilisation of natural resources.

Article 11
Historical and cultural monuments and other cultural values are under the care and protection of the state. Within the framework of the principles and norms of international law the Republic of Armenia shall promote the

protection of Armenian cultural and historical values in other countries and support the development of Armenian culture and education.

Article 12
The state language of the Republic of Armenia is Armenian.

Article 13
The flag of the Republic of Armenia is a tricolour: red, blue, orange with equal horizontal stripes.
The coat of arms of the Republic of Armenia is as follows: in the centre of the shield Mount Ararat with Noah's ark and the coats of arms of the four kingdoms of historical Armenia are drawn. The shield is supported by a lion and an eagle. On the bottom of the shield a sword, a branch, a sheaf, a chain and a ribbon are drawn.
The anthem of the Republic of Armenia is "Our Mother Country".
The capital of the Republic of Armenia is Yerevan.

Chapter 2 – Fundamental human and civil rights and freedoms

Article 14
The procedure for the acquisition and termination of citizenship of the Republic of Armenia is established by law. In the Republic of Armenia people of Armenian origin acquire citizenship in a simplified manner.
The citizen of the Republic of Armenia shall not be simultaneously a citizen of another state.

Article 15
Citizens regardless of nationality, race, sex, language, creed, political or other opinion, social origin, property and other status, enjoy all the rights, freedoms and duties established by the Constitution and laws.

Article 16
All are equal before the law and are equally protected by the law without discrimination.

Article 17
Everyone has the right to life.
Capital punishment, as an exclusive penalty, until its abolition, may be determined by law in case of capital crimes.

Article 18
Everyone has the right to freedom and immunity. No-one shall be searched or arrested otherwise than in the manner prescribed by law. He/she may be detained solely by court order as determined by law.

Article 19
No-one shall be subjected to torture, cruel treatment or punishment degrading human dignity. No-one shall be subjected without his/her own consent to medical or scientific experimentation.

Article 20
Everyone has the right to defend his/her private life and the life of his/her family from unlawful interference and to protect his/her dignity and reputation from assault. It is prohibited to collect, keep, use and disseminate illegally any information about a person's or his/her family's life. Everyone has the right to secrecy of his/her correspondence, telephone conversations, mail, telegraph and other messages, which can be restricted solely by a court decision.

Article 21
Everyone has the right to immunity of his/her dwelling. It is prohibited to enter a person's house against his/her will, save for cases prescribed by law. The dwelling shall be searched solely by a court decision as determined by law.

Article 22
Every citizen has the right to freedom of movement and residence within the borders of the Republic. Everyone has the right to leave the Republic. Every citizen has the right to return to the Republic.

Article 23
Everyone has the right to freedom of thought, conscience, and religion. Freedom to express one's religion and beliefs can be restricted solely by law based on the provisions of Article 45 of the Constitution.

Article 24
Everyone has the right to assert his/her opinion. No-one shall coerce a person to recant or change his/her opinion.
Everyone has the right to freedom of speech, including freedom to seek, receive and impart information and ideas through any source of media regardless of state borders.

Article 25
Everyone has the right to establish associations together with other persons, including the right to establish or join trade unions.
Every citizen has the right to the establishment and membership of political parties with other citizens. These rights can be restricted as regards people in the armed forces and law enforcement bodies.
No-one shall be compelled to join a political party or association.

Article 26
The citizens have the right to hold peaceful unarmed meetings, rallies, demonstrations and processions.

Article 27
Citizens of the Republic of Armenia who have attained eighteen years of age are entitled to participate in state government through their representatives elected directly by expression of their free will.

Citizens found incapable by court decision and those citizens on whom a sentence passed has entered into force and who are serving a sentence are not entitled to vote and to be elected.

Article 28
Everyone has the right to property and inheritance. Foreign citizens and persons without citizenship, save for cases prescribed by law, shall not have the right to own property. In cases prescribed by law only courts can deprive people of the property.
Confiscation of property for the needs of society and the state can be carried out in exceptional cases on the basis of law and upon preliminary equivalent compensation.

Article 29
Everyone has the right to free choice of employment. Everyone has the right to a fair salary not less than the minimum determined by the state and to working conditions which meet sanitary and safety requirement.
Citizens have the right to strike for the protection of their economic, social, and labour interests. The procedure for exercising this right and restrictions upon it are determined by law.

Article 30
Everyone has the right to rest. The maximum duration of the working day, rest-days and the minimum duration of annual paid vacations are established by law.

Article 31
Every citizen has the right to a standard of living adequate for the well-being of himself/herself and his/her family, including the improvement of housing and living conditions. The state shall take appropriate steps to ensure the exercise of this right.

Article 32
The family is the natural and fundamental group unit of society. The family, motherhood, and childhood are under the auspices and protection of the society and the state.
Men and women enjoy equal rights as to marriage, during marriage, and at its dissolution.

Article 33
Every citizen has the right to social insurance in the event of old age, disability, sickness, widowhood, unemployment and other cases prescribed by law.

Article 34
Everyone has the right to maintain his/her health. The order of medical care and services is determined by law. The state shall implement health care programmes for the population and promote the development of sports and physical culture.

Article 35
Every citizen has the right to education. Education shall be free of charge in state secondary educational institutions. Every citizen has the right to get higher education in state educational institutions on a competitive basis.
The establishment and activities procedure of private educational institutions is determined by law.

Article 36
Everyone has the right to freedom of producing works of literature, art and science, to participate in the cultural life of society, and to benefit from the achievements of scientific progress.
Intellectual property is protected by law.

Article 37
Citizens belonging to national minorities have the right to preserve their traditions, and to develop their language and culture.

Article 38
Everyone has the right to defend his/her rights and freedoms by means not prohibited by law. Everyone has the right to judicial defence of his/her freedoms and rights set forth in the Constitution and laws.

Article 39
Everyone has the rights to restore his/her violated rights, as well as the right to a public hearing of his/her case under equal conditions by an independent and impartial tribunal with observance of all requirements of justice for revealing the substantiation of the accusation indicted.
For the purposes of protection of public morals, order, national security, private life of parties or protection of the interests of justice the participation of the press and public in all or part of a trial may be prohibited by law.

Article 40
Everyone has the right to receive juridical assistance. In cases prescribed by law juridical assistance is rendered free of charge. Everyone has the right to a defence from the moment of arrest, detention, or accusation. Every convict has the right to reconsideration of a sentence by a higher court. Every convict has the right to be acquitted or to appeal for mitigation of the punishment.
Compensation of the damage caused to the victim shall be ensured as determined by law.

Article 41
Everyone charged with a penal offence has the right to be presumed innocent until proved guilty as determined by law by a court sentence entered into force.
The defendant is not bound to prove his/her innocence. Unproved suspicions are construed in favour of the defendant.

Article 42

No-one shall be compelled to testify against him/herself, his/her spouse and relatives. The law may prescribe other cases of release from the duty to testify.

The use of unlawfully obtained evidence shall be prohibited. It is prohibited to impose a heavier penalty than the one that was applicable at the time when the offence was committed.

No-one shall be held guilty of an offence on account of any act or omission which did not constitute a criminal offence under national law at the time when it was committed. Laws determining responsibility or increasing severity of the responsibility do not have retroactive power.

Article 43

The rights and freedoms set forth in the Constitution are not exhaustive and shall not be construed as an exclusion of other universal human and civil rights and freedoms.

Article 44

The fundamental human and civil rights and freedoms set forth in Articles 23-27 of the Constitution, may be restricted solely by law, if need be for the protection of national and public security, public order, health, morals, rights and freedoms and reputation of other persons.

Article 45

Particular human and civil rights and freedoms, save for those provided for in Articles 17, 19, 20, 39, 41-43 of the Constitution, may be temporarily restricted in the event of martial law or in cases prescribed by paragraph 14 of Article 55 of the Constitution.

Article 46

Everyone shall pay taxes and fees and make other compulsory payments in the manner and amount determined by law.

Article 47

Everyone shall participate in the defence of the Republic of Armenia as determined by law.

Article 48

Everyone shall observe the Constitution and laws and respect the rights, freedoms and dignity of other persons.

It is prohibited to use the rights and freedoms for the purposes of the violent overthrow of the constitutional order, advocacy of national, racial and religious hatred, and propaganda for violence and war.

Chapter 3 – The President of the Republic

Article 49

The President of the Republic of Armenia shall ensure the observance of the Constitution, and normal activities of the legislative, executive and judicial powers. The President of the Republic shall be the guarantor of the independence, territorial integrity and security of the Republic.

Article 50
The President of the Republic shall be elected by the citizens of the Republic of Armenia for a term of five years.
Anyone who has attained the age of 35 years, has been a citizen of the Republic of Armenia for the past ten years, has been a resident of the Republic of Armenia for the past ten years, and has the right to vote is eligible for the office of the President.
One and the same person shall not be elected President of the Republic for more than two successive terms.

Article 51
The presidential election of the Republic shall be held in accordance with the procedure established by the Constitution and law, fifty days before the powers of the acting President of the Republic expire.
A candidate is considered the President-elect of the Republic if he has received in his favour more than half of the votes of the candidates. If more than two candidates run for the elections and none of them have received enough votes, on the fourteenth day after voting, the second round of election is held, in which the two top candidates may participate. In the second round the candidate who has received more votes is considered elected. In case one candidate runs for President, he is considered elected if he has received more than half of the votes. In case the President is not elected, on the fortieth day after voting new elections shall be held.
The President-elect enters into office on the day the powers of the previous President of the Republic expire. The President of the Republic elected by new or extraordinary elections enters into office within ten days after the election.

Article 52
In case insuperable obstacles hinder the running of one of the candidates for the presidency of the Republic, presidential elections of the Republic shall be postponed for a period of two weeks. If within this period the obstacles, recognised insuperable, are not removed or in case of the death of one of the candidates prior to the voting day, new elections shall be held. The new elections shall be held on the fortieth day after the obstacles are recognised as insuperable.

Article 53
In the event of resignation, death, impossibility of execution of powers of the President of the Republic, or removing him from office as determined by Article 57 of the Constitution, on the fortieth day after presidential vacancy extraordinary presidential elections are held.

Article 54
The President of the Republic enters into office by taking an oath at a special meeting of the National Assembly.

Article 55

The President of the Republic:

1. Shall make an address to the people and the National Assembly;
2. Within a period of twenty-one days on receipt of a law passed by the National Assembly shall sign and promulgate it. Within that period the President without signing the law returns it requiring reconsideration together with his objections and proposals, to the National Assembly. Within five days after the law is repassed by the National Assembly, he signs and promulgates it;
3. Can dissolve the National Assembly and appoint extraordinary elections after consultation with the Prime Minister and the Chairman of the National Assembly. Extraordinary elections shall be held no sooner than thirty and no later than forty days after the dissolution of the National Assembly. The President shall not dissolve the National Assembly during the last six months of his office;
4. Shall appoint and remove the Prime Minister of the Republic. Appoints and removes the members of the Government at the proposal of the Prime Minister. In case the National Assembly carries a vote of no confidence in the Government, within twenty days the President shall receive the resignation of the Government, appoint the Prime Minister and form the Government;
5. In cases prescribed by law, shall appoint civil servants;
6. Can set up deliberative bodies;
7. Shall represent the Republic of Armenia in international relations, implement the guidance of foreign policy, conclude international treaties, sign the international treaties ratified by the National Assembly, and ratify intergovernmental agreements;
8. Shall appoint and recall the diplomatic representatives of the Republic of Armenia to foreign countries and international organisations, and receive the credentials and letters of recall of diplomatic representatives of foreign countries;
9. At the proposal of the Prime Minister shall appoint and remove from office the General Prosecutor;
10. Shall appoint members and the Chairman of the Constitutional Court. On the basis of the findings of the Constitutional Court may terminate the powers of judges of the Constitutional Court appointed by him or give consent to subjecting him/her to administrative or criminal responsibility by court order.
11. In accordance with the procedure provided for in Article 95 of the Constitution shall appoint the Chairmen and judges of the Court of Appeals and its chambers, courts of review, court of first instance and other courts, deputies of the General Prosecutor and prosecutors heading the structural subdivisions of the prosecutor's office, can terminate the powers of a judge to administrative or criminal responsibility, and remove the public prosecutors appointed by him;
12. Is the Commander-in-Chief of the armed forces and appoints the highest commanding staff;
13. Shall make a decision on the use of the armed forces. In the event of an armed attack on the Republic, existence of its immediate danger, or in case the National Assembly declares war, the President shall impose martial law and may declare total or partial call-up.

In the event of the imposition of martial law a special meeting of the National Assembly shall be convened;

14. In the event of an immediate danger to constitutional order, after consultation with the Chairman of the National Assembly and the Prime Minister, he shall take appropriate steps and send out a message thereof to the people;

15. Shall grant citizenship of the Republic of Armenia and settle matters on granting political asylum;

16. Shall award orders and medals of the Republic of Armenia and grant titles of honour, highest military, diplomatic and other ranks;

17. Shall grant amnesty to convicts.

Article 56
The President of the Republic shall issue decrees and orders obligatory for execution in the whole territory of the Republic. The decrees and orders of the President of the Republic shall not contravene the Constitution and laws.

Article 57
The President of the Republic may be removed from office on impeachment for treason or other felony.

For the purposes of receiving findings on removing the President of the Republic from office the National Assembly shall apply to the Constitutional Court with a resolution by a majority vote of the total number of deputies.

The National Assembly shall adopt a resolution on the basis of the findings of the Constitutional Court on removing the President of the Republic from office by at least a two-thirds vote of the total number of deputies.

Article 58
The resignation of the President of the Republic of Armenia shall be accepted by the National Assembly by a majority vote of the total number of deputies.

Article 59
In case of disability of the President of the Republic or existence of other insuperable obstacles hindering the performance of his duties, at the proposal of the Government and on the basis of the findings of the Constitutional Court, by at least a two-thirds vote of the total number of deputies the National Assembly shall pass a resolution on the impossibility of executing the powers of the President of the Republic.

Article 60
In case the presidency is vacated before a President-elect enters into office, the Chairman of the National Assembly and should it be impossible the Prime Minister, shall perform the duties of the President of the Republic. Within this period it is prohibited to dissolve the National Assembly, appoint a referendum, and appoint or remove the Prime Minister or the General Prosecutor.

Article 61
The procedure for the remuneration of the President, service and ensuring security is established by law.

Chapter 4 – The National Assembly

Article 62

The legislative power in the Republic of Armenia is executed by the National Assembly.

In cases provided for in Articles 59, 66, 73, 74, 78, 81, 83, 84, 111, 112 of the Constitution, as well as for the purposes of organising its activities the National Assembly shall pass resolutions which are signed and promulgated by the Chairman of the National Assembly.

The powers of the National Assembly are determined by the Constitution. The National Assembly shall operate in accordance with its Rules of Procedure.

Article 63

The National Assembly shall consist of 131 deputies. The powers of the National Assembly expire in June of the fourth year after its election, on the day of the opening of the initial session of the newly elected National Assembly when the newly elected National Assembly assumes its powers.

The National Assembly may be dissolved in accordance with the procedure prescribed by the Constitution.

The newly elected National Assembly shall not be dissolved within one year after its election. The National Assembly shall not be dissolved in the event of martial law or in cases provided for in paragraph 14 of Article 55 of the Constitution, or when the issue of the removal of the President of the Republic from office is raised.

Article 64

Anyone who has attained the age of 25 years, has been a citizen of the Republic of Armenia for the past five years, has been a resident of the Republic of Armenia for the past five years and has the right to vote may be elected deputy.

Article 65

The deputy shall not hold any public office or engage in a paid occupation, save for scientific, academic and creative work. The remuneration and guarantees for the activities of the deputy are established by law.

Article 66

The deputy shall not be bound by the mandate, and shall be guided by his/her conscience and convictions. The deputy shall not be persecuted or called to liability for actions proceeding from his/her status including opinion expressed in the National Assembly if it does not mean insult or slander.

The deputy shall not be arrested and subjected to administrative or criminal responsibility by court order without the consent of the National Assembly.

Article 67

The powers of the deputy terminate in case the term of powers of the National Assembly expires, the National Assembly is dissolved, he/she violates the provisions of Part 1 of Article 65 of the Constitution, he/she loses citizenship of the Republic of Armenia, is absent from half of the voting during one session for an insufficient reason, is sentenced to imprisonment, is recognised as disabled, resigns.

The procedure for termination of powers of the deputy is determined by the Rules of Procedure of the National Assembly.

Article 68

Regular elections to the National Assembly shall be held within sixty days prior to the expiration of its powers. The procedure of elections to the National Assembly is determined by law. Elections shall be appointed by the decree of the President of the Republic. The initial session of the newly elected National Assembly shall be convened on the second Thursday following the election of at least two-thirds of the total number of deputies. Until the election of the Chairman of the National Assembly the oldest deputy shall chair its meetings.

Article 69

Regular sessions of the National Assembly shall be convened twice a year; from the second Monday of September up to the second Wednesday of December; from the first Monday of February up to the second Wednesday of June. The meetings of the National Assembly shall be public. Meetings in camera may be convened by the resolution of the National Assembly.

Article 70

An extraordinary session of the National Assembly may be convened by the President of the Republic on the initiative of at least one-third of the total number of deputies or the Government. On the demand of the majority of the total number of deputies an extraordinary session of the National Assembly shall be held with the agenda and date determined by the initiator. The extraordinary session shall not last more than six days. An extraordinary session of the National Assembly shall be convened by the Chairman of the National Assembly on the initiative of the Government or at least one-third of the total number of deputies. The extraordinary session of the National Assembly shall be held with the agenda and date determined by the initiator.

Article 71

Save for cases under Articles 57, 58, 59, 72, 74, 84, 111, Part 4 of Article 75, Part 1 of Article 79 and paragraph 3 of Article 83 of the Constitution, laws and resolutions of the National Assembly shall be passed by a majority vote of the deputies present if more than half of the total number of deputies take part in voting.

Article 72

The National Assembly shall consider a law returned by the President of the Republic with priority. In case the National Assembly does not accept the proposals and objections of the President of the Republic, the returned law shall be reconsidered and passed by a majority vote of the deputies.

Article 73

Six standing committees shall be set up in the National Assembly. If need be, temporary committees may be set up as well. The standing committees shall be set up for the preliminary consideration of bills and other proposals and for the submission of findings to the National Assembly thereof.

Temporary committees shall be set up for the preliminary consideration of particular bills or submission of findings or references on definite events and facts.

Article 74

Within twenty days after the formation of the newly elected National Assembly or its formation, the Government submits its Programme of Actions to the National Assembly raising the issue of its confidence at the meeting of the National Assembly.

The draft resolution on carrying a vote of no confidence in the Government may be submitted by at least one-third of the total number of deputies within 24 hours after the issue of confidence is raised.

The draft resolution on carrying a vote of no confidence in the Government shall be voted no sooner than within 48 and no later than within 72 hours after it has been submitted. The resolution shall be passed by a majority vote of the total number of deputies.

In case no draft resolution on carrying a vote of no confidence in the Government is submitted or a resolution is not passed, the Programme of Actions of the Government is deemed approved.

In case a resolution on carrying a vote of a no confidence is passed, the Prime Minister submits and application to the President of the Republic on the resignation of the Government.

Article 75

The right to legislative initiative in the National Assembly shall belong to the deputies and the Government. The Government determines the order of priority of the consideration of submitted bills and may demand these bills be votes with acceptable amendments.

Any bill considered urgent by the decision of the Government shall be discussed and voted by the National Assembly within one month. Bills reducing the national revenues or increasing the expenditure shall be considered by the National Assembly based on the findings of the Government and passed by a majority vote of the total number of deputies. In respect to the passage of the submitted bill the Government may raise the issue of its confidence. If the National Assembly does not pass a resolution on carrying a vote of no confidence in the Government in accordance with the procedure provided for in Article 74 of the Constitution, the bill is considered approved. The Government shall not, in relation to the submitted bill, raise the issue of confidence more than twice a session.

Article 76

The National Assembly shall approve the state budget submitted by the Government. In case the state budget is not approved until the beginning of a new fiscal year, the expenditure shall be performed in the same proportion as the previous year. The procedure for consideration and approval of the state budget is determined by law.

Article 77
The National Assembly shall supervise the implementation of the state budget, as well as the use of loans and credits received from foreign countries and international organisations. The National Assembly shall consider and approve the annual report on the implementation of the state budget based on the findings of the National Assembly's Control Chamber.

Article 78
For the purposes of legislative ensurance of the Programme of Actions of the Government, the National Assembly may authorise the Government to make decisions with legal force which operate within the period determined by the National Assembly and shall not contravene laws. The decisions are signed by the President of the Republic.

Article 79
By a majority vote of the total number of deputies the National Assembly shall elect the Chairman of the National Assembly for the whole term of its powers. The Chairman of the National Assembly shall conduct the meetings, dispose of the National Assembly's material and financial resources, and ensure its normal activities. The National Assembly shall elect 2 Deputy Chairmen of the National Assembly.

Article 80
The deputies have the right to pose questions to the Government. At one of the meetings of a regular session each week the Prime Minister and the members of the Government shall answer the deputies' questions. The National Assembly shall not pass resolutions regarding the questions of the deputies.

Article 81
At the proposal of the President of the Republic the National Assembly:
1.   shall declare an amnesty;
2.   shall ratify or annul international treaties of the Republic of Armenia. The framework of international treaties subject to ratification in the National Assembly is determined by law;
3.   shall declare war.
Based on the findings of the Constitutional Court the National Assembly may terminate the implementation of measures provided for in paragraphs 13 and 14 of Article 55 of the Constitution.

Article 82
At the proposal of the Government the National Assembly shall approve the territorial-administrative division of the Republic.

Article 83

The National Assembly:

1.   at the proposal of the President of the Republic shall appoint the Chairman and the Deputy Chairman of the Central Bank;

2.   at the proposal of the Chairman of the National Assembly shall appoint the Chairman of the National Assembly's Control Chamber, members of the Constitutional Court, and from among the membership of the Constitutional Court shall appoint the Chairman of the Constitutional Court. If within 30 days after the formation of the Constitutional Court the National Assembly fails to appoint the Chairman of the Constitutional Court, the President of the Republic shall appoint the Chairman of the Constitutional Court;

3.   based on the findings of the Constitutional Court it may terminate the powers of any member of the Constitutional Court appointed by itself, give its consent to detain him/her, and call him/her to administrative or criminal responsibility.

Article 84

By a majority vote of the total number of deputies the National Assembly may carry a vote of no confidence in the Government. The National Assembly shall not exercise this right in the event of martial law or in cases provided for in paragraph 14 of Article 55 of the Constitution.

Chapter 5 – The Government

Article 85

The executive power in the Republic of Armenia is exercised by the Government of the Republic of Armenia. The Government is composed of the Prime Minister and the Ministers. The powers of the Government are determined by the Constitution and laws. The structure and order of activities of the Government are determined by the President of the Republic at the presentation of the Prime Minister.

Article 86

Meetings of the Government shall be convened and chaired by the President of the Republic or, at his recommendation, by the Prime Minister. Decisions of the Government are signed by the Prime Minister and ratified by the President of the Republic.

In cases provided for in Article 59 of the Constitution, at the demand of the majority of the Cabinet members the Prime Minister shall convene and chair a meeting of the Government.

Article 87

The Prime Minister shall guide the routine business of the Government and co-ordinate the activities of Ministers.

The Prime Minister shall make decisions. In cases determined by the procedure of Government activities, decisions of the Prime Minister shall be signed also by the Ministers responsible for the implementation of decisions.

Article 88
A Cabinet member shall not be a member of any representative body, hold other public office or engage in a paid occupation;

Article 89
The Government:
1. in accordance with the procedure prescribed by Article 74 of the Constitution shall submit its Programme of Actions to the National Assembly for approval;
2. shall submit the Budget bill to the National Assembly for approval, ensure the implementation of the budget and submit a report thereof to the National Assembly;
3. shall administer state property;
4. shall ensure the implementation of a single financial-economic, loan and tax national policy;
5. shall ensure the implementation of national policy in the fields of science, education, culture, health care, social insurance and environmental protection;
6. shall ensure the implementation of the defence, national security and foreign policy of the Republic;
7. shall take measures to strengthen lawfulness, ensure the rights and freedoms of citizens, protect public order and the property of citizens.

Article 90
The Government shall submit the Budget bill to the National Assembly for consideration at least sixty days prior to the beginning of the fiscal year and shall require, with amendments made by it, that it be voted before the expiration of the above-mentioned date. In relation to the adoption of the budget, the Government may raise the issue of its confidence. If the National Assembly does not pass a resolution on carrying a vote of no confidence in the Government in accordance with the procedure provided for in Article 74 of the Constitution, the state budget with the amendments adopted by the Government is considered approved.
In case a vote of no confidence in the Government is carried by the National Assembly regarding the adoption of the budget, within 20 days a new Government shall submit a Budget bill, which shall be considered and approved within 30 days in accordance with the procedure prescribed by the present Article.

Chapter 6 – Judicial power

Article 91
In the Republic of Armenia justice is administered solely by the courts in accordance with the Constitution and laws. In the cases prescribed by law, trial by jury is held.

Article 92
In the Republic of Armenia the courts of general jurisdiction are as follows: courts of first instance, courts of review and the Court of Appeals.

Economic courts, military tribunals and other courts prescribed by law operate in the Republic of Armenia. The establishment of emergency courts is prohibited.

Article 93
Sentences, judgements and decisions entered into legal force shall be
reviewed in the Court of Appeals based on the appeals of the General Prosecutor, and his deputies or lawyers registered in the Court of Appeals with
special licences.

Article 94
The President of the Republic shall be the guarantor of the independence of
judicial bodies. He is the head of the Council of Justice. The Minister of Justice and the General Prosecutor are the deputy chairmen of the Council of
Justice. 14 members appointed by the President of the Republic for a term of
5 years shall sit on the Council, of which 2 shall be legal scholars, 9 shall be
judges, and 3 shall be public prosecutors. 3 Council members each shall be
appointed from among the judges of the courts of first instance, courts of
review and the Court of Appeals. For each seat general meetings of judges
nominate 3 candidates by secret ballot. The General Prosecutor shall nominate the candidacies for the prosecutor members of the Council.

Article 95
The Council of Justice:
1.   at the proposal of the Minister of Justice shall form and submit for the
approval of the President of the Republic the annual lists of professional fitness and official advancement of judges on the basis of which appointments
are made;
2.   at the proposal of the General Prosecutor shall form and submit for the
approval of the President of the Republic the annual lists of professional fitness and official advancement of pubic prosecutors on the basis of which
appointments are made;
3.   shall propose the candidacies for the chairmen and judges of the Court
of Appeals and its chambers, the chairmen of the courts of review, courts of
first instance and other courts and submit its findings as regards the candidacies for other judges presented by the Minister of Justice;
4.   shall present its findings as regards the candidacies presented by the
General Prosecutor for the deputy General Prosecutors and prosecutors and
heads of structural subdivisions of the prosecutor's office;
5.   shall present a proposal for granting qualification ranks to judges and
public prosecutors;
6.   shall present a proposal for giving consent to the termination of powers
of a judge, to the detention and the subjecting of him/her to administrative
or criminal responsibility by court order;
7.   shall subject judges to disciplinary liability.
The Chairman of the Court of Appeals shall chair the meetings of the Council of Justice while considering matters of subjecting a judge to liability. The
President of the Republic, the Minister of Justice and the General Prosecutor
shall not take part in these meetings;

8.   shall express its opinion on issues of pardon upon the inquiry of the President of the Republic.

The procedure of activities of the Council of Justice is determined by law.

Article 96
Judges and members of the Constitutional Court shall be irreplaceable. The judge shall hold office until he/she attains the age of 65 and the member of the Constitutional Court shall hold office until he/she attains the age of 70. Their powers shall be terminated solely in cases and in accordance with the procedure prescribed by the Constitution and law.

Article 97
In administering justice, judges and members of the Constitutional Court shall be independent and subordinate only to law. The guarantees for the activities, principles and order of liability of the judge and the member of the Constitutional Court are determined by law.

Article 98
Judges and members of the Constitutional Court shall not hold other pubic office or engage in paid occupations, save for scientific, educational and creative work. Judges and members of the Constitutional Court shall not be affiliated with any political party or engage in political activity.

Article 99
The Constitutional Court shall be composed of 9 members of which 5 shall be appointed by the National Assembly and 4 shall be appointed by the President of the Republic.

Article 100
As determined by law the Constitutional Court:

1.   shall determine the conformity of resolutions of the National Assembly, decrees and orders of the President of the Republic and Government decisions with the Constitution;

2.   prior to the ratification of an international treaty shall decide whether the obligations set forth in it are in conformity with the Constitution;

3.   shall settle disputes relating to referendums and results of presidential and parliamentary elections;

4.   shall recognise insuperable or eliminated obstacles for a presidential candidate;

5.   shall submit its findings on the existence of a basis for removing the President of the Republic from office;

6.   shall submit its findings on measures under paragraphs 13 and 14 of Article 55 of the Constitution;

7.   shall submit its findings on the impossibility of performing his powers by the President of the Republic;

8.   shall submit its findings on the termination of the powers of a member of the Constitutional Court, detention and subjecting him/her to administrative or criminal responsibility by court order;

9. shall make a decision on the suspension or prohibition of the activities of a political party in cases prescribed by law.

Article 101
The following persons may apply to the Constitutional Court:
1. the President of the Republic;
2. at least one-third of the deputies;
3. presidential and parliamentary candidates regarding the disputes on election results;
4. the Government in cases provided for in Article 59 of the Constitution.
The Constitutional Court shall examine cases only if a corresponding application is submitted.

Article 102
The Constitutional Court shall make its decisions and findings no later than 30 days after the receipt of an application. The decisions of the Constitutional Court shall be final, not subject to review and shall enter into force from the moment of promulgation.
The Constitutional Court shall settle matters provided for in paragraphs 1-4 of Article 100 of the Constitution by a majority vote of the total number of its members, and matters provided for in paragraphs 5-9 of Article 100 by at least a two-thirds vote.

Article 103
The prosecutor's office of the Republic of Armenia is a single centralised system headed by the General Prosecutor.
the prosecutor's office:
1. shall claim criminal prosecution in cases and in accordance with the procedure prescribed by law;
2. shall oversee the legality of preliminary investigation and investigations;
3. shall perform the prosecution in the court;
4. shall bring actions in the court to defend state interests;
5. shall appeal against judgements, verdicts and decisions of courts;
6. shall oversee the application of punishment and other means of coercion.
The prosecutor's office shall operate within the framework of powers reserved to it by the Constitution on the basis of a law on the prosecutor's office.

Chapter 7 – Territorial administration and local self-government

Article 104
The administrative-territorial units of the Republic of Armenia are the provinces and communities. Provinces consist of village and city communities.

Article 105
For the purposes of disposing of community property and settling important community matters, bodies of local self-government are elected for a term of 3 years: community elders with 5 to 15 members and the head of the community: city mayor, village head.
The head of the community forms his/her staff.

Article 106
At the presentation of the head of the community, community elders approve the community budget, supervise the realisation of the budget, and as determined by law establish local fees and payments.

Article 107
National government is realised in provinces. In provinces the Government shall appoint and remove governors who carry out the territorial policy of the Government and co-ordinate the activities of territorial services of republican executive bodies.

Article 108
The city of Yerevan has the status of a province. At the presentation of the Prime Minister the President of the Republic shall appoint and remove from office the mayor of Yerevan.
Local self-government in Yerevan shall be exercised in district communities.

Article 109
At the presentation of the governor, the Government in cases prescribed by law may remove the head of community from office. In case of the removal of the head of the community by decision of the Government, extraordinary elections are held within 30 days. Before the newly elected head of community assumes his/her powers, the Prime Minister shall appoint an acting head of the city community and the governor shall appoint an acting head of the village community.

Article 110
The election procedure and powers of the bodies of local self-government are determined by the Constitution and laws.

Chapter 8 – Adoption of the Constitution, amendments and referendum

Article 111
The Constitution is adopted or amended through a referendum on the initiative of the President of the Republic or the National Assembly.
The President of the Republic shall appoint a referendum at the proposal or upon the agreement of the majority of the total number of deputies of the National Assembly.
Within 21 days upon the receipt of the draft Constitution or amendments to it, the President of the Republic may return it to the National Assembly with his objections and proposals and require a new consideration.
The President of the Republic puts up for referendum the draft Constitution or draft amendments proposed once again by at least a two-thirds vote of the total number of deputies within the period determined by the National Assembly.

Article 112
Laws are put up for referendum at the proposal of the National Assembly or the Government in accordance with the procedure determined by Article 111 of the Constitution.
Laws adopted by referendum shall be amended solely by referendum.

Article 113
The draft put up for a referendum is considered adopted if more than half of the participants in the voting, but not less than one-third of the citizens on the voter lists, are in favour.

Article 114
Articles 1, 2 and 114 of the Constitution are not subject to amendments.

Chapter 9 – Transitory provisions

Article 115
The present Constitution enters into force on the basis of the results of a referendum upon its promulgation.

Article 116
From the moment the Constitution enters into force:
1.   the operation of the 1978 Constitution with subsequent amendments and supplements, as well as the operation of constitutional laws, shall terminate;
2.   laws and other legal acts of the Republic of Armenia shall operate to the extent they do not contravene the Constitution;
3.   the President of the Republic shall exercise the powers reserved to him by the Constitution. The Vice-President of the Republic until the expiration of his powers shall fulfil the instructions of the President of the Republic;
4.   the National Assembly shall exercise the powers reserved to it by the Constitution. The provisions of Part 1 of Article 63 and Part 1 of Article 65 of the Constitution shall be applied for the subsequent convocations of the National Assembly. Until then Articles 4 and 5 of the Constitutional law of 27 March 1995 shall be in operation;
5.   until the formation of the Constitutional Court international treaties shall be ratified without its findings;
6.   village, settlement, city, regional councils of deputies and their executive bodies shall continue to exercise their powers determined by law until the adoption of legislation on bodies of territorial administration and local self-government in accordance with the Constitution.
Until the adoption of legislation on territorial government and local self-government the right to carry a vote of no confidence in the chairmen of city and regional councils of deputies shall belong to the National Assembly;
7.   regional (city) people's courts and the Supreme Court shall continue to operate within the framework of their former powers until the adoption of legislation on court structure and judicial procedure and the formation of a new judicial system in accordance with the Constitution;

8. the state Arbitration Court shall continue to operate within the framework of its former powers until the formation of an Economic Court;

9. the powers of judges of regional (city) people's courts shall be extended for a period of up to 6 months, during which, at the proposal of the Council of Justice, the President of the Republic shall appoint judges of regional (city) courts of a period of 3 years;

10. the powers of the members of the Supreme Court shall be extended until the formation of the Court of Appeals, but for no longer than 3 years;

11. until the formation of a new judicial system 11 members appointed by the President of the Republic, including 2 legal scholars, 6 judges and 3 public prosecutors, shall be included in the Council of Justice. 3 members of the Council shall be appointed each from among the judges of regional (city) people's courts and the Supreme Court, in the procedure prescribed by Article 94 of the Constitution. The President of the Republic shall head the Council. The Minister of Justice and the General Prosecutor shall be the Deputy Chairmen of the Council. The Council of Justice shall exercise the powers reserved to it by the Constitution;

12. the prosecutor's office shall exercise the powers reserved to it by the Constitution in accordance with the legislation in operation until the passage of a law on the prosecutor's office;

13. the Supreme Court shall review court sentences and judgements and decisions entered into force on the basis of the appeals of the General Prosecutor, his deputies and lawyers registered in the Supreme Court with special licences.

14. until the conformity of the legislation on criminal procedure with the Constitution the previous procedure for search and arrest shall be preserved.

Article 117
The day of the adoption of the Constitution is declared a holiday, called "Constitution Day".

Translator:
Zabela Movsissian

Azerbaijan

Chronology

1989

July 12: In Nagorno-Karabakh, the predominantly Armenian enclave in Azerbaijan, the regional Soviet votes for immediate secession from Azerbaijan and incorporation into Armenia. The Presidium of the Azerbaijan Supreme Soviet declares the vote illegal.

July 29: Demonstrations are held demanding economic and political autonomy for the republic, fresh elections in Azerbaijan to the USSR Congress of People's Deputies and legal recognition for the Azerbaijani Popular Front, as a political party.

September 22: Arkady Volsky, special representative of the USSR, imposes a "special status" because of inter-ethnic clashes in Nagorno-Karabakh.

September 23: The Supreme Soviet adopts a new law defining the republic's sovereignty. Notable clauses assert the Azerbaijani sovereignty over Nagorno-Karabakh and the inviolability of the republic's frontiers, Azerbaijan's rights to secede from Soviet Union, the right of the Azerbaijan Supreme Soviet to veto any legislation imposed by the Moscow authorities and Azerbaijan's full control over its natural resources. The law also makes Azeri the republic's state language.

September 25: President Mikhail Gorbachev issues an ultimatum to the leaders of Azerbaijan and Armenia to negotiate the lifting of several blockades, strikes and demonstrations with the aim of Azerbaijan autonomy and restoration of full Azerbaijan control over Nagorno-Karabakh.

October 3: The USSR Supreme Soviet approves special measures in order to lift the blockades.

October 5: The Azerbaijan Popular Front is registered as an official organisation by the Azerbaijan authorities.

November 28: The USSR Supreme Soviet votes to end direct rule from Moscow over Nagorno-Karabakh. It is decided, with only four votes against and 20 abstentions, to give the Azerbaijani authorities two months to pass new legislation guaranteeing full and real autonomy to Nagorno-Karabakh and establishing new government bodies for the enclave.

1990

January 8: Mass demonstrations in Baku on sovereignty over Nagorno-Karabakh.

January 13-15: The Popular Front is on the verge of taking power with mass support. Declaration of state of emergency and despatch of Soviet troops follows inter-ethnic riots.

January 20: Communist Party (CP) first secretary, Abdul Rakman Verzirov, is dismissed.

January 24: Prime Minister Ayaz Mutalibov is elected as the new first secretary of the CP.

January 26: Gasan Gasanov is appointed as Prime Minister.

March 30: The Prime Ministers of Armenia and Azerbaijan meet for preliminary talks in Tbilisi (Georgia).

May 18: Ayaz Mutalibov is elected President of the Republic and Elmira Kafarova Chairman of the Supreme Soviet (previously Chairman of the Presidium of the Supreme Soviet).

October 14: The CP emerges as clear winner in elections to the 360-seat Azerbaijan Supreme Soviet held in two rounds. The communists advocate keeping Azerbaijan within the Soviet Union, but attract nationalist support by opposing any compromise on Nagorno-Karabakh.

December 1: The adoption of the name Republic of Azerbaijan is proclaimed by a decree of President Ayaz Mutalibov. A new state flag is adopted.

1991

February 7: The Supreme Soviet re-elects Gasan Gasanov as Prime Minister.

March 17: Azerbaijan holds the all-union referendum on the preservation of the Soviet Union. 69.7% of the vote is in favour, with a turnout of 75.1%.

April 23: President Mikhail Gorbachev signs, with nine of the fifteen union republics including Azerbaijan, a pact aimed at achieving stable relations between the central government and the governments of the republics. It sets out a timetable for major political changes, starting with the signing of the new Union Treaty. No longer than six months after signature of the Treaty a new Union constitution would be promulgated, followed by elections to the Congress of People's Deputies.

August 19: Attempted *coup d'état* in Moscow.

August 30: Azerbaijan declares itself independent.

September 8: Direct presidential elections endorse the current president Ayaz Mutalibov, the sole candidate, in a turnout cited by the republic's central electoral commission as 83.7%.

October 18: The Supreme Soviet declares the country independent.

November 27: At the meeting of the Soviet State Council, the presidents of Armenia and Azerbaijan adopt a resolution calling on them to "abrogate all acts that change Nagorno-Karabakh's legal status", but they refuse Gorbachev's proposition for a 10 km buffer zone.

December 8: Belarus, The Russian Federative Republic and Ukraine sign the Minsk Agreement, establishing the Commonwealth of Independent States (CIS).

December 12: Azerbaijan signs the Alma Ata Agreement, thus joining the CIS.

December 21: The CIS formally replaces the Soviet Union, grouping eleven republics with the exception of Georgia. The Russian Federative Republic takes over many of the former Union functions, including its seat in the UN Security Council. The Azerbaijani Supreme Soviet, however, refuses to ratify the membership.

December 28: The autonomous region Nagorno-Karabakh holds elections to a parliament, after proclaiming itself a republic.

1992

March 6: Setbacks in the war with Armenia over Nagorno-Karabakh precipitate a power struggle leading to the resignation of President Ayaz Mutalibov.

May 14: An emergency session of the Supreme Council blames acting President Mamedov and reinstates ex-President Mutalibov who immediately declares a state of emergency in Baku.

May 18: Pending new elections, Kambarov is appointed acting President and deputy leader of the Azerbaijani Popular Front.

June 7: Presidential elections: A nationally-elected presidency is introduced. Abulfez Elchibey, leader of the Azerbaijani Popular Front, is sworn in as President after obtaining 59.4% of the votes in a 76% turnout in elections; there were five candidates in all.

October 12: Russian President Boris Yeltsin and President Abulfaz Elchibey sign a treaty of "friendship, co-operation and mutual security" in Moscow.

1993

January 3: Russian President Yeltsin and United States President Bush issue a joint statement on the Nagorno-Karabakh conflict.

April 28: Panakh Guseinov is appointed Prime Minister, after Rakhim Guseinov resigned as such on January 28.

June 2: The *manat* is introduced as new currency, but the rouble remains in use.

June 4: The rebel forces of cashiered Col. Surat Guseinov clash with the national army.

June 7: Prime Minister Panakh Guseinov resigns.

June 15: Parliament elects Geidar Aliyev, member of the Yeni Azerbaijan Party and leader of the Nakhichevan Autonomous Region, as Chair of Parliament, after the resignation of Isa Gambarov.

June 18: President Elchibey flees to Nakhichevan, after a *coup d'état* led by Col. Surat Guseinov.

June 21: Col. Guseinov declares himself "Head of State".

June 24: The Parliament impeaches Elchibey and declares Geidar Aliyev to be the acting President.

June 27: Parliament appoints Col. Guseinov as Prime Minister and "Supreme Commander", after being nominated by Aliyev.

June 29: The Popular Front announces that until Elchibey returns to authority, it will suspend its activities.

July 16: Former Prime Minister Panakh Guseinov is arrested in connection with an alleged plot to assassinate Aliyev.

August 31: Former President Elchibey confidence poll results: in the question "Do you trust Abulfaz Elchibey as your President", 97.5% of the answers are negative and 2% positive (turnout 92%).

September 20: The *Milli Majlis* (National Assembly) decides that Azerbaijan should seek full membership of the CIS.

October 3: Presidential elections are held. Geidar Aliyev is sworn in as President after securing 98.8% of the vote in the presidential election. The turnout is recorded as 97%.

1994

April 4: Natig Hasanov is elected Chairman of the Parliament of Nakhichevan, in succession to Aliyev.

September 30: Afiyaddin Jalilov, a deputy Chair of the *Milli Majlis* and strong supporter of the President Aliyev, is shot dead.

October 3: Aliyev announces a state of emergency in Baku.

October 5: Aliyev censures alleged Russian destabilisation and allegations against former President. Prime Minister Guseinov denies taking any part in the rebel activity, nevertheless Aliyev announces Guseinov's dismissal.

October 6: Fuad Kuliyev, the First Deputy Prime Minister is named as Guseinov's successor.

1995

March 7: Azerbaijan and Armenia reach an agreement over the operation of the ceasefire originally announced in May 1994.

May 2: The *Milli Majlis* confirms Fuad Kuliyev, acting Prime Minister since October 1994, in his post.

August 12: A new electoral law governing the forthcoming legislative elections is adopted: the one-chamber legislative body will consist of 125 deputies; 80% (100 deputies) will be elected in single-member constituencies with a requirement of 50% voter participation, and 20% (25 deputies) by proportional representation, with a threshold of 8%.

September 19: The Supreme Court reverses a ban on the CP which it had issued on 1 September, after allegations of the Minister of Justice that the party had engaged in anti-state activities seeking to build a new communist union across the former Soviet Union.

October: During this month further restrictions are imposed on the activities of Popular and Communist political parties and party-members who are expected to contest the first legislative elections, on 12 November.

November 12: Eight parties participate in the first legislative elections since independence. Ninety-six seats are decided including all 25 proportional representation seats, with a turnout of 86%. The electoral observers of the Council of Europe, OSCE and the UN report irregularities. In a referendum 91.9% of the registered voters approve the new constitution, which defines Azerbaijan as a presidential republic, with executive powers residing in the head of the state and legislative power in the new 125-seat parliament. The President is given power to declare a state of emergency.

November 26: A second election round is held for 29 seats remaining to be filled in the constituencies where no candidates secured an absolute majority during the first round. Another 13 seats are filled.

1996

February 4: Final voting is held in the constituencies where the voter participation has been less than 50%. Run-off elections for 15 parliamentary seats. Final results: New Azerbaijan Party, 54 seats; National Independence Front, 4 seats; Popular Front, 4 seats; Democratic Independence Party,

2 seats; Democratic Entrepreneurs Party, 1 seats; Citizens' Solidarity Party, 1 seat; Musavat Party, 1 seat; Social Justice Party, 1 seat; Motherland Party, 1 seat; and the Independents gain the remaining 55 seats. One seat is reserved for a member from Karabakh. Turnout 60.9%.

June 28: Azerbaijan obtains special guest status with the Parliamentary Assembly of the Council of Europe.

July 20: President Aliyev accepts the resignation of Prime Minister Fuad Kuliyev and appoints Artur Rasizade, currently First Deputy Prime Minister, as acting Prime Minister.

September: Rasul Guliev resigns as President of Parliament. His successor is Murtuz Nadjafoglu Alzsqerov, one of the founders and now deputy chairman of the Yeni Azerbaijan Party.

Constitution of the Azerbaijan Republic[1]

Approved by referendum, 12 November 1995

Section 1 – General

Chapter 1 – People's power

Article 1 – The source of power
1. The sole source of state power in the Azerbaijan Republic is the people of Azerbaijan.
2. People of Azerbaijan are citizens of the Azerbaijan Republic living in the territory of the Azerbaijan Republic and outside it who are subordinate to the Azerbaijan state and its laws which do not exclude standards of international legislation.

Article 2 – Sovereignty of people
1. Sovereign right of the Azerbaijan people is the right of free and independent determination of their destiny and establishment of their own form of governance.
2. The people of Azerbaijan exercise their sovereign right directly – by way of nation-wide voting – referendum, and through their elected representatives based on universal, equal and direct suffrage by way of free, secret and personal ballot.

Article 3 – Questions solved by way of nation-wide voting – referendum
1. People of Azerbaijan may solve any questions involving their rights and interests by way of referendum.
2. The following questions may be solved only by way of referendum:
    a. acceptance of the Constitution of the Azerbaijan Republic and introduction of amendments thereto;
    b. change of state borders of the Azerbaijan Republic.

Article 4 – Right to represent the people
No-one except authorized representatives elected by the people will have the right to represent the people, speak on behalf of people and to make statements on behalf of the people.

---

1. European Commission for Democracy through Law

Article 5 – Unity of the people
1.   The people of Azerbaijan are united.
2.   Unity of the Azerbaijan people constituted the basis of the Azerbaijanian state. Azerbaijan Republic is the mutual and indivisible motherland for all citizens of the Azerbaijan Republic.

Article 6 – Inadmissibility of the usurpation of power
1.   No part of the people of Azerbaijan, no social group or organisation and no individual may usurp the right for execution of power.
2.   Usurpation of power is the most grave crime against the people.

Article 7 – The Azerbaijanian state
1.   The Azerbaijanian state is a democratic, legal, secular, unitary republic.
2.   In terms of internal problems state power in the Azerbaijan Republic is limited only by law, in terms of foreign policy by provisions resulting from international agreements, wherein the Azerbaijan Republic is one of the parties.
3.   State power in the Azerbaijan Republic is based on a principle of division of powers:
     –   the Milli Majlis of the Azerbaijan Republic exercises legislative power;
     –   executive power belongs to the President of the Azerbaijan Republic;
     –   the law courts of the Azerbaijan Republic exercise judicial power.
4.   According to provisions of the present Constitution legislative, executive and judicial power interact and are independent within the limits of their authority.

Article 8 – The Head of the Azerbaijanian state
1.   The President of the Azerbaijan Republic is the Head of the Azerbaijanian state. He represents the Azerbaijanian state both within the country and in its relations with foreign countries.
2.   The President of the Azerbaijan Republic represents the unity of the Azerbaijanian people and provides continuity of Azerbaijanian statehood.
3.   The President of the Azerbaijan Republic is the guarantor of independence and territorial integrity of the Azerbaijanian state and of observance of international agreements wherein the Azerbaijan Republic is one of the parties.
4.   The President of the Azerbaijan Republic is the guarantor of independence of judicial power.

Article 9 – Military forces
1.   In order to provide for its safety and defend itself, the Azerbaijan Republic establishes military forces and other military troops.
2.   The Azerbaijan Republic rejects war as a means of infringement on the independence of other states and way of settlement of international conflicts.
3.   The President of the Azerbaijan Republic is the Supreme Commander-in-Chief of the military forces of the Azerbaijan Republic.

Article 10 – Principles of international relations
The Azerbaijan Republic develops its relations with other countries based on principles recognised in international legal standards.

Article 11 – Territory
1.   The territory of the Azerbaijan Republic is sole, inviolable and indivisible.
2.   Internal waters of the Azerbaijan Republic, the sector of the Caspian Sea (lake) belonging to the Azerbaijan Republic and air space over the Azerbaijan Republic are integral parts of the territory of the Azerbaijan Republic.
3.   No part of territory of the Azerbaijan Republic may be estranged. The Azerbaijan Republic will not give any part of its territory to anybody; the state borders of the Azerbaijan Republic may be changed only by free decision of its peoples made by way of referendum declared by Mili Majlis of the Azerbaijan Republic.

Article 12 – The highest priority objective of the state
1.   The highest priority objective of the state is to provide rights and liberties of a person and citizen.
2.   Rights and liberties of a person and citizen listed in the present Constitution are implemented in accordance with international treaties wherein the Azerbaijan Republic is one of the parties.

Article 13 – Property
1.   Property in the Azerbaijan Republic is inviolable and is protected by the state.
2.   Property may be state, private or municipal.
3.   Property may not be used for restriction of rights and liberties of a person and citizen, interests of society and state, dignity of a person.

Article 14 – Natural resources
Without prejudice to the rights and interests of any physical persons and legal entities, natural resources belong to the Azerbaijan Republic.

Article 15 – Economic development and the state
1.   The development of the economy based on various forms of property in the Azerbaijan Republic is aimed at ensuring the prosperity of the people.
2.   Based on market relationships the Azerbaijanian state creates conditions for the development of the economy, guarantees free business activity and prevents monopoly and unfair competition in economic relations.

Article 16 – Social development and the state
1.   The Azerbaijan state takes care to improve the prosperity of all people and each citizen, their social protection and proper living conditions.
2.   The Azerbaijan state participates in the development of culture, education, public health, science and the arts and protects the environment and the historical, material and spiritual heritage of the people.

Article 17 – Family and the state
1.   The family as a basic element of society is under special protection of the state.
2.   Parents must take care of their children and their education. The state controls implementation of this responsibility.

Article 18 – Religion and the state
1.   Religion in the Azerbaijan Republic is separated from the state. All religions are equal before the law.
2.   The spreading and propaganda of religions which humiliate people's dignity and contradict the principles of humanism are prohibited.
3.   The state educational system is secular.

Article 19 – Monetary unit
1.   The monetary unit of the Azerbaijan Republic is the manat.
2.   Only the National Bank has the right of introducing money into circulation and withdrawing it from circulation. The National Bank of the Azerbaijan Republic belongs exclusively to the state.
3.   The use of other monetary units, besides the manat, on the territory of the Azerbaijan Republic is prohibited.

Article 20 – Restrictions concerning state debts
Debts incurred as result of intending to assist revolts or coups against the Azerbaijanian state shall not be accepted as liabilities and paid by the Azerbaijan Republic.

Article 21 – Official language
1.   Azerbaijanian language is the official language of the Azerbaijan Republic. The Azerbaijan Republic promotes the development of the Azerbaijanian language.
2.   The Azerbaijan Republic ensures the free use and development of other languages spoken by the people.

Article 22 – Capital
Baku is the capital of the Azerbaijan Republic.

Article 23 – Symbols of the Azerbaijanian state
1.   The state flag of the Azerbaijan Republic, the state emblem of the Azerbaijan Republic and state hymn of the Azerbaijan Republic are state symbols of the Azerbaijan Republic.
2.   The state flag of the Azerbaijan Republic consists of three horizontal stripes of the same width. The upper stripe is blue, the middle stripe is red, and the lower one is green; in the middle of the red stripe on both sides of the flag a white crescent with eight-pointed star is depicted. The width of the flag is half of its length.
3.   The appearance of state flag of the Azerbaijan Republic and state emblem of the Azerbaijan Republic, music and text of state hymn of the Azerbaijan Republic are specified by the Constitutional Law of the Azerbaijan Republic.

Section 2 – Basic rights, liberties and responsibilities

Chapter 3 – Basic rights and liberties of a person and citizen

Article 24 – Main principle of rights and liberties of a person and citizen
1.   Everyone from the moment of birth possesses inviolable and inalienable rights and liberties.

2.   Rights and liberties envisage also responsibility and obligations of every-one to society and other persons.

Article 25 – Right of equality
1.   All people are equal with respect to the law and law courts.
2.   Men and women possess equal rights and liberties.
3.   The state guarantees equality of rights and liberties of everyone, irre-spective of race, nationality, religion, language, sex, origin, financial position, occupation, political convictions, membership in political parties, trade unions and other public organisations. Rights and liberties of a person or citizen can-not be restricted due to race, nationality, religion, language, sex, origin, con-viction, political and social belonging.

Article 26 – Protection of rights and liberties of a person and citizen
1.   Everyone has the right to protect his/her rights and liberties using means and methods not prohibited by law.
2.   The state guarantees protection of rights and liberties of all people.

Article 27 – Right to life
1.   Everyone has the right to life.
2.   Except for the extermination of enemy soldiers in the case of military aggression, when carrying out the death sentence and in other cases envis-aged by law, right to life of every person is inviolable.
3.   The death penalty, until it is completed abolished, may be applied legal-ly only in cases of especially grave crimes against the state, or against the life and health of a human being.
4.   Arms shall not be used against human beings except for cases of neces-sary defence, urgent situations, whenever a criminal should be caught, to pre-vent a prisoner from running away, to prevent revolt or coup against the state, to carry out orders given by authorised persons during martial law or state of emergency, military aggression.

Article 28 – Right to freedom
1.   Everyone has the right to freedom.
2.   The right to freedom may be restricted only as specified by law, by way of detention, arrest or imprisonment.
3.   Everyone legally present on the territory of the Azerbaijan Republic may travel without restrictions, choose his/her place of residence and travel abroad.
4.   Any citizen of the Azerbaijan Republic has the right to return to his/her country whenever he/she so desires.

Article 29 – Right to ownership of property
1.   Everyone has the right to own property.
2.   Neither kind of property has priority. The right of ownership including private ownership is protected by law.
3.   Everyone may possess movable and real property. The right of owner-ship envisages the right of the owner to possess, use and dispose of the prop-erty himself/herself or jointly with others.

4.   Nobody shall be deprived of his/her property without the decision of a court of law. Total confiscation of property is not permitted. Compulsory purchase of the property for state or public needs is permitted only after preliminary fair reimbursement of its cost.
5.   The state guarantees the right to inherit property.

Article 30 – Right to intellectual property
1.   Everyone has the right to intellectual property.
2.   Copyright, patent rights and other rights to intellectual property are protected by law.

Article 31 – Right to live in safety
1.   Everyone has the right to live in safety.
2.   Except in cases envisaged by law it is prohibited to infringe on anybody's life, physical and spiritual health, property, living premises, or to commit acts of violence.

Article 32 – Right to personal immunity
1.   Everyone has the right to personal immunity.
2.   Everyone has the right to confidentiality concerning his/her personal and family life. Except in cases envisaged by legislation, interference in a person's private life is prohibited.
3.   Gaining, storing, use and spreading information about a person's private life without his/her consent is not permitted.
4.   The state guarantees everyone the right to confidentiality with respect to correspondence, telephone communications, post, telegraph messages and information sent by other means of communication. This right may be restricted, as specified by legislation, to prevent crime or to find out true facts when investigating a criminal case.

Article 33 – Right to sanctity of the home
1.   Everyone has the right to sanctity of his/her home.
2.   Except in cases specified by law, or by the decision of a court of law nobody has the right to enter a private home against the will of its inhabitants.

Article 34 – Right to marriage
1.   Everyone has the right to marry on reaching the age specified by legislation.
2.   Marriages shall be concluded voluntarily. Nobody should be forced into marriage.
3.   The family and marriage are protected by the state. Maternity, paternity and childhood are protected by the law. The state provides support to large families.
4.   The rights of wife and husband are equal. The care and education of children constitutes both a right and a responsibility of parents.
5.   It is the responsibility of children to respect parents and look after them. Children who are of age (18) and capable of working must support disabled parents.

Article 35 – Right to work

1. Labour is the basis of personal and public prosperity.
2. Everyone has the right to choose independently, based on his/her abilities, a kind of activity, profession, occupation and place to work.
3. Nobody may be forced to work.
4. Labour agreements are concluded voluntarily. Nobody may be forced to conclude a labour agreement.
5. Based on decisions of a court of law there may be cases of forced labour, with the terms and conditions being specified by legislation; forced labour is permissible due to orders of authorised persons during the term of army service, state of emergency or martial law.
6. Everyone has the right to work in safe and healthy conditions, to get remuneration for his/her work without any discrimination, not less than the minimum wages rate established by the state.
7. Unemployed persons have the right to receive social allowances from the state.
8. The state will do its best to eliminate unemployment.

Article 36 – Right to strike

1. Everyone has the right to strike, both individually and together with others.
2. The right for strike for those working based on labour agreements may be restricted only in cases envisaged by the law. Soldiers and civilians employed in the Army and other military formations of the Azerbaijan Republic have no right to strike.
3. Individual and collective labour disputes are settled in line with legislation.

Article 37 – Right to rest

1. Everyone has the right to rest.
2. For those whose work is based on labour agreements, an eight-hour working day, national holidays and at least one paid vacation with a duration of at least 21 calendar days are guaranteed.

Article 38 – Right to social protection

1. Everyone has the right to social protection.
2. Most vulnerable persons must get support, in the first place, from members of their families.
3. Everyone has the right to social protection on reaching specific age according to legislation, in the case of illness, disability, loss of bread-winner in the family, unemployment and in other cases envisaged by legislation.
4. The minimum sum of pensions and social allowances is specified by law.
5. The state creates possibilities for the development of charitable activity, voluntary social insurance and other forms of social protection.

Article 39 – Right to live in a healthy environment

1. Everyone has the right to live in a healthy environment.
2. Everyone has the right to gain information about the true ecological situation and to receive compensation for damage done to his/her health and property because of the violation of ecological requirements.

Article 40 – Right to culture
1.   Everyone has the right to take part in cultural life, to use the organisations and values of culture.
2.   Everyone must respect historical, cultural and spiritual heritage, take care of it and protect historical and cultural memorials.

Article 41 – Right to protection of health
1.   Everyone has the right to protection of his/her health and to medical care.
2.   The state takes all necessary measures for the development of all forms of health services based on various forms of property, guarantees sanitary-epidemiological safety and creates possibilities for various forms of medical insurance.
3.   Officials concealing facts and cases dangerous to life and public health will bear legal responsibility.

Article 42 – Right to education
1.   Every citizen has the right to education.
2.   The state guarantees free obligatory secondary education.
3.   The system of education is under state control.
4.   The state guarantees continuation of education for the most gifted persons irrespective of their financial position.
5.   The state establishes minimum educational standards.

Article 43 – Right to a home
1.   Nobody may be deprived of his/her home.
2.   The state assists in the construction of living premises, takes special measures for the realisation of the right to a home.

Article 44 – Right to nationality
1.   Everyone has the right to keep his/her nationality.
2.   Nobody may be forced to change his/her nationality.

Article 45 – Right to use mother tongue
1.   Everyone has the right to use his/her mother tongue. Everyone has the right to be educated, and to carry out creative activity in any language, as desired.
2.   Nobody may be deprived of right to use his/her mother tongue.

Article 46 – Right to defend persnal honour and dignity
1.   Everyone has the right to defend his/her honour and dignity.
2.   Dignity is protected by state. Nothing must lead to the humiliation of the dignity of a human being.
3.   Nobody must be subject to tortures and torment, treatment or punishment humiliating the dignity of human beings. Medical, scientific and other experiments must not be carried out on any person without his/her consent.

Article 47 – Freedom of thought and speech
1.   Everyone may enjoy freedom of thought and speech.
2.   Nobody should be forced to promulgate his/her thoughts and convictions or to renounce his/her thoughts and convictions.

3.   Propaganda provoking racial, national, religious and social discord and animosity is prohibited.

Article 48 – Freedom of conscience
1.   Everyone enjoys the freedom of conscience.
2.   Everyone has the right to define his/her attitude to religion, to profess, individually or together with others, any religion or to profess no religion, to express and spread his/her beliefs concerning religion.
3.   Everyone is free to carry out religious ritual; however, this should not violate public order or contradict public morals.
4.   Religious beliefs and convictions do not excuse infringements of the law.

Article 49 – Freedom of meetings
1.   Everyone has the right to meetings.
2.   Everyone has the right, having notified the relevant governmental bodies in advance, peacefully and without arms, to meet with other people, to organise meetings, demonstrations and processions and to place pickets.

Article 50 – Freedom of information
1.   Everyone is free to look for, acquire, transfer, prepare and distribute information.
2.   The freedom of the mass media is guaranteed. State censorship in the mass media, including the press is prohibited.

Article 51 – Freedom of creative activity
1.   Everyone is free to carry out creative activity.
2.   The state guarantees freedom in literary-artistic, scientific-technical and other kinds of creative activity.

Article 52 – Right to citizenship
A person having political and legal relations with the Azerbaijan Republic and also mutual rights and obligations is the citizen of the Azerbaijan Republic. A person born on the territory of the Azerbaijan Republic or to citizens of the Azerbaijan Republic is the citizen of the Azerbaijan Republic. A person is a citizen of the Azerbaijan Republic if one of his/her parents is a citizen of the Azerbaijan Republic.

Article 53 – Guarantee of right to citizenship
1.   In no circumstances may a citizen of the Azerbaijan Republic be deprived of citizenship of the Azerbaijan Republic.
2.   In no circumstances may a citizen of the Azerbaijan Republic be expelled from the Azerbaijan Republic or extradited to a foreign state.
3.   The Azerbaijan Republic ensures legal protection for citizens of the Azerbaijan Republic temporarily or permanently living outside the Republic.

Article 54 – Right to take part in political life of society and state
1.   Citizens of the Azerbaijan Republic have the right to take part in the political life of society and state without restrictions.

2.   Any citizen of the Azerbaijan Republic has the right himself to stand up to attempted rebellion against the state or attempted coup d'état.

Article 55 – Right to take part in governing the state

1.   Citizens of the Azerbaijan Republic have the right to take part in governing the state. They may exercise the said right themselves or through their representatives.

2.   Citizens of the Azerbaijan Republic have the right to work in governmental bodies. Officials of state bodies are appointed from citizens of the Azerbaijan Republic. Foreign citizens and stateless citizens may be employed in state organisations in an established order.

Article 56 – Electoral right

1.   Citizens of the Azerbaijan Republic have the right to elect and be elected to state bodies and also to take part in referendum.

2.   Those recognised as incapable by a court of law have no right to take part in elections and in referendums.

3.   Participation in elections by military personnel, judges, state employees, religious officials, persons imprisoned by decision of a court of law, and other persons specified in the present Constitution and laws may be restricted by law.

Article 57 – Right to appeal

1.   Citizens of the Azerbaijan Republic have the right to appeal personally and also to submit individual and collective written applications to state bodies. Each application should be responded to in an established order and period of time.

2.   Citizens of the Azerbaijan Republic have the right to criticise activity or work of state bodies, their officials, political parties, trade unions, other public organisations and also activity or work of individuals. Prosecution for criticism is prohibited. Insult or libel shall not be regarded as criticism.

Article 58 – Right of freedom of membership

1.   Everyone is free to join other people.

2.   Everyone has the right to establish any union, including political party, trade union and other public organisation or enter existing organisations. Unrestricted activity of all unions is ensured.

3.   Nobody may be forced to join any union or remain its member.

4.   Activity of unions intended for forcible overthrow of legal state power on the whole territory of the Azerbaijan Republic or on a part thereof is prohibited. Activity of unions which violates the Constitution and laws may be stopped by decision of a court of law.

Article 59 – Right to business activity

Everyone may, using his/her possibilities, abilities and property, according to existing legislation, individually or together with other citizens, carry out business activity or other kinds of economic activity not prohibited by the law.

Article 60 – Guarantee of rights and liberties by court of law
1.   The legal protection of rights and liberties of every citizen is ensured.
2.   Everyone may appeal to a court of law regarding decisions and activity (or inactivity) of state bodies, political parties, trade unions, other public organisations and officials.

Article 61 – Right to legal advice
1.   Everyone has the right to obtain qualified legal advice.
2.   In specific cases envisaged by legislation legal advice shall be rendered free to the applicant, at the expense of the government.
3.   Every citizen has the right to a lawyer's advice from the moment of detention, arrest or being charged with a crime by competent state bodies.

Article 62 – Inadmissibility of change of legal jurisdiction
Everyone has the right for consideration of his/her case in the court of law specified by the legislation. Case of the person shall not be considered in another court without the person's consent.

Article 63 – Presumption of innocence
1.   Everyone is entitled to the presumption of innocence. Everyone who is charged with a crime shall be considered innocent until his guilt is proven legally and if no verdict of law court has been brought into force.
2.   A person under suspicion of crime must not be considered guilty.
3.   A person accused of a crime does not need to prove his/her innocence.
4.   Evidence obtained illegally must not be used when presenting a legal case.
5.   Nobody may be convicted of a crime without the verdict of law court.

Article 64 – Inadmissibility of repeated conviction for one and the same crime
Nobody may be repeatedly sentenced for one and the same crime.

Article 65 – Right for repeated appeal to the law court
Every person convicted by a court of law has the right to appeal, as specified by the law, to the higher court asking for reconsideration of the verdict and also for pardon and mitigation of the sentence.

Article 66 – Inadmissibility of testifying against relations
Nobody may be forced to testify against him/herself, spouse, children, parents, brother or sister. The complete list of relations against whom testifying is not obligatory is specified by law.

Article 67 – Rights of a person detained, arrested or charged with a crime
Every person, detained, arrested or charged with a crime should be immediately advised by competent state bodies about his/her rights, reasons for his/her arrest and institution of criminal proceedings against him/her.

Article 68 – Right for compensation of losses
1.   The rights of a person who has been a victim of crime and also of usurpation of power are protected by law. A victim of crime has the right to take part in the administration of justice and demand compensation for losses.

2.   Everyone has the right for compensation by the state for losses born as a result of illegal actions or non-action of state bodies or their officials.

Article 69 – Right of foreign citizens and stateless persons
1.   Foreign citizens and stateless persons staying in the Azerbaijan Republic may enjoy all rights and must fulfil all obligations like citizens of the Azerbaijan Republic if not specified by legislation or international agreement in which the Azerbaijan Republic is one of the parties.
2.   Rights and liberties of foreign citizens and stateless persons permanently living or temporarily staying in the territory of the Azerbaijan Republic may be restricted only according to international legal standards and the laws of the Azerbaijan Republic.

Article 70 – Right of political asylum
1.   In accordance with recognised international legal standards the Azerbaijan Republic grants political asylum to foreign citizens and stateless persons.
2.   The extradition of persons persecuted for their political beliefs and also for acts which are not regarded as a crime in the Azerbaijan Republic is not permitted.

Article 71 – Protection of rights and liberties of a human being and citizen
1.   To observe and to protect rights and liberties of a human being and citizen specified in the Constitution is the responsibility of bodies of legislative, executive and legal power.
2.   No-one may restrict implementation of rights and liberties of a human being and citizen.
3.   Rights and liberties of a human being and citizen may be partially and temporarily restricted only on announcement of war, martial law and state of emergency, and also mobilisation, taking into consideration international obligations of the Azerbaijan Republic. The population of the Republic shall be notified in advance about restrictions as regards its rights and liberties.
4.   Nobody, in any circumstances, may be forced to promulgate his/her religious and other beliefs, thoughts or be persecuted for such.
5.   None of the provisions of the Constitution may be interpreted as a regulation directed at the prohibition of rights and liberties of a human being and citizen.
6.   The rights and liberties of a human being and citizen act on the territory of the Azerbaijan Republic by themselves.
7.   Any arguments related to the violation of rights and liberties of a human being and citizen are settled in courts of law.
8.   No-one will be responsible for acts which were not considered criminal at the time of their being carried out. If, after the crime, a new law was introduced envisaging no responsibility or a mitigation of responsibility, the said new law shall apply.

Chapter 4 – Main responsibilities of citizens

Article 72 – Main responsibilities of citizens
1.   Everyone has obligations to the state and society directly resulting from his/her rights and liberties.

2.   Everyone must follow the provisions of the Constitution and laws of the Azerbaijan Republic, respect rights and liberties of other persons and fulfil other obligations envisaged by the law.
3.   Ignorance of the law does not release a citizen from responsibility.

Article 73 – Taxes and other state duties
1.   Everyone must pay taxes and other state duties in time and in full as required.
2.   Nobody may be forced to pay taxes and other state duties if they are not envisaged in the law and in excess of the amount specified therein.

Article 74 – Loyalty to motherland
1.   Loyalty to the motherland is sacred.
2.   Persons working in legislative, executive or judicial power bodies who were elected and appointed to their posts are responsible for accurate and conscientious fulfilment of their obligations and, whenever required by the law, to make an oath.
3.   A person working in legislative, executive or judicial power bodies who was elected and appointed to his/her post and made an oath regarding the Constitution of the Azerbaijan Republic shall be considered dismissed and will not be able to take this position if he/she was charged with crime against the state, including rebellion or *coup d'état* and has been sentenced based on his charge.

Article 75 – Respect for state symbols
Every citizen must respect the state symbols of the Azerbaijan Republic: its banner, state emblem and hymn.

Article 76 – Defence of the motherland
1.   The defence of the motherland is the duty of every citizen. Citizens of the Republic serve in the army according to legislation.
2.   If beliefs of citizens come into conflict with service in the army, then in some cases envisaged by legislation alternative service instead of regular army service is permitted.

Article 77 – Protection of historical and cultural monuments
Every citizen is responsible for protection of historical and cultural monuments.

Article 78 – Protection of the environment
Every citizen is responsible for protection of the environment.

Article 79 – Inadmissibility of fulfilment of obligations contravening the legislation
No one may be forced to carry out obligations contravening the Constitution and laws of the Azerbaijan Republic.

Article 80 – Responsibility
Violation of provisions of the present Constitution and laws of the Azerbaijan Republic including usurpation of rights and liberties and also failure to fulfil responsibilities specified in the present Constitution and laws of the Azerbaijan Republic will be prosecuted.

Section 3 – State power
Chapter 5 – Legislative power

Article 81 – Implementation of legislative power
Legislative power in the Azerbaijan Republic is implemented by Milli Majlis of the Azerbaijan Republic.

Article 82 – Number of deputies in Milli Majlis of the Azerbaijan Republic
Milli Majlis of the Azerbaijan Republic consists of 125 deputies.

Article 83 – Procedure of elections of deputies of Milli Majlis of the Azerbaijan Republic
Deputies of Milli Majlis of the Azerbaijan Republic are elected based on majority and proportional voting systems and general, equal and direct elections by way of free, individual and secret voting.

Article 84 – Term of authority of a calling of Milli Majlis of the Azerbaijan Republic
1.   The term of authority of each calling of Milli Majlis of the Azerbaijan Republic is five years.
2.   Elections for each calling of Milli Majlis of the Azerbaijan Republic take place every five years on the first Sunday in November.
3.   The term of authority of deputies of Milli Majlis of the Azerbaijan Republic is restricted by the term of authority of respective calling of Milli Majlis of the Azerbaijan Republic.
4.   If new elections of deputies to replace retired deputies of Milli Majlis of the Azerbaijan Republic are carried out, then the term of authority of the newly elected deputy corresponds to the remaining term of authority of the respective retired deputy.

Article 85 – Requirements to be fulfilled by candidates to the posts of deputies of Milli Majlis of the Azerbaijan Republic
1.   Every citizen of the Azerbaijan Republic not younger than 25 may be elected a deputy of Milli Majlis of the Azerbaijan Republic in an established order.
2.   Persons having dual citizenship, those having obligations to other states, those working in the bodies of executive or judicial power, persons involved in other payable activity except scientific, pedagogical and creative activity, religious men, persons whose incapacity has been confirmed by a court of law, those condemned for grave crime and those serving a sentence due to verdict a court of law may not be elected deputies of Milli Majlis of the Azerbaijan Republic.

Article 86 – Inspection and approval of results of elections of deputies of Milli Majlis of the Azerbaijan Republic
The accuracy of results of elections is checked and approved by Constitutional Court of the Azerbaijan Republic as specified in the law.

Article 87 – End of the term of authority of deputies of Milli Majlis of the Azerbaijan Republic
1.   The term of authority of deputies of Milli Majlis of the Azerbaijan Republic ends on the day of the first meeting of new calling of Milli Majlis of the Azerbaijan Republic.
2.   Elections of deputies to replace those who left Milli Majlis of the Azerbaijan Republic shall not be held if less than 25 days remains to the end of term of authority of Milli Majlis of the Azerbaijan Republic.
3.   Milli Majlis of the Azerbaijan Republic will have powers after the authority of 83 of its deputies has been approved.

Article 88 – Sessions of Milli Majlis of the Azerbaijan Republic
1.   Every year two sessions of Milli Majlis of the Azerbaijan Republic are held.
The spring session begins on 1 February and continues until 31 May.
The autumn session begins on 30 September and continues until 30 December.
If 1 February and 30 September fall on holidays the session will begin on the following working day.
After approval of the authority of 83 deputies of Milli Majlis of the Azerbaijan Republic the first meeting of Milli Majlis of the Azerbaijan Republic shall be summoned within one week beginning from the day of approval.
If after elections to Milli Majlis of the Azerbaijan Republic, authority of 83 its deputies has not been approved before 1 February, then the day of opening the first meeting of Milli Majlis of the Azerbaijan Republic will be established by the Constitutional Court of the Azerbaijan Republic.
2.   Extraordinary sessions of Milli Majlis of the Azerbaijan Republic will be summoned by the Chairman of Milli Majlis of the Azerbaijan Republic at request of the President of the Azerbaijan Republic or 42 deputies of Milli Majlis of the Azerbaijan Republic.
3.   The agenda of an extraordinary session will be prepared by those who summoned the said session. After the questions of the agenda have been discussed, the extraordinary session ends.

Article 89 – Deprivation of deputies of Milli Majlis of the Azerbaijan Republic of their mandates and loss of powers by a deputy of Milli Majlis of the Azerbaijan Republic
1.   A deputy of Milli Majlis of the Azerbaijan Republic loses his/her mandate in the following cases:
  a.   whenever during the elections there was falsification in calculation of votes;
  b.   on giving up citizenship of the Azerbaijan Republic or accepting other citizenship;
  c.   on commitment of crime and whenever there is a valid verdict of court of law;

    d.   on accepting a post in state bodies or in religious organisations, involvement in business, commercial or other paid activity (except scientific, pedagogical and creative activity);

    e.   on a voluntary basis;

    f.   on abolition of the party the deputy belongs to.

Decisions about deprivation of the deputy of Milli Majlis of the Azerbaijan Republic of his mandate are taken as specified in legislation.

2.   Whenever deputies of Milli Majlis of the Azerbaijan Republic are not able to fulfil their obligations, and in other cases specified by law, their authority is considered terminated. The procedure of taking respective decision is determined by the law.

Article 90 – Immunity of deputies of Milli Majlis of the Azerbaijan Republic

1.   A deputy of Milli Majlis of the Azerbaijan Republic enjoys immunity during the whole term of his powers. Except in cases when the deputy may be caught in the act of a crime, a deputy of Milli Majlis of the Azerbaijan Republic may not during the whole term of his/her authority be called to criminal responsibility, or arrested, disciplinary measures may not be applied to him by a court, nor may he be searched. The deputy of Milli Majlis of the Azerbaijan Republic may be arrested only if he/she has been caught at a place of crime. In such case the body which detained the deputy of Milli Majlis of the Azerbaijan Republic must immediately notify the General Procurator of the Azerbaijan Republic of this fact.

2.   The immunity of a deputy of Milli Majlis of the Azerbaijan Republic may be stopped only by decision of Milli Majlis of the Azerbaijan Republic based on application of the General Procurator of the Azerbaijan Republic.

Article 91 – Prohibition on institution of proceedings against deputies of Millis Majlis of the Azerbaijan Republic

Deputies of Milli Majlis of the Azerbaijan Republic cannot be made responsible for their activity in Milli Majlis of the Azerbaijan Republic, voting in Milli Majlis of the Azerbaijan Republic and statements made in Milli Majlis of the Azerbaijan Republic. Without the deputies' consent, in connection with such cases, they are not obliged to give explanations and evidence.

Article 92 – Organisation of work of Milli Majlis of the Azerbaijan Republic

Milli Majlis of the Azerbaijan Republic determines the procedure of its activities, elects its chairman and his deputies, organises permanent and other commissions and establishes a Counting Chamber.

Article 93 – Acts of Milli Majlis of the Azerbaijan Republic

1.   Milli Majlis of the Azerbaijan Republic accepts Constitutional laws and decrees regarding the questions of its competence.

2.   Constitutional laws, laws and decrees are taken in Milli Majlis of the Azerbaijan Republic in an order specified in the present Constitution.

3.   Deputies of Milli Majlis of the Azerbaijan Republic exercise their voting right personally.

4. Specific orders to the bodies of executive power and law courts cannot be envisaged in laws and decrees of Milli Majlis of the Azerbaijan Republic.

Article 94 – General rules established by Milli Majlis of the Azerbaijan Republic
1. Milli Majlis of the Azerbaijan Republic establishes general rules concerning the following matters:
    i. use of rights and liberties of a person and citizen specified in the present Constitution, state guarantees of these rights and liberties;
    ii. elections of the President of the Azerbaijan Republic;
    iii. elections to Milli Majlis of the Azerbaijan Republic and status of deputies of Milli Majlis of the Azerbaijan Republic;
    iv. referendums;
    v. judicial system and status of judges; procurator's office, the bar and notary's offices;
    vi. legal proceedings, execution of court verdicts;
    vii. elections to municipalities and status of municipalities;
    viii. state of emergency; martial law;
    ix. state awards;
    x. status of physical persons and legal entities;
    xi. objects of civil law;
    xii. transactions, civil legal agreements, representation and inheritance;
    xiii. right of property, including legal régime of state, private and municipal property, right of intellectual property, other proprietary rights; liability right;
    xiv. family relationships, including guardianship and trusteeship;
    xv. basis of financial activity – taxes, duties and charges;
    xvi. labour of relationships and social maintenance;
    xvii. interpretation of crime and other violations of law; establishment of responsibility for these acts;
    xviii. defence and military service;
    xix. government employment;
    xx. basis of security;
    xxi. territorial arrangement; régime of state borders;
    xxii. ratification and denunciation of international treaties;
    xxiii. communications and transport;
    xxiv. statistics; metrology and standards;
    xxv. customs;
    xxvi commerce and stock exchange activity;
    xxvii. banking business, accounting, insurance.
2. Questions specified in paragraphs 2, 3 of the present article the laws are approved by majority of 83 votes, other questions – by majority of 63 votes.
3. The first part of the present Article may be supplemented with the Constitutional law.

Article 95 – Competence of Milli Majlis of the Azerbaijan Republic
1. The following questions fall under the competence of Milli Majlis of the Azerbaijan Republic;

  i. organisation of work of Milli Majlis of the Azerbaijan Republic;

  ii. based on recommendation by the President of the Azerbaijan Republic establishment of diplomatic representations of the Azerbaijan Republic;

  iii. administrative-territorial division;

  iv. ratification and denunciation of international agreements;

  v. based on recommendation by the President of the Azerbaijan Republic approval of state budget of the Azerbaijan Republic and control over its execution;

  vi. amnesty;

  vii. based on recommendation by the President of the Azerbaijan Republic approval of military doctrine of the Azerbaijan Republic;

  viii. in cases specified in the present Constitution, approval of decrees of the President of the Azerbaijan Republic;

  ix. based on recommendation by the President of the Azerbaijan Republic, giving consent for appointment of Prime Minister of the Azerbaijan Republic;

  x. based on recommendation by the President of the Azerbaijan Republic, appointment of judges of the Constitutional Court of the Azerbaijan Republic, the Supreme Court of the Azerbaijan Republic and Economic Court of the Azerbaijan Republic;

  xi. based on recommendation by the President of the Azerbaijan Republic, giving consent for appointment and dismissal of the General Procurator of the Azerbaijan Republic;

  xii. dismissal of the President of the Azerbaijan Republic by way of impeachment based on the recommendation of the Constitutional Court of the Azerbaijan Republic;

  xiii. based on recommendation by the President of the Azerbaijan Republic, dismissal of judges;

  xiv. taking decision regarding a vote of confidence in the Cabinet of Ministers of the Azerbaijan Republic;

  xv. based on recommendation by the President of the Azerbaijan Republic, appointment and dismissal of members of the Administration Board of the National Bank of the Azerbaijan Republic;

  xvi. based on recommendation by the President of the Azerbaijan Republic, giving consent for enlistment of military forces of the Azerbaijan Republic to operations other than their normal duties;

  xvii. based on request of the President of the Azerbaijan Republic giving consent for announcement of war and conclusion of peace treaty;

  xviii. announcement of referendum;

  xix. establishment of Auditor Chamber.

2. Questions specified in paragraphs 1-4 of the present article – the laws are approved by a majority of 63 votes, other questions – decrees are approved in the same order if not specified otherwise by the present Constitution.

3. Decrees are also taken regarding other questions which due to the present Constitution fall under the competence of Milli Majlis of the Azerbaijan Republic.

4. The first part of the present Article may be supplemented with the Constitutional law.

Article 96 – Right of legislative initiative
1.   The right of legislative initiative in Milli Majlis of the Azerbaijan Republic (the right to submit for consideration by Milli Majlis of the Azerbaijan Republic drafts of laws and other questions) belongs to deputies of Milli Majlis of the Azerbaijan Republic, the President of the Azerbaijan Republic, Supreme Court of the Azerbaijan Republic and Alli Majlis of Nakhichevan Autonomous Republic.
2.   Drafts of laws or decrees submitted for consideration by Milli Majlis of the Azerbaijan Republic by the President of the Azerbaijan Republic, Supreme Court of the Azerbaijan Republic or Alli Majlis of Nakhichevan Autonomous Republic, as legislative initiative, are put to the vote as they are.
3.   Amendments to such drafts of laws or decrees are introduced by consent of the body which used the right of legislative initiative.
4.   Drafts of laws or decrees submitted for consideration by Milli Majlis of the Azerbaijan Republic by the President of the Azerbaijan Republic, Supreme Court of the Azerbaijan Republic or Alli Majlis of Nakhichevan Autonomous Republic, as legislative initiative, are put to the vote in Milli Majlis of the Azerbaijan Republic within two months.
5.   If draft of the law or decree has been declared by the President of the Azerbaijan Republic, Supreme Court of the Azerbaijan Republic or Alli Majlis of Nakhichevan Autonomous Republic urgent, then above specified term shall constitute 20 days.

Article 97 – Term for submitting laws for signing
1.   Drafts of the laws are submitted to the President of the Azerbaijan Republic for signing within 14 days from the day of their acceptance.
2.   An urgent draft of the law is submitted to the President of the Azerbaijan Republic for signing within 24 hours from the moment of its acceptance.

Article 98 – Validity of acts of Milli Majlis of the Azerbaijan Republic
If not specified otherwise in the law and decree of Milli Majlis of the Azerbaijan Republic themselves, the law and decree become valid from the date of their publication.

Chapter 6 – Executive power

Article 99 – Possession of executive power
Executive power in the Azerbaijan Republic belongs to the President of the Azerbaijan Republic.

Article 100 – Requirements to be fulfilled by candidates for the post of the President of the Azerbaijan Republic
A citizen of the Azerbaijan Republic not younger than 35, permanently living in the territory of the Azerbaijan Republic for longer than 10 years, possessing the right to vote, with no previous convictions, having no liabilities in other states, with a university degree, not having dual citizenship may be elected the President of the Azerbaijan Republic.

Article 101 – Procedure of elections of the President of the Azerbaijan Republic

1.   The President of the Azerbaijan Republic is elected for a five-year term by way of general, direct and equal elections, with free, personal and secret ballot.

2.   The President of the Azerbaijan Republic is elected by a majority of two-thirds of the votes cast.

3.   If the required majority has not been achieved in the first round of voting, then a second round will be held on the second Sunday after the first round. Only the leading two candidates in the first round, or the next two candidates if the first two should withdraw, will take part in the second round of elections.

4.   The candidate who obtains a simple majority of the votes cast in the second round of elections is considered to have been elected the President of the Azerbaijan Republic.

5.   No one may be elected the President of the Azerbaijan Republic for more than two terms.

6.   The procedure for implementating the present Article is specified in legislation.

Article 102 – Results of elections of the President of the Azerbaijan Republic

Results of elections of the President of the Azerbaijan Republic are officially announced by the Constitutional Court of the Azerbaijan Republic within seven days from the day of voting.

Article 103 – Oath of a person elected the President of the Azerbaijan Republic

1.   A person elected the President of the Azerbaijan Republic, within three days from the day when results of elections of the President of the Azerbaijan Republic have been announced, with the participation of judges of the Constitutional Court of the Azerbaijan Republic takes an oath: "In carrying out the powers of the President of the Azerbaijan Republic I swear to follow the Constitution of the Azerbaijan Republic, protect the sovereignty and territorial integrity of the state, and to serve people".

2.   It is considered that the President of the Azerbaijan Republic begins carrying out his official powers from the day when he takes his oath.

Article 104 – Inability of the President of the Azerbaijan Republic to carry out his powers

1.   The President of the Azerbaijan Republic is considered to have left his post ahead of time on resignation, complete inability to fulfil his powers due to illness, dismissal from his post in cases or in an order envisaged in the present Constitution.

2.   When the President of the Azerbaijan Republic is going to resign, his application to resign is presented to the Constitutional Court of the Azerbaijan Republic. The Constitutional Court of the Azerbaijan Republic, having confirmed that the President of the Azerbaijan Republic himself sent in his resignation makes the decision to accept this resignation. From that moment the President is considered to have left his post due to resignation.

3.   Having received notification of the complete inability of the President of the Azerbaijan Republic to fulfil his powers due to poor health, Milli Majlis of the Azerbaijan Republic applies to the Constitutional Court of the Azerbaijan Republic for clarification of this fact. Should the Constitutional Court of the Azerbaijan Republic confirm this fact, the question is settled.

Article 105 – Implementation of powers of the President of the Azerbaijan Republic on his resignation
1.   Whenever the President of the Azerbaijan Republic resigns from his post ahead of time, extraordinary elections of the President of the Azerbaijan Republic are held within three months. In such case, until a new president of the Azerbaijan Republic is elected, the Chairman of Milli Majlis of the Azerbaijan Republic will carry out powers of the President of the Azerbaijan Republic.
2.   If during the said term the Chairman of Milli Majlis of the Azerbaijan Republic carrying out the powers of the President of the Azerbaijan Republic resigns or becomes incapable of carrying out his powers due to illness, the Prime Minister of the Azerbaijan Republic will carry out powers of the President of the Azerbaijan Republic.
3.   If the Prime Minister of the Azerbaijan Republic is unable to fulfil the powers of the President of the Azerbaijan Republic due to reasons given in Paragraph 2 of the present Article, Milli Majlis of the Azerbaijan Republic passes a decree about the delegation of powers of the President of the Azerbaijan Republic to another official.

Article 106 – Immunity of the President of the Azerbaijan Republic
The President of the Azerbaijan Republic enjoys the right of personal immunity. The honour and dignity of the President of the Azerbaijan Republic are protected by law.

Article 107 – Dismissal of the President of the Azerbaijan Republic from his post
1.   In the case of grave crime committed by the President of the Azerbaijan Republic, the question of dismissal of the President may be submitted to Milli Majlis of the Azerbaijan Republic on the initiative of the Constitutional Court of the Azerbaijan Republic based on conclusions of the Supreme Court of the Azerbaijan Republic presented within 30 days.
2.   The President of the Azerbaijan Republic may be dismissed from his post by decree of Milli Majlis of the Azerbaijan Republic taken by a majority of 95 votes of deputies. This decree is signed by the Chairman of the Constitutional Court of the Azerbaijan Republic. If the Constitutional Court of the Azerbaijan Republic fails to sign the said decree within one week it shall not come into force.
3.   The decree about the dismissal of the President of the Azerbaijan Republic from his post must be accepted within two months from the date of application of the Constitutional Court of the Azerbaijan Republic to Milli Majlis of the Azerbaijan Republic. If the said decree is not taken within this term, then the accusation against the President of the Azerbaijan Republic is considered to have been rejected.

Article 108 – Provisions for the President of the Azerbaijan Republic
The President of the Azerbaijan Republic and his family are provided for by the state. Security of the President of the Azerbaijan Republic and his family is ensured by special security teams.

Article 109 – Competence of the President of the Azerbaijan Republic
The President of the Azerbaijan Republic:

    i.   announces elections to Milli Majlis of the Azerbaijan Republic;

    ii.   submits for approval by Milli Majlis of the Azerbaijan Republic the state budget of the Azerbaijan Republic;

    iii.   approves state economic and social programmes;

    iv.   by consent of Milli Majlis of the Azerbaijan Republic appoints and dismisses the Prime Minister of the Azerbaijan Republic;

    v.   appoints and dismisses members of the Cabinet of Ministers of the Azerbaijan Republic; whenever necessary takes the chair at the meetings of the Cabinet of Ministers of the Azerbaijan Republic;

    vi.   takes decisions about the resignation of Cabinet of Ministers of the Azerbaijan Republic;

    vii.   establishes central and local executive power bodies within the limits of sums allocated in the state budget of the Azerbaijan Republic;

    viii.   cancels decrees and orders of the Cabinet of Ministers of the Azerbaijan Republic and the Cabinet of Ministers of Nakhichevan Autonomous Republic, as well as acts of central and local executive power bodies;

    ix.   submits proposals to Milli Majlis of the Azerbaijan Republic about the appointment of judges of the Constitutional Court of the Azerbaijan Republic, the Supreme Court of the Azerbaijan Republic and the Economic Court of the Azerbaijan Republic; appoints judges of other courts of the Azerbaijan Republic; by consent of Milli Majlis of the Azerbaijan Republic appoints and dismisses the General Procurator of the Azerbaijan Republic;

    x.   submits recommendations to Milli Majlis of the Azerbaijan Republic about appointment and dismissal of members of the Administration Board of the National Bank of the Azerbaijan Republic;

    xi.   submits to Milli Majlis of the Azerbaijan Republic for approval military doctrine of the Azerbaijan Republic;

    xii.   appoints and dismisses officers of higher rank to military forces of the Azerbaijan Republic;

    xiii.   forms the executive office of the President of the Azerbaijan Republic, appoints its head;

    xiv.   appoints and dismisses authorised representatives of the President of the Azerbaijan Republic;

    xv.   submits recommendations to Milli Majlis of the Azerbaijan Republic about the establishment of diplomatic representations of the Azerbaijan Republic in foreign countries and in international organisations, appoints and dismisses diplomatic representatives of the Azerbaijan Republic in foreign countries and in international organisations;

    xvi.   receives credence and letters of recall from diplomatic representatives of foreign countries;

    xvii.   concludes interstate and intergovernmental agreements, presents interstate agreements to Milli Majlis of the Azerbaijan Republic for ratification and denunciation; signs decrees on ratification of international agreements;

xviii. announces referendum;

xix. signs and issues laws;

xx. settles questions concerning citizenship;

xxi. settles questions concerning granting political asylum;

xxii. grants pardons;

xxiii. gives state awards;

xxiv. assigns higher military and higher special ranks;

xxv. announces total or partial mobilisation and also demobilisation;

xxvi. takes the decision about calling up citizens of the Azerbaijan Republic to urgent military service and transfer to the reserve of soldiers of urgent military service;

xxvii. forms Security Council of the Azerbaijan Republic;

xxviii. submits recommendation to Milli Majlis of the Azerbaijan Republic about consent for the use of military forces of the Azerbaijan Republic in implementation of duties other than their normal duties;

xxix. announces a state of emergency and martial law;

xxx. on consent of Milli Majlis of the Azerbaijan Republic announces a war and concludes peace agreements;

xxxi. forms special security bodies within the limits of sums allocated from the state budget of the Azerbaijan Republic;

xxxii. settles other questions which under the present Constitution do not pertain to the competence of Milli Majlis of the Azerbaijan Republic and law courts of the Azerbaijan Republic.

Article 110 – Signing of the laws
1. The President of the Azerbaijan Republic signs the laws within 56 days after their presentation. If the President of the Azerbaijan Republic has objections against a law he may return it to Milli Majlis of the Azerbaijan Republic within the specified term without signing, together with his comments.
2. Should the President of the Azerbaijan Republic fail to sign Constitutional laws they will not come into force. If Milli Majlis of the Azerbaijan Republic accepts by majority of 95 votes laws that have been accepted previously by majority of 83 votes, and by majority of 83 votes the laws that have been accepted previously by majority of 63 votes, the said laws come into force after repeated voting.

Article 111 – Declaration of martial law
In cases of actual occupation of some part of the territory of the Azerbaijan Republic, announcement of war by foreign country or countries against the Azerbaijan Republic, blockade of the territory of the Azerbaijan Republic and also whenever there is real danger of armed attack against the Azerbaijan Republic, blockade of the territory of the Azerbaijan Republic and also in case of real threat of such blockade, the President of the Azerbaijan Republic announces martial law all over the territory of the Azerbaijan Republic or in individual areas, and within 24 hours submits the relevant decree for approval by Milli Majlis of the Azerbaijan Republic.

Article 112 – State of emergency
Whenever natural calamities take place, epidemic, epizootic, grave ecological and other disasters and also on accomplishment of acts aimed at violation of the territorial integrity of the Azerbaijan Republic, revolt or *coup d'état,* with mass disorders accompanied by violence, other conflicts threatening the life and safety of citizens or the normal activity of state bodies, the President of the Azerbaijan Republic announces a state of emergency in individual areas of the Azerbaijan Republic and within 24 hours submits the relevant decree for approval by Milli Majlis of the Azerbaijan Republic.

Article 113 – Acts of the President of the Azerbaijan Republic
1.   Establishing general procedures the President of the Azerbaijan Republic issues decrees, all other questions, he issues orders.
2.   If not specified otherwise in decrees and orders of the President of the Azerbaijan Republic, they become valid from the day of their publication.

Article 114 – Status of the Cabinet of Ministers of the Azerbaijan Republic
1.   For implementation of executive powers, the President of the Azerbaijan Republic establishes a Cabinet of Ministers of the Azerbaijan Republic.
2.   The Cabinet of Ministers of the Azerbaijan Republic is the highest body of executive power of the President of the Azerbaijan Republic.
3.   The Cabinet of Ministers of the Azerbaijan Republic is subordinate to the President of the Azerbaijan Republic and reports to him.
4.   The procedure of activities of the Cabinet of Ministers of the Azerbaijan Republic is defined by the President of the Azerbaijan Republic.

Article 115 – Composition of Cabinet of Ministers of the Azerbaijan Republic
The Cabinet of Ministers of the Azerbaijan Republic includes Prime Minister of the Azerbaijan Republic, his deputies, ministers and heads of other central bodies of executive power.

Article 116 – Resignation of the Cabinet of Ministers of the Azerbaijan Republic
On a day when the newly elected President of the Azerbaijan Republic comes into his rights and begins carrying out his powers, the Cabinet of Ministers of the Azerbaijan Republic resigns.

Article 117 – Meetings of the Cabinet of Ministers of the Azerbaijan Republic
As a rule, the Prime Minister of the Azerbaijan Republic takes the chair at meetings of the Cabinet of Ministers of the Azerbaijan Republic.

Article 118 – Procedure of appointment of Prime Minister of the Azerbaijan Republic
1.   The Prime Minister of the Azerbaijan Republic is appointed by the President of the Azerbaijan Republic at the consent of Milli Majlis of the Azerbaijan Republic.

2. The proposed candidature for the post of Prime Minister of the Azerbaijan Republic is submitted for consideration to Milli Majlis of the Azerbaijan Republic by the President of the Azerbaijan Republic no later than one month from the day when the President begins carrying out his powers, or not later than two weeks from the day of resignation of the Cabinet of Ministers of the Azerbaijan Republic.

3. Milli Majlis of the Azerbaijan Republic takes the decision concerning the candidate to the post of Prime Minister of the Azerbaijan Republic not later than one week from the day when the candidature was proposed. Should this procedure be violated, or candidatures proposed by the President of the Azerbaijan Republic for the post of Prime Minister of the Azerbaijan Republic be rejected three times, then the President of the Azerbaijan Republic may appoint the Prime Minister of the Azerbaijan Republic without the consent of Milli Majlis of the Azerbaijan Republic.

Article 119 – Authority of Cabinet of Ministers of the Azerbaijan Republic
The Cabinet of Ministers of the Azerbaijan Republic:
  – prepares the draft of the state budget of the Azerbaijan Republic and submits it to the President of the Azerbaijan Republic;
  – provides implementation of the state budget of the Azerbaijan Republic;
  – provides implementation of financial-credit and monetary policy;
  – provides implementation of state economic programmes;
  – carries out control over ministries and other central bodies of executive power and annuls their acts;
  – solves other questions delegated to it by the President of the Azerbaijan Republic.

Article 120 – Acts of Cabinet of Ministers of the Azerbaijan Republic
1. In establishing general procedures the Cabinet of Ministers of the Azerbaijan Republic issues decrees, as for all other questions it issues orders.
2. If not specified otherwise in decrees and orders of the Cabinet of Ministers of the Azerbaijan Republic, they become valid from the day of their publication.

Article 121 – Requirements to be fulfilled by candidates for the posts of members of the Cabinet of Ministers of the Azerbaijan Republic
1. The Prime Minister of the Azerbaijan Republic shall be a citizen of the Azerbaijan Republic not younger than 30, having right to vote, with a university degree, having no liabilities in other states.
2. The Deputy Prime Minister of the Azerbaijan Republic, minister, head of other central body of executive power shall be a citizen of the Azerbaijan Republic not younger than 25, having the right to vote, with a university degree, having no liabilities in other states.

Article 122 – Requirements to members of the Cabinet of Ministers of the Azerbaijan Republic

The Prime Minister of the Azerbaijan Republic, his deputies, ministers and heads of other central bodies of executive power may not occupy any posts, irrespective of the procedure, elections or appointment, may not be involved in business, commercial and other payable activity except scientific, pedagogical and creative activity, may not get remuneration other than their wages and money for scientific, pedagogical and creative activity.

Article 123 – Immunity of the Prime Minister of the Azerbaijan Republic
1.   The Prime Minister of the Azerbaijan Republic enjoys immunity throughout his term of office.
2.   The Prime Minister of the Azerbaijan Republic may not be arrested, called to criminal responsibility except in cases when he has been caught in the act of crime; disciplinary measures may not be applied to him by law court, nor may he be searched.
3.   The Prime Minister of the Azerbaijan Republic may be arrested if he has been caught in the act of committing a crime. In such case the deputy of Milli Majlis of the Azerbaijan Republic must immediately notify the General Procurator of the Azerbaijan Republic about the fact.
4.   Immunity of the Prime Minister of the Azerbaijan Republic might be stopped only by the President of the Azerbaijan Republic, based on application of the General Procurator of the Azerbaijan Republic.

Article 124 – Local bodies of executive power
1.   Heads of executive power bodies carry out executive power locally.
2.   Heads of executive power bodies are appointed to their posts and dismissed by the President of the Azerbaijan Republic.
3.   Limits of authority of local executive power bodies are determined by the President of the Azerbaijan Republic.

Chapter 7 – Judicial power

Article 125 – Judicial power
1.   Judicial power in Azerbaijan is implemented by courts of law.
2.   Judicial power is implemented through the Constitutional Court of the Azerbaijan Republic, the Supreme Court of the Azerbaijan Republic, the Economic Court of the Azerbaijan Republic, ordinary and specialised law courts of the Azerbaijan Republic.
3.   Judicial power is implemented by way of constitutional, civil and criminal legal proceedings and other forms of legislation provided for by law.
4.   In all legal proceedings, except constitutional proceedings, the Procurator's Office of the Azerbaijan Republic and lawyers take part.
5.   The judicial system and legal proceedings in the Azerbaijan Republic are determined by law.
6.   The use of legal means aimed at changing the authority of courts of law and the establishment of extraordinary courts of law which are not envisaged by the law are prohibited.

Article 126 – Requirements to be fulfilled by candidates for judges' posts

1. Judges shall be citizens of the Azerbaijan Republic not younger than 30, having the right to vote, higher juridical education and at least five years working experience in the sphere of law.
2. Judges may not occupy any other posts, irrespective of the procedure, elections or appointment, may not be involved in business, commercial and other payable activity, except scientific, pedagogical and creative activity, may not be involved in political activity and join political parties, may not receive remuneration other than their wages and money for scientific, pedagogical and creative activity.

Article 127 – Independence of judges, main principles and conditions of implementation of justice
1. Judges are independent, they are subordinate only to the Constitution and laws of the Azerbaijan Republic, they cannot be replaced during the term of their office.
2. In their consideration of legal cases judges must be impartial and fair; they should treat the parties as juridically equal and act based on facts and according to the law.
3. Direct and indirect restriction of legal proceedings from whatever quarter and due to some reason, illegal influence, threats and interference is not allowed.
4. Justice shall be implemented based on equality of citizens before the law and the court of law.
5. In all courts of law cases shall be heard in public.
6. It is allowed to have closed hearing of legal cases only if the law court decides that open hearings may result in the disclosure of state, professional or commercial secrets, or that it is necessary to keep confidentiality with respect to personal or family life.
7. Except for cases envisaged by law it is prohibited to carry out legal proceedings by correspondence.
8. Law proceedings are carried out based on the principle of contest.
9. Everyone has the right of defence at all stages of legal proceedings.
10. Justice is based on the presumption of innocence. In the Azerbaijan Republic legal proceedings are carried out in the standard language of the Azerbaijan Republic or in a language of the majority population in a specific area. Participants in legal proceedings not knowing the language of proceedings have the right to be acquainted with the materials of proceedings, to take part in legal proceedings using an interpreter and to make statements in the court in their native language.

Article 128 – Immunity of judges
1. Judges are immune.
2. A judge may be called to criminal responsibility only in accordance with the law.
3. Authority of judges may be stopped only for reasons and rules envisaged by the law.
4. Whenever judges commit crime, the President of the Azerbaijan Republic, based on conclusions of Supreme Court of the Azerbaijan Republic, may make a statement in Milli Majlis of the Azerbaijan Republic with the intention

to dismiss judges from their posts. Relevant conclusions of the Supreme Court of the Azerbaijan Republic must be presented to the President of the Azerbaijan Republic within 30 days after his request.

5.   A decision about the dismissal of judges of the Constitutional Court of the Azerbaijan Republic, Supreme Court of the Azerbaijan Republic and the Economic Court of the Azerbaijan Republic is taken by Milli Majlis of the Azerbaijan Republic with a majority of 83 votes; a decision about the dismissal of other judges is taken by Milli Majlis of the Azerbaijan Republic with a majority of 63 votes.

Article 129 – Decisions of law courts and their implementation
Law courts take decisions on behalf of the state; implementation of these decisions is obligatory.

Article 130 – Constitutional Court of the Azerbaijan Republic
1.   Constitutional Court of the Azerbaijan Republic consists of nine judges.
2.   Judges of the Constitutional Court of the Azerbaijan Republic are appointed by Milli Majlis of the Azerbaijan Republic on the recommendation by the President of the Azerbaijan Republic.
3.   The Constitutional Court of the Azerbaijan Republic based on inquiry of the President of the Azerbaijan Republic, Milli Majlis of the Azerbaijan Republic, the Cabinet of Ministers of the Azerbaijan Republic, the Supreme Court of the Azerbaijan Republic, the Procurator's Office of the Azerbaijan Republic and Alli Majlis of the Nakhichevan Autonomous Republic takes decisions regarding the following:
        i.   correspondence of laws of the Azerbaijan Republic, decrees and orders of the President of the Azerbaijan Republic, decrees of Milli Majlis of the Azerbaijan Republic, decrees and orders of the Cabinet of Ministers of the Azerbaijan Republic and normative-legal acts of central bodies of executive power to the Constitution of the Azerbaijan Republic;
        ii.   correspondence of decrees of the President of the Azerbaijan Republic, decrees of the Cabinet of Ministers of the Azerbaijan Republic, decrees of the Cabinet of Ministers of the Azerbaijan Republic, normative-legal acts of central bodies of executive power to the laws of the Azerbaijan Republic;
        iii.   correspondence of decrees of the Cabinet of Ministers of the Azerbaijan Republic and normative-legal acts of central bodies of executive power to decrees of the President of the Azerbaijan Republic;
        iv.   in cases envisaged by law, correspondence of decisions of the Supreme Court of the Azerbaijan Republic to the Constitution and laws of the Azerbaijan Republic;
        v.   correspondence of acts of municipalities to Constitution of the Azerbaijan Republic, laws of the Azerbaijan Republic, decrees of the President of the Azerbaijan Republic, decrees of the Cabinet of Ministers of the Azerbaijan Republic (in Nakhichevan Autonomous Republic also to the Constitution and laws of Nakhichevan Autonomous Republic and decrees of the Cabinet of Ministers of Nakhichevan Autonomous Republic);
        vi.   correspondence of interstate agreements of the Azerbaijan Republic, which have not yet become valid, to the Constitution of the Azer-

baijan Republic; correspondence of intergovernmental agreements of the Azerbaijan Republic to the Constitution and laws of the Azerbaijan Republic;

vii.   prohibition of political parties or other public unions;

viii.   correspondence of the Constitution and laws of Nakhichevan Autonomous Republic, decrees of Alli Majlis of Nakhichevan Autonomous Republic, decrees of the Cabinet of Ministers of Nakhichevan Autonomous Republic to the Constitution of the Azerbaijan Republic; correspondence of the laws of Nakhichevan Autonomous Republic and decrees of the Cabinet of Ministers of Nakhichevan Autonomous Republic to the laws of the Azerbaijan Republic; correspondence of decrees of the Cabinet of Ministers of Nakhichevan Autonomous Republic to decrees of the President of the Azerbaijan Republic and decrees of the Cabinet of Ministers of the Azerbaijan Republic;

ix.   settlement of disputes connected with division of authority between legislative, executive and judicial powers.

4.   Constitutional Court of the Azerbaijan Republic gives its interpretation of the Constitution and laws of the Azerbaijan Republic based on inquiries of the President of the Azerbaijan Republic, Milli Majlis of the Azerbaijan Republic, Cabinet of Ministers of the Azerbaijan Republic, Supreme Court of the Azerbaijan Republic, Procurator's Office of the Azerbaijan Republic and Alli Majlis of Nakhichevan Autonomous Republic.

5.   Constitutional Court of the Azerbaijan Republic also exercises other authorities envisaged in the present Constitution.

6.   Constitutional Court of the Azerbaijan Republic takes decisions as regards the questions of its competence. Decisions of the Constitutional Court of the Azerbaijan Republic are obligatory all over the territory of the Azerbaijan Republic.

7.   Laws and other acts, individual provisions of these documents, intergovernmental agreements of the Azerbaijan Republic cease to be valid under terms specified in the decision of the Constitutional Court of the Azerbaijan Republic, and interstate agreements of the Azerbaijan Republic do not come into force.

Article 131 – Supreme Court of the Azerbaijan Republic

1.   The Supreme Court of the Azerbaijan Republic is the highest judicial body on civil, criminal, administrative and other cases directed to general and specialised law courts; it exercises control over activity of general and specialised courts of law and gives explanations regarding practices in activity of courts of law in an order envisaged by legislation;

2.   The judges of the Supreme Court of the Azerbaijan Republic are appointed by Milli Majlis of the Azerbaijan Republic on recommendation of the President of the Azerbaijan Republic.

Article 132 – Economic Court of the Azerbaijan Republic

1.   Economic Court of the Azerbaijan Republic is the highest law court for the settlement of economic disputes. It carries out control over the activities of the respective specialised law courts in an order envisaged by legislation.

2.   Judges of the Economic Court of the Azerbaijan Republic are appointed by Milli Majlis of the Azerbaijan Republic on the recommendation by the President of the Azerbaijan Republic.

Article 133 – Procurator's Office of the Azerbaijan Republic

1.   In an order specified by legislation, the Procurator's Office of the Azerbaijan Republic exercises control over accurate and uniform fulfilment and application of laws; in cases envisaged by legislation it undertakes prosecution and carries out investigation; supports state incrimination in the law court; brings in an action in the law court; remonstrates against decisions of law court.

2.   The Procurator's Office of the Azerbaijan Republic is an integral centralised body based on the subordination of territorial and specialised procurators to the General Procurator of the Azerbaijan Republic.

3.   The General Procurator of the Azerbaijan Republic is appointed to his post and dismissed from it by the President of the Azerbaijan Republic, at the consent of Milli Majlis of the Azerbaijan Republic.

4.   Deputies of General Procurator of the Azerbaijan Republic, procurators supervising specialised republican procurator's offices and the procurator of Nakhichevan Autonomous Republic are appointed to their posts and dismissed from their posts by the President of the Azerbaijan Republic on the recommendation of General Procurator of the Azerbaijan Republic.

5.   Territorial and specialised procurators are appointed to their posts and dismissed by the General Procurator of the Azerbaijan Republic on agreement with the President of the Azerbaijan Republic.

Chapter 8 – Nakhichevan Autonomous Republic

Article 134 – Status of Nakhichevan Autonomous Republic

1.   The Nakhichevan Autonomous Republic is an autonomous state within the Azerbaijan Republic.

2.   The status of Nakhichevan Autonomous Republic is defined in the present Constitution.

3.   The Nakhichevan Autonomous Republic is an integral part of the Azerbaijan Republic.

4.   The Constitution of the Azerbaijan Republic, the laws of the Azerbaijan Republic, decrees of the President of the Azerbaijan Republic and decrees of the Cabinet of Ministers of the Azerbaijan Republic are obligatory on the territory of Nakhichevan Autonomous Republic.

5.   The Constitution and laws of the Nakhichevan Autonomous Republic accepted by Alli Majlis of Nakhichevan Autonomous Republic shall not contradict respectively the Constitution and laws of the Azerbaijan Republic; decrees accepted by the Cabinet of Ministers of Nakhichevan Autonomous Republic – to the Constitution and laws of the Azerbaijan Republic and decrees of the Cabinet of Ministers of the Azerbaijan Republic.

Article 135 – Division of powers in Nakhichevan Autonomous

1.   Legislative power in Nakhichevan Autonomous Republic is implemented by Alli Majlis of Nakhichevan Autonomous Republic, executive power by the Cabinet of Ministers of Nakhichevan Autonomous Republic and judicial power by law courts of Nakhichevan Autonomous Republic.

2.   Alli Majlis of Nakhichevan Autonomous Republic independently settles questions which according to the Constitution and laws of the Azerbaijan Republic fall under its competence; the Cabinet of Ministers of Nakhichevan

Autonomous Republic independently settles questions which according to the Constitution and laws of the Azerbaijan Republic and decrees of the President of the Azerbaijan Republic fall under its competence; law courts of Nakhichevan Autonomous Republic independently settle questions which according to the Constitution and laws of the Azerbaijan Republic fall under their competence.

Article 136 – The highest official of Nakhichevan Autonomous Republic
1.   The Chairman of Alli Majlis of Nakhichevan Autonomous Republic is the highest official of Nakhichevan Autonomous Republic. Alli Majlis of Nakhichevan Autonomous Republic consists of 45 members.
2.   The term of authority of Alli Majlis of Nakhichevan Autonomous Republic is five years.
3.   Alli Majlis of Nakhichevan Autonomous Republic elects chairman of Alli Majlis of Nakhichevan Autonomous Republic and his deputies and establishes permanent and other commissions.

Article 137 – Alli Majlis of Nakhichevan Autonomous Republic
1.   Alli Majlis of Nakhichevan Autonomous Republic consists of 45 members.
2.   Term of authority of Alli Majlis of Nakhichevan Autonomous Republic is five years.
3.   Alli Majlis of Nakhichevan Autonomous Republic elects chairman of Alli Majlis of Nakhichevan Autonomous Republic and his deputies, establishes permanent and other commissions.

Article 138 – Competence of Alli Majlis of Nakhichevan Autonomous Republic
1.   Alli Majlis of Nakhichevan Autonomous Republic establishes general procedures concerning the following:
   i.   elections to Alli Majlis of Nakhichevan Autonomous Republic;
   ii.   taxes;
   iii.   routes of economic development of Nakhichevan Autonomous Republic;
   iv.   social maintenance;
   v.   protection of environment;
   vi.   tourism;
   vii.   protection of health, science and culture.
2.   Alli Majlis of Nakhichevan Autonomous Republic accepts laws related to questions specified in the present Article.

Article 139 – Questions solved by Alli Majlis of Nakhichevan Autonomous Republic
1.   Alli Majlis of Nakhichevan Autonomous Republic takes decisions concerning the following questions:
   i.   organisation of work in Alli Majlis of Nakhichevan Autonomous Republic;
   ii.   approval of the budget of Nakhichevan Autonomous Republic;

iii.   approval of economic and social programmes of Nakhichevan Autonomous Republic;

iv.   appointment and dismissal of the Prime Minister of Nakhichevan Autonomous Republic;

v.   approval of composition of the Cabinet of Ministers of Nakhichevan Autonomous Republic;

vi.   decisions concerning a vote of confidence in the Cabinet of Ministers of Nakhichevan Autonomous Republic.

2.   Alli Majlis of Nakhichevan Autonomous Republic issues decrees concerning questions specified in the present Article.

Article 140 – Cabinet of Ministers of Nakhichevan Autonomous Republic

1.   The composition of the Cabinet of Ministers of Nakhichevan Autonomous Republic recommended by the Prime Minister of Nakhichevan Autonomous Republic is approved by Alli Majlis of Nakhichevan Autonomous Republic.

2.   The Prime Minister of Nakhichevan Autonomous Republic is appointed by Alli Majlis of Nakhichevan Autonomous Republic on the recommendation of the President of the Azerbaijan Republic.

3.   Cabinet of Ministers of Nakhichevan Autonomous Republic:

–   prepares the draft of the budget of the Autonomous Republic and presents it for approval by Alli Majlis of Nakhichevan Autonomous Republic;

–   implements the budget of the Autonomous Republic;

–   provides implementation of economic programmes of the Autonomous Republic;

–   provides implementation of social programmes of the Autonomous Republic;

–   settles other questions delegated to it by the President of the Azerbaijan Republic.

4.   The Cabinet of Ministers of Nakhichevan Autonomous Republic issues orders and decrees.

Article 141 – Local executive power in Nakhichevan Autonomous Republic

In Nakhichevan Autonomous Republic heads of local executive power bodies are appointed by the President of the Azerbaijan Republic on the recommendation of the Chairman of Alli Majlis of Nakhichevan Autonomous Republic.

Section 4 – Local self-government

Chapter 9 – Municipalities

Article 142 – Organisation of local self-government

1.   Local self-government is carried out by municipalities.

2.   Municipalities are formed based on elections.

3.   Procedure of elections to municipalities and status of municipalities are specified in laws.

Article 143 – Organisation of work of municipalities
1.   Activity of municipalities is carried out by way of meetings, permanent and other commissions.
2.   Meetings of municipalities are summoned by their chairmen.

Article 144 – Authority of municipalities
1.   The following questions are settled at the meetings of municipalities:
    i.   recognition of the authority of municipality members, loss of their authority and termination of their authority according to legislation;
    ii.   approval of in-house regulations of the municipality;
    iii.   elections of the chairman of the municipality, his deputies, permanent and other commissions;
    iv.   establishment of local taxes and duties;
    v.   approval of local budget and reports on its implementation;
    vi.   possession of municipal property, use and disposal thereof;
    vii.   acceptance and implementation of local programmes of social protection and social development;
    viii.   acceptance and implementation of local programmes of economic development;
    ix.   acceptance and implementation of local ecological programmes.
2.   Municipalities may be given additional authorities of legislative and executive power. To implement these authorities respective financing is required. Implementation of such authorities will be controlled respectively by legislative and executive power bodies.

Article 145 – Decisions of municipalities
1.   Decisions shall be taken on the agenda items of the meetings of municipality.
2.   Decisions at the meetings of the municipality are taken by a simple majority of voting members of the municipality.
3.   Decisions related to local taxes and duties are taken by majority of two thirds of votes of municipality members.

Article 146 – Guarantee of inviolability of municipalities
Legal protection of municipalities and compensation of additional expenditures resulting from decisions made by state bodies are guaranteed.

Section 5 – The right and the law

Chapter 10 – Legislative system

Article 147 – Legal force of the Constitution of the Azerbaijan Republic
1.   The Constitution of the Azerbaijan Republic possesses the highest legal power.
2.   The Constitution of the Azerbaijan Republic possesses direct legal power.
3.   The Constitution of the Azerbaijan Republic is the basis of the legislative system of the Azerbaijan Republic.

Article 148 – Acts constituting the legislative system of the Azerbaijan Republic
1.   The legislative system consists of the following normative-legal acts:
    i.   Constitution;
    ii.   acts accepted by referendum;
    iii.   laws;
    iv.   orders;
    v.   decrees of the Cabinet of Ministers of the Azerbaijan Republic;
    vi.   normative acts of central executive power bodies.
2.   International agreements wherein the Azerbaijan Republic is one of the parties constitute an integral part of the legislative system of the Azerbaijan Republic.
3.   In Nakhichevan Autonomous Republic Constitution and laws of Nakhichevan Autonomous Republic, decrees of the Cabinet of Ministers of Nakhichevan Autonomous Republic also possess legal power.
4.   The legislative system of Nakhichevan Autonomous Republic should conform to legislative system of the Azerbaijan Republic.
5.   Within the limits of their authority local bodies of executive power may accept normative acts not contradicting acts constituting the legislative system.

Article 149 – Normative-legal acts
1.   Normative-legal acts should be based on law and justice (the same attitude to equal interests).
2.   The use and implementation of acts taken by referendum is obligatory for citizens, legislative, executive and judicial power bodies, legal entities and municipalities only after their publication.
3.   The laws should not contradict the Constitution. The use and implementation of published laws is obligatory for all citizens, legislative, executive and judicial power bodies, legal entities and municipalities.
4.   Decrees of the President of the Azerbaijan Republic should not contradict the Constitution and laws of the Azerbaijan Republic. The use and implementation of published decrees is obligatory for all citizens, executive power bodies, legal entities.
5.   Decrees of the Cabinet of Ministers of the Azerbaijan Republic should not contradict the Constitution, laws of the Azerbaijan Republic and decrees of the President of the Azerbaijan Republic. The use and implementation of published decrees of the Cabinet of Ministers is obligatory for citizens, central and local executive power bodies and legal entities.
6.   Acts of central bodies of executive power should not contradict the Constitution, laws of the Azerbaijan Republic, decrees of the President of the Azerbaijan Republic, decrees of Cabinet of Ministers of the Azerbaijan Republic.
7.   Normative-legal acts improving the legal situation of physical persons and legal entities, eliminating or mitigating their legal responsibility have reverse power. Other normative-legal acts have no reverse power.

Article 150 – Acts of municipalities
1.   Acts taken by municipalities should be based on law and fairness (the same attitude and equal interests), should not contradict the Constitution and

laws of the Azerbaijan Republic, decrees of the President of the Azerbaijan Republic, decrees of the Cabinet of Ministers of the Azerbaijan Republic (in Nakhichevan Autonomous Republic, also to Constitution and laws of Nakhichevan Autonomous Republic, decrees of the Cabinet of Ministers of Nakhichevan Autonomous Republic).

2.   Implementation of acts taken by the municipality is obligatory for citizens living in this territory and legal entities located in this territory.

Article 151 – Legal value of international acts
Whenever there is disagreement between normative-legal acts in the legislative system of the Azerbaijan Republic (except the Constitution of the Azerbaijan Republic and acts accepted by way of referendum) and international agreements wherein the Azerbaijan Republic is one of the parties, provisions of international agreements shall dominate.

Chapter 11 – Changes in the Constitution of the Azerbaijan Republic

Article 152 – Procedure of introduction of changes into the Constitution of the Azerbaijan Republic
Changes in the text of the Constitution of the Azerbaijan Republic may be made only by way of referendum.

Article 153 – Procedure of submitting proposed changes in the text of the Constitution of the Azerbaijan Republic
If proposed changes in the text of the Constitution of the Azerbaijan Republic are presented by Milli Majlis of the Azerbaijan Republic or the President of the Azerbaijan Republic, then the Constitutional Court of the Azerbaijan Republic should give its conclusion beforehand.

Article 154 – Limitations on authority of the Constitutional Court of the Azerbaijan Republic
Constitutional Court of the Azerbaijan Republic shall not take decisions concerning changes in the text of the Constitution of the Azerbaijan Republic made by way of referendum.

Article 155 – Limitations on the initiative of introduction of changes into the Constitution of the Azerbaijan Republic
Proposals about changes in Articles 1, 2, 6, 7, 8 and 21, about restriction of provisions envisaged in Chapter 3 of the present Constitution are not subject to referendum.

Chapter 12 – Amendments to the Constitution of the Azerbaijan Republic

Article 156 – Procedure of introduction of amendments to the Constitution of the Azerbaijan Republic
1.   Amendments to the Constitution of the Azerbaijan Republic are taken in the form of Constitutional laws in Milli Majlis of the Azerbaijan Republic, by a majority of 95 votes.

2.   Constitutional laws on amendments to the Constitution of the Azerbaijan Republic are put to the vote in Milli Majlis of the Azerbaijan Republic twice. The second ballot shall be held six months after the first one.

3.   Constitutional laws on amendments to the Constitution of the Azerbaijan Republic are submitted to the President of the Azerbaijan Republic for signing in an order envisaged in the present Constitution for laws, both after the first and after the second ballot.

4.   Constitutional laws and amendments to the Constitution of the Azerbaijan Republic become valid after they have been signed by the President of the Azerbaijan Republic after the second ballot.

5.   Constitutional laws on amendments are an integral part of Constitution of the Azerbaijan Republic and should not contradict the main text of the Constitution of the Azerbaijan Republic.

Article 157 – Initiative on introduction of amendments to Constitution of the Azerbaijan Republic

Amendments to theConstitution of the Azerbaijan Republic may be proposed by the President of the Azerbaijan Republic or by at least 63 deputies of Milli Majlis of the Azerbaijan Republic.

Article 158 – Limitations on initiative on introduction of amendments to the Constitution of the Azerbaijan Republic

Neither the President of the Azerbaijan Republic nor deputies of Milli Majlis of the Azerbaijan Republic may propose amendments to the Constitution of the Azerbaijan Republic as stated in the provisions contained respectively in Chapters 5 and 6 of the present Constitution.

Transitional clauses

1.   The Constitution of the Azerbaijan Republic comes into force after it has been accepted by referendum, from the day of its official publication. The Constitution (Main Law) of the Azerbaijan Republic accepted on 21 April 1978 becomes null and void from the day when the present Constitution comes into force.

2.   The President of the Azerbaijan Republic elected before the present Constitution of the Azerbaijan Republic came into force shall carry out powers delegated to the President of the Azerbaijan Republic by the present Constitution.

3.   Paragraph 5 of Article 101 of the present Constitution is valid for the President of the Azerbaijan Republic elected after the acceptance of the present Constitution.

4.   Powers of people's deputies of the Azerbaijan Republic and Milli Majlis formed by the Supreme Council of the Azerbaijan Republic expire on the day of the first meeting of the newly elected Milli Majlis of the Azerbaijan Republic.

The first meeting of the newly elected Milli Majlis of the Azerbaijan Republic shall be held a week after at least 83 deputies of Milli Majlis of the Azerbaijan Republic have been elected. The first session of Milli Majlis of the Azerbaijan Republic will continue until 31 May 1996.

Article 85 of the Law of the Azerbaijan Republic "On elections to Milli Majlis of the Azerbaijan Republic" accepted on 15 August 1995 remains valid until the expiration of the powers of the first calling of Milli Majlis of the Azerbaijan Republic elected based on the basis of this law.

5.   From the day of acceptance of the present Constitution the Cabinet of Ministers of the Azerbaijan Republic carries out powers delegated to it by the present Constitution.

6.   From the day when the present Constitution comes into force the authority of local councils of people's deputies of the Azerbaijan Republic is terminated.

Authority delegated by legislation of the Azerbaijan Republic to local councils of people's deputies of the Azerbaijan Republic is carried out by local executive power bodies.

7.   After the present Constitution comes into force, the law on local self-government should be taken and elections to municipalities must take place within two years.

8.   Provisions of laws and other normative-legal acts acting in the territory of the Azerbaijan Republic before acceptance of the present Constitution remain valid if they do not contradict the present Constitution.

9.   Law courts of the Azerbaijan Republic acting before acceptance of the present Constitution shall carry out justice in accordance with authority and principles specified in the present Constitution.

10. From the day when the present Constitution comes into force, within one year laws on status of judges, judicial system and judicial reform should be taken in line with the present Constitution and judges of the Azerbaijan Republic must be appointed anew.

Until said laws are taken, appointment of judges to their posts and their dismissal will be done based on legislation which existed before the present Constitution came into force.

11. From the day when the present Constitution comes into force, within one year the Law of the Azerbaijan Republic about the Constitutional Court of the Azerbaijan Republic shall be taken and the Constitutional Court of the Azerbaijan Republic shall be established. Until the Constitutional Court of the Azerbaijan Republic is established the authority of the Constitutional Court of the Azerbaijan Republic envisaged by the present Constitution shall not be implemented. The question envisaged in Paragraph 7, Clause 3 of Article 130 of the present Constitution will be solved by the Supreme Court of the Azerbaijan Republic.

12. From the day when the present Constitution comes into force the Higher Arbitration Court of the Azerbaijan Republic is called the Economic Court of the Azerbaijan Republic and carries out powers defined by existing legislation.

Belarus

Chronology

1989

June 24: Having been prevented from holding its constituent congress in Byelorussia, the Byelorussian Popular Front is founded in Vilnius and elects Zenon Paznyak as chairman of the party.

July 28: Nikolai Dementei is elected Chairman of the Presidium of the Supreme Soviet, replacing Georgy Tarazevich.

1990

March 4: Elections for the Supreme Soviet are held. The allocation of a quota of reserved Supreme Soviet seats for official organisations is decided. In direct elections for 272 of the 360 Supreme Soviet seats, an average of five candidates contested each seat. Candidates endorsed by the nationalist Popular Front-style organisation *Adradzhenne* do better than expected, despite alleged harassment during the campaign.

April 7: Vyacheslav Kebich is appointed as Prime Minister.

May 19: The Supreme Soviet narrowly elects Nikolai Dementei as its Chairman, i.e. Head of the Byelorussian Socialist Soviet Republic (BSSR), from a field of three candidates.

July 27: The Supreme Soviet adopts a declaration proclaiming supremacy, independence and indivisibility of the republic's power on its territory, and independence and equality in external relations. It also authorises the BSSR to have its own armed forces, internal security troops and state security bodies. The declaration proclaims the intention to make Byelorussia a permanently neutral state, and the right to demand compensation for damages caused to the republic's ecology by Union bodies. The declaration alludes to secession by ascribing to the republic the right to voluntary unions with other states and free withdrawal from such unions.

December 12: The Byelorussian Communist Party (CP) elects Anatoly Malofeyev as its first secretary.

1991

March 17: Byelorussia holds the all-union referendum on the preservation of the Soviet Union. 82.7% of the population vote in favour of the preservation of the Soviet Union and 16.1% vote against. The turnout is 83.3%.

April 23: President Mikhail Gorbachev signs, with nine of the fifteen union republics including Byelorussia, a pact aimed at achieving stable relations between the central government and the governments of the republics. It sets out a timetable for major political changes, starting with the signing of the new Union Treaty. No longer than six months after signature of the Treaty a new Union constitution would be promulgated, followed by elections to the Congress of People's Deputies.

End of June: The Supreme Soviet decides that the post of President be elected directly.

August 19: Attempted *coup d'état* in Moscow.

August 25: President Dementei, who expresses support for the coup, resigns. The Supreme Soviet declares the country independent. The Communist Party (CP) leaves the Communist Party of the Soviet Union (CPSU), its first secretary Anatoly Malofeyev resigns from the CPSU politburo.

August 28: The members of the government suspend their party membership and the CP is temporarily suspended by the Ministry of Justice.

September 18: Byelorussia is renamed to become the Republic of Belarus. The Supreme Soviet elects, by 214 votes out of a total of 312, Stanislav Shushkevich, an active supporter of democratic change, President of the Supreme Soviet.

December 8: Belarus, the Russian Federative Republic and Ukraine sign the Minsk (Viskuli) agreement, establishing a Commonwealth of Independent States (CIS).

December 10: The Supreme Soviet ratifies the CIS declaration.

December 21: The CIS formally replaces the Soviet Union, grouping eleven republics with the exception of Georgia. The Russian Federative Republic takes over many of the former Union functions, including its seat in the UN Security Council. The post of President of the USSR is abolished.

1992

March 4: The Belarus Popular Front proposes a referendum on the dissolution of the Supreme Soviet.

May 25: Belarus introduces its own internal currency, the rubel.

September 16: The Parliamentary Assembly of the Council of Europe grants special guest status to the Supreme Soviet.

October 29: The Supreme Soviet defeats another attempt of the Popular Front to hold a referendum calling for the dissolution of parliament and elections in December.

1993

February 3: The Supreme Soviet lifts the bans imposed in August 1991 on the CPSU and on the CP of Belarus, but the property of both parties remains under state control.

April 9: The Supreme Soviet votes by 188 votes to 34 in favour of Belarus joining the collective security agreement of the CIS.

July 1: The chairman of the Supreme Soviet and Head of the Belorussian state, Stanislav Shushkevich, is defeated in a vote of confidence in the Supreme Soviet, but remains in office, because the chamber is not quorate at the time of the vote. Twenty-seven deputies support Shushkevich and 168 vote against him. Shushkevich is criticised for failing to sign the CIS treaty on collective security.

July 7: Shushkevich agrees to postpone a referendum on the CIS treaty until August.

1994

January 28: The Supreme Soviet elects Mechyslav Grib as its Chairman.

February 11: The Speaker of the Supreme Soviet advocates the introduction of a presidential system of government to replace the current parliamentary system.

February 22: The Supreme Soviet elects Ivan Bambiza as its deputy chairman.

March 15: The Supreme Soviet adopts with 236 votes in favour, 6 against and 8 abstentions a new constitution proclaiming that Belarus becomes a presidential republic. It is declared "a unitary democratic social law-governed state". The Parliament will be reduced to 260 deputies.

April 12: A Treaty on Monetary Union is signed by the Prime Minister Kebich and his Russian counterpart Chernomyrdin in Moscow.

June 23: Presidential elections are held. Aleksandr Lukashenko, an independent candidate, emerges as the front-runner, taking 44.8% of the votes (Turnout: 79%).

July 10: Aleksandr Lukashenko is elected as Belarus's first President, having won 80.1% of the vote in a run-off presidential election (Turnout: 69.9%). His rival, the sitting Prime Minister, Vyacheslau Kebich, a former communist, wins only 14.1% of the vote.

July 21: Mikhail Chigir is elected Prime Minister.

August 9: The Prime Minister announces a restructuring of ministries. The government, comprising 24 ministries plus the State Security Committee (KGB), will be accountable to the Prime Minister rather than to the Council of Ministers. An inner Cabinet or Collegium is to be composed of the Prime Minister, deputy prime ministers and the ministers of Finance, Interior and Foreign Affairs. In the restructuring, 12 ministries and a significant portion of the government bureaucracy are to be abolished.

September 7: The Russian Prime Minister Chernomyrdin rules out monetary union with Belarus, on the ground that the economies of the two countries diverged.

October 11: The Belorussian rouble will be the sole currency by the end of 1994.

November 14: A new party, supporting the President, the Belarus Patriotic Movement is registered with the Ministry of Justice.

November 29: In a decree, President Lukashenko acquires control over the appointment and dismissal of senior local officials, creating a vertical chain of power from the presidency down.

1995

February 1: The Supreme Soviet approves a law whereby the president can be removed from office if at least two-third of the deputies back the dismissal. Three possible grounds: (i) an expression of no confidence by the people in a nation-wide referendum (ii) criminal activity by the president (iii) infringement of the constitution.

May 14: In four referendums voters back the resumption of cultural and economic links with Russia and the increase of presidential powers. The results: (i) equal status for Russian and Belorussian language: 83.1%; (ii) new state flag and emblem: 75%; (iii) support for economic integration: 82.4%; (iv) giving the president the right to terminate the parliament's mandate in the event of violation of the constitution: 77.6%. Turnout 64.7%.

May 14: The first round of legislative elections produces a turnout of 64.7%.

May 28: A second round of elections is held in 141 of the 260 constituencies, with a turnout of 56%. 119 deputies are elected, 55 deputies short of the required 174 deputies to form a quorum.

June 14: In an extraordinary session, the Supreme Soviet accepts a resolution to hold a new round of elections to a newly reconstituted Supreme Soviet on November 29.

October 1: The United Democratic Party and the Civic Party merge to form the United Civic Party (UCP).

October: Confrontation between the executive and the legislature on account of the inconclusive general elections held in May. The President holds that the existing Supreme Soviet, which was elected in March 1990 under the old constitution, has no legitimacy since its mandate expired in May 1995. Conversely the Supreme Soviet states that it remains the legislative power until the election of a new parliament.

November 29: Third round of elections is repeated in 141 constituencies where the turnout was below 50% in May. The results are inconclusive.

December 10: Fourth round of general elections is held, resulting in 59 elected deputies bringing the total elected seats to 198. At last the minimum of 174 seats for a quorum is exceeded. Turnout 52%. Party affiliation: Party of Communists of Belarus, 42 seats; Agrarian Party, 33 seats; UCP, 9 seats; Party of People's Accord, 8 seats; Unaffiliated, 96 seats; 10 seats are taken by the remaining parties and 62 seats remain unfilled.

December 11: The Constitutional Court rules that 11 decrees, out of the examined 14, issued by the President are wholly or partially unconstitutional.

1996

January 11: Syamyon Sharetski, leader of the Agrarian Party, is elected Chairman of the new Supreme Soviet.

March 29: The Russian State Duma adopts a resolution approving the plan to sign a union treaty with Belarus.

April 2: President Lukashenko and Russian President Boris Yeltsin sign a union treaty in Moscow forming a Community of Sovereign Republics (SSR). The treaty contains wide-ranging provisions covering political, economic and military co-operation. The Russian Prime Minister, Viktor Chernomyrdin is appointed as chair of the SSR executive committee.

November 24: A referendum on a new constitution takes place. 70.5% of the population votes in favour of a new constitution, in the version favoured by Lukashenko, and 7.9% vote against (Turnout: 84%). The Supreme Soviet is replaced by a 110-member House of Representatives.

November 26: President Lukashenko signs a law closing impeachment proceedings against himself.

November 27: The new constitution comes into force.

November 28: The Supreme Soviet passes legislation, first, to establish a 110-member House of Representatives and, secondly, to abolish the Supreme Soviet.

November 30: The Communist Party of Belarus, headed by Viktar Chykin, is registered.

December 4: The Chairman of the Constitutional Court, Valeryy Tsikhinya, and three judges resign after the adoption of the new constitution. The

Chairman argues that the results of the 24 November referendum are not legitimate, and he accuses the President of not taking into account the opinion of the Constitutional Court.

December 5: A decree from the President sets up a State Control Committee of the Republic, responsible for conducting cases formerly under the jurisdiction of the Control Chamber. The President signs a decree that stipulates that a second round of voting for deputies of the Supreme Soviet will not be held.

December 8: The deputies of the Supreme Soviet who were elected on 24 November 1996 in parliamentary by-elections are not to be registered.

December 11: The deputies of the Supreme Soviet, opposing the President, declare the new parliament unlawful and running counter to the republic's legislation.

December 13: President Lukashenko signs a decree on elections to the upper house of parliament. Each of the six Belorussian regions and the capital, Minsk, will elect eight members to the Council of the Republic (Senate). Another eight members of the new parliament's upper house will be appointed by the president. The National Assembly's upper house has a total of 64 members. The president, deputies of the House of Representatives (parliament's lower chamber), members of the government and judges cannot be elected to the Council of the Republic.

December 17: Aleksandr Lukashenko takes part in the first session of the House of Representatives of the National Assembly. It consists of 110 deputies, and another 34 applications have been received from deputies of the Supreme Soviet of the 13th convocation. The House contains representatives of ten political parties and movements. Lukashenko calls for close cooperation with the Russian Parliament and fosters peace and stability within the country.

Law of the Republic of Belarus "on the procedure governing the entry into force of the Constitution of the Republic of Belarus"

Article 1
The Constitution of the Republic of Belarus shall enter into force on the day on which it is promulgated, apart from the one specified in this Law.

Article 2
The day on which the Constitution of the Republic of Belarus is adopted shall be declared a national holiday.

Article 3
On the day on which the Constitution of the Republic of Belarus enters into force, the articles of the 1978 Constitution of the Republic of Belarus, together with any subsequent amendments and addenda thereto, shall cease to apply, unless otherwise specified in this Law, as shall the articles of the Law of the Republic of Belarus on granting the status of a constitutional law to the Declaration of the Supreme Soviet of the Republic of Belarus on the State Sovereignty of the Republic of Belarus of 25 August 1991.

Article 4
The laws referred to in the Constitution of the Republic of Belarus shall be adopted within two years of its entry into force. To ensure that the adopted Constitution of the Republic of Belarus is implemented in full, a Constitutional Court of the Republic of Belarus shall be set up within one month of the day on which the Constitution of the Republic of Belarus enters into force.

Article 5
Until the laws and other enforceable enactments are brought into line with the Constitution of the Republic of Belarus, they shall apply in the particular parts thereof that are not contrary to the Constitution of the Republic of Belarus.

Article 6
Within two years of the entry into force of the Constitution of the Republic of Belarus, the laws governing the transition to the exercise of the rights specified in Articles 30 (where it refers to free movement and choice of place of residence within the Republic of Belarus) and 46 of the Constitution of the Republic of Belarus shall be adopted. The transition shall be completed no later than five years after the entry into force of the relevant laws.

Article 7

People's deputies of the Republic of Belarus shall retain their powers until the opening of the first sitting of the Supreme Council of the Republic of Belarus of the 13th convocation.

The powers of the Supreme Soviet of the Republic of Belarus of the 12th convocation, the Presidium thereof and the Chairman of the Supreme Soviet of the Republic of Belarus, together with any subsequent amendment and addenda shall be retained until the President of the Republic of Belarus takes office, and the powers of the Council of Ministers of the Republic of Belarus shall be retained until the formation of the Cabinet of Ministers of the Republic of Belarus under the procedure specified in the 1994 Constitution.

After the President of the Republic of Belarus has taken office, the Supreme Soviet of the Republic of Belarus of the 12th convocation, the Presidium thereof and the Chairman of the Supreme Soviet of the Republic of Belarus shall exercise the powers specified in the 1994 Constitution.

Officials who have been elected or appointed by the Supreme Soviet of the Republic of Belarus of the 12th convocation shall retain their powers for the periods specified in law.

Article 8

It is hereby established that during 1994-1995 the use of the words "Council of People's Deputies" shall be permitted in place of "Council of Deputies" on official forms, seals, stamps and other official documents.

Article 9

The Chairman of the Supreme of the Supreme Council of the Republic of Belarus is hereby instructed to sign the Constitution of the Republic of Belarus.

[Signed] M. Grib, the Chairman of the Supreme Council of the Republic of Belarus.

Minsk, 15 March 1994

Declaration of state sovereignty of the Republic of Belarus

27 July 1990

The Supreme Soviet of the Republic of Belarus, expressing the will of the people of the Republic of Belarus, aware of its responsibility for the destiny of the Belarusian nation,
reaffirming its respect for the dignity and the rights of the people of all nationalities residing in the Republic of Belarus,
expressing its respect for the sovereign rights of all the peoples of the Union of Soviet Socialist Republics and of the world,
considering the Republic a full and independent member of the world community,
acting in conformity with the principles of the Universal Declaration of Human Rights and other universally recognised international legal instruments,
hereby solemnly proclaims the full state sovereignty of the Republic of Belarus as the supremacy, the independence and the absolute state power of the Republic within its territory, the competence of its laws, the independence of the Republic in foreign relations, and declares its determination to establish a state, based on law.

Article 1
The Republic of Belarus is a sovereign state established on the basis of the realisation by the Belarusian nation of its inalienable right to self-determination, state-language status of the Belarusian language, and the supremacy of the people in the determination of its destiny.
The inalienable rights of the Republic of Belarus as a sovereign state shall be realised in conformity with the universally recognised norms of international law. The Republic of Belarus shall safeguard and protect the right of the Belarusian people to have its own state.
The Republic of Belarus shall have its own emblem, flag and anthem.
Any forcible acts against the national statehood of the Republic of Belarus committed by political parties, public associations or individuals shall be punishable by law.

Article 2
The citizens of the Republic of Belarus of all nationalities constitute the Belarusian people, which shall be endowed with the sovereignty and shall be the sole source of state power in the Republic. The sovereignty of the people shall be realised both directly and through representative organs of state power.

The right to act in the name of all the people of the Republic shall be vested exclusively in the Supreme Soviet of the Republic of Belarus.

Article 3
The state sovereignty of the Republic of Belarus shall be proclaimed in the name of the supreme goal: free development and prosperity, a dignified life for every citizen of the Republic on the basis of ensuring human rights of the individual in conformity with the Constitution of the Republic of Belarus and its international obligations.

Article 4
Citizenship of the Republic of Belarus shall be an integral part of its sovereignty. The Republic shall protect the honour, the health, the rights and the legal interests of its citizens, and shall ensure their social protection. They shall enjoy protection of the Republic of Belarus outside its territory. The Republic may confer and terminate citizenship.

Article 5
The land, its mineral wealth, the other natural resources on the territory of the Republic of Belarus, and its air space shall be the property of the Belarusian people which shall have the exclusive rights of their possession, use and disposal.
The determination of the legal status of all kinds of property shall be within the exclusive competence of the Republic of Belarus.
The Republic of Belarus shall have the right to its portion of the all-Union property according to the contribution of the Belarusian people and, as a founding Republic of the Soviet Union having legal capacity, shall have the right to its portion of the diamond, currency, and reserves of the USSR.
The Republic of Belarus shall establish the National Bank, accountable to the Supreme Soviet of the Republic, shall organise its financial and credit system, shall confirm the right of ownership of specialised banks based on its territory at the time of the adoption of this Declaration, shall organise its own taxation and customs services, and shall have the right to establish its own monetary system.

Article 6
The territory of the Republic of Belarus shall be indivisible and inviolable and shall not be altered or used without the consent of the Republic of Belarus.
All questions concerning borders shall be decided only on the basis of the mutual consent of the Republic of Belarus and the adjacent sovereign states by the conclusion of appropriate agreements, subject to ratification by the Supreme Soviet of the Republic of Belarus.

Article 7
Within the territory of the Republic of Belarus the Constitution of the Republic of Belarus and the laws of the Republic of Belarus shall have supremacy.
All citizens and stateless persons, state organs, enterprises, institutions and organisations based or functioning on the territory of the Republic of Belarus shall obey the laws of the Republic of Belarus.

The delimitation of legislative, executive, and judicial power shall be the most important principle of the functioning of the Republic of Belarus as a state, based on law.
The supreme supervision over the strict and uniform observance of the laws shall be exercised by the Procurator-General appointed by the Supreme Soviet of the Republic of Belarus.

Article 8
The Republic of Belarus shall independently establish a procedure for organising nature preservation, utilisation of natural resources of the territory of the Republic and shall ensure ecological security for the people of the Republic.
The Republic of Belarus shall have the right to compensation for the damage incurred as a result of activities of all-Unions organs, Union republics, and other states.
The Republic of Belarus demands from the Government of the USSR an unconditional and prompt compensation for the damage connected with the elimination of the effects of the Chernobyl disaster.
The Republic of Belarus shall use its freedom and sovereignty first and foremost to save the people of the Republic of Belarus from the effects of the Chernobyl disaster.

Article 9
The Republic of Belarus shall be independent in deciding on the questions of culture and spiritual development of the Belarusian nation, and in organising its own system of information, education, and upbringing.
The Republic of Belarus shall ensure functioning of the Belarusian language in all spheres of social life, and the preservation of national traditions and historical symbols.
National, cultural, and historical values on the territory of the Republic of Belarus shall be the exclusive property of the Republic and its citizens.

Article 10
The Republic of Belarus shall have the right to its own armed forces, internal security forces, organs of state and public security, which shall be controlled by the Supreme Soviet of the Republic of Belarus.
The Republic of Belarus shall have the sovereign right to determine for its citizens the procedure and conditions of military service, and service in the organs of state and public security, and to decide on the questions of deployment of troops and armaments on its territory.
No military units, military bases or installations of other countries shall be deployed on the territory of the Republic of Belarus without the consent of its Supreme Soviet.
The Republic of Belarus sets the aim to make its territory a nuclear-free zone and to become a neutral state.

Article 11
The Republic of Belarus shall independently exercise the right to enter into voluntary unions with other states and to withdraw freely from these unions.

The Republic of Belarus proposes to commence immediately the elaboration of an agreement on a union of sovereign socialist states.

Article 12

The provisions of the present Declaration shall be implemented by the Supreme Soviet of the Republic of Belarus through the adoption of a new Constitution (Fundamental Law) of the Republic of Belarus, and laws of the Republic of Belarus.

Constitution of the Republic of Belarus[1]

Adopted by the Supreme Soviet of the Republic of Belarus on 15 March 1994

We, the People of the Republic of Belarus (of Belarus),
emanating from the responsibility for the present and future of Belarus;
recognising ourselves as a subject, with full rights, of the world community and confirming our adherence to values common to all mankind;
founding ourselves on our inalienable right to self-determination;
supported by the centuries-long history of development of Belarusian statehood;
striving to assert the rights and freedoms of every citizen of the Republic of Belarus;
desiring to maintain civic harmony, stable foundations of democracy and a state based on the rule of law;
hereby adopt this Constitution as the Basic Law of the Republic of Belarus.

Section 1 – Principles of the constitutional system

Article 1

The Republic of Belarus shall be a unitary, democratic, social state based on the rule of law. The Republic of Belarus shall have supreme control and absolute authority in its territory and shall implement domestic and foreign policy independently.
The Republic of Belarus shall defend its independence and territorial integrity, its constitutional system, and safeguard legality and law and order.

Article 2

The individual shall be of supreme importance to society and the State.
The State shall bear responsibility towards the citizen to create the conditions for the free and dignified development of his identity. The citizen bears a responsibility towards the State to discharge unwaveringly the duties imposed upon him by the Constitution.

---

1. Information Centre at the Ministry of Foreign Affairs of the Republic of Belarus

Article 3

The people shall be the sole source of state power in the Republic of Belarus. The people shall exercise their power directly and through representative bodies in the form and within the limits specified in the Constitution.

Any actions aimed at seizing state power by forcible means or by way of any other violation of the laws of the Republic of Belarus laws shall be punishable by law.

Article 4

Democracy in the Republic of Belarus shall be exercised on the basis of a variety of political institutions, ideologies and views.

The ideology of political parties, religious or other public associations, or social groups may not be made compulsory for citizens.

Article 5

Political parties and other public associations acting within the framework of the Constitution and laws of the Republic of Belarus, shall contribute towards ascertaining and expressing the political will of citizens and participate in elections.

Political parties and other public associations shall have the right to use state mass media under the procedure determined by the law.

The creation and activities of political parties and other public associations that aim to change the constitutional system by force, or conduct a propaganda of war, ethnic, religious and racial hatred, shall be prohibited.

Article 6

The State shall rely on the principle of dividing power into legislative, executive and judicial power. State bodies, within the limits of their powers, shall be independent. They shall cooperate among themselves and check and counterbalance one another.

Article 7

The State and all the bodies and officials thereof shall be bound by the law and operate within the limits of the Constitution and the laws adopted in accordance therewith.

Legal enactments or specific provisions thereof which are deemed under the procedure specified in law to be contrary to the provisions of the Constitution shall have no legal force.

Enforceable enactments of state bodies shall be promulgated or published by some means specified in law.

Article 8

The Republic of Belarus shall recognise the supremacy of the universally acknowledged principles of international law and ensures that its laws comply with such principles.

The conclusion of international agreements that are contrary to the Constitution shall not be permitted.

Article 9

The territory of the Republic of Belarus shall be the natural condition of the existence and spatial limit of the people's self-determination, and the basis for its prosperity and the sovereignty of the Republic of Belarus.

The territory of Belarus shall be unified and inalienable.

The territory shall be divided into regions, districts, cities and other administrative-territorial units. The administrative-territorial division of the state is determined by the law.

Article 10

A citizen of the Republic of Belarus shall be guaranteed the protection and patronage of the State both in the territory of Belarus and beyond. No one may be stripped of citizenship of the Republic of Belarus or the right to change his citizenship.

A citizen of the Republic of Belarus may not be extradited to a foreign state, unless otherwise stipulated in international agreements to which the Republic of Belarus is party.

Citizenship shall be acquired or lost in accordance with the law.

Article 11

Foreign nationals and stateless persons in the territory of Belarus shall enjoy rights and liberties and discharge duties on a par with the citizens of the Republic of Belarus, unless otherwise specified in the Constitution, the laws and international agreements.

Article 12

The Republic of Belarus may grant the right of asylum to persons persecuted in other states for political or religious beliefs or their ethnic affiliation.

Article 13

The State shall grant equal rights to all to conduct economic and other activities, other than those prohibited by law, and guarantee equal protection and equal conditions for the development of all forms of ownership.

The State shall regulate economic activities on behalf of the individual and society.

The law may specify facilities that may be the property of the State alone and grant the State an exclusive right to conduct certain types of activity.

Article 14

The State shall regulate relations among social, ethnic and other communities on the basis of the principles of equality before the law and respect of their rights and interests.

Article 15

The State shall bear responsibility for preserving the historic and cultural heritage, and the free development of the cultures of all the ethnic communities that live in the Republic of Belarus.

Article 16

All religions and faiths shall be equal before the law. The establishment of any privileges or restrictions with regard to a particular religion or faith in relation to others shall not be permitted.

The activities of denominational organisations, their bodies and representatives, that are directed against the sovereignty of the Republic of Belarus, its constitutional system and civic harmony, or involve a violation of civil rights and liberties, shall be prohibited.

Relations between the State and religious denominations shall be governed by the law.

Article 17

The official language of the Republic of Belarus shall be Belarusian.

The Republic of Belarus shall safeguard the right to use the Russian language freely as a language of interethnic communication.

Article 18

In its foreign policy the Republic of Belarus shall proceed from the principles of the equality of states, the non-use or threatened use of force, the inviolability of frontiers, the peaceful settlement of disputes, non-interference in internal affairs and other universally acknowledged principles and standards of international law.

The Republic of Belarus shall endeavour to make its territory a nuclear-free zone, and the State neutral.

Article 19

The symbols of the Republic of Belarus as a sovereign state shall be its national flag, national emblem and national anthem.

Article 20

The capital of the Republic of Belarus is the city of Minsk.

The status of the city of Minsk shall be determined by the law.

Section 2 – The individual, society, and the state

Article 21

Safeguarding the rights and liberties of the citizens of the Republic of Belarus shall be the supreme goal of the State.

The State shall guarantee the rights and liberties of the citizens of Belarus that are enshrined in the Constitution and the laws, and specified in the State's international obligations.

Article 22

All shall be equal before the law and entitled, without discrimination, to equal protection of their rights and legitimate interests.

Article 23

Restriction of personal rights and liberties shall be permitted only in the instances specified in law, in the interest of national security, public order, the

protection of the morals and health of the population, as well as rights and liberties of other persons.
No one may enjoy advantages and privileges that are contrary to the law.

Article 24
Everyone shall have the right to life.
The State shall protect the life of the individual against any unlawful threat.
Until its abolition, the death penalty may be applied in accordance with the law as an exceptional penalty for particularly serious crimes and only in accordance with the verdict of a court of law.

Article 25
The State shall safeguard personal liberty, inviolability and dignity. The restriction or denial of personal liberty is possible in the instances and under the procedure specified in law.
A person who has been taken into custody shall be entitled to a judicial investigation into the legality of his detention or arrest.
No one shall be subjected to torture or cruel, inhuman or undignified treatment or punishment, or be subjected to medical or other experiments without his consent.

Article 26
No one may be found guilty of a crime unless his guilt is proven under the procedure specified in law and established by the verdict of a court of law that has acquired legal force. A defendant shall not be required to prove his innocence.

Article 27
No one shall be forced to give evidence or provide explanations against himself, members of his family or close relations. Evidence obtained in violation of the law shall have no legal force.

Article 28
Everyone shall be entitled to protection against unlawful interference with his private life, including encroachments on the privacy of his correspondence and telephone and other communications, and on his honour and dignity.

Article 29
The inviolability of the home and other legitimate property of citizens shall be guaranteed. No one shall have the right, without just cause, to enter the dwelling and other lawful property of a citizen against his will.

Article 30
Citizens of the Republic of Belarus shall have the right to move freely and choose their place of residence within the Republic of Belarus, to leave it and to return to it without hindrance.

Article 31
Everyone shall have the right independently to determine his attitude towards religion, to profess any religion individually or jointly with others, or to profess none at all, to express and spread beliefs connected with his attitude towards religions, and to participate in the performance of acts of worship and religious rituals and rites.

Article 32
Marriage, the family, motherhood, fatherhood, and childhood shall be under the protection of the State.
On reaching the age of consent women and men shall have the right to enter into marriage on a voluntary basis and start a family. A husband and wife shall be equal in family relationships. Parents or persons *in loco parentis* shall be entitled and required to raise their children and to take care of their health, development and education. No child shall be subjected to cruel treatment or humiliation or used for work that may be harmful to its physical, mental or moral development. Children shall care for their parents or persons *in loco parentis* and render them assistance.

Article 33
Everyone is guaranteed freedom of thought and beliefs and their free expression.
No one shall be forced to express his beliefs or to deny them.
No monopolisation of the mass media by the State, public associations or individual citizens and no censorship shall be permitted.

Article 34
Citizens of the Republic of Belarus shall be guaranteed the right to receive, store and disseminate complete, reliable and timely information on the activities of state bodies and public associations, on political, economic and international life, and on the state of the environment.
State bodies, public associations and officials shall afford citizens of the Republic of Belarus an opportunity to familiarise themselves with material that affects their rights and legitimate interests.

Article 35
The freedom to hold assemblies, rallies, street marches, demonstrations and pickets that do not disturb law and order or violate the rights of other citizens of the Republic of Belarus, shall be guaranteed by the State. The procedure for conducting the above events shall be determined by the law.

Article 36
Everyone shall be entitled to freedom of association.
Judges, employees of the Procurator's Office, the staff of bodies of internal affairs, the Supervisory Authority of the Republic of Belarus and security bodies, as well as servicemen may not be members of political parties or other public associations that pursue political goals.

Article 37

Citizens of the Republic of Belarus shall have the right to participate in the solution of state matters, both directly and through freely elected representatives. The direct participation of citizens in the administration of the affairs of society and the State shall be safeguarded by the holding of referendums, the discussion of draft laws and issues of national and local significance, and by other means specified in law.

Article 38

Citizens of the Republic of Belarus shall have the right to vote freely and to be elected to state bodies on the basis of universal, equal and direct suffrage by secret ballot.

Article 39

Citizens of the Republic of Belarus, in accordance with their capabilities and vocational training, shall be entitled to equal access to any post in state bodies.

Article 40

Everyone shall have the right to address personal or collective appeals to state bodies.

State bodies, as well as the officials thereof, shall consider any appeal and furnish a reply in point of substance within the period specified in law. Any refusal to consider an appeal that has been submitted shall be justified in writing.

Article 41

Citizens of the Republic of Belarus shall be guaranteed the right to work as the worthiest means of an individual's self-assertion, type of occupation and work in accordance with one's vocation, capabilities, education and vocational training, and having regard to social needs, and the right to healthy and safe working conditions. The State shall create the conditions necessary for full employment of the population. Where a person is unemployed for reasons which are beyond his control, he shall be guaranteed training in new specialisations and an upgrading of his qualifications having regard to social needs, and to unemployment benefit in accordance with the law.

Citizens shall have the right to protection of their economic and social interests, including the right to form trade unions and conclude collective contracts (agreements), and the right to strike.

Forced labour shall be prohibited, other than work or service specified in the verdict of a court of law or in accordance with the law on state of emergency or martial law.

Article 42

Employees shall be entitled to remuneration for the work they have done in accordance with the quantity, quality and social significance of such work, but it shall not be less than the minimum specified by the State. Women and men and adults and minors shall be entitled to equal remuneration for work of equal value.

Article 43
Working people shall be entitled to holidays. For employees, this right shall be safeguarded by the establishment of a working week of no more than 40 hours, shorter working hours at night and the provision of annual paid leave and weekly rest days.

Article 44
The State shall guarantee everyone the right of property.
A proprietor shall have the right to possess, enjoy and dispose of assets either individually or jointly with others. The inviolability of property and the right to inherit property shall be protected by law.
The compulsory alienation of assets shall be permitted only by reason of public need, under the conditions and the procedure specified by law, with timely and full compensation for the value of the alienated assets, and in accordance with a verdict of a court of law.
The exercise of the right of property shall not be harmful to the environment or historical and cultural treasures, or infringe upon the rights and legally protected interests of others.

Article 45
Citizens of the Republic of Belarus shall be guaranteed the right to health care, including free treatment at state health-care establishments. The right of citizens of the Republic of Belarus to health care shall also be secured by the development of physical training and sport, measures to improve the environment, the opportunity to use fitness establishments and improvements in occupational safety.

Article 46
Everyone shall be entitled to a pleasant environment and to compensation for loss or damage caused by the violation of this right.

Article 47
Citizens of the Republic of Belarus shall be guaranteed the right to social security in old age, in the event of illness, disability, loss of fitness for work and loss of a bread-winner and in other instances specified in law. The State shall display particular concern for those who lost their health in the defence of national and public interests.

Article 48
Citizens of the Republic of Belarus shall be entitled to housing. This right shall be safeguarded by the development of state, public and private housing and assistance for citizens in the acquisition of housing.
No one may be deprived of housing arbitrarily.

Article 49
Everyone shall have the right to education.
Accessible and free general, secondary and vocational-technical education shall be guaranteed.

Secondary specialised and higher education shall be accessible to all in accordance with the capabilities of each individual. Everyone may, on a competitive basis, obtain the appropriate education at state educational establishments free of charge.

Article 50
Everyone shall have the right to preserve his ethnic affiliation, and equally, no one may be compelled to define or indicate his ethnic affiliation.
Insults to ethnic dignity shall be prosecuted by law.
Everyone shall have the right to use his native language and to choose the language of communication. In accordance with the law, the State shall guarantee the freedom to choose the language of education and teaching.

Article 51
Everyone shall have the right to take part in cultural life. This right shall be safeguarded by universal accessibility to the treasures of domestic and world culture that are held in state and public collections and by the development of a network of cultural and educational establishments.
Freedom of artistic, scientific and technical creativity and teaching shall be guaranteed.
Intellectual property shall be protected by law.

Article 52
Everyone in the territory of the Republic of Belarus shall abide by its Constitution and laws and respect national traditions.

Article 53
Everyone shall respect the dignity, rights, liberties and legitimate interests of others.

Article 54
Everyone shall preserve the historical and cultural heritage and other cultural treasures.

Article 55
It shall be the duty of everyone to protect the environment.

Article 56
Citizens of the Republic of Belarus shall contribute towards the funding of public expenditure through the payment of state taxes, dues and other payments.

Article 57
It shall be the responsibility and sacred duty of every citizen of the Republic of Belarus to defend the Republic of Belarus.
The procedure governing military service, the grounds and conditions for exemption from military service and the substitution thereof by alternative service shall be determined by the law.

Article 58
No one shall be compelled to discharge duties that are not specified in the Constitution of the Republic of Belarus and its laws or renounce his rights.

Article 59
The State shall take all measures at its disposal to create the domestic and international order necessary for the exercise in full of the rights and liberties of the citizens of the Republic of Belarus that are specified in the Constitution.

Article 60
State bodies, official and other persons that are entrusted with the discharge of state functions shall, within the limits of their competence, take measures necessary for the exercise and protection of personal rights and liberties.
These bodies and persons shall be held liable for actions that violate personal rights and liberties.

Article 61
Everyone shall be guaranteed protection of his rights and liberties by a competent, independent and impartial court of law within time periods specified in law.
To defend their rights, liberties, honour and dignity, citizens shall be entitled to recover, through the courts, both property damage and financial compensation for moral injury.

Article 62
Everyone shall have the right to legal assistance to exercise and defend his rights and liberties, including the right to make use, at any time, of the assistance of lawyers and one's other representatives in court, other state bodies, bodies of local government, enterprises, establishments, organisations and public associations, and also in relations with officials and citizens. In the instances specified in law, legal assistance shall be rendered from public funds. Opposition to the rendering of legal assistance shall be prohibited in the Republic of Belarus.

Article 63
The exercise of the personal rights and liberties specified in this Constitution may be suspended only during a state of emergency or martial law under the procedure and within the limits specified in the Constitution and the law.
In carrying out special measures during a state of emergency, the rights specified in Article 24, part three of Article 25 and Articles 26 and 31 of the Constitution may not be restricted.

Section 3 – Electoral system and referendum

Chapter 1 – Electoral system

Article 64
The elections of deputies and other persons elected to state office by the people shall be universal: citizens of the Republic of Belarus who have reached the age of 18 shall be eligible to vote.

Citizens who are deemed incapable by a court of law or held in places of confinement in accordance with the verdict of a court shall not take part in elections. Persons in respect of whom preventive punishment (detention) is selected under the procedure specified in the law on criminal proceedings shall not take part in voting. Any direct or indirect restrictions on citizen's voting rights in other instances shall be impermissible and punishable by law.

Article 65
The age qualifications of deputies and other persons elected to state office shall be determined by the relevant laws, unless otherwise specified in the Constitution.

Article 66
Elections shall be free. A voter shall decide personally whether to take part in elections and for whom to vote.
The preparation and conduct of elections shall be open and in public.

Article 67
Elections shall be held according to the principle of equal suffrage. Voters shall have equal number of votes.
The number of the votes in each constituency shall be approximatively equal. Candidates standing for public office shall take part in elections on an equal basis.

Article 68
Elections shall be direct. Deputies shall be elected by citizens directly.

Article 69
Voting at elections shall be secret. The monitoring of voters' preferences while voting is in progress shall be prohibited.

Article 70
Public associations, individual work forces and citizens shall have the right to nominate candidates for deputy in accordance with the law.

Article 71
Expenditure incurred in the preparation and conduct of elections shall be covered by the State within the limits of the funds assigned for that purpose.

Article 72
Elections shall be conducted by electoral commissions.
The procedure governing the conduct of elections shall be determined by the laws of the Republic of Belarus.
No elections shall be held during a state of emergency or martial law.

Chapter 2 – Referendum

Article 73
National and local referendums may be held to resolve the most important issues of the State and society.

Article 74
National referendums shall be called by the Supreme Council of the Republic of Belarus, on the recommendation of the President of the Republic of Belarus or no fewer than 450 000 citizens eligible to vote.
The Supreme Council shall set the date of a national referendum within thirty days of the submission, for reconsideration in accordance with the law, of a recommendation by the President of the Republic of Belarus or no fewer than 450 000 citizens eligible to vote.
The issue of holding a national referendum may also be considered by the Supreme Council on the initiative of no fewer than 70 deputies of the Supreme Council of the Republic of Belarus.

Article 75
Local referendums shall be called by the relevant local representative bodies on their initiative or on the recommendation of no less than ten per cent of the citizens who are eligible to vote and resident in the area concerned.

Article 76
Referendums shall be conducted by means of universal, free, equal and secret ballot.
Citizens of the Republic of Belarus eligible to vote shall take part in referendums.

Article 77
The decisions adopted by referendum may be reversed or amended only by means of another referendum, unless otherwise specified by the referendum.

Article 78
The procedure governing the conduct of national and local referendums and a list of issues that may not be put to a referendum shall be determined by the law of the Republic of Belarus.

Section 4 – Legislative, executive and judicial power

Chapter 3 – The Supreme Council of the Republic of Belarus

Article 79
The Supreme Council of the Republic of Belarus shall be the highest representative, standing and sole legislative body of state power of the Republic of Belarus.

Article 80
The Supreme Council of the Republic of Belarus shall consist of 260 deputies elected by the citizens of the Republic of Belarus.
Any citizen of the Republic of Belarus who is eligible to vote and has reached the age of 21 may become a deputy of the Supreme Council.

Article 81

The term of the Supreme Council shall be five years.

The powers of the Supreme Council may be terminated prematurely in accordance with a resolution of the Supreme Council that is adopted by a majority of no less than two-thirds of the elected deputies.

Elections for a new Supreme Council shall be called no later than three months prior to the expiry of the powers of the current Supreme Council.

Article 82

The first sitting of the Supreme Council shall be convened by the Central Commission of the Republic of Belarus on Elections and National Referendums no later than 30 days after the elections.

Article 83

The Supreme Council of the Republic of Belarus shall:

1.   call national referendums;
2.   adopt and amend the Constitution;
3.   adopt laws and resolutions and monitor their implementation;
4.   provide interpretation of the Constitution and laws;
5.   call regular elections of deputies of the Supreme Council and local councils of deputies and presidential elections;
6.   form the Central Commission on Elections and National Referendums;
7.   elect the Constitutional Court of the Republic of Belarus, the Supreme Court of the Republic of Belarus, the Supreme Economic Court of the Republic of Belarus, the Procurator-General of the Republic of Belarus, and the chairman and the council of the Supervisory Authority of the Republic of Belarus, the chairman and members of the board of the National Bank of the Republic of Belarus;
8.   determine the procedure for resolving issues relating to the administrative-territorial structure of the State;
9.   determine the guidelines of the domestic and foreign policy of the Republic of Belarus;
10. approve the national budget, the national account and the allowance quotas from national taxes and revenue to local budgets;
11. set national taxes and dues and monitor the issue of money;
12. ratify and denounce international treaties of the Republic of Belarus;
13. adopt decisions on amnesty;
14. determine military doctrine;
15. declare war and conclude peace;
16. institute state awards, ranks and titles of the Republic of Belarus;
17. adopt resolutions on the dissolution of local councils of deputies and call new elections where they systematically and flagrantly violate the requirements of the law;
18. repeal orders of the Chairman of the Supreme Council of the Republic of Belarus where they are contrary to the laws and resolutions of the Supreme Council.

The Supreme Council may resolve other issues in accordance with the Constitution.

Article 84
Deputies shall vote in person at sitting of the Supreme Council.
Laws and resolutions of the Supreme Council shall be deemed to have been adopted provided that a majority of elected deputies has voted for them, unless otherwise specified in the Constitution.
Adopted laws shall be sent to the President for signature within ten days of their adoption.

Article 85
The Supreme Council shall elect, from the ranks of the deputies of the Supreme Council, a Chairman of the Supreme Council, a First Vice-Chairman of the Supreme Council and vice-chairmen of the Supreme Council.

Article 86
The Chairman of the Supreme Council shall be elected by secret ballot. He shall be accountable to the Supreme Council.

Article 87
The Chairman of the Supreme Council of the Republic of Belarus shall:
1.   exercise general leadership in the preparation of issues to be considered by the Supreme Council;
2.   chair sittings of the Supreme Council;
3.   represent the Supreme Council in relations with bodies and organisations within the country and abroad;
4.   sign resolutions adopted by the Supreme Council;
5.   put forward to the Supreme Council nominations for the posts of First Vice-Chairman and vice-chairmen of the Supreme Council, the Procurator-General and the Chairman of the Supervisory Authority;
6.   manage the work of the staff of the Supreme Council.
The First Vice-Chairman and the vice-chairmen of the Supreme Council of the Republic of Belarus shall, on the instructions of the Chairman of the Supreme Council, discharge certain of his duties and stand in for the Chairman of the Supreme Council where he is unavailable or unable to discharge his duties.

Article 88
The Supreme Council shall elect, from the ranks of the deputies, standing committees and other bodies to draft laws, give preliminary consideration to, and prepare, issues that fall within the jurisdiction of the Supreme Council, and monitor the implementation of laws.
Where necessary, the Supreme Council may set up investigatory, audit and other ad hoc commissions.

Article 89
A Presidium of the Supreme Council of the Republic of Belarus shall be set up to organise the work of the Supreme Council.
The Presidium of the Supreme Council shall include the Chairman of the Supreme Council, the First Vice-Chairman of the Supreme Council, the vice-chairmen of the Supreme Council and deputies in accordance with the Rules of Procedure by the Supreme Council.

The Chairman of the Supreme Council shall be the head of the Presidium of the Supreme Council.

Article 90
The right of legislative initiative in the Supreme Council of the Republic of Belarus shall belong to deputies of the Supreme Council, standing committees of the Supreme Council, the President, the Supreme Court, the Supreme Economic Court, the Procurator-General, the Supervisory Authority, the National Bank, and citizens who are eligible to vote, in a number of no less than 50 000.

Article 91
The powers of the Supreme Council shall be retained until the opening of the first sitting of the Supreme Council of a new convocation.

Article 92
A deputy of the Supreme Council shall exercise his powers in the Supreme Council on a professional basis or, if he so desires, without suspending his activity in industry or administration.
The President, members of the Cabinet of Ministers, judges and other persons appointed to posts by the President, or following consultation with the President, may not become deputies of the Supreme Council.

Article 93
A deputy of the Supreme Council may not be held legally liable for his activity in the Supreme Council which is carried out in accordance with the Constitution both during the period he exercises his powers and after the termination of such powers.
A deputy of the Supreme Council may not be arraigned on criminal charges, arrested or otherwise deprived of his personal liberty without consent of the Supreme Council, except where he is detained at the scene of a crime. Criminal proceedings against a deputy of the Supreme Council may be instituted by the Procurator-General with the consent of the Supreme Council, and in the period between sessions, with consent of the Presidium of the Supreme Council.

Article 94
The procedure governing the activities of the Supreme Council, the bodies thereof and the deputies shall be determined by the Rules of Procedure of the Supreme Council, which shall be adopted by the Supreme Council and signed by its Chairman, and other legislative instruments of the Republic of Belarus.

Chapter 4 – The President of the Republic of Belarus

Article 95
The President of the Republic of Belarus shall be the Head of State and the Executive.

Article 96
Any citizen of the Republic of Belarus at least 35 years of age who is eligible to vote and has been resident in the Republic of Belarus for at least ten years may be elected President.

Article 97
The President shall be elected directly by the people of the Republic of Belarus. The President's term of office shall be five years. The same person may be President for no more than two terms.
Presidential candidates shall be nominated by no fewer than 70 deputies of the Supreme Council or by citizens of the Republic of Belarus where the signatures of no less than 100 000 voters have been collected.
Presidential elections shall be called by the Supreme Council no later than five months and held no later than two months prior to the expiry of the term of office of the previous President. Where the office of the President becomes vacant, elections shall be held no sooner than 30 days, and no later than 70 days, from the day on which the office fell vacant.

Article 98
The elections shall be deemed to have taken place where over half the citizens of the Republic of Belarus on the electoral roll have taken part in the poll. The President shall be deemed elected where over half the citizens of the Republic of Belarus who took part in the poll voted for him.
Where no candidate polls the requisite number of votes, within two weeks a second round of voting shall be conducted between the two candidates who obtained the largest number of votes. The presidential candidate who obtains more than half the votes of those who took part in the second poll shall be deemed to be elected. The procedure governing the conduct of presidential elections shall be determined by the law of the Republic of Belarus.

Article 99
The President shall take office after taking the following oath:
"Assuming the office of President of the Republic of Belarus, I solemnly swear to serve the people of the Republic of Belarus, to abide by the Constitution and laws of the Republic of Belarus, and to discharge conscientiously the lofty duties that have been imposed upon me."
The oath shall be administered in a ceremonial setting at a special sitting of the Supreme Council of the Republic of Belarus no later than two months from the day on which the President is elected. The powers of the previous President shall terminate the moment the President-elect takes the oath.

Article 100
The President of the Republic of Belarus shall:
1.   take measures to protect the sovereignty, national security and territorial integrity of the Republic of Belarus and safeguard political and economic stability and the respect of civil rights and liberties;
2.   manage the system of bodies of executive power and ensure their cooperation with the representative bodies;

3.   set up and abolish ministries, state committees and other central bodies of administration of the Republic of Belarus;
4.   appoint and dismiss, with the consent of the Supreme Council, the prime minister, his deputies, ministers of foreign affairs, finance, defence, internal affairs and chairman of the Committee for State Security; appoint and dismiss other members of the Cabinet of Ministers; accept the resignation of the persons referred to in this paragraph;
5.   introduce to the Supreme Council candidates for election for the post of chairman of the Constitutional Court, chairman of the Supreme Court, chairman of the Supreme Economic Court, chairman of the board of the National Bank;
6.   annually present to the Supreme Council reports on the state of the nation, on his own initiative or on the recommendation of the Supreme Council, inform the Supreme Council of the Republic of Belarus of the implementation of the domestic and foreign policy of the Republic of Belarus;
7.   deliver addresses to the people of the Republic of Belarus and the Supreme Council;
8.   report to the Supreme Council on the Programme of Action of the Cabinet of Ministers;
9.   have the right to take part in the work of the Supreme Council and its bodies and make a speech or deliver a report to them at any time;
10. appoint judges of the Republic of Belarus, other than those whose election falls within the competence of the Supreme Council;
11. appoint other officials whose offices are determined by the law, unless otherwise specified in the Constitution;
12. resolve issues regarding the granting of citizenship of the Republic of Belarus, the termination thereof and the granting of asylum;
13. confer state awards and bestow ranks and titles;
14. grant pardons to convicted citizens;
15. represent the State in relations with other countries and international organisations;
16. conduct negotiations and sign international treaties and appoint and recall diplomatic representatives of the Republic of Belarus in foreign countries and at international organisations;
17. receive the credentials and letters of recall of the accredited diplomatic representatives of foreign countries;
18. in the event of a natural disaster, a catastrophe, or unrest involving violence or the threat of violence on the part of a group of persons or organisations that endangers peoples' lives and health or jeopardises the territorial integrity and existence of the State, declare a state of emergency in the territory of the Republic of Belarus or in specific areas thereof and submit the decision to the Supreme Council for approval within three days;
19. have the right, in instances specified in law, to defer a strike or suspend it for a period not exceeding two months;
20. sign laws and have the right, within ten days of receiving a law, to return it with his objections to the Supreme Council for further discussion and a second vote. Where, by a majority of no less than two-thirds of the elected deputies, the Supreme Council upholds the decision it had adopted previously, the President shall be required to sign the law within three days. Any law that is not returned within the above period shall be deemed to be signed;

21. be entitled to repeal instruments of bodies of executive power subordinate to him;

22. suspend the decisions of local councils of deputies where they are contrary to the law;

23. head the Security Council of the Republic of Belarus;

24. be the Commander-in-Chief of the Armed Forces of the Republic of Belarus;

25. impose, in the event of military threat or attack, martial law in the territory of the Republic of Belarus and announce general or partial mobilisation;

26. exercise other powers entrusted to him by the Constitution and the laws. The President shall have no right to delegate to any bodies or officials his powers as the Head of State.

Article 101
The President shall, within the limits of his powers, issue edicts and orders and organise and monitor their implementation.

Article 102
The President may not hold other offices or receive any monetary remuneration other than his salary, apart from royalties for works of science, literature and art.

The President shall suspend his membership of political parties and other public associations that pursue political goals for the whole of his term in office.

Article 103
The President may tender his resignation at any time. The President's resignation shall be accepted by the Supreme Council.

Article 104
The President may be removed from office where he violates the Constitution or commits a crime and relieved of office prematurely, where he is unable to discharge his duties on account of the state of his health, by a resolution of the Supreme Council adopted by a majority of no less two-thirds of the elected deputies of the Supreme Council.

The issue of removing the President may be raised on the recommendation of no fewer than 70 deputies of the Supreme Council. Findings concerning a violation by the President of the Constitution shall be provided by the Constitutional Court, and on the commission of the Supreme Council. From the moment the Constitutional Court presents its findings concerning a violation of the Constitution, or an ad hoc commission presents its finding concerning the commission of a crime, the President may not discharge his duties until the Supreme Council pronounces a corresponding decision.

Where the President is removed in connection with the commission of a crime, the case shall be examined on the merits of the charge by the Supreme Court.

Article 105
Whether the office of President falls vacant or he is unable to discharge his duties, his powers shall be transferred to the Chairman of the Supreme Council until the President-elect is sworn in. In that case, the duties of the

Chairman of the Supreme Council shall be transferred to the First Vice-Chairman of the Supreme Council.

Article 106
A Cabinet of Ministers of the Republic of Belarus shall be formed under the auspices of the President of the Republic of Belarus to exercise the powers of the executive in the fields of economy, foreign policy, defence, national security, maintenance of public order and other spheres of state administration.

Article 107
The Cabinet of Ministers shall relinquish its powers to the President-elect.
Members of the Cabinet of Ministers shall be appointed and dismissed by the President. The prime minister, his deputies, ministers for foreign affairs, finance, defence and internal affairs, and the chairman of the Committee for State Security shall be appointed and dismissed by the President with the consent of the Supreme Council.
The prime minister shall manage directly the activities of the Cabinet of Ministers, sign the acts of the Cabinet of Ministers that have binding force in the entire territory of the Republic of Belarus and discharge other functions entrusted to him.
The Supreme Council shall be entitled to obtain a report from any member of the Cabinet of Ministers regarding the implementation of the law. Where a member of the Cabinet of Ministers violates the Constitution and the laws, the Supreme Council shall be entitled to raise the issue of his premature dismissal with the President.

Article 108
The competence of the Cabinet of Ministers and the procedure governing its activities shall be determined on the basis of the Constitution and the Law on the Cabinet of Ministers of the Republic of Belarus.

Chapter 5 – The Courts

Article 109
The courts shall exercise judicial power in the Republic of Belarus.
The judicial system in the Republic of Belarus shall be determined by the law.
The formation of special courts shall be prohibited.

Article 110
In administering justice judges shall be independent and subordinate to law alone.
Any interference in judges' activities in the administration of justice shall be impermissible and liable to legal action.

Article 111
Judges may not engage in business activities or perform any paid work apart from teaching and scientific research that does not involve holding a regular staff position.
The grounds for electing (appointing) judges and their dismissal shall be determined by the law.

Article 112
The courts shall administer justice on the basis of the Constitution, the laws and other enforceable enactments adopted in accordance therewith.
If, during the hearing of a specific case, a court concludes that an enforceable enactment is contrary to the Constitution or other law, it shall make a ruling in accordance with the Constitution and the law, and raise, under the established procedure, the issue of whether the enforceable enactment in question should be deemed unconstitutional.

Article 113
Cases before a court shall be tried collegially, and in the instances specified in law, by judges individually.

Article 114
The trial of cases in all courts shall be open. The hearing of cases in closed court session shall be permitted only in the instances specified in law and in accordance with all the rules of legal procedure.

Article 115
Justice shall be administered on the basis of the adversarial proceedings and equality of the parties involved in the trial.

Article 116
The parties have the right to appeal rulings, sentences and other judicial decisions.

Section 5 – Local government and self-government

Article 117
Citizens shall exercise local government and self-government through local councils of deputies, executive and administrative bodies, bodies of public territorial self-government, local referendums, assemblies and other forms of direct participation in state and public affairs.

Article 118
Local councils of deputies shall be elected by the citizens of the relevant administrative-territorial units for a four-year term.

Article 119
Local councils of deputies and executive and administrative bodies shall, within the limits of their competencies, resolve issues of local significance, proceeding from national interests and the interests of the people who reside in the relevant territory, and implement the decisions of higher state bodies.

Article 120
The following shall fall within the exclusive competence of the local councils of deputies:

- the approval of programmes of economic and social development, and local budgets and accounts;
- the setting of local taxes and dues in accordance with the law;
- the determination, within the limits specified by law, of the procedure governing the management and disposal of municipal property;
- the calling of local referendums.

Article 121
Local councils of deputies and executive and administrative bodies shall, on the basis of existing laws, adopt decisions that have binding force in the relevant territory.

Article 122
Decisions of local councils of deputies that are contrary to the law shall be reversed by higher councils of deputies.
Decisions of local executive and administrative authorities that are contrary to the law shall be reversed by the relevant councils of deputies, higher executive and administrative bodies and the President of the Republic of Belarus.
Decisions of local councils of deputies and their executive and administrative bodies that restrict or violate civil rights and liberties and the legitimate interests of citizens, and in other instances specified in law, may be challenged in a court of law.

Article 123
Where a local council of deputies systematically or flagrantly violates the requirements of the law, it may be dissolved by the Supreme Council. Other grounds for the premature termination of the powers of local councils of deputies shall be determined by the law.

Article 124
The competence and the procedure governing the establishment and activities of bodies of local government and self-government shall be determined by the law.

Section 6 – State monitoring and supervision

Chapter 6 – The Constitutional Court of the Republic of Belarus

Article 125
The Constitutional Court of the Republic of Belarus shall monitor the constitutionality of enforceable enactments in the State.

Article 126
The Constitutional Court of the Republic of Belarus shall be elected by the Supreme Council of the Republic of Belarus from among qualified specialists in the field of law and number eleven judges. The term of the members of the Constitutional Court shall be eleven years. The age limit for members of the Constitutional Court shall be 60.

Persons elected to the Constitutional Court may not engage in business activities or perform any other paid work, apart from teaching and scientific research that does not involve holding a regular staff position.

Persons elected to the Constitutional Court shall be entitled to tender their resignation at any time.

Direct or indirect pressure on the Constitutional Court or its members in connection with the monitoring of the Constitution shall be impermissible and liable to legal action.

Article 127
On the recommendation of the President, the Chairman of the Supreme Council, standing committees of the Supreme Council, no fewer than 70 deputies of the Supreme Council, the Supreme Court, the Supreme Economic Court or the Procurator-General, the Constitutional Court shall produce a ruling on:

– the conformity of laws, international agreements, other obligations of the Republic of Belarus to the Constitution and other instruments of international law ratified by the Republic of Belarus;

– the conformity of the legal instruments of interstate formations of which the Republic of Belarus is part, edicts of the President, ordinances of the Cabinet of Ministers and orders of the Supreme Court, the Supreme Economic Court and the Procurator-General that are a proscriptive nature to the Constitution, the laws and instruments of international law ratified by the Republic of Belarus.

The Constitutional Court shall be entitled, at its discretion, to examine the question of whether the enforceable enactments of a state body or public association conform to the Constitution, the laws and instruments of international law ratified by the Republic of Belarus.

Article 128
Enforceable enactments, international agreements and other obligations that are deemed by the Constitutional Court to be unconstitutional because they violate human rights and liberties shall be deemed as having no legal force as a whole or in a particular part thereof from the time the relevant enactment is adopted.

Other enforceable enactments of state bodies and public associations, international treaty or other obligations that are deemed by the Constitutional laws or instruments of international law ratified by the Republic of Belarus shall be deemed invalid as a whole or in a particular part thereof from a time determined by the Constitutional Court.

The Constitutional Court shall make rulings by a simple majority of votes of the full complement of judges.

Article 129
The findings of the Constitutional Court shall be final and not subject to appeal or protest.

Article 130
The Constitutional Court shall be entitled to submit proposals to the Supreme Council on the need for amendments and addenda to the Constitution and

on the adoption and amendment of laws. Such proposals shall be subject to compulsory consideration by the Supreme Council.

Article 131
Persons elected to the Constitutional Court may not be arraigned on criminal charges, arrested or otherwise deprived of their personal liberty without the consent of the Supreme Council, except where they are detained at the scene of a crime.
Criminal proceedings against members of the Constitutional Court may be instituted by the Procurator-General with the consent of the Supreme Council.

Article 132
The competence, organisation and procedure governing the activities of the Constitutional Court shall be determined by the law.

Chapter 7 – The Procurator's Office

Article 133
Supervision of the strict and uniform implementation of the laws by ministries and other bodies subordinate to the Cabinet of Ministers, local representative and executive bodies, enterprises, organisations and establishments, public associations, officials and citizens shall be entrusted to the Procurator-General of the Republic of Belarus and the procurators subordinate to him.
The Procurator's Office shall supervise the implementation of laws in the investigation of crimes, the conformity to the law of judicial decisions in civil and criminal cases and cases involving administrative offences; in the instances specified in law, conduct preliminary inquiries and support public prosecutions in the courts.

Article 134
The Procurator-General elected by the Supreme Council shall be the head of the uniform and centralised system of bodies of the Procurator's Office.
Subordinate procurators shall be appointed by the Procurator-General.

Article 135
The Procurator-General and the subordinate procurators shall be independent in the exercise of their powers and guided by the law alone. The Procurator-General shall be accountable in his activities to the Supreme Council.

Article 136
The competence, organisation and procedure governing the activities of bodies of the Procurator's Office shall be determined by the law.

Chapter 8 – The Supervisory Authority of the Republic of Belarus

Article 137
The Supervisory Authority shall monitor the implementation of the national budget, the use of public property and the implementation of the acts of the

Supreme Council governing public property relationships and economic, financial and tax relations.

Article 138
The Supervisory Authority shall be formed by the Supreme Council, operate under its direction and be accountable to it.

Article 139
The Chairman of the Supervisory Authority shall be elected by the Supreme Council for a five-year term.

Article 140
The competence, organisation and procedure governing the activities of the Supervisory Authority shall by determined by the law.

Section 7 – Financial and credit system of the Republic of Belarus

Article 141
The financial and credit system of the Republic of Belarus shall include the budget system, the banking system, as well as the financial resources of non-budget funds, funds of enterprises, establishments, organisations and citizens.
A unified fiscal, tax, credit and currency policy shall be pursued in the territory of the Republic of Belarus.

Article 142
The budget system of the Republic of Belarus shall include the national budget and local budgets.
Budget revenue shall be raised from the taxes specified in law, other mandatory payments, as well as other receipts.
National expenditure shall be covered by the national budget on its expenditure side.
In accordance with the law, non-budgetary funds may be created in the Republic of Belarus.

Article 143
The procedure for drawing up, approving and implementing budgets and public non-budgetary funds shall be determined by the law.

Article 144
A national account shall be submitted to the Supreme Council for consideration no later than five months from the end of the fiscal year in review.
Local accounts shall be submitted to the relevant councils of deputies for the consideration within time specified in law.
National and local accounts shall be published.

Article 145
The banking system of the Republic of Belarus shall consist of the National Bank of the Republic of Belarus and other banks. The National Bank shall

regulate credit relations and monetary circulation, determine the procedure for making payments and have an exclusive right to issue money.

Section 8 – The application of the Constitution of the Republic of Belarus and the procedure for amending the Constitution

Article 146
The Constitution shall have the supreme legal force. Laws and other instruments of state bodies shall be promulgated on the basis of, and in accordance with, the Constitution of the Republic of Belarus.
Where there is a discrepancy between a law and the Constitution, the Constitution shall apply, and where there is a discrepancy between an enforceable enactment and a law, the law shall apply.

Article 147
The issue of amending and supplementing the Constitution shall be considered by the Supreme Council on the initiative of no fewer than 150 000 citizens of the Republic of Belarus who are eligible to vote, no fewer than 40 deputies of the Supreme Council, the President or the Constitutional Court.

Article 148
A law on amending or supplementing the Constitution may be adopted after it has been debated and approved twice by the Supreme Council with at least three months' interval.
The Constitution shall not be amended or supplemented during a state of emergency or the last six months of the term of a Supreme Council.

Article 149
The Constitution, laws on amendments and addenda thereto, on the entry into force of the Constitution and the said laws and instruments on interpretation of the Constitution shall be deemed to have been adopted where no less than two-thirds of the elected deputies of the Supreme Council have voted in favour of them.
The Constitution may be amended or supplemented via a referendum. A decision to amend or supplement the Constitution by means of a referendum shall be deemed adopted where a majority of citizens on the electoral roll have voted in favour of it.

[Signed] M. Grib, the Chairman of the Supreme Council of the Republic of Belarus
15 March 1994
Minsk,

Constitution of the Republic of Belarus[1]

Adopted by referendum, 27 November 1996

We, the People of the Republic of Belarus, (of Belarus),
proceeding from the assumption of responsibility for the present and future of Belarus,
recognising ourselves as a fully-fledged subject of the international community and conforming our adherence to values common to all mankind,
founding ourselves on our inalienable right to self-determination,
supported by the centuries-long history of development of Belarusian statehood,
striving to assert the rights and freedoms of every citizen of the Republic of Belarus,
desiring to maintain civic concord, stable foundations of government by the people and a state based on the rule of law,
hereby adopt and enact this Constitution as the Fundamental Law of the Republic of Belarus.

Section 1 – Principles of the constitutional system

Article 1
The Republic of Belarus is a unitary, democratic, social state based on the rule of law.
The Republic of Belarus exercises supreme control and absolute authority over the whole of its territory, and shall implement an independent internal and foreign policy.
The Republic of Belarus shall defend its independence and territorial integrity, its constitutional system, and safeguard legality and law and order.

Article 2
The individual, his rights, freedoms and guarantees for their attainment manifest the supreme goal and value of society and the State.
The State shall bear responsibility towards the citizen to create the conditions for the free and dignified development of his identity. The citizen bears a responsibility towards the State to discharge unwaveringly the duties imposed upon him by the Constitution.

---

1. Information Centre at the Ministry of Foreign Affairs of the Republic of Belarus

Article 3
The people shall be the sole source of state power and the repository of sovereignty in the Republic of Belarus. The people shall exercise their power directly through representative and other bodies in the forms and within the bounds specified by the Constitution.
Any actions aimed at changing the constitutional system and seizing state power by forcible means or by way of any other violation of the laws of the Republic of Belarus shall be punishable by law.

Article 4
Democracy in the Republic of Belarus shall be exercised on the basis of diversity of political institutions, ideologies and views.
The ideology of political parties, religious or other public associations, social groups may not be made mandatory for citizens.

Article 5
Political parties and other public associations acting within the framework of the Constitution and laws of the Republic of Belarus, shall contribute towards ascertaining and expressing the political will of the citizens and shall participate in elections.
Political parties and other public associations shall have the right to use state mass media under the procedure determined by the legislation.
The creation and activities of political parties and other public associations that aim to change the constitutional system by force, or conduct a propaganda of war, social, ethnic, religious and racial hatred, shall be prohibited.

Article 6
State power in the Republic of Belarus is exercised on the principle of division of powers between the legislature, executive and judiciary. State bodies' within the confines of their powers, shall be independent: they shall co-operate among themselves acting on the principle of checks and balances.

Article 7
The Republic of Belarus shall be bound by the principle of supremacy of law. The State and all the bodies and officials thereof shall operate within the confines of the Constitution and the laws enacted in accordance therewith.
Legal enactments or specific provisions thereof which are deemed under the procedure specified in law to be contrary to the provisions of the Constitution shall have no legal force.
Enforceable enactments of state bodies shall be published or promulgated by some means specified in law.

Article 8
The Republic of Belarus shall recognise the supremacy of the universally acknowledged principles of international law and ensure that its laws comply with such principles.
The Republic of Belarus in conformity with principles of international law may on a voluntary basis enter interstate formations and withdraw from them.

The conclusion of international treaties that are contrary to the Constitution shall not be permitted.

Article 9
The territory of the Republic of Belarus shall be the natural condition of the existence and spatial limit of the people's self-determination, and the basis for its prosperity and the sovereignty of the Republic of Belarus.

The territory of Belarus shall be unified and inalienable.

The territory shall be divided into regions (oblasts), districts, cities and other administrative-territorial units. The administrative-territorial division of the State is determined by the legislation.

Article 10
A citizen of the Republic of Belarus shall be guaranteed the protection and patronage of the State both on the territory of Belarus and beyond.

No one may be deprived of citizenship of the Republic of Belarus or the right to change his citizenship.

A citizen of the Republic of Belarus may not be extradited to a foreign state, unless otherwise stipulated in international treaties to which the Republic of Belarus is party.

Citizenship shall be acquired or lost in accordance with the law.

Article 11
Foreign nationals and stateless persons on the territory of Belarus shall enjoy rights and liberties and execute duties on equal terms with the citizens of the Republic of Belarus, unless otherwise specified in the Constitution, the laws and international treaties.

Article 12
The Republic of Belarus may grant the right of asylum to persons persecuted in other states for political or religious beliefs or their ethnic affiliation.

Article 13
Property may be in state or private ownership.

The State shall grant equal rights to all to conduct economic and other activities, other than those prohibited by law, and guarantee equal protection and equal conditions for the development of all forms of ownership.

The State shall promote the development of co-operation.

The State shall guarantee to everyone equal opportunities for free utilisation of abilities and assets for business and other types of economic activities which are not banned by law.

The State shall regulate economic activities on behalf of the individual and society, and shall ensure the direction and co-ordination of state and private economic activity for social purposes.

The mineral wealth, waters and forests are the sole and exclusive property of the State. The land for agricultural use is the property of the State.

The law may specify facilities that may be the property of the State alone, or specify the special terms for their transition to private ownership, or grant the State an exclusive right to conduct certain types of activity.

The State shall guarantee the workers the right to participate in the management of enterprises, organisations and establishments to enhance their efficiency and improve social and economic living standards.

Article 14
The State shall regulate relations among social, ethnic and other communities on the basis of the principles of equality before the law and respect for their rights and interests.
The relations in the social sphere and in labour between the organs of state management, associations of employers and trade unions shall be exercised on the principles of social partnership and interaction of parties.

Article 15
The State shall bear responsibility for preserving the historic, cultural and spiritual heritage, and the free development of the cultures of all the ethnic communities that live in the Republic of Belarus.

Article 16
Religions and faiths shall be equal before the law.
Relations between the State and religious organisations shall be regulated by the law with regard to their influence on the formation of the spiritual, cultural and state traditions of the Belarusian people.
The activities of confessional organisations, their bodies and representatives, that are directed against the sovereignty of the Republic of Belarus, its constitutional system and civic harmony, or involve a violation of civil rights and liberties of its citizens as well as impede the execution of state, public and family duties by its citizens or are detrimental to their health and morality shall be prohibited.

Article 17
The Belarusian and Russian languages shall be the official languages of the Republic of Belarus.

Article 18
In its foreign policy the Republic of Belarus shall proceed from the principles of the equality of states, the non-use of force or the threat of force, the inviolability of frontiers, the peaceful settlement of disputes, non-interference in internal affairs of states and other universally acknowledged principles and standards of international law.
The Republic of Belarus pledges itself to make its territory a neutral, nuclear-free state.

Article 19
The symbols of the Republic of Belarus as a sovereign state shall be its national flag, national emblem and national anthem.

Article 20
The capital of the Republic of Belarus is the city of Minsk.
The status of the city of Minsk shall be determined by the law.

Section 2 – The individual, society and the state

Article 21
Safeguarding the rights and liberties of the citizens of the Republic of Belarus shall be the supreme goal of the State.

Every individual shall exercise the right to a dignified standard of living, including appropriate food, clothing, housing and likewise a continuous improvement of necessary living conditions.

The State shall guarantee the rights and liberties of the citizens of Belarus that are enshrined in the Constitution and the laws, and specified in the state's international obligations.

Article 22
All shall be equal before the law and entitled without discrimination to equal protection of their rights and legitimate interests.

Article 23
Restriction of personal rights and liberties shall be permitted only in the instances specified in law, in the interest of national security, public order, the protection of the morals and health of the population as well as rights and liberties of other persons.

No one may enjoy advantages and privileges that are contrary to the law.

Article 24
Every person shall have the right to life.

The State shall protect the life of the individual against any illegal infringements.

Until its abolition, the death sentence may be applied in accordance with the law as an exceptional penalty for especially grave crimes and only in accordance with the verdict of a court of law.

Article 25
The State shall safeguard personal liberty, inviolability and dignity. The restriction or denial of personal liberty is possible in the instances and under the procedure specified in law.

A person who has been taken into custody shall be entitled to a judicial investigation into the legality of his detention or arrest.

No-one shall be subjected to torture or cruel, inhuman or undignified treatment or punishment, or be subjected to medical or other experiments without his consent.

Article 26
No-one may be found guilty of a crime unless his guilt is proven under the procedure specified in law and established by the verdict of a court of law that has acquired legal force. A defendant shall not be required to prove his innocence.

Article 27
No person shall be compelled to be a witness against himself, members of his

family or next-of-kin. Evidence obtained in violation of the law shall have no legal force.

Article 28
Everyone shall be entitled to protection against unlawful interference with his private life, including encroachments on the privacy of his correspondence and telephone and other communications, and on his honour and dignity.

Article 29
The right of the people to be secure in their homes and other legitimate effects shall be guaranteed. No person shall have the right, save in due course of law, to enter the premises or other legal property of a citizen against his will.

Article 30
Citizens of the Republic of Belarus shall have the right to move freely and choose their place of residence within the Republic of Belarus, to leave it and to return to it without hindrance.

Article 31
Everyone shall have the right independently to determine his attitude towards religion, to profess any religion individually or jointly with others, or to profess none at all, to express and spread beliefs connected with his attitude towards religion, and to participate in the performance of acts of worship and religious rituals and rites, which are not prohibited by the law.

Article 32
Marriage, the family, motherhood, fatherhood, and childhood shall be under the protection of the State.
On reaching the age of consent women and men shall have the right to enter into marriage on a voluntary basis and start a family. A husband and wife shall be equal in family relationships.
Parents or persons *in loco parentis* shall be entitled and required to raise their children and to take care of their health, development and education. No child shall be subjected to cruel treatment or humiliation or used for work that may be harmful to its physical, mental or moral development. Children shall care for their parents or persons *in loco parentis* and render them assistance.
Children may be separated from their family against the consent of their parents or persons *in loco parentis* only according to the verdict of the court of law, if the parents or persons *in loco parentis* fail in their duty towards their children.
Women shall be guaranteed equal rights with men in their opportunities to receive education and vocational training, promotion in labour, socio-political, cultural and other spheres of activity, as well as in creating conditions safeguarding their labour and health.
Young people are guaranteed the right for their spiritual, moral and physical development.

The State shall create all necessary conditions for the free and effective participation of young people in the political, social, economic and cultural development of society.

Article 33
Everyone is guaranteed freedom of thought and belief and their free expression.

No one shall be forced to express his beliefs or to deny them.

No monopolisation of the mass media by the State, public associations or individual citizens and no censorship shall be permitted.

Article 34
Citizens of the Republic of Belarus shall be guaranteed the right to receive, store and disseminate complete, reliable and timely information of the activities of state bodies and public associations, on political, economic, cultural and international life, and on the state of the environment.

State bodies, public associations and officials shall afford citizens of the Republic of Belarus an opportunity to familiarise themselves with material that affects their rights and legitimate interests.

The use of information may be restricted by legislation with the purpose safeguarding the honour, dignity, personal and family life of citizens and the full implementation of their rights.

Article 35
The freedom to hold assemblies, rallies, street marches, demonstrations and pickets that do not disturb law and order or violate the rights of other citizens of the Republic of Belarus shall be guaranteed by the State. The procedure for conducting the above events shall be determined by the law.

Article 36
Everyone shall be entitled to freedom of association.

Judges, employees of the Procurator's Office, the staff of bodies of internal affairs, the State Supervisory Committee and security bodies, as well as servicemen may not be members of political parties or other public associations that pursue political goals.

Article 37
Citizens of the Republic of Belarus shall have the right to participate in the solution of state matters, both directly and through freely elected representatives.

The direct participation of citizens in the administration of the affairs of society and the State shall be safeguarded by the holding of referendums, the discussion of draft laws and issues of national and local significance, and by other means specified in law.

In instances determined by the law the citizens of the Republic of Belarus shall take part in the discussion of issues of state and public life at national and local meetings.

Article 38

Citizens of the Republic of Belarus shall have the right to vote freely and to be elected to state bodies on the basis of universal, equal, direct or indirect suffrage by secret ballot.

Article 39

Citizens of the Republic of Belarus, in accordance with their capabilities and vocational training, shall be entitled to equal access to any post in state bodies.

Article 40

Everyone shall have the right to address personal or collective appeals to state bodies.

State bodies, as well as the officials thereof, shall consider any appeal and furnish a reply in point of substance within the period specified in law. Any refusal to consider an appeal that has been submitted shall be justified in writing.

Article 41

Citizens of the Republic of Belarus shall be guaranteed the right to work as the worthiest means of an individual's self-assertion, that is, the right to choose one's profession, type of occupation and work in accordance with one's vocation, capabilities, education and vocational training, and having regard to social needs, and the right to healthy and safe working conditions. The State shall create conditions necessary for full employment of the population. Where a person is unemployed for reasons which are beyond his control, he shall be guaranteed training in new specialisations and an upgrading of his qualifications having regard to social needs, and an unemployment benefit in accordance with the law.

Citizens shall have the right to protection of their economic and social interests, including the right to form trade unions and conclude collective contracts (agreements), and the right to strike.

Forced labour shall be prohibited, other than work or service specified in the verdict of a court of law or in accordance with the law on the state of emergency or martial law.

Article 42

Employees shall be guaranteed a just share of remuneration for the economic results of their labour in accordance with the quantity, quality and social significance of such work, but it shall not be less than the level which shall ensure them and their families a life of independence and dignity.

Women and men and adults and minors shall be entitled to equal remuneration for work of equal value.

Article 43

Working people shall be entitled to holidays. For employees, this right shall be safeguarded by the establishment of a working week of no more than 40 hours, shorter working hours at night and the provision of an annual paid leave and weekly rest days.

Article 44
The State shall guarantee everyone the right of property and shall contribute to its acquisition.

A proprietor shall have the right to possess, enjoy and dispose of assets either individually or jointly with others. The inviolability of property and the right to inherit property shall be protected by law.

Property acquired in accordance with the law shall be safeguarded by the State.

The State shall encourage and protect the savings of citizens and guarantee conditions for the return of deposits.

The compulsory purchase of assets shall be permitted only by reason of public need, under the conditions and the procedure specified by law, with timely and full compensation for the value of the alienated assets, and in accordance with a ruling of a court of law.

The exercise of the right of property shall not be contrary to social benefit and security, or be harmful to the environment or historical and cultural treasures, or infringe upon the rights and legally protected interests of others.

Article 45
Citizens of the Republic of Belarus shall be guaranteed the right to health care, including free treatment at state health-care establishments.

The State shall make health care facilities accessible to all of its citizens.

The right of citizens of the Republic of Belarus to health care shall also be secured by the development of physical training and sport, measures to improve the environment, the opportunity to use fitness establishments and improvements in occupational safety.

Article 46
Everyone shall be entitled to a conducive environment and to compensation for loss or damage caused by the violation of this right.

The State shall supervise the rational utilisation of natural resources to protect and improve living conditions, and to preserve and restore the environment.

Article 47
Citizens of the Republic of Belarus shall be guaranteed the right to social security in old age, in the event of illness, disability, loss of fitness for work and loss of a bread-winner and in other instances specified in law. The State shall display particular concern for veterans of war and labour, as well as for those who lost their health in the defence of national and public interests.

Article 48
Citizens of the Republic of Belarus shall be entitled to housing. This right shall be safeguarded by the development of state and private housing, and assistance for citizens in the acquisition of housing.

The State and local self-government shall grant housing free of charge or at available prices in accordance with the law to citizens who are in need of social protection.

No-one may be deprived of housing arbitrarily.

Article 49
Everyone shall have the right to education.
Accessible and free general, secondary and vocation-technical education shall be guaranteed.
Secondary specialised and higher education shall be accessible to all in accordance with the capabilities of each individual. Everyone may, on a competitive basis, obtain the appropriate education at state educational establishments free of charge.

Article 50
Everyone shall have the right to preserve his ethnic affiliation, and equally, no one may be compelled to define or indicate his ethnic affiliation.
Insults to ethnic dignity shall be prosecuted by law.
Everyone shall have the right to use his native language and to choose the language of communication. In accordance with the law, the State shall guarantee the freedom to choose the language of education and teaching.

Article 51
Everyone shall have the right to take part in cultural life. This right shall be safeguarded by universal accessibility to the treasures of domestic and world culture that are held in state and public collections and by the development of a network of cultural and educational establishments.
Freedom of artistic, scientific and technical creativity and teaching shall be guaranteed.
Intellectual property shall be protected by law.
The State shall contribute to the development of culture and scientific and technical research for the benefit of the common interest.

Article 52
Everyone in the territory of the Republic of Belarus shall abide by its Constitution and laws and respect national traditions.

Article 53
Everyone shall respect the dignity, rights, liberties and legitimate interests of others.

Article 54
Everyone shall preserve the historical, cultural and spiritual heritage and other national treasures.

Article 55
It shall be the duty of everyone to protect the environment.

Article 56
Citizens of the Republic of Belarus shall contribute towards the funding of public expenditure through the payment of state taxes, dues and other payments.

Article 57
It shall be the responsibility and sacred duty of every citizen of the Republic of Belarus to defend the Republic of Belarus.
The procedure governing military service, the grounds and conditions for exemption from military service and the substitution thereof by alternative service shall be determined by the law.

Article 58
No one shall be compelled to discharge duties that are not specified in the Constitution of the Republic of Belarus and its laws or renounce his rights.

Article 59
The State shall take all measures at its disposal to create the domestic and international order necessary for the exercise in full of the rights and liberties of the citizens of the Republic of Belarus that are specified in the Constitution. State bodies, officials and other persons who have been entrusted to exercise state functions shall take necessary measures to implement and safeguard the rights and liberties of the individual.
These bodies and persons shall be held responsible for actions violating the rights and liberties of an individual.

Article 60
Everyone shall be guaranteed protection of his rights and liberties by a competent, independent and impartial court of law within time periods specified in law.
To defend their rights, liberties, honour and dignity, citizens shall be entitled in accordance with the law to recover, through the courts, both property damage and financial compensation for moral injury.

Article 61
Everyone shall have the right in accordance with the international instruments ratified by the Republic of Belarus to appeal to international organisations to defend their rights and liberties, provided all available intrastate means of legal defence have been exhausted.

Article 62
Everyone shall have the right to legal assistance to exercise and defend his rights and liberties, including the right to make use, at any time, of the assistance of lawyers and his other representatives in court, other state bodies, bodies of local government, enterprises, establishments, organisations and public associations, and also in relations with officials and citizens. In the instances specified in law, legal assistance shall be rendered from public funds. Opposition to the rendering of legal assistance shall be prohibited in the Republic of Belarus.

Article 63
The exercise of the personal rights and liberties specified in this Constitution may be suspended only during a state of emergency or martial law under the procedure and within the limits specified in the Constitution and the law.

In carrying out special measures during a state of emergency, the rights specified in Article 24, part three of Article 25 and Articles 26 and 31 of the Constitution may not be restricted.

Section 3 – Electoral system and referendum

Chapter 1 – Electoral system

Article 64

The elections of deputies and other persons elected to state office by the people shall be universal: citizens of the Republic of Belarus who have reached the age of l8 shall be eligible to vote.

Citizens who are deemed incapable by a court of law or held in places of confinement in accordance with the verdict of a court shall not take part in elections. Persons in respect of whom preventive punishment (detention) is selected under the procedure specified in the law on criminal proceedings shall not take part in voting. Any direct or indirect restrictions on citizens' voting rights in other instances shall be impermissible and punishable by law.

The age qualification of deputies and other persons elected to state positions shall be determined by corresponding laws, unless otherwise provided by the Constitution.

Article 65

Elections shall be free. A voter shall decide personally whether to take part in elections and for whom to vote.

The preparation and conduct of elections shall be open and in public.

Article 66

Elections shall be held according to the principle of equal suffrage. Voters shall have equal number of votes.

Candidates standing for public office shall take part in elections on an equal basis.

Article 67

Elections of deputies shall be direct. Deputies shall be elected by citizens directly.

Article 68

Voting at elections shall be secret. The monitoring of voters' preferences while voting is in progress shall be prohibited.

Article 69

Public associations, work collectives and citizens shall have the right to nominate candidates for deputy in accordance with the law.

Article 70

Expenditure incurred in the preparation and conduct of elections shall be covered by the State within the limits of the funds assigned for that purpose. In instances determined by the law, the expenditure for the preparation and conduct of elections may be carried out at the expense of public associations, enterprises, offices, organisations and citizens.

Article 71
Elections shall be conducted by electoral commissions, unless otherwise specified in the Constitution.
The procedure governing the conduct of elections shall be determined by the laws of the Republic of Belarus.
No elections shall be held during a state of emergency or martial law.

Article 72
The recall of deputies shall be exercised according to the order and instances as determined by the law.
The voting for the recall of a deputy shall be exercised to the order determined for the election of the deputy, and on the initiative of no less than 20% of the citizens eligible to vote and resident in the corresponding area.
The reason and order for the recall of a member of the Council of the Republic shall be determined by the law.

Chapter 2 – Referendum (Plebiscite)

Article 73
National and local referendums may be held to resolve the most important issues of the State and society.

Article 74
National referendums shall be called on the initiative of the President of the Republic of Belarus, as well as on the initiative of the Council of the Republic or House of Representatives, which is taken at their separate sittings by a majority of the full number of deputies of each house, or on the initiative of no fewer than 450 000 citizens eligible to vote, including no fewer than 30 000 citizens from each of the regions (oblasts) and the city of Minsk.
The President shall call a national referendum after its submission by the Council of the Republic and House of Representatives in accordance with the law, or by the citizens themselves.
The date of the referendum shall be no later than three months after the President issued the decree on holding a referendum.
The decisions taken by the national referendum shall be signed by the President of the Republic of Belarus.

Article 75
Local referendums shall be called by the relevant local representative bodies on their initiative or on the recommendation of no less than 10% of the citizens who are eligible to vote and resident in the area concerned.

Article 76
Referendums shall be conducted by means of universal, free, equal and secret ballot.

Citizens of the Republic of Belarus eligible to vote shall take part in referendums.

Article 77
The decisions adopted by referendum may be reversed or amended only by means of another referendum, unless otherwise specified by the referendum.

Article 78
The procedure governing the conduct of national and local referendums and a list of issues that may not be put to a referendum shall be determined by the law of the Republic of Belarus.

Section 4 – The President, Parliament, Government, the Courts

Chapter 3 – The President of the Republic of Belarus

Article 79
The President of the Republic of Belarus shall be the Head of State, the guarantor of the Constitution of the Republic of Belarus, the rights and liberties of man and citizen.
The President shall personify the unity of the nation, the implementation of the main guidelines of the domestic and foreign policy, shall represent the State in relations with other states and international organisations. The President shall provide the protection of the sovereignty of the Republic of Belarus, its national security and territorial integrity, shall ensure its political and economic stability, continuity and interaction of bodies of state power, shall maintain the intermediation among the bodies of state power.
The President shall enjoy immunity, and his honour and dignity shall be protected by the law.

Article 80
Any citizen of the Republic of Belarus by birth, who is at least 35 years of age, eligible to vote and has been resident in the Republic of Belarus for at least ten years to the elections may be elected President.

Article 81
The President shall be elected directly by the people of the Republic of Belarus for a term of office of five years by universal, free, equal, direct and secret ballot. The same person may be President for no more than two terms.
Presidential candidates shall be nominated by citizens of the Republic of Belarus where the signatures of no less than 100 000 voters have been collected.
Presidential elections shall be called by the House of Representatives no later than five months and shall be conducted no later than two months prior to the expiry of the term of office of the previous President.
Where the office of the President becomes vacant, elections shall be held no sooner than 30 days and no later than 70 days, from the day on which the office fell vacant.

Article 82

The elections shall be deemed to have taken place where over half the citizens of the Republic of Belarus on the electoral roll have taken part in the poll. The President shall be deemed elected where over half the citizens of the Republic of Belarus who took part in the poll voted for him.

Where no candidate polls the requisite number of votes, within two weeks a second round of voting shall be conducted between the two candidates who obtained the largest number of votes. The presidential candidate who obtains more than half the votes of those who took part in the second poll shall be deemed to be elected.

The procedure governing the conduct of presidential elections shall be determined by the law of the Republic of Belarus.

Article 83

The President shall assume office after taking the following Oath:

"Assuming the office of President of the Republic of Belarus, I solemnly swear to faithfully serve the people of the Republic of Belarus, to respect and safeguard the rights and liberties of man and citizen, to abide by and protect the Constitution of the Republic of Belarus, and to discharge strictly and conscientiously the lofty duties that have been bestowed upon me".

The Oath shall be administered in a ceremonial setting attended by members of the House of Representatives and the Council of the Republic, the judges of the Constitutional, Supreme and Economic Courts no later than two months from the day on which the President is elected. The powers of the previous President shall terminate the moment the President-elect takes the Oath.

Article 84

The President of the Republic of Belarus shall:

1.   call national referendums;
2.   call regular and extraordinary elections to the House of Representatives, the Council of the Republic and local representative bodies;
3.   dissolve the chambers of the Parliament according to the order and instances determined by the Constitution;
4.   appoint six members of the Central Commission of the Republic of Belarus on Elections and National Referendums;
5.   form, dissolve and reorganise the Administration of the President of the Republic of Belarus, other bodies of state administration, as well as consultative advisory councils, other bodies attached to the Presidency;
6.   appoint the Prime Minister of the Republic of Belarus with the consent of the House of Representatives;
7.   determine the structure of the Government of the Republic of Belarus, appoint and dismiss the deputy Prime ministers, ministers and other members of the Government, take the decision on the resignation of the Government, or any of its members;
8.   appoint with the consent of the Council of the Republic the Chairperson of the Constitutional, Supreme and Economic Courts from among the judges of these courts;
9.   appoint with the consent of the Council of the Republic the judges of the Supreme and Economic Courts, Chairperson of the Central Commission of

the Republic of Belarus on Elections and National Referendums, the Procurator-General, the Chairperson and members of the Governing Board of the National Bank;

10. appoint six members of the Constitutional Court, and other judges of the Republic of Belarus;

11. dismiss the Chairperson and judges of the Constitutional, Supreme and Economic Courts, the Chairperson of the Central Commission of the Republic of Belarus on Elections and National Referendums, the Procurator-General, the Chairperson and members of the Board of the National Bank according to the order and instances determined by the law and to the notification of the Council of the Republic;

12. appoint and dismiss the Chairperson of the State Supervisory Committee;

13. deliver messages to the people of the Republic of Belarus on the state of the nation and on the guidelines of the domestic and foreign policy;

14. deliver annual messages to the Parliament which are not open to discussion at the sittings of the House of Representatives and Council of the Republic; have the right to participate in the sessions of Parliament and its bodies; deliver speeches and addresses to Parliament at any requested time;

15. have the right to chair the meetings of the Government of the Republic of Belarus;

16. appoint leading officials of bodies of state administration and determine their status; appoint official representatives of the President in the Parliament and other officials whose offices are determined by the law, unless otherwise specified in the Constitution;

17. resolve issues regarding the granting of citizenship of the Republic of Belarus, the termination thereof and the granting of asylum;

18. institute state holidays and red-letter days, bestow state awards, ranks and titles;

19. grant pardons to convicted citizens;

20. conduct negotiations and sign international treaties, appoint and recall diplomatic representatives of the Republic of Belarus in foreign countries and to international organisations;

21. receive the credentials and letters of recall of the accredited diplomatic representatives of foreign countries;

22. in the event of a natural disaster, a catastrophe, or unrest involving violence or the threat of violence on the part of a group of persons or organisations that endangers peoples' lives and health or jeopardises the territorial integrity and existence of the State, declare a state of emergency in the territory of the Republic of Belarus or in specific areas thereof and submit the decision to the Council of the Republic for approval within three days;

23. have the right, in instances specified in the law, to defer a strike or suspend it for a period not exceeding three months;

24. sign bills and have the right to the order determined by the Constitution to return it or some of its provisions with the objections to the House of Representatives;

25. have the right to abolish acts of the Government;

26. exercise supervision directly or through specially formed bodies of observance of laws by local organs of administration or self-government and have the right to suspend decisions of local councils of deputies, or abolish deci-

sions of local executive and administrative bodies where they do not conform to the requirements of the law;

27. form and head the Security Council of the Republic of Belarus, and appoint and dismiss the State Secretary of the Security Council;

28. be the Commander-in-Chief of the Armed Forces of the Republic of Belarus; appoint and dismiss the Supreme Command of the Armed Forces;

29. impose, in the event of military threat or attack, martial law in the territory of the Republic of Belarus and announce general or partial mobilisation with the submission within 3 days of the taken decision for approval of the Council of the Republic;

30. exercise other powers entrusted to him by the Constitution and the laws.

Article 85
The President shall issue decrees and orders on the basis and in accordance with the Constitution which are mandatory in the territory of the Republic of Belarus.

In instances determined by the Constitution, the President shall issue decrees which have the force of the law. The President shall ensure directly or through specially formed bodies the execution of the decrees, orders and instructions.

Article 86
The President may not hold other offices or receive any monetary remuneration other than his salary, apart from royalties for works of science, literature and art.

The President shall suspend his membership of political parties and other public associations that pursue political goals during the whole of his term in office.

Article 87
The President may tender his resignation at any time. The President's resignation shall be accepted by the House of Representatives.

Article 88
The President of the Republic of Belarus may be prematurely removed from office where he is persistently incapable of discharging his duties on account of the state of his health. The issue of removing the President shall be taken by a resolution of the House of Representatives adopted by a majority of no less than two-thirds of the elected deputies as determined by the Constitution and a majority of no less than two-thirds of the full composition as determined by the Constitution of the Council of the Republic on the basis of the findings of an ad hoc Commission formed by the Chambers of the Parliament. The President may be removed from office for acts of state treason and other grave crimes. The decision to file a charge against the President shall be supported by a majority of the whole House of Representatives on behalf of no less than one-third of the number of deputies. The investigation of the charge shall be exercised by the Council of the Republic. The President shall be deemed to be removed from office if the decision is adopted by no less than two-thirds of the full composition of the Council of the Republic, and no less than two-thirds of the full House of Representatives.

The failure of the Council of the Republic and House of Representatives to take a decision to remove the President from office within a month since it was initiated shall make the move invalid. The move to remove the President from office may not be initiated in accordance with the provision of the Constitution in the course of the hearings on the premature termination of the powers of Parliament.

Where the President is removed in connection with the commission of a crime, the case shall be examined on the merits of the charge by the Supreme Court.

Article 89
Whether the office of President falls vacant or the President is unable to discharge his duties to the order as determined by the Constitution, his powers shall be transferred to the Prime Minister until the President-elect is sworn in.

Chapter 4 – Parliament – The National Assembly

Article 90
The Parliament – the National Assembly – is a representative and legislative body of the Republic of Belarus.

The Parliament shall consist of two chambers: the House of Representatives and the Council of the Republic.

Article 91
The House of Representatives shall consist of 110 deputies. The election of deputies to the House of Representatives shall be carried out in accordance with the law on the basis of universal, equal, free, direct electoral suffrage and by secret ballot.

The Council of the Republic shall be a chamber of territorial representation. The Council of the Republic shall consist of eight deputies from every region (oblast) and the city of Minsk, elected at the meetings of deputies of local Councils of deputies of base level of every region (oblast) and the city of Minsk from their ranks. Eight members of the Council of the Republic shall be appointed by the President of the Republic of Belarus.

Elections for a new composition of the chambers of Parliament shall be set no later than four months and held no later than 30 days prior to the expiry of the powers of the current Parliament.

Extraordinary elections for the chambers of the Parliament shall be held within three months of the premature expiry of the powers of the chambers of the Parliament.

Article 92
Any citizen of the Republic of Belarus who has reached the age of 21 may become a deputy of the House of Representatives.

Any citizen of the Republic of Belarus who has reached the age of 30, and who has been resident on the territory of a corresponding region (oblast), or the city of Minsk for no less than five years may become a member of the Council of the Republic.

A deputy of the House of Representatives shall exercise his powers in the Parliament on a professional basis unless otherwise determined by the Constitution. A deputy of the House of Representatives may simultaneously be member of the Government.

No person may be simultaneously a member of both chambers of the Parliament. A member of the House of Representatives may not be a member of a local council of deputies. A member of the Council of the Republic may not be simultaneously a member of the Government. No person may exercise his duties as a member of the House of Representatives, or member of the Council of the Republic and simultaneously hold the office of President or a judge.

Article 93

The term of the Parliament shall be four years. The powers of the Parliament may be extended by law only in the event of a war.

The first session of Parliament after the elections shall be called by the Central Commission on Elections and National Referendums and shall be convened no later than 30 days after the elections. The countdown of the 30-day period for calling and beginning of the first session of the House of Representatives shall start from the day of the second round of elections for the new Parliament. If the second round of elections for the House of Representatives is not held, then the countdown of the 30-day period shall start from the day of the first round of general elections in the Republic of Belarus. The countdown of the 30-day period for calling and convening the first session of the Council of the Republic shall start from the day of the first meeting of the deputies of the local councils of deputies of base level for the elections of the members of the Council of the Republic from the regions (oblasts) or the city of Minsk.

The powers of the House of Representatives or the Council of the Republic may be terminated prematurely according to the order determined by the Constitution. With the termination of the powers of the House of Representatives or the Council of the Republic, the President may take the decision to terminate the powers of the House of Representatives or the Council of the Republic consequently.

Article 94

The powers of the House of Representatives may be terminated prematurely where no confidence is expressed or a no-confidence vote is expressed in the Government, or where the House fails twice to give its consent for the appointment of the Prime Minister.

The powers of the House of Representatives or the Council of the Republic may be prematurely terminated in accordance with the conclusion of the Constitutional Court due to systematic and gross violation of the Constitution by the chambers of the Parliament.

The decision on this issue shall be taken by the President after official consultations with the Chairs of the chambers.

The chambers may not be dissolved during a state of emergency or martial law, in the last six months of the term of office of the President or in the course of proceedings of both chambers on the premature removal of the President from office.

Both chambers may not be dissolved in the course of the first year since the first sittings were held.

Article 95
The chambers shall hold their regular sessions twice a year.

The first session shall open on 2 October; its duration may not exceed 80 days.

The second session shall open on 2 April and its duration may not exceed 90 days.

If 2 October or 2 April is a non-working day, then the session shall begin its proceedings on the first day following the said non-working day.

The House of Representatives and the Council of the Republic may in instances of urgent necessity be convened for an extraordinary session at the request of the President, or initiative of no less than a two-thirds majority of the full composition of every chamber for a special agenda.

The extraordinary sessions shall be called by the decrees of the President.

Article 96
The House of Representatives shall elect from the ranks of the deputies the Chairperson of the House and the deputy.

The Council of the Republic shall elect from the ranks of senators the Chairperson of the Council of the Republic and the deputy.

The Chairpersons of the House of Representatives and the Council of the Republic or their deputies shall conduct the proceedings and shall be in charge of the regulations of the operation of the chambers.

The House of Representatives and the Council of the Republic shall elect from the ranks of the deputies standing committees and other bodies to draft laws, give preliminary consideration to, and prepare issues that fall within the jurisdiction of the chambers.

Article 97
The House of Representatives shall:

1.   consider draft laws put forward by the President or submitted by no less than 150 000 citizens of the Republic of Belarus, who are eligible to vote, to make amendments and alterations in the Constitution and give its interpretation;

2.   consider draft laws, including the guidelines of the domestic and foreign policy of the Republic of Belarus; the military doctrine; ratification and denunciation of international treaties; the fundamental concept and principles of execution of rights, liberties and duties of its citizens; citizenship issues, the status of foreigners and persons without citizenship; the rights of ethnic minorities; the approval of the budget of the republic and the account on its implementation; the introduction of national taxes and dues; the principles of ownership; the basics of social security; the principles regulating labour and employment, marriage, the family, childhood, maternity, paternity, education, upbringing, culture and public health; environmental protection and the rational utilisation of natural resources; determination of the procedure for resolving issues relating to the administrative-territorial structure of the State; local self-government; the administration of justice and the status of judges;

issues of criminal responsibility and amnesty; declaration of war and conclusion of peace; martial law and a state of emergency; institution of state awards; interpretation of laws;

3.   call elections for the Presidency;

4.   grant consent to the President concerning the appointment of the Prime Minister;

5.   consider the report of the Prime Minister on the policy of the Government and approve or reject it; a second rejection by the House of the policy of the Government shall be deemed as an expression of no-confidence in the Government;

6.   consider on the initiative of the Prime Minister a call for a vote of confidence;

7.   on the initiative of no less than one-third of the full composition of the House of Representatives express a no-confidence vote in the Government; the issue of liability of the Government may not be discussed in the course of the year after the approval of the programme of government policy;

8.   accept the resignation of the President;

9.   be entitled with a majority of the full composition of the House of Representatives to forward charges of treason or of some other grave crime against the President; on the basis of the decision of the Council of the Republic and with no less than a two-thirds majority of the full composition of the House take the decision to remove the President from office;

10. cancel the order of the Chairperson of the House of Representatives.

The House of Representatives may take decisions on other issues which are determined by the Constitution.

Article 98
The Council of the Republic shall:

1.   approve or reject draft laws adopted by the House of Representatives with regard to alterations and addenda to the Constitution; and on the interpretation of the Constitution, as well as other draft laws;

2.   give its consent for the appointment by the President of the Chairperson of the Constitutional Court, Chairperson and judges of the Supreme Court, the Chairperson and judges of the Supreme Economic Court, the Chairperson of the Central Commission on Elections and National Referendums, the Procurator-General, the Chairperson and members of the National Bank;

3.   elect six judges of the Constitutional Court;

4.   elect six members of the Central Commission on Elections and National Referendums;

5.   reverse decisions of local Councils of deputies which do not conform to legislation;

6.   adopt resolutions on the dissolution of local Councils of deputies where they systematically and flagrantly violate the requirements of the law and other instances determined by the law;

7.   consider charges of treason or of some other grave crime forwarded by the House of Representatives against the President and take a decision on its investigation. Given the presence of substantial evidence take the decision to remove the President from office with no less than two-thirds of the full composition of the House;

8.   consider Presidential decrees on the introduction of a state of emergency, martial law, general or partial mobilisation no later than three days after their submission and take the appropriate decision.
The Council of the Republic may take decisions on other issues determined by the Constitution.

Article 99

The right of legislative initiative shall belong to the President, members of the House of Representatives, the Council of the Republic, and the Government, as well as to citizens who are eligible to vote, in a number of no less than 50 000, and is implemented in the House of Representatives.
Draft laws, the adoption of which may reduce state resources or increase expenditure, may be introduced in the House of Representatives only with the consent of the President, or at his delegation, by the Government.
The President or at his delegation the Government shall have the right to forward proposals to the House of Representatives and Council of the Republic for urgent consideration of a draft law. In this case the House of Representatives and the Council of the Republic shall consider the draft law within ten days of its submission.
At the request of the President or at his consent the Government, the House of Representatives and Council of the Republic shall take decisions at their sessions voting in general for the whole draft law or a part of it, which was forwarded by the President or Government preserving only those amendments which were forwarded or accepted by the President or Government.

Article 100

Any bill, unless otherwise specified by the Constitution, shall be initially considered in the House of Representatives and then in the Council of the Republic.
A bill, unless otherwise specified in the Constitution, shall become law after its approval by a majority of votes of the full composition of the House of Representatives and the Council of the Republic.
Bills adopted by the House of Representatives shall be sent to the Council of the Republic for consideration within five days, where they shall be considered within no more than twenty days unless otherwise specified in the Constitution.
A bill shall be deemed to have been approved by the Council of the Republic provided that a majority of votes of the full composition of the Council of the Republic has been cast for it, or if within twenty days, and in cases of urgency within ten days, after its submission, the Council of the Republic failed to consider it. If the bill is rejected by the Council of the Republic, both chambers may form a conciliation commission on a parity basis to overcome the existing differences. The text of the bill drafted by the conciliatory commission shall be submitted for approval to both chambers.
If the conciliatory commission fails to draft a compromise bill, the President, or at his delegation the Government, may request that the House of Representatives take a final decision. The bill shall be deemed to have been adopted by the House of Representatives if no less than two-thirds of its full composition has voted for it.

A bill adopted by the House of Representatives and approved by the Council of the Republic, or in the instance determined by the present article adopted by the House of Representatives shall be submitted to the President for signature within ten days. If the President is in agreement with the bill, he shall sign it. If the President does not return the bill within two weeks after its submission, it shall be deemed to have been signed by the President. The bill shall not be deemed to have been signed and shall be invalid if it failed to be returned to Parliament due to the end of the session.

If the President does not agree with the text of the bill, he shall return it together with his objections to the House of Representatives, which shall consider it with the President's objections within thirty days. If the bill has been adopted by the House of Representatives by no less than two-thirds of its full composition, it together with the President's objections shall be submitted within five days to the Council of the Republic, which shall consider it for a second hearing within twenty days. The bill shall be deemed to have been approved if no less than two-thirds of the full composition of the Council of the Republic has voted for it. The bill, after the House of Representatives and the Council of the Republic have overruled the President's objections, shall be signed by the President within five days. The bill shall become law even if it is not signed by the President within the time.

The President's objections to the provisions of the bill, which are returned for a second hearing, shall be considered to the same order. In this instance, prior to the appropriate decision of the House of Representatives and the Council of the Republic the bill shall be signed by the President and become law without the provisions which have been rejected by the President.

Article 101

At the proposal of the President, the House of Representatives and the Council of the Republic may adopt a law supported by a majority of the full composition of both chambers, delegating to him legislative powers to issue decrees which have the power of law. The latter shall determine the subject of the issue and the term of the powers of the President to issue such decrees. There shall be no delegation of powers to the President to issue decrees which provide alterations and addenda to the Constitution and its interpretation; alteration and addendum of policy laws; the approval of the national budget and an account of its implementation alterations with regard to the election of the President and Parliament; or limitation of constitutional rights and liberties of the citizens. The law on delegating legislative powers to the President shall not permit him to alter the said law, nor shall it permit the adoption of regulations which are retroactive.

In instances of necessity the President may personally initiate or at the proposal of the Government may issue temporary decrees which have the power of law. If such decrees are issued at the initiative of the Government, they shall be signed by the Prime Minister. Temporary decrees shall be submitted for further approval within three days of their adoption to the House of Representatives, and then to the Council of the Republic. These decrees shall be valid if they are not rejected by a majority of no fewer than two-thirds of votes of the full composition of both chambers. The chambers may regulate through legislation issues which have emerged due to decrees which have been abolished.

Article 102

The deputies of the House of Representatives and members of the Council of the Republic shall enjoy immunity in the expression of their views and execution of their powers. This shall not refer to charges of slander and insult.

During the period they exercise their powers the deputies and the members of Council of the Republic may be arrested or deprived of personal liberty in other manner only with the prior consent of the appropriate chamber with the exception of instances of high treason, or some other grave crime, as well as detention at the site where the crime was committed.

A criminal case involving a deputy of the House of Representatives or a member of the Council of the Republic shall be tried by the Supreme Court.

Article 103

Sittings of the chambers shall be open. The chambers, in the instance of state interests, may take the decision to hold a closed session by majority of the full composition of the corresponding chamber. The President, his representatives, the Prime Minister and members of the Government shall address the sessions out of turn as many times as they deem it necessary.

One sitting monthly shall be reserved for question time to the Government for the deputies of the Houses of Representatives and members of the Council of the Republic.

A deputy of the House of Representatives or member of the Council of the Republic shall have the right to make an inquiry to the Prime Minister or members of the Government and the heads of state bodies which are formed or elected by Parliament. The inquiry shall be included in the agenda of the chamber. The answer to the inquiry shall be given within twenty days of the current session in the order determined by the chamber of the Parliament.

The sitting of the chamber shall be deemed quorate if no less than two-thirds of the number of elected deputies of the Houses of Representatives or members of the Council of the Republic are present.

Voting in the House of Representatives and Council of the Republic shall be open and exercised by the deputy of the House or member of the Council of the Republic in person by a 'yes' vote or a 'nay' vote. A secret vote shall be held only in the instance of addressing personnel issues.

Article 104

Decisions of the House of Representatives shall be taken by laws or enactments. Enactments of the House of Representatives shall be taken with regard to issues of order and supervision.

The decisions of the Council of the Republic shall be taken in the form of enactments.

The decisions of the chambers shall be deemed to have been adopted by a majority of the full composition of the chambers unless otherwise specified in the Constitution.

Laws with regard to basic guidelines of domestic and foreign policy of the Republic of Belarus and military doctrine thereof shall be considered to be of policy character and shall be deemed to have been adopted provided that a two-thirds majority of elected deputies of both chambers has voted for them.

The laws shall be published immediately after their signature and shall become valid ten days after their publication unless the law determines another term. The decrees of the President shall come into force to the same order therein.

The law shall have no retrospective action unless it extenuates or revokes the responsibility of citizens.

Article 105

The procedure governing the activities of the House of Representatives, Council of the Republic, the bodies thereof and the deputies and members of the Council of the Republic shall be determined by the Rules of Procedure of the chambers, which shall be signed by the Chairpersons of the chambers.

Chapter 5 – The Government – The Council of Ministers of the Republic of Belarus

Article 106

Executive power in the Republic of Belarus shall be exercised by the Government – the Council of Ministers of the Republic of Belarus – the central body of state administration.

The Government in its actions shall be accountable to the President of the Republic of Belarus and responsible to the Parliament of the Republic of Belarus.

The Government shall relinquish powers to the President-elect of the Republic of Belarus.

The Government of the Republic of Belarus shall consist of the Prime Minister, his deputies and ministers. The heads of other central bodies of state administration may be members of the Government.

The Prime Minister shall be appointed by the President of the Republic of Belarus with the consent of the House of Representatives. The decision on this order shall be taken by the House of Representatives within two weeks of the nomination of the candidacy of the Prime Minister. If the House of Representatives rejects the nomination submitted for Prime Minister twice, the President shall appoint the acting Prime Minister on his own, and dissolve the House of Representatives and call new elections.

The Prime Minister shall manage the activities of the Government.

The Prime Minister shall:

1.   manage directly the activities of the Government and hold personal responsibility for its activities;

2.   sign the acts of the Government;

3.   submit to Parliament a report on the programme of the Government within two months of his appointment, and in the instance of its rejection submit the second report on the programme of the Government within two months;

4.   inform the President on the basic guidelines of the activities of the Government, and on all the most important decisions;

5.   exercise other functions connected with the organisation and activities of the Government.

The Government or any member therein shall be entitled to tender the resignation to the President, if he deems it impossible to discharge the duties entrusted to him. The Government shall tender its resignation to the

President if the House of Representatives has passed a vote of no confidence in the Government.

The Prime Minister may request from the House of Representatives a vote of confidence with regard to the governmental programme or any other issue submitted to the House. If a no-confidence vote is passed by the House of Representatives, the President shall be entitled to accept the resignation of the Government, or dissolve the House of Representatives within ten days, and call new elections. If the resignation of the Government is rejected the latter shall continue to discharge its duties.

The President shall be entitled to take the decision on the resignation of the Government on his own initiative, and dismiss any member of the Government.

In the instance of the resignation of the Government of the Republic of Belarus or termination of its powers, the latter at the assignment of the President shall continue to hold office until a new Government shall have been formed.

Article 107

The Government of the Republic of Belarus shall:

administer the system of subordinate bodies of state administration and other executive organs;

elaborate the basic guidelines of domestic and foreign policy, and take measures to implement them;

elaborate and submit to the President for further parliamentary consideration the draft national budget and an account of its implementation;

ensure the execution of a uniform economic, financial, credit and monetary policy, and state policy in the field of science, culture, education, health care, ecology, social security and remuneration of labour;

take measures to secure the rights and liberties of citizens, safeguard the interests of the state, national security and defence, protection of property, maintain public order and eliminate crime;

act on behalf of the property owner with regard to assets which are the sole property of the Republic of Belarus, and exercise management of state property;

ensure the implementation of the Constitution, the laws, decrees, edicts and instructions of the President;

repeal acts of ministries and other central bodies of state administration;

exercise other powers entrusted to it by the Constitution, laws and acts of the President.

Article 108

The Government of the Republic of Belarus shall issue acts that have binding force in the entire territory of the Republic of Belarus.

The Prime Minister shall issue orders which are under his jurisdiction.

The competence of the Government and the procedure governing its activities shall be determined on the basis of the Constitution and the Law on the Council of Ministers of the Republic of Belarus.

Chapter 6 – The Courts

Article 109

The courts shall exercise judicial power in the Republic of Belarus.

The judicial system shall be based upon the principles of territorial delineation and specialisation.

The judicial system in the Republic of Belarus shall be determined by the law.

The formation of special courts shall be prohibited.

Article 110

In administering justice judges shall be independent and subordinate to law alone.

Any interference in judges' activities in the administration of justice shall be impermissible and liable to legal action.

Article 111

Judges may not engage in business activities or perform any paid work, apart from teaching and academic research.

The grounds for electing (appointing) judges and their dismissal shall be determined by the law.

Article 112

The courts shall administer justice on the basis of the Constitution, the laws and other enforceable enactments adopted in accordance therewith.

If, during the hearing of a specific case, a court concludes that an enforceable enactment is contrary to the Constitution, it shall make a ruling in accordance with the Constitution and raise, under the established procedure, the issue of whether the enforceable enactment in question should be deemed unconstitutional.

Article 113

Cases before a court shall be tried collegially, and in the instances specified in law, by judges individually.

Article 114

The trial of cases in all courts shall be open.

The hearing of cases in closed court session shall be permitted only in the instances specified in law and in accordance with all the rules of legal procedure.

Article 115

Justice shall be administered on the basis of the adversarial proceedings and equality of the parties involved in the trial.

The rulings of courts are mandatory for all citizens and officials.

The parties and the persons have the right to appeal against rulings, sentences and other judicial decisions.

Article 116

Supervision of the constitutionality of enforceable enactments of the state shall be exercised by the Constitutional Court of the Republic of Belarus.

The Constitutional Court of the Republic of Belarus shall be formed of 12 judges from among highly qualified specialists in the field of law, who as a rule have a scientific degree.

Six judges of the Constitutional Court shall be appointed by the President of the Republic of Belarus and six elected by the Council of the Republic. The Chairperson of the Constitutional Court shall be appointed by the President with the consent of the Council of the Republic. The term of the members of the Constitutional Court shall be 11 years, and the permissible age limit shall be 70 years.

The Constitutional Court on the recommendations of the President of the Republic of Belarus, the House of Representatives, the Council of the Republic, the Supreme Court of the Republic of Belarus, the Supreme Economic Court of the Republic of Belarus, the Cabinet of Ministers of the Republic of Belarus shall produce a ruling on:

the conformity of laws, decrees and edicts of the President, international agreements and other obligations of the Republic of Belarus to the Constitution and other instruments of international law ratified by the Republic of Belarus;

the conformity of instruments of interstate formations of which the Republic of Belarus is part, edicts of the President of the Republic of Belarus which are issued in execution of the law, the Constitution, the laws, decrees and instruments of international law ratified by the Republic of Belarus;

the conformity of the ordinances of the Council of Ministers and orders of the Supreme Court, the Supreme Economic Court, Procurator-General to the Constitution, laws and instruments of international law ratified by the Republic of Belarus, laws, decrees and edicts;

the conformity of enactments of any other state body to the Constitution, laws and decrees as well as to the laws and instruments of international law ratified by the Republic of Belarus.

Enforceable enactments or their particular provisions which are considered unconstitutional shall be deemed invalid according to the order determined by the law.

In instances specified by the Constitution, the Constitutional Court with regard to the proposal of the President shall give its conclusion on the presence of instances of systematic or flagrant violation of the Constitution of the Republic of Belarus by the chambers of Parliament.

The competence, organisation and procedure governing the activities of the Constitutional Court shall be determined by the law.

Section 5 – Local government and self-government

Article 117

Citizens shall exercise local government and self-government through local councils of deputies, executive and administrative bodies, bodies of public territorial self-government, local referendums, assemblies and other forms of direct participation in state and public affairs.

Article 118

Local councils of deputies shall be elected by the citizens of the relevant administrative-territorial units for a four-year term.

Article 119

The heads of local executive and administrative bodies shall be appointed and dismissed by the President of the Republic of Belarus or in accordance with the order determined by the latter, and their appointment shall be subject to the approval of the local councils of deputies.

Article 120

Local councils of deputies and executive and administrative bodies shall, within the limits of their competence, resolve issues of local significance, proceeding from national interests and the interests of the people who reside in the relevant territory, and implement the decisions of higher state bodies.

Article 121

The following shall fall exclusively within the exclusive competence of the local councils of deputies:
the approval of programmes of economic and social development, and local budgets and accounts;
the setting of local taxes and dues in accordance with the law;
the determination, within the limits specified by law, of the procedure governing the management and disposal of municipal property;
the calling of local referendums.

Article 122

Local councils of deputies and executive and administrative bodies shall, on the basis of existing laws, adopt decisions that have binding force in the relevant territory.
Decisions of local councils of deputies that are contrary to the law shall be reversed by higher representative bodies.
Decisions of local executive and administrative authorities that are contrary to the law shall be reversed by the relevant councils of deputies, superior executive and administrative bodies and the President of the Republic of Belarus.
Decisions of local councils of deputies and their executive and administrative bodies that restrict or violate civil rights and liberties and the legitimate interests of citizens, and other instances specified in law, may be challenged in a court of law.

Article 123

Where a local council of deputies systematically or flagrantly violates the requirements of the law, it may be dissolved by the Council of the Republic. Other grounds for the premature termination of the powers of local councils of deputies shall be determined by the law.

Article 124

The competence and the procedure governing the establishment and activities of bodies of local government and self-government shall be determined by the law.

Section 6 – The Procurator's Office and the State Supervisory Committee

Chapter 7 – The Procurator's Office

Article 125

The Procurator-General of the Republic of Belarus and subordinate public prosecutors shall be entrusted to supervise the strict and unified implementation of the laws, decrees, regulations and other enforceable enactments by ministers and other bodies subordinate to the Council of Ministers, as well as by local representative and executive bodies, enterprises, organisations, establishments, public associations, officials and citizens.

The Procurator's office shall exercise supervision over the implementation of the laws determining the execution of the verdicts of the courts in civil, criminal and administrative cases in instances determined by the law, as well as carry out preliminary investigation and support state charges in the courts.

Article 126

The Procurator-General shall head the unified and centralised system of bodies of the Procurator's office, and shall be appointed by the President with the consent of the Council of the Republic.

The subordinate public prosecutors shall be appointed by the Procurator-General.

Article 127

The Procurator-General and subordinate public procurators shall be independent in the exercise of their powers and guided by the legislation. The Procurator-General shall be accountable to the President.

Article 128

The competence, organisation and procedure governing the activities of bodies of the Procurator's office shall be determined by the law.

Chapter 8 – The State Supervisory Committee

Article 129

The Supervisory Authority shall monitor the implementation of the national budget, the use of public property and the implementation of the acts of the President, Parliament, Government and other state bodies governing public property relationships and economic, financial and tax relations.

Article 130

The State Supervisory Committee shall be formed by the President.

The Chairperson of the State Supervisory Committee shall be appointed by the President.

Article 131

The competence, organisation and procedure governing the activities of the State Supervisory Committee shall be determined by the law.

Section 7 – Financial and credit system of the Republic of Belarus

Article 132

The financial and credit system of the Republic of Belarus shall include the budget system, the banking system, as well as the financial resources of non-budget funds, funds of enterprises, establishments, organisations and citizens.

A unified fiscal, tax, credit and currency policy shall be pursued in the territory of the Republic of Belarus.

Article 133

The budget system of the Republic of Belarus shall include the national budget and local budgets.

Budget revenue shall be raised from the taxes specified in law, other mandatory payments, as well as other receipts.

National expenditure shall be covered by the national budget on its expenditure side.

In accordance with the law, non-budgetary funds may be created in the Republic of Belarus.

Article 134

The procedure for drawing up, approving and implementing budgets and public non-budgetary funds shall be determined by the law.

Article 135

A national account shall be submitted to the Parliament for consideration no later than five months from the end of the fiscal year in review.

Local accounts shall be submitted to the relevant councils of deputies for the consideration within the time specified in law.

National and local accounts shall be published.

Article 136

The banking system of the Republic of Belarus shall consist of the National Bank of the Republic of Belarus and other banks. The National Bank shall regulate credit relations and monetary circulation, determine the procedure for making payments and have an exclusive right to issue money.

Section 8 – The application of the Constitution of the Republic of Belarus and the procedure for amending the Constitution

Article 137

The Constitution shall have supreme legal force. Laws, decrees, ordinances and other instruments of state bodies shall be promulgated on the basis of, and in accordance with, the Constitution of the Republic of Belarus.

Where there is a discrepancy between a law, decree or ordinance and the Constitution, the Constitution shall apply.

Where there is a discrepancy between a decree or ordinance and a law, the law shall apply when the powers for the promulgation of the decree or ordinance were provided by the law.

Article 138

The issue of amending and supplementing the Constitution shall be considered by the chambers of the Parliament on the initiative of the President or of no fewer than 150 000 citizens of the Republic of Belarus who are eligible to vote.

Article 139

A law on amending and supplementing the Constitution may be adopted after it has been debated and approved twice by both chambers of the Parliament with at least a three months' interval.

The Constitution shall not be amended or supplemented by the Parliament during a state of emergency or the last six months of the term of the House of Representatives.

Article 140

The Constitution, laws on amendments and addenda thereto, on the entry into force of the said laws and instruments on the interpretation of the Constitution shall be deemed to have been adopted where no less than two-thirds of the elected deputies of both chambers of the Parliament have voted in favour of them.

The Constitution may be amended or supplemented via a referendum. A decision to amend or supplement the Constitution by means of a referendum shall be deemed adopted where a majority of citizens on the electoral roll have voted in favour of it.

Sections 1, 2, 4 and 8 of the Constitution may be reconsidered only by means of a referendum.

Section 9 – Final and transitional clauses

Article 141

The 1994 Constitution of the Republic of Belarus together with the alterations and addenda, adopted at the national referendum (the present Constitution) shall enter into force on the day on which it is promulgated, apart from the specific provisions thereof, that are to enter into force under the procedure and at the times specified in the present Constitution. Simultaneously the Law of the Republic of Belarus "On the Procedure Governing the Entry into Force of the Constitution of the Republic of Belarus" shall cease to apply.

Article 142

The laws, decrees and other acts which were applied in the territory of the Republic of Belarus prior to the entry into force of the present Constitution shall apply in the particular parts thereof that are not contrary to the Constitution of the Republic of Belarus.

Article 143

Within a month of the entry into force of the Constitution of the Republic of Belarus the Supreme Council of the Republic of Belarus and the President of the Republic of Belarus shall form the House of Representatives from among the deputies of the Supreme Council who were elected by the appointed date of the referendum held in 1996. The deputies of the Supreme Council of the Republic of Belarus shall retain their powers within the term stipulated by the present Constitution. The term of their powers shall be assessed from the day on which the present Constitution enters into force.

The Council of the Republic shall be formed according to the order specified in Article 91 of the present Constitution.

If within the assigned time the House of Representatives is not formed due to controversies between the President and the Supreme Council, the former shall in accordance with clauses 2 and 3 of Article 84 of the present Constitution dissolve the Supreme Council and call on new elections to Parliament.

Article 144
The President of the Republic of Belarus shall retain his powers. The term of his powers shall be assessed from the day on which the present Constitution enters into force.

Article 145
The Government of the Republic of Belarus shall exercise its duties and powers from the day on which the present Constitution enters into force.

Article 146
The President, Parliament and the Government within two months of the date the present Constitution enters into force shall form assigned bodies of power according to the order as determined by the present Constitution, unless otherwise specified by part 3 of Article 143 of the Constitution.

A. Lukashenko, President of the Republic of Belarus

Minsk, 27 November 1996

Georgia

Chronology

1988

September 21-23: Nationalist demonstrations in Tbilisi.

November 5, 12 and 23: Demonstrations in Tbilisi against the "russification" of Georgia.

1989

March 29: Otar Cherkeziya succeeds Pavel Gilashvili as President of the Presidium of the Supreme Soviet.

April 9: Triggered by separatist demands in Abkhazia, mass pro-independence demonstrations culminate in brutal action of the security forces, killing 20 demonstrators.

April 14: The first Secretary of the Georgian Communist Party (CP) Dzumbar Patiashvili resigns on account of the brutalities of 9 April.

June 24-26: Nationalist demonstrations in Tbilisi voice independence demands.

June 28: Constituent congress of the People's Front of Georgia.

November 17: The Supreme Soviet approves amendments to the constitution, which declares a sovereign Georgian ownership of natural resources, the republic's right to secede and the assertion of the right to "suspend Soviet laws and regulatory enactments" if considered contrary to Georgian interests.

November 17: The Supreme Soviet dismisses Otar Cherkeziya as President of the Supreme Soviet Presidium, replacing him by Givi Gumbaridze.

1990

March 9: The Supreme Soviet declares the treaties of 1921-22, by which Georgia joined the Soviet Union, an international crime and demands that the authorities in Moscow enter negotiations on restoring Georgia's independence.

March 20: The Supreme Soviet amends the constitution, abolishing the monopoly of power of the CP.

August 20: The Supreme Soviet adopts a law providing for multiparty parliamentary elections in October.

August 25: The Supreme Soviet of the Abkhaz Autonomous Soviet Socialist Republic declares its independence from Georgia.

August 25: The Georgian Supreme Soviet pronounces the Abkhaz declaration invalid.

August 31: The Abkhaz Supreme Soviet annuls the declaration.

September 20: The autonomous *oblast* South Ossetia proclaims its independence from Georgia.

September 21: The Georgian Supreme Soviet rules this proclamation invalid.

October 28: The Round Table/Free Georgia coalition, a bloc of pro-independence parties, wins the elections to the 250-seat Supreme Soviet, by 54.03%, gaining 114 seats. The CP gains 24.42% of the votes and 60 seats. A second round will be held on 11 November for the remaining 76 seats.

November 11: In the second round of parliamentary elections the Round Table/Free Georgia bloc affirms its victory by raising its share of votes to 62% and 155 seats, 12 seats short of a two-thirds majority in the Supreme Soviet. The CP raises the number of its seats to 64. The remaining 31 seats go to the other parties and Independents.

November 14: The Supreme Soviet elects, by 323 votes to 5, the Round Table leader Zviad Gamsakhurdia as Chair of the Supreme Soviet, *de facto* head of state, and proclaims the Republic of Georgia, dropping the adjectives "Soviet" and "Socialist".

November 15: The Supreme Soviet appoints the Round Table member Tengiz Sigua as Prime Minister.

December 8: The CP announces that it is seceding from the Communist Party of the Soviet Union (CPSU) and affirms the party's goal of securing Georgia's secession.

December 10: South Ossetia reaffirms its September proclamation of independence and state sovereignty within the Soviet Union.

December 11: The Georgian Supreme Soviet passes a law stripping South Ossetia of its autonomy.

1991

January 7: The President of the Soviet Union issues a decree annulling South Ossetia's proclamation and the Georgian Supreme Soviet's law of December 1990.

February 18: D. Mikeladze replaces Avtandil Margiani as First Secretary of the CP.

March 17: In all the Soviet Republics an All-Union referendum is held on the preservation of the USSR. The Georgian Government refuses to participate.

March 31: A referendum is held on the "restoration of state independence", in which 98.93% vote in favour, with a turnout of 99.6%.

April 9: The Supreme Soviet adopts a formal declaration of the "restoration of state independence" and calls for negotiations with Soviet authorities.

April 14: The Supreme Soviet elects Zviad Gamsakhurdia to the new post of President of Georgia.

May 26: In Georgia's first presidential elections, Zviad Gamsakhurdia is re-elected as President, gaining 87% of the votes, with a turnout of 80%.

August 18: Vissarion Gugushvili replaces Tengiz Sigua as Prime Minister, after the latter's resignation.

August 19: Attempted *coup d'etat* in Moscow.

August 27: The Supreme Soviet bans the CP.

September 2: First day of a series of demonstrations, demanding the resignation of the President.

September 6: The Chair of the Supreme Soviet, Akaky Asatiani, announces the breaking-off all official relations with the Soviet Union.

September 24: The President declares a state of emergency.

November 25: The Supreme Soviet lifts the state of emergency.

December 8: The Russian Federative Republic, Belarus and Ukraine sign the Minsk Agreement, establishing a Commonwealth of Independent States (CIS).

December 12: The remaining former Soviet republics sign the Alma Ata Agreement, thus joining the CIS. Georgia sends observers, but internal power struggles prevent its participation in the CIS.

December 21: The CIS formally replaces the Soviet Union, grouping eleven republics with the exception of Georgia.

December 21: The South Ossetian Supreme Soviet declares the region independent and confirms the unification with Russia.

1992

January 2: The head of the national guard Dzhaba Iosseliani and the commander of the nationalist militia Tengiz Kitovani declare that a military council has taken power, they announce a state of emergency and depose the President, who flees the country. The Council reinstates Tengiz Sigua as acting Prime Minister and gives him the responsibility of forming a temporary government.

February 21: The Military Council announces the restoration of the 1921 Constitution.

March 6: Former Soviet Union Minister for Foreign Affairs Edward Shevardnadze returns to his native Georgia.

March 10: The Military Council transfers its legislative and executive powers to a newly created 50-member State Council, chaired by Shevardnadze. Shevardnadze becomes *de facto* head of state.

July 23: The Abkhazian Supreme Council restores the 1925 Constitution and proclaims the country's sovereignty.

July 25: The Georgian State Council declares the Abkhaz Constitution null and void.

August 4: The State Council lifts the state of emergency.

October 11: Elections are held to the 234-member parliament; 84 members are chosen by absolute majority and 150 members by proportional representation. Shevardnadze is re-elected as Chair of the State Council, *de facto* head of state, with 95.9% of the votes.

November 6: The Parliament confirms Shevardnadze as head of state and issues a decree on the division of powers, which serves as an interim Constitution; the head of state together with the government enjoys the supreme executive power.

November 8: The Parliament re-elects Tengiz Sigua as Prime Minister.

1993

April 5: In addition to the rouble, a temporary currency is introduced.

July 1: The Parliament grants the President extended powers, including the power to issue decrees without parliamentary approval.

August 5: Prime Minister Tengiz Sigua and his government resign, after the State Council refuses to approve the budget.

August 20: The Parliament approves Otar Patsatsia as Prime Minister.

September 13: A Parliamentary majority, of 134 deputies, backs the government nominations made by President Shevardnadze.

September 14: The Parliament approves a plan to introduce a two-month state of emergency, which starts on September 20, following the civil unrest in Georgia.

September 15: The Parliament votes to suspend itself for a two-month period, on account of the state of emergency.

November 20: President Shevardnadze decrees an extension of the state of emergency until January 20.

November 21: The Union of Citizens of Georgia Party (UCGP) holds its constituent congress and elects Shevardnadze as its leader.

1994

January 18: The Parliament extends the state of emergency until February 20.

February 3: Russian President Yeltsin and President Shevardnadze sign a Treaty of Friendship and Co-operation.

March 1: The Parliament, in its first plenary session since its suspension, ratifies Georgia's membership of the CIS.

May 25: Representatives of political and public organisations sign a Declaration of National Union and Accord.

June 25: At a founding congress, the Georgian Communist Party (CP) revives and Major-General Panteleimon Giorgadze is elected as its leader.

July 21: The UN Security Council adopts a resolution approving the presence of Russian peacekeeping troops in Georgia.

September 28: The Parliament rejects, by 32 votes to 127, a motion of no confidence in the President.

November 26: The Abkhaz Supreme Council adopts a new constitution, establishing itself as a sovereign state, instituting a strong presidency and changing its parliament's name into the National Assembly.

November 28: President Shevardnadze denounces the Abkhaz Constitution.

1995

April 4: A new centre-left political party is founded: the People's Socialist Party of Georgia.

August 24: The Parliament adopts, by 159 votes to 8, a new constitution replacing the 1992 decree on State Power which had served as an interim constitution. The new constitution states that Georgia is a republic with federal elements, a unicameral parliament of 150 deputies for a four-year period and an executive president elected for five years. The Parliament seats 235 members of which 85 are chosen by simple majority in single-member constituencies and 150 by proportional representation, with a 5% threshold. If no candidate obtains at least 33% of the votes cast in the constituency, a run-off simple majority election will be held between the two best candidates.

September 2: Security Service Minister Igor Giorgadze and Deputy Minister Temur Khachisvili are dismissed, following an assassination attempt against President Shevardnadze on August 29.

September 25: The new currency, the *lari,* is introduced.

September 26: Registration for the presidential elections due on 5 November. Six candidates gain enough signatories: Edward Shevardnadze representing the UCGP and the Socialist Party (SP); Dzumber Patiashvili representing the CP; Kartlos Gharibashvili representing the DPG; Roin Liparteliani representing the Agrarian Party of Georgia (APG); Anaki Bakradze, an opposition figure; and Panteleimon Giorgadze representing the United Communist Party of Georgia (UCPG).

October 17: The constitution adopted in August comes into effect.

November 5: Edward Shevardnadze is re-elected as President, gaining 75% of the votes cast. In the first round of the parliamentary elections only three parties achieve the 5% threshold for the representation according to the proportional system. These are: the UCGP, the NDP and the All Georgian Union of Revival Party.

November 19: Second round of elections is held in 36 constituencies for the majority seats. The UCGP gains 23.71% of the votes and 107 seats, the NDP 7.95% of the votes and 35 seats, the All Georgian Union of Revival Party 6.84% of the votes and 31 seats, the Socialist Party of Georgia 3.79% and 4 seats, the Union of Georgian Traditionalists 4.22% and 2 seats, the Reformers Union of Georgia-National Concord 2.89% and 2 seats, the remaining parties gain 22 seats and independents win 29 seats and 4 seats remain to be filled. Turnout 68.18%.

November 25: President Shevardnadze is sworn in.

1996

May 28: The Council of Europe grants Georgia Special Guest Status.

July 14: Georgia applies for membership of the Council of Europe.

The Constitution of Georgia¹

Adopted by the Parliament, 4 April 1995

Preamble

The people of Georgia whose strong will is to establish a democratic social order, economic independence, a social and legal state, to guarantee universally recognised human rights and freedoms and to strengthen state independence and peaceful relations with other countries, universally announce this constitution based upon many centuries of state tradition and the main principles of the Constitution of 1921.

Chapter 1 – General provisions

Article 1
1.   Georgia is an independent, unified and indivisible law-based state, ratified by the referendum carried out on 31 March 1991 throughout the territory of the country, including the then Autonomous Soviet Socialist Republic of Abkhazia and the former autonomous oblast of South Ossetia and further adduced by the act of 9 April 1991 restoring the independence of the Georgian state.
2.   The form of political order of the Republic of Georgia is a democratic Republic.
3.   "Georgia" is the name of the Georgian state.

Article 2
1.   The territory of the Georgian state is determined by the condition of the country as at 21 December 1991. The territorial integrity of Georgia and the inviolability of state borders is confirmed and recognised by the Constitution and the laws of Georgia and also by the world concord of states and international organisations.
2.   The transfer of the territory of Georgia is forbidden. Changes to the state borders are possible only through bilateral agreement with neighbouring states.
3.   The internal territorial state arrangement of Georgia is determined by constitutional law on the basis of the authority demarcation principle

---

1. European Commission for Democracy through Law

effective over the whole territory of Georgia at such a time when there is the full restoration of Georgian jurisdiction.

4.   Citizens of Georgia regulate matters of local importance through self-government as long as this does not encroach upon state sovereignty. The right to create self-governing bodies, their powers and their relationship with state bodies, is determined by organic law.

Article 3

1.   The special administration of Georgian supreme state bodies is responsible for:

   a.   legislation on Georgian citizenship, human rights and freedoms, emigration and immigration, entrance to and departure from Georgia, foreign nationals and stateless persons temporarily or permanently residing on the territory of Georgia;

   b.   the status and protection of boundaries and their protection; the status of territorial waters, airspace, continental shelf and special economic zones;

   c.   state defence and security; military forces, military industry and the trading of arms;

   d.   the issue of war and peace; the determination of a legal régime for a state of emergency and a state of war and their introduction;

   e.   foreign policy and international relations;

   f.   custom and tariff regimes and foreign trade;

   g.   state finances and state loans; the minting of money; legislation on banking, credit and insurance;

   h.   standards and models; geodesy and cartography; time; state statistics;

   i.   universal system and régime of energy; communications; the merchant fleet; flags of ships; harbours of state importance; airports and airfields; the control of airspace; transit and air transport; registration of air transport; meteorological services and the system of environmental protection;

   j.   railways and roads of importance to the whole state;

   k.   fishing in oceans and open seas;

   l.   boundary-sanitary cordon;

   m.   legislation on pharmaceutical medicines;

   n.   certification and accreditation of secondary and high schools, legislation on academic, scientific and professional titles and honours;

   o.   legislation on intellectual property rights;

   p.   legislation on trade, criminal and civil law;

   r.   criminal police and investigation;

   s.   legislation on land, minerals and natural resources.

2.   Matters relating to joint administration are determined separately.

Article 4

1.   Once there are appropriate conditions and when self-governing bodies have been created over the whole territory of Georgia, Parliament will be formed with two chambers; namely the Council of the Republic and the Senate.

2.   The Council of the Republic will consist of members elected proportionally.

3.   The Senate will consist of members elected from Abkhazia, Adjaria and other territorial units of Georgia as well as five members appointed by the President.
4.   The composition, powers and right of election to the chambers are determined by organic law.

Article 5
1.   The people are the only source of state power in Georgia. State power is exercised only within the framework of the Constitution.
2.   Power is exercised by the people through referendums, through their representatives and through other forms of direct democracy.
3.   No individual or group of individuals has the right to seize or unlawfully take state power.
4.   State power is exercised and based upon legal state principles.

Article 6
1.   The Constitution is the first law of the state. All other legal acts shall be issued in accordance with the Constitution.
2.   The legislation of Georgia corresponds with universally recognised norms and principles of international law. International treaties or agreements concluded with and by Georgia, if they are not in contradiction to the Constitution of Georgia, have prior legal force over internal normative acts.

Article 7
The state recognises and defends generally recognised rights and freedoms of the individual as everlasting and the highest values. The people and the state are bound by these rights and freedoms as well as by current legislation for the exercise of state power.

Article 8
The state language of Georgia is Georgian, but in Abkhazia, Abkhazian is also the state language.

Article 9
The state recognises the special importance of the Georgian Orthodox Church in Georgian history but simultaneously announces complete freedom in religious belief and the independence of the church from the state.

Article 10
Tbilisi is the capital of Georgia.

Article 11
State symbols of Georgia are determined by organic law.

Chapter 2 – Citizenship of Georgia – Rights and freedoms of the individual

Article 12
1.   Citizenship is attained by birth or by naturalisation.

2. A citizen of Georgia may not be a citizen of another country at the same time.
3. The order of naturalisation and loss of citizenship is determined by organic law.

Article 13
1. The state shall protect its citizens irrespective of their location.
2. No person may be deprived of his citizenship.
3. The expulsion of a citizen from the country is prohibited.
4. The extradition of a citizen of Georgia to another country is prohibited, except in cases defined by international agreement. A decision on extradition may be appealed against in court.

Article 14
Everyone is born free and is equal before the law, regardless of race, skin colour, language, sex, religion, political and other beliefs, national, ethnic and social origin, property and title status or place of residence.

Article 15
1. A person's life is inviolable and is protected by law.
2. Special forms of punishment – capital punishment before its full abrogation – may be envisaged by organic law for extremely serious crimes directed against a person's life. Only the supreme court has the right to make such a decision.

Article 16
Everyone has the right to free personal development.

Article 17
1. A person's conscience and dignity are inviolable.
2. Torture, inhumane, brutal or degrading treatment or punishment is inadmissible.

Article 18
1. The freedom of a person is inviolable.
2. Arrest or other kinds of restrictions of personal freedoms are prohibited without the decision of a court.
3. The detention of an individual is permissible in cases determined by law by a designated authorised official. The individual who has been detained or whose freedoms have been otherwise restricted must be conveyed to court (for a hearing) not later than 48 hours following arrest. If within the next 24 hours the court has not made a decision concerning the arrest or other kind of freedom restriction, the individual must be released forthwith.
4. The physical or moral coercion of an individual who has been detained or whose freedom has been otherwise restricted is inadmissible.
5. A detained individual must immediately be made aware of his rights and the basis of his detention. The detained individual may demand the assistance of a lawyer. This right must always be satisfied.

6.   The term of detention of a suspected individual should not exceed 72 hours before a charge is made and the accused cannot be held on remand for more than 9 months.

7.   Failure to comply with the enactments of this article is punishable by law. An individual detained or unlawfully arrested has the right to compensation.

Article 19
1.   Every individual has the right to freedom of speech, thought, conscience, religion and belief.

2.   The persecution of an individual for his thought, beliefs or religion is prohibited as is also the compulsion to express opinions about them.

3.   These rights may not be restricted unless the exercise of these rights infringes upon the rights of other individuals.

Article 20
1.   Every individual's private life, place of personal activity, personal papers and correspondence are inviolable, communication by telephone and other kinds of technical means are inviolable. The interference of these rights is permissible only by a court's decision or without such a decision by the necessity determined by law.

Article 21
1.   The right to inheritance and property is recognised and guaranteed. The abrogation of the universal right of property, its acquisition, transfer and inheritance is prohibited.

2.   Restriction of these rights is possible for the necessary social need in cases determined by law and by established right.

3.   Sequestration of property for necessary social need is permissible in cases directly determined by law, by a decision of the court or through urgent necessity by organic law but only if full compensation is made.

Article 22
1.   Every individual lawfully within the territory of Georgia is free to move within that territory and is free to choose his place of residence.

2.   Everyone lawfully within the territory of Georgia is free to leave the country. A citizen of Georgia can freely enter the country.

3.   Restriction upon these rights is permissible only in accordance with the law, in order to guarantee state and public security and what is necessary for the existence of a democratic society, a healthy defence and the prevention of crime and the fulfilment of justice.

Article 23
1.   The freedom of intellectual creativity and intellectual property rights are guaranteed.

2.   Interference in creative activity or censorship in this sphere is prohibited.

3.   The prevention and seizure of creative work is not permissible if the distribution of such creative work does not violate the legal rights of other individuals.

Article 24
1.   Every individual has the right to receive freely and to disseminate information and to express and disseminate his opinion orally, in written or any other form.
2.   Mass media are free. Censorship is prohibited.
3.   Monopolisation of the mass media or the means of spreading information by the state, legal or natural persons is prohibited.
4.   Points 1 and 2 of this article can be restricted by law and by the conditions necessary in a democratic society for the guarantee of state and public security, territorial integrity, prevention of crime, and the defence of the rights and dignities of others to avoid the revelation of information received in confidence or to guarantee the independence and impartiality of justice.

Article 25
1.   Every individual except members of the armed forces, police and the security services has the right to hold a public assembly without arms either inside or in the open air without prior permission.
2.   The necessity for prior notification to the authorities is determined by law, if a public assembly is held in a public thoroughfare.
3.   The government may halt a public assembly only if it is deemed to be of a criminal nature.

Article 26
1.   Every individual has the right to create and join any association, including trade unions.
2.   Citizens of Georgia have the right to create political parties or other political organisations in accordance with organic law and participate in their activities.
3.   The creation and activities of such public and political entities whose goal is to overthrow or change the Constitutional order of Georgia by force, or violate the independence of the country or violate the country's territorial integrity or advocate war and violence, or attempt to induce ethnic, racial, social or national unrest are impermissible.
4.   The creation of armed formations by public and political organisations is prohibited.
5.   Persons enrolled in the staff of state security bodies, foreign affairs and the armed forces or who have been appointed judges or procurators must cease to be a member of any political organisation.
6.   The prohibition of activities of public and political parties or groups is possible only by court decision in cases and rights determined by organic law and established right.

Article 27
The state is authorised to establish restrictions on the political activity of citizens of foreign countries and stateless persons.

Article 28
1.   A citizen who has attained the age of 18 has the right to participate in referendums and elections of state and self-governing bodies. The free will of constituents is guaranteed.

2.   Only individuals who are confirmed as incompetent by the court or who have been deprived of their liberty by the due process of law, are deprived of the right to participate in elections and referendums.

Article 29
1.   Every citizen is allowed to hold any official state position as long as he satisfies established requirements.
2.   The requirements for positions of state institutions are defined by law.

Article 30
1.   Labour is free.
2.   The state is obliged to foster conditions for the development of free enterprise and competition. Except in cases envisaged by law the monopolisation of activity is prohibited. Consumer rights are protected by law.
3.   On the basis of international agreements regulating labour relationships, the state protects the labour rights of Georgian citizens abroad.
4.   The defence of labour rights, legal payment for labour and healthy working conditions, the working conditions of minors and women are determined by law.

Article 31
The state is obliged to develop the whole territory of the country equally. With respect to the high mountains regions special privileges are envisaged in law.

Article 32
1.   The state must help the unemployed to find work. Conditions for the provision of a minimum standard of living and the status of the unemployed are determined by law.
2.   The conditions for the provision of a minimum standard of living and the status of the unemployed are determined by law.

Article 33
The right to strike is recognised. Rules for realising this right are determined by law which also guarantees the continuance of work in areas deemed to be of vital importance.

Article 34
1.   The state fosters the development of culture, the unrestricted participation of nationals in cultural life the revelation and enrichment of cultural origins, the recognition of national and generic values and the deepening of international cultural relationships.
2.   Each citizen is obliged to care for and protect and preserve the cultural heritage. The state protects cultural heritage by law.

Article 35
1.   Each citizen has the right to education. Freedom of choice in education is recognised.

2.   The state guarantees that educational programmes conform to international standards and rights.
3.   The state guarantees pre-school education. Primary education is mandatory for all. The state provides free primary education for all. Citizens have the right to free secondary, professional and tertiary education at state institutes within the framework and according to the rules established in law.
4.   The state supports educational institutions by the right established in law.

Article 36
1.   Marriage is based upon equality of rights and freedom of will.
2.   The state supports the prosperity of the family.
3.   The rights of mothers and children are protected by law.

Article 37
1.   Everyone has the right to health insurance as a means of gaining medical assistance. In cases determined by law, free medical services are guaranteed.
2.   The state controls every health institution, enterprise of medical means and their trade.
3.   Everyone has the right to live in a healthy environment and use natural and cultural surroundings. Everyone is obliged to protect the natural and cultural surroundings.
4.   The state guarantees the protection of nature and the rational use of it to ensure a healthy environment, corresponding to the ecological and economic interests of society, and taking into account the interests of current and future generations.
5.   Individuals have the right to complete, objective and timely information on their working and living conditions.

Article 38
1.   Citizens of Georgia are equal in social, economic, cultural and political life regardless of national, ethnic, religious or linguistic origin according to universally recognised principles and norms of international law all have the right to develop their culture freely without any discrimination and interference. They may use their language in private and public life.
2.   In accordance with universally recognised principles of international law the exercise of minority rights should not oppose the sovereignty, integrity and political independence of Georgia.

Article 39
The Constitution does not deny other universally recognised rights, freedoms and guarantees of the individual and citizen, which are not specifically stated, but are the natural outcome of the principles contained within the Constitution.

Article 40
1.   Each individual is considered innocent until proven guilty through the due process of law.

2.	No individual is obliged to prove his innocence.

3.	A person can only be proven guilty if the evidence is incontrovertible. Every suspicion or allegation not proven by the right established by law must be decided in favour of the defendant.

Article 41

1.	Every citizen has the right according to the law to know information about himself which exists in state institutions as well as official records existing there, as long as they do not contain state, professional or commercial secrets.

2.	Information existing in official papers connected with health, finances or other private matters of an individual are not available to other individuals without the prior consent of the individual concerned, except in cases determined by law, when it is necessary for the state and public security, defence of health, rights and freedoms of others.

Article 42

1.	Each individual has the right of appeal to the court to protect his rights and freedoms.

2.	Every individual can only be judged by the court which has jurisdiction over the particular case.

3.	The right to defence is guaranteed.

4.	No individual can be brought to court twice for the same case.

5.	No individual has to answer for an action if it was not considered as a violation of law at the moment it was performed. A law that does not lessen the responsibility or remit a punishment has no retroactive force.

6.	Anybody charged with a criminal offence has the right to obtain the attendance and examination of witnesses on his behalf under the same conditions as those brought by the prosecution.

7.	Evidence obtained by breaking the law is impermissible and has no legal force.

8.	No individual is obliged to give evidence against himself or a relative as defined by law.

9.	Any individual who suffers damage illegally caused by state and self-governing bodies and officers is guaranteed full compensation through the court from state resources.

Article 43

1.	The defence of human rights and freedoms on the territory of Georgia is supervised by the Public Defender, who is elected for five years by the majority of the whole of Parliament.

2.	The Public Defender is authorised to reveal facts about the violation of human rights and freedoms and to report on it to corresponding bodies and individuals.

3.	The power of the Public Defender is determined by organic law.

Article 44

1.	Every individual living in Georgia is obliged to obey the constitution and legislation of Georgia and exercise his rights.

2.   The rights and freedoms of one individual shall not violate the rights and freedoms of others.

Article 45

The main rights and freedoms enunciated in the Constitution apply to legal persons as well as individuals.

Article 46

1.   During a state of emergency or martial law the President of the Republic is authorised to restrict the action of rights and freedoms contained in Articles 18, 20, 21, 22, 24, 25, 30 and 33 of the Constitution either in the whole country or a part of it. The President is obliged to submit a decision on a state of emergency or martial law to Parliament for ratification within 48 hours.

2.   If a state of emergency or martial law is introduced, elections for the President, and other representative bodies of Georgia, can be held only once the state of emergency or martial law has been removed.

Article 47

1.   Foreign citizens and stateless persons living in Georgia have rights and obligations equal to the rights and obligations of citizens of Georgia with some exceptions envisaged by the Constitution and law.

2.   By the right determined by law and in accordance with universally acknowledged norms of international justice Georgia gives shelter to foreign citizens and stateless persons.

3.   Extradition of a sheltered person to another state, who is pursued on political grounds or pursued for an activity which is not regarded as a crime by the legislation of Georgia is prohibited.

Chapter 3 – The Parliament of Georgia

Article 48

The Parliament of Georgia is the supreme representative body of the country which exercises legislative power, determines the main direction of domestic and foreign policy and exercises general control over the Cabinet of Ministers and other functions within the framework determined by the Constitution.

Article 49

1.   The Parliament of Georgia consists of 150 deputies elected for a term of four years by a proportional system and 85 elected by a majority system for a period of four years on the basis of free, universal, equal and direct suffrage by secret ballot.

2.   A citizen having attained the age of 25 and with the right to vote, may be elected a deputy.

3.   The internal structure of each chamber, the order of work is determined by the Parliament.

Article 50

1.   The right to participate in elections is granted to a political party or group of citizens registered by the right determined by law, whose initiative is

supported by the signatures of not less than 5 000 voters or which has a representative in the Parliament at the time elections are called. The right to participate in elections through the majority system is recognised if the individual is confirmed by 1 000 signatories or was a member of the Parliament at the previous elections.

2.   The mandates of an MP shall be distributed only among those political parties or groups which receive at least 5% of the votes of those who participate in the elections held under the proportional system.

3.   Regular elections for Parliament are held within 15 days of the expiration of its power. If the date for holding the elections falls under a state of emergency or a state of war, elections are held in not more than 60 days before the next election.

4.   The authority of the previous Parliament ceases immediately after the first meeting of the newly elected Parliament.

5.   The right of election of an MP and also his inadmissibility in participating in elections is determined by the Constitution and organic law.

Article 51
The first sitting of the newly elected Parliament shall be held within 20 days after the elections. The day of the first sitting is determined by the President. The Parliament will begin its work when confirmed by two-thirds of the deputies.

Article 52
1.   A Member of the Parliament of Georgia is the representative of the whole of Georgia and uses a free mandate. His call-up for military service is impermissible.

2.   Bringing an action against a Member of Parliament, his detention or arrest, or the search of his person or place of residence, is permissible only with the consent of the Parliament, except in cases where he is caught committing a crime. In such a case Parliament must be notified immediately. If Parliament does not agree to the Member's detention, he must be released immediately.

3.   A Member of Parliament has the right not to give evidence on facts disclosed to him as a Member of Parliament. No seizure of documents connected with this matter may take place. A Member of Parliament reserves this right after the expiry of his term.

4.   A Member of Parliament is not answerable for the ideas and opinions expressed in and out of Parliament while performing his duties.

5.   The conditions allowing an MP to carry out his duties are guaranteed. State bodies guarantee his personal security.

6.   Preventing an MP from carrying out his duties is punishable by law.

Article 53
1.   A Member of Parliament may not occupy any position in a state office or carry out industrial activities. Cases of incompatibility are determined by law.

2.   An individual cannot simultaneously be a Member of Parliament and a territorial representative body. Exemption of this are Members of Parliament

and simultaneously the Abkhazian or Adjarian supreme representative bodies.

3.   In cases of the violation of the enactments of the two preceding clauses, the individual will cease to be a Member of Parliament.

4.   Members of Parliament receive a salary as determined by law.

Article 54

1.   The question of the recognition of the authority of a Member of Parliament, or the pre-term expiry of his duties, is decided by the Parliament. This decision may be appealed against to the Constitutional court.

2.   The pre-term expiry of duties of a Member of Parliament is possible in the following cases:

    a.   resignation;

    b.   recognition of the validity of charges by a court conviction;

    c.   inability to work as recognised by a court, bankruptcy or death;

    d.   occupation of a position or carrying out of activities incompatible with the status of a deputy;

    e.   loss of citizenship of Georgia;

    f.   failure to participate in the work of Parliament for a period of four months without good reason.

Article 55

1.   The Parliament of Georgia for the term of its authority, by the right determined by the regulations, elects the Speaker of the Parliament and the Deputy Speakers, one from Abkhazia and one from Adjaria by secret ballot.

2.   The Speaker leads the work of the appropriate chamber, guarantees the free expression of opinions, signs acts adopted by at chamber and performs other duties envisaged by regulations.

3.   The Deputy Speakers perform the duties of the Speaker by his order, in cases where the Speakers is unable to exercise his authority or where it is discussed.

4.   The Speaker on behalf of the Parliament performs the complete administrative functions in the House of Parliament by the right envisaged by the regulations.

Article 56

1.   Committees are created in the Parliament for the term of its authority, for the preliminary preparation of legislation, for assistance in fulfilling decisions and as accountable bodies before the Parliament and for the purpose of control over government activities.

2.   In cases envisaged by the Constitution and the regulations and also at the request of one-quarter of the deputies, temporary committees are created in the Parliament. Representation of the Parliamentary majority in these committees shall not exceed one-half of the total number of members of such a committee.

3.   By the request of the investigative committee presence at sessions and also the receipt of necessary documents for investigation of any particular issue are obligatory.

Article 57
1.   A bureau is created for the organisation of Parliamentary work. It comprises the Speaker, Deputy Speakers, deputies of Parliamentary Committees and Parliamentary Groups.
2.   The bureau considers questions of officials determined by this law by the right envisaged by the regulations and on the judgement of corresponding committees.

Article 58
1.   Members of Parliament can create Parliamentary groups. The number necessary to create a group must be not less than ten.
2.   The creation and functioning of a faction, as well as its authority are determined by the laws and regulations.

Article 59
1.   A Member of Parliament has the right to question bodies created by it or responsible before it, members of the government, mayors of cities, governors of executive bodies of territorial units at every level and state institutions and receive answers from them. In terms of the courts and judges this rule may be applied only by rights determined by organic law.
2.   A group of at least ten deputies and a Parliamentary group have the right to question any body responsible before Parliament, or particular members of the government, who are due to answer these questions at the sittings of Parliament. The answer may become the matter of consideration of the Parliament.

Article 60
1.   Sittings of Parliament and its chambers are public. By a vote of the majority of those present Parliament is authorised to declare a sitting or a part of it closed, while considering a specific issue.
2.   Officials that are elected or appointed and confirmed by Parliament are authorised and may be required to attend sittings of the Parliament its committees and commissions. Such officials should be heard immediately.
3.   Voting is always open except in cases envisaged by the Constitution and law.
4.   Proceedings of the Parliament's sittings, except for secret matters, are issued in the printing body of Parliament.

Article 61
1.   The Parliament gathers of its own accord for regular sessions twice a year. The autumn session opens on the first Tuesday of September and closes on the third Friday of December. The spring session opens on the first Tuesday of February and closes on the last Friday of June.
2.   The President of Georgia at the request of the Speaker, or one quarter of the deputies or on his own initiative may convene an extraordinary sitting of Parliament in the period between regular sessions. If 48 hours after the written submission has been made for this to happen, Parliament has not convened, Parliament is obliged to convene within a further 48 hours according to its regulations.

3.   Extraordinary sittings must have a specific agenda and the sitting closes once the agenda has been completed.

4.   The declaration of war or a state of emergency by the President causes the convening of Parliament within 48 hours. Parliament sits until the end of the particular situation.

Article 62

Decisions of Parliament on war and peace, emergency situations and issues determined by Article 46 of the Constitution are adopted by the majority of the total number of the Parliament.

Article 63

1.   To introduce the motion for impeachment of the President of Georgia, a third of the Members of Parliament must agree, in the cases envisaged by Article 75.2 of this constitution. The case is submitted to the Supreme Court or the Constitutional Court for judgement.

2.   If the Supreme Court confirms by its judgement that the President has committed the crime adduced or the Constitutional Court confirms the President's violation of the Constitution, the Parliament by a simple majority can vote to put the impeachment of the President to the vote.

3.   The President is considered removed and impeached if two-thirds of all the Parliament vote in favour of the motion on impeachment.

4.   If the Parliament does not vote within 30 days, the motion is considered dropped and introduction of the same motion is impermissible for one year.

5.   Discussion of the charge brought against the President and the passing of a decision in the case of war, state of emergency and martial law is impermissible in the Parliament.

Article 64

1.   The right to raise the question of the removal of the Head of the Supreme Court, Members of the Government, the General Prosecutor, Chairman of the Chamber of Control and members of the Council of the National Bank is vested in one-third of the total number of Parliament, by the right of impeachment in the cases of violation of the Constitution, high treason, and commitment of capital crimes.

2.   By the right envisaged in Article 63.2 Parliament is authorised to remove officials listed in the first part of this article by the majority of the total members of Parliament.

Article 65

1.   The Parliament of Georgia ratifies international treaties and agreements or denounces them or abrogates them by the majority of the total members of Parliament.

2.   Except for those international treaties and agreements which envisage ratification, ratification of such international treaties is mandatory which:

   a.   envisages entrance into an international organisation or into inter-state unity;

   b.   is of a military character;

c.   concerns the territorial integrity of the state or the changing of the state's borders;

d.   concerns the borrowing and distribution of a loan to the state;

e.   requires a change in international legislation or the adoption of necessary laws and acts possessing the power of law for the fulfilment of changed obligations.

3.   The Parliament must be immediately notified about the conclusion of other international agreements and treaties.

4.   In the case where a constitutional application to the Constitutional court is submitted, ratification of international treaties or agreement is prohibited before a decision is made by the Constitutional Court.

Article 66

1.   A bill is considered passed if supported by the majority of those present as long as those present are not less than one-third of the total of deputies or in those cases not envisaged by the Constitution.

2.   The draft of an organic law is considered adopted if supported by the majority of the total number of Parliament.

3.   The decision of the Parliament is adopted as a decree unless other rights are envisaged by the Constitution.

4.   The right to adopt other kinds of decision is determined by the regulations of the Parliament.

Article 67

1.   The right of legislative initiative is vested in the President, a Member of Parliament, a Parliamentary group, a committee of Parliament, supreme representative bodies from Abkhazia and Adjaria or 30 000 electors.

2.   A bill submitted by the President may be considered out of term or in an accelerated way.

Article 68

1.   A bill adopted by Parliament is passed to the President of Georgia within five days.

2.   The President either signs and issues the law within ten days or returns it to the Parliament with further amendments.

3.   If the President returns the bill to Parliament, Parliament votes on the President's amendments. For adoption of his amendments the same amount of votes is required as in Article 66 of this Constitution. If the amendments are adopted, the President is obliged to sign and publish the law within seven days.

4.   If Parliament votes against the President's amendments, the bill as passed from Parliament to the President is voted on again. The original is considered passed if supported by three-fifths of the total number of deputies in the cases of laws and organic laws; by two-thirds of the total number of deputies in the case of Constitutional amendments.

5.   If the President refuses to sign the law within the determined period, it is signed and issued by the Speaker.

6.   The law enters into force only on the fifteenth day after its official publication, unless another date is provided.

Chapter 4 – The President of the Republic

Article 69
1.   The President of Georgia is the Head of State and of the executive.
2.   The President of Georgia heads and exercises domestic and foreign policy of the state. He guarantees the unity and integrity of the country and the activity of state bodies according to the Constitution.
3.   The President of the Republic is the supreme representative of Georgia in foreign relations.

Article 70
1.   The President shall be elected in free, universal, equal and direct suffrage by secret ballot with a term of five years. One and the same person can serve only two consecutive terms as President.
2.   Any citizen of Georgia who is eligible to vote, has attained 35 years of age, has lived in Georgia for at least fifteen years and is living in Georgia on the day elections are scheduled may be elected as the President of the Republic.
3.   The right to nominate a candidate for the Presidency is vested in a political party or an initiative group whose initiative is confirmed by the signatures of 50 000 electors.
4.   A candidate is considered elected if he/she receives the absolute majority of votes of the participants, on condition that more than half the total number of electors have participated in the elections.
5.   If elections are considered held, but none of the candidates received the necessary votes, then the second round of the elections is held two weeks later.
6.   The second round of elections is held between the two candidates who had the best result in the first round. The candidate who receives more votes will be considered elected President on condition that at least one-third of the total number of electors participated in the ballot.
7.   In the event that it is acknowledged that elections are not held or are held but the only candidate balloting in the first round could not receive enough votes or the President was not elected on the second round, new elections are to be held within two months.
8.   During a state of emergency, a state of war or martial law, no elections can be held.
9.   The first round of regular elections for the Presidency is held on the second Sunday of April five years after the previous elections.
10.   The orders and means of the elections of the President are determined by the Constitution and organic law.

Article 71
1.   Before occupying his position the newly elected President makes a speech delivering his programme and swears:
"I, the President of Georgia, solemnly pledge before God and my nation to defend the Constitution of Georgia, independence, the unity and inseparability of my country. I will honestly perform the duties of President. I will protect the welfare and security of my people, and will care for the renaissance and power of my nation and my homeland."

2.   The ceremony mentioned in the first point of this article is to take place on the third Sunday after the holding of Presidential elections.

Article 72
The President cannot hold any other position, carry out any commercial activity or receive any other salary or compensation from any other occupation.

Article 73
1.   The President of the Federal Republic:
     a.   concludes international agreements and treaties, negotiates with foreign states, with the consent of Parliament, appoints and relieves ambassadors and other diplomatic agents, receives and accredits ambassadors and other diplomatic representatives of foreign states and international organisations;
     b.   appoints members of his government with the consent of Parliament;
     c.   is authorised to remove ministers;
     d.   receives the resignation of ministers; is authorised to task them to perform their duties until a new government is appointed;
     e.   submits the draft of the Georgian state budget to the Parliament following agreement with the Parliamentary committees over the main principles;
     f.   submits to the Parliament the appointment and release of officials by the rights envisaged in the Constitution, law and established right;
     g.   in cases of war, massive disorder, violation of territorial integrity of the country, military coup, armed rising, ecological disaster or epidemic or in other cases when bodies of the state are deprived of their authority, declares a state of emergency throughout the whole territory of the state or its parts and submits it to Parliament within 48 hours for approval. In the case of a state of emergency, the President is authorised to issue decrees with the power of law and take special measures. The decrees are submitted to the Parliament when it gathers. Emergency powers exist only on the territory where the emergency is declared for the reasons mentioned in this part;
     h.   is authorised to halt or dismiss the activity of representative bodies of local self-government, or other representative bodies of territorial units if their activities endanger the sovereignty, territorial integrity of the country or the exercise of Constitutional authority of states authorities within the country;
     i.   on the basis of the Constitution and the law, issues enactments and orders;
     j.   signs and issues laws by the order determined by the Constitution;
     k.   decides questions on granting citizenship and shelter;
     l.   awards state honours, high-ranking military awards, special and honorary titles, and the highest diplomatic ranks;
     m.   has the right to grant pardons.
2.   The President sets elections for the Parliament and representative bodies by the right determined by law.
3.   The President is authorised to abrogate acts of bodies of the executive accountable to him.

4.   The President is the supreme commander-in-chief of the armed forces of Georgia. He appoints members of the national security Council, presides over its sittings and appoints and dismisses generals.

5.   The President is authorised to address people and the Parliament, and once a year he submits a report to Parliament on the most important questions of the state situation.

6.   The President exercises other authorities determined by the Constitution and law.

Article 74

1.   By the request of 20 000 electors or on his own initiative, the President fixes the referendum within 30 days following receipt of its request on issues determined by the Constitution and law.

2.   The holding of referendums for the adoption of the abrogation of law, amnesty or pardon or on ratification and denunciation of international treaties and agreement, also on questions which restrict main constitutional guarantees and freedoms of the individual is prohibited.

3.   Questions connected with fixing and holding referendums are determined by organic law.

Article 75

1.   The President has personal immunity. While occupying his position, his arrest or the bringing of criminal proceedings against him is impermissible.

2.   Parliament has the right to relieve the President of his duties according to the procedures of Article 63 of the Constitution and according to orders determined by organic law, for gross or continuing violation of the Constitution and law, or high treason or other capital crimes:

     a.   for violation of the Constitution if this is confirmed by the Constitutional Court;

     b.   on high treason or other capital crimes by the Supreme Court;

Article 76

1.   In cases where the President is unable to perform his duties or in the case of pre-term expiry, the powers of the President are delegated to the Speaker. Within this period the duties of the Speaker are performed by one of his deputies.

2.   A person holding the position of President in these cases cannot use the rights formulated in Article 73, and the rights envisaged in Article 74.

3.   Elections for the President are held within 45 days of the expiry of the President's duties and their holding is guaranteed by the Parliament.

Article 77

1.   After taking the oath, the President in order to exercise his executive role, accepts the resignation of the government but he can charge it to perform its duties until a new government is formed. The President is obliged to form a government within two weeks and submit it for ratification to Parliament. After consideration by the appropriate Parliamentary committee, the Parliament confirms it by the majority of the total number of deputies.

2.   In cases where Parliament does not ratify the government, the President is authorised to submit the same government for ratification or a new one. One and the same government can be submitted twice. The right to a second submission is determined by law.

3.   In the event of the removal of a minister a new minister is submitted to the Parliament within two weeks.

Article 78

1.   By the submission of the President the Parliament confirms the structure and the right of activity of the executive.

2.   The armed forces, state security forces, and the police shall not be united.

Article 79

1.   Members of the government are responsible to the President.

2.   Members of the government resign before the President.

Article 80

1.   Members of the government may hold no other position, except a party position, may not be involved in commercial activities nor receive a salary or other permanent remuneration from any other activity.

2.   A member of the government is authorised to resign by the right determined by law.

3.   The removal of a member of the government is possible only by the President or by the Parliament by the right determined in Article 64 of this Constitution.

Article 81

1.   Ministries are created on the basis of law in the fields necessary for the functioning of the state and public life.

2.   A ministry is directed by a minister who takes decisions independently on matters under his jurisdiction. Ministers issue orders on the basis of law and its fulfilment.

3.   A state minister who directs chancellery and fulfils separate tasks under the direction of the President is considered to be in the government.

Chapter 5 – The Judiciary

Article 82

1.   Judicial power is exercised with the help of the constitutional control, justice and other forms determined by law.

2.   Acts of courts are mandatory on the whole territory of the country for all state bodies and persons.

3.   The judiciary is independent and operates only through the courts.

4.   Courts make decisions on behalf of Georgia.

Article 83

1.   The legal body for constitutional control is the Constitutional Court of Georgia. Its authority, rights of creation and activity is determined by the Constitution and organic law.

2.   Justice is performed by general courts. Their system and rights of jurisdiction are determined by law.
3.   The creation of military courts is possible in war conditions and only in
the system of general courts.
4.   The creation of emergency or special courts is prohibited.

Article 84
1.   A judge is independent in his activity and is subject only to the Constitution and law. Any interference in a judge's activities in order to influence his
decision is prohibited and punishable by law.
2.   The removal of a judge from a case, his preliminary dismissal or transfer
to another position is permissible only by law in determined cases.
3.   No-one has the right to make a judge accountable in a particular case.
4.   All acts which restrict the independence of a judge are annulled.
5.   The repeal, arrestation or halting of a court decision is possible only by a
court by the right determined by law.

Article 85
1.   Cases in court are considered in open sittings. Consideration of a case to
be closed is possible only in cases envisaged by law. Decisions of courts are
announced publicly.
2.   The jurisdiction is exercised in the state language. Persons not having
command of the legal language of the court are provided with interpreters.
In regions where the population does not have command of the state language, the state guarantees to provide teaching in the state language and
explanations of matters pertaining to jurisdiction.
3.   Law is exercised on the basis of equality and competition of the parties.

Article 86
1.   A judge must be a citizen of Georgia who has attained the age of 30,
who has high legal education and at least five years' experience in the field.
2.   A judge is appointed for a period of not less than ten years.
3.   The position of a judge is incompatible with any other occupation or
remunerative activity, except pedagogical activities. A judge cannot be a
member of a political party, or participate in political activities.

Article 87
1.   Judges have personal immunity. Bringing a judge before a criminal court,
his detention or arrest, the search of his workplace or car or place of residence
without the consent of the head of the Supreme Court is impermissible. In
cases where he is caught committing a crime this should be immediately notified to the head of the Supreme Court. If the head of the Supreme Court does
not give his consent the detained or arrested judge must be released forthwith.
2.   The state guarantees the security of a judge and his family.

Article 88
1.   The Constitutional Court of Georgia exercises court authority by right of
Constitutional jurisdiction.

2. The Constitutional Court of Georgia consists of nine judges. Three members of the court are appointed by the President, three members are elected by the Parliament by three-fifths of the total number of deputies and three members are appointed by the Supreme Court. The term for a member of the Constitutional Court is ten years. The Constitutional Court selects the chairman of the Court for a period of five years. The election of a chairman for a second period is not permissible.

3. A member of the Constitutional Court may not be a person who has held the position before.

4. A member of the Constitutional Court must be a citizen of Georgia who has attained the age of 35 and has a higher legal education. The right of selection, appointment and election, release from duties and other activities of constitutional jurisdiction are determined by law.

5. Members of the Constitutional Court have personal immunity. Bringing a member of the Constitutional Court before a Criminal Court, his detention or arrest, the search of his workplace or car or place of residence without the consent of the head of the Supreme Court is impermissible. In cases where he is caught committing a crime this should be immediately notified to the Constitutional Court. If the Constitutional Court does not give its consent, the detained or arrested member must be released forthwith.

Article 89

1. The Constitutional Court of Georgia on the basis of the application and nomination of the President, of one-fifth of the Members of Parliament, of the courts, of the supreme representative bodies of Abkhazia and Adjaria, public defenders and citizens and by the rights established by organic law:

   a. takes decisions on correspondence of the Constitution to the law, to the President and to the normative acts of the supreme representative bodies of Abkhazia and Adjaria;

   b. considers disputes on the competence between state bodies;

   c. considers questions of constitutionality of the creation and activity of political parties;

   d. considers disputes connected with the question of the Constitutionality of referendums and elections;

   e. considers disputes connected with the question of the Constitutionality of international treaties and agreements;

   f. on the basis of applications of citizens considers questions of Constitutionality of normative acts on the issues envisaged by the second chapter of this Constitution;

   g. exercises other authority determined by the Constitution and organic law of Georgia.

2. The decision of the Constitutional Court is final. Normative acts or their part recognised as unconstitutional have no legal power from the moment of the publishing of the appropriate decision of the Constitutional Court.

Article 90

1. The Supreme Court of Georgia in accordance with a determined procedure supervises the enforcement of justice of every court of Georgia and reconsiders cases determined by law in the court of first instance.

2.   The Chairman and judges of the Supreme Court of Georgia, at the President's nomination, are elected by the Parliament by the majority of the total number of deputies for a period of not less than ten years.
3.   The authority, organisation and order of activity of the Supreme Court as well as the release of the Chairman and judges released from duties are determined by law.
4.   The Chairman and members of the Supreme Court have personal immunity. Bringing a member before a Criminal Court, his detention or arrest, the search of his workplace or car or place of residence without the consent of the head of the Supreme Court is impermissible. In cases where he is caught committing a crime, this should be immediately notified to Parliament. If Parliament does not give its consent the detained or arrested member must be released forthwith.

Article 91
1.   The procurator's office of Georgia is the institution of the judiciary which performs capital prosecution, supervises investigation, enforces sentences handed down by the courts and is the state prosecutor.
2.   The procurator's office of Georgia is one, centralised system. The procurator-general is appointed by Parliament upon the President's nomination, by the majority of the total number of deputies for a period of five years. Subordinate procurators are appointed by the procurator-general.
3.   The authority, organisation and order of activity of the procurator's office is determined by organic law.

Chapter 6 – State Finances and Control

Article 92
1.   The Parliament of Georgia by the majority of the total number of deputies, annually passes the state budget law which is signed by the President.
2.   The orders for making and passing the budget are determined by law.

Article 93
1.   Only the President has the right to submit the draft budget to Parliament.
2.   The President is obliged to submit the draft budget to the Council not later than three months before the end of the current budget year. Together with the draft budget the President submits a report on the fulfilment of the budget for the current year. The President submits a report on the fulfilment of the state budget not later than three months following the end of the budget year.
3.   Without the consent of the President, it is impossible to introduce changes to the draft budget. The President can require from Parliament additional state expenditure only on condition that he indicates from where the resources derive and on what they are to be spent.
4.   If Parliament cannot pass the budget by the beginning of the new budget year, in accordance with the relative budget of the previous fiscal year the expenditure necessary to carry out state obligations is covered.

Article 94
1.   Everyone is obliged to pay taxes to the amount and right determined by law.
2.   The structure of taxes and their introduction are determined by law.
3.   Exemption from state taxes and payments from the state treasury is permissible only by law.

Article 95
1.   The Georgian National Bank guarantees the appropriate functioning of a steady fiscal credit system of Georgia.
2.   The Georgian National Bank carries out fiscal credit and currency policies in accordance with the main directions determined by Parliament.
3.   The National Bank supervises other banks and is the banker of the government of Georgia and its fiscal agent.
4.   The National Bank is independent in its activities. The authority, right of activity and guarantee of independence are determined by organic law.
5.   The name and units of money are determined by law. Only the National Bank has the right of to issue money.

Article 96
1.   The highest body of the National Bank is the Board of the National Bank, whose members are approved by Parliament by the majority of the total number of deputies upon the nomination of the President, for a period of seven years. The removal of members of the Board is possible only by Parliament according to Article 64 of this Constitution.
2.   The President of the National Bank is appointed and relieved of his duties by the President of Georgia, upon the nomination of the Board of the National Bank.
3.   The National Bank is responsible before the Parliament and annually submits a report of the Bank's activities.

Article 97
1.   Financial-economic oversight of state revenues and other expenditure of the state is carried out by the Chamber of Control of Georgia. It is authorised to check the financial entries relating to the activities of other bodies of fiscal-economic activity and it submits proposals to the President of Georgia on improving tax legislation.
2.   The Chamber of Control is independent. It is responsible to Parliament. The Chairman of the Chamber of Control is appointed by Parliament, upon the nomination of the President, for a term of five years. His removal is possible only by a decision of Parliament in accordance with Article 64 of this Constitution.
3.   Twice a year while submitting the preliminary and final report on the fulfilment of the budget, the Chamber of Control submits a report to Parliament connected with the account of government expenditure. Once a year it submits a report of its own activities.
4.   The authority, organisation, right of activity and guarantee of the Chamber of Control are determined by law.
5.   Other bodies of state control are created according to law.

Chapter 7 – State Defence

Article 98
1.   Defensive war is a sovereign right of Georgia.
2.   Georgia has military forces for the defence of independence, sovereignty and territorial integrity of the country and for the fulfilment of international obligations.
3.   The structure and composition of military forces is determined by law. The structure of the military forces is confirmed by the President and its size is confirmed by the Parliament by the majority of the total number of deputies upon the nomination of the Council of National Defence.

Article 99
1.   The Council of National Defence is created for military construction and organisation of the defence of the country, which is headed by the President.
2.   The composition, the authority and the order of activity of the Council of National Defence is determined by organic law.

Article 100
1.   The use of military force during a state of emergency or for the fulfilment of international obligations is prohibited without the agreement of Parliament.
2.   For the purpose of state defence, in special cases, or cases envisaged by law, the decision to permit the entrance, use and movement of military forces of other countries on the territory of Georgia is made by the President. The decision is immediately submitted to Parliament for approval and it enters into force upon the consent of Parliament.

Article 101
1.   The defence of Georgia is the duty of every citizen.
2.   The defence of the country and the fulfilment of military duties is obligatory for every able-bodied citizen. The form of military duty is obligatory for every able-bodied citizen. The form of military duty is determined by law.

Chapter 8 – Revision of the Constitution

Article 102
1.   Those allowed to submit a bill for the general or partial revision of the Constitution are:
     a.   the President;
     b.   more than half the total number of either chamber of Parliament;
     c.   200 000 electors.
2.   Any bill proposing a revision to the Constitution shall be submitted to Parliament, which promulgates it for general discussion.
3.   Discussion of the draft begins in Parliament one month after it has been promulgated.
4.   The bill to revise the Constitution is considered passed if supported by at least two-thirds of the total number of deputies of the Parliament.
5.   The law on the revision of the Constitution is signed and published by the President of Georgia by the right envisaged in Article 68.

Article 103
The announcement of a state of emergency or martial law stops the process of the revision of the Constitution until the end of the abolition of the state of emergency or martial law.

Chapter 9 – Transitional provisions

Article 104
1.   The Constitution of Georgia enters into force from the day of the recognition of the authority of the newly elected President and Parliament of Georgia.
2.   Articles 49, 50 and 70 of the Constitution enter into force immediately after the promulgation of the Constitution.

Article 105
1.   The right to participate in the elections of 1995, have political unions of citizens registered by the right determined by law, whose initiative is confirmed by 50 000 signatories, or which had a representative in the Parliament on the day this Constitution was adopted.
2.   Proportional elections are held under a one party list.
3.   The political union or electoral bloc has the right to submit to the majority electoral district a candidate who is also on a party list for the elections held under the proportional system.
4.   The candidate who receives the most votes, but not less than one-third of the participants in the poll in that district, is considered elected as the member of Parliament for that district.
5.   If a member of Parliament is not elected on the first round of voting, a second round will be held, in which the candidates who came first and second will participate. The candidate who receives the most votes is considered elected.
6.   This article enters into force immediately after the promulgation of this Constitution and functions before the authorities of the newly elected Parliament are recognised.

Article 106
1.   After the Constitution enters into force, only those laws or parts of them which are not in contradiction to this Constitution have legal force.
2.   Two years after the Constitution comes into force, the President and Parliament guarantee the state registration of normative acts adopted before the Constitution came into force and their correspondence with the Constitution and laws.
3.   Two years after the Constitution enters into force the Parliament of Georgia must adopt organic laws envisaged by the Constitution, or confirm the legality of normative acts which exist in those areas.

Article 107
1.   Before the adoption of organic laws of legal force, current legislation remains valid according to the Constitution.
2.   Article 18 points 1 and 2 enter into force after the adoption of the appropriate legislative acts of criminal procedure.

3.   The organic law on the Constitutional Court is to be adopted before 1 February 1996.

Article 108
Article 102.2 excepted, the making of changes or additions connected with the complete restoration of jurisdiction on the whole territory of Georgia is possible without promulgating the bill on the revision of the Constitution for general public reconsideration.

Article 109
1.   The Head of State signs and promulgates the Constitution adopted by the appropriate right.
2.   Members of the current Georgian Parliament and the Constitutional Commission sign the text of the Constitution. For at least one year after the Constitution enters into force, the text of the Constitution must be displayed openly in the buildings of every local body of Georgia, in order that everyone may be allowed to know its contents.

Kazakhstan

Chronology

1990

February 22: The Supreme Soviet elects Nursultan Nazarbayev as Chairman of the Presidium, i.e. *de facto* head of state.

April 24: The Supreme Soviet re-elects Nursultan Nazarbayev.

October 25: The Supreme Soviet issues a sovereignty declaration intended to assert the primacy of its own legislation (republican laws) over all-union laws.

1991

March 17: In an all-union referendum 94.1% vote in favour of the preservation of the USSR. (Turnout 88.2%)

April 23: President Mikhail Gorbachev signs, with nine of the fifteen union republics including Kazakhstan, a pact aimed at achieving stable relations between the central government and the governments of the republics. It sets out a timetable for major political changes, starting with the signing of the new Union Treaty. No longer than six months after signature of the Treaty a new Union constitution would be promulgated, followed by elections to the Congress of People's Deputies.

August 19: Attempted *coup d'état* in Moscow.

August 22: Nazarbayev resigns as first secretary of the Kazakh Communist Party (KCP) and as a member of the Communist Party of the Soviet Union (CPSU) Politburo.

August 28: The KCP dissolves itself.

September 8: The Socialist Party of Kazakhstan (SPK) replaces the KCP.

December 1: Presidential elections are held. Nursultan Nazarbayev wins with 98.76%.

December 8: Belarus, the Russian Federative Republic and Ukraine sign the Minsk Agreement, establishing the Commonwealth of Independent States (CIS).

December 12: Kazakhstan signs the Alma Ata Agreement, thus joining the CIS.

December 16: The Supreme Soviet declares the country independent.

December 21: The CIS formally replaces the Soviet Union, grouping eleven republics including Kazakhstan, with the exception of Georgia. The Russian Federative Republic takes over many of the former Union functions, including its seat in the UN Security Council.

1992

June 2: The Supreme Council adopts a draft constitution, defining the President as head of the government and a smaller full-time parliament, which cannot be disbanded by the President. It stipulates that Russian is the language of inter-ethnic communication.

June 24: The Supreme Court orders the registration by the Ministry of Justice of the new KCP, while it had refused to register in April.

October 11: The oppositional Freedom Party, the National Democratic Party and the Republican Party merge under the name of the Republican Party.

1993

January 28: The Supreme Council adopts the first Constitution of the Republic of Kazakhstan, establishing the Supreme Council, and a new unicameral 177-member parliament.

February 6: The People's Unity Party is founded, chaired by President Nursultan Nazarbayev.

December 8: The Supreme Council votes for the elections of a new parliament.

December 13: The Supreme Council dissolves itself. The President will temporarily rule by decree.

1994

March 7: Elections to the new 177-member parliament are held, with a turnout of 73.52%. The People's Unity Party gains 30 seats, the Trade Union Federation, 11 seats; the People's Congress of Kazakhstan (NKK), 9 seats; the Socialist Party, 8 seats; the Peasants Union, 4 seats; the Harmony Movement, 4 seats; the independents, 59 seats; and 10 seats to the remaining parties. CSCE monitors note violations in the election procedure.

May 27: The Supreme Council passes a motion of no confidence in the Government.

October 11: Prime Minister Tereschenko and his Government resign.

October 12: The President appoints Kazhageldin Akezhan Magzhan Ulu (Congress of People's Unity of Kazakhstan) as Prime Minister.

1995

March 4: The Congress of People's Unity (SNEK) constitutes itself as a political party.

March 6: The Constitutional Court rules that procedural infringement during the elections of March 1994 renders the results invalid.

March 8: The President files an official complaint against the ruling.

March 10: The Supreme Council orders the suspension of the Constitutional Court ruling.

March 11: The Supreme Council approves a constitutional amendment allowing the Parliament to overrule Constitutional Court decisions and suspending the operation of the Court until June. Nevertheless, the President accedes to the Constitutional Court ruling, announcing the dissolution of the Supreme Council and the holding of new elections. He also express doubt as to the legal validity of legislation approved by the Supreme Council since it convened in March 1994, and argues that the government appointed by the Supreme Council is also invalid. The Government resigns, but stays in office in an interim capacity and the President declares that he will rule by decree until the election of the new assembly and the formal appointment of the new government.

April 29: A referendum is held on the extension of the presidential term. 95.46% vote in favour of the extension of President Nazarbayev's term until 2000 (Turnout 91.21%).

May 22: The President establishes a Council of Experts giving it the mandate to draft the new constitution.

July 4: The Constitutional Court and minority groups criticise the published draft constitution. Among the more controversial provisions are those (i) changing the name of the Republic of Kazakhstan into the Kazakh Republic, (ii) recognising Kazakh as the only official language, (iii) preventing dual citizenship, (iv) banning trade unions in state institutions and (v) restricting foreign funding for trade unions. Furthermore the Constitution defines the state as a presidential state and establishes a new bicameral parliament: the Supreme *Kenges;* of the 47-member Senate, 40 members are elected by government officials from a state list and 7 appointed by the President. The 67 members from the *Mazhilis* are elected by absolute majority.

August 1: The President agrees to abandon the proposal to change the name of the Republic.

August 30: In a referendum 89.14% of the voters approve the new constitution. Turnout (90.58%)

October 20: The President dismisses the members of the Constitutional Court replacing it by a Constitutional Council whose decisions will be subject to a presidential veto.

September 15: The Kazakh capital is transferred from Alma Ata to the city of Akmola, formerly known as Tselinograd.

December 5 and 9: Elections to a new bicameral Supreme *Kenges:* 38 out of the 40 members of the Senate are chosen, 2 seats remain vacant on account of not achieving the 50% threshold; 43 out of 67 members of the *Mazhilis* are elected, 2 short of a quorum. Turnout 78.16%. The OSCE criticises family-voting and lack of information.

December 23: Run-off elections to the *Mazhilis* are held.

1996

February 4: Last round of run-off elections are held. The Party of National Unity (PNU; the successor of SNEK) gains 11 seats, the Democratic Party of Kazakhstan, 7 seats; the Popular Cooperative Party, 2 seats; the Communist Party, 2 seats; NKK, 1 seat; the Socialist Party, 1 seat; the Harmony Movement, 1 seat; and the independents, 42 seats. Neither in the *Mazhilis* nor in the Senate does a seat remain vacant.

February 6: A new Constitutional Court is constituted.

March 15: The Russian State Duma passes a resolution in order to "deepen the integration of the peoples previously united in the USSR". This resolution revokes the 1991 agreement which established the CIS, and the Supreme Soviet's resolution of 12 December 1991 which abrogates the treaty on the formation of the USSR. The Duma also adopts a resolution upholding the legal validity of the results of the 17 March 1991 referendum on the future of the USSR.

March 17: President Nazarbayev expresses his concern on the resolution adopted by the Russian State Duma on March 15.

March 18: The Ministry of Justice suspends the Communist Party, after it organised rallies for the revival of the USSR.

November 11: President Nazarbayev appoints the government's first woman minister, Natalya Korzhova as Minister of Labour and Social Security.

Constitution of Kazakhstan[1]

Adopted by referendum, 30 August 1995

First part of constitution

We, the people of Kazakhstan, united by a common historical destiny, creating statehood on the ancient Kazakh land, recognising ourselves to be a peace-loving, civil society committed to the ideals of liberty, equality and harmony, wishing to occupy a fitting place in the world community, recognising our lofty responsibility to present and future generations, and proceeding from our sovereign right, adopt this Constitution.

Section 1 – General provisions

Article 1
1.   The Republic of Kazakhstan affirms itself to be a democratic, secular, law-based and social state, whose highest values are man, his life, rights and liberties.
2.   The fundamental principles for action of the Republic of Kazakhstan are social harmony and political stability; economic development for the good of all the people; Kazakhstan patriotism; the solution of the most important questions of state life by democratic methods, including through voting in a republican referendum or in parliament.

Article 2
1.   The Republic of Kazakhstan is a unitary state with a presidential form of rule.
2.   The sovereignty of the republic shall extend throughout its territory. The state shall ensure the integrity, inviolability and inalienability of its territory.
3.   The administrative-territorial structure of the republic and the location and status of its capital shall be defined by law.
4.   The appellations Republic of Kazakhstan and Kazakhstan are equivalent.

---

1. Text of constitution of the Republic of Kazakhstan as published by the *Vecherniy Almaty* newspaper, in Russian on 11 September 1995. Subheadings are as published.

Article 3
1.   The sole source of state power is the people.
2.   The people shall exercise power directly via a republican referendum and free elections and shall also delegate the exercise of their power to state bodies.
3.   No one may appropriate power in the Republic of Kazakhstan. The appropriation of power shall be prosecuted according to the law. The right to speak on behalf of the people and the state belongs to the president and also the Parliament of the Republic of Kazakhstan within the bounds of its constitutional powers. The government of the republic and other state authorities shall act in the name of the state only within the bounds of the authorities delegated to them.
4.   State power in the republic is unified and is exercised on the basis of the Constitution and laws, in accordance with the principle that it is separated into legislative, executive and judicial branches, and that these interact, with a system of checks and balances being applied.

Article 4
1.   The provisions of the Constitution, the laws relating to it, other normative legal documents, the international contractual and other obligations of the republic, and also normative decisions of the Constitutional Council and the Supreme Court of the republic represent the effective law in the Republic of Kazakhstan.
2.   The Constitution has supreme legal force and direct application throughout the republic.
3.   International treaties ratified by the republic take precedence over its laws and shall apply directly, except in instances where it follows from an international treaty that promulgation of a law is required in order for it to be applied.
4.   All laws and international treaties to which the republic is party shall be published. The official publication of regulatory legal documents concerning the rights, liberties and obligations of citizens is an obligatory condition for their application.

Article 5
1.   Ideological and political diversity are recognised in the Republic of Kazakhstan. It is forbidden to merge public and state institutions or set up political party organisations in state bodies.
2.   Public associations are equal before the law. It is forbidden for the state to interfere illegally in the affairs of public associations, for public associations to interfere illegally in the affairs of the state, for public associations to be granted the functions of state authorities, or for public associations to receive state funding.
3.   The creation or activity of public associations whose objectives or actions are aimed at forcibly changing the constitutional system, violating the integrity of the republic, undermining the security of the state, or inciting social, racial, ethnic, religious, class or tribal discord, and also the creation of paramilitary formations not provided for by legislation, are prohibited.
4.   The activities of political parties and trade unions of other states, and of parties of a religious orientation, as well as the funding of political parties and

trade unions by foreign legal entities and citizens, foreign states and international organisations are prohibited in the republic.

5.   The activities of foreign religious associations on the territory of the republic and the appointment by foreign religious centres of leaders of religious associations in the republic shall take place by arrangement with the appropriate state bodies of the republic.

Article 6

1.   State and private property are recognised and afforded equal protection in the Republic of Kazakhstan.

2.   Property carries obligations and its use should simultaneously serve the public good. The subjects and objects of property, the extent and limits of owners' exercise of their rights and the guarantees of their protection shall be determined by law.

3.   The land and its underground resources, waters, flora and fauna and other natural resources are owned by the state. Land may also be privately owned on the terms and conditions and within the limits established by law.

Article 7

1.   In the Republic of Kazakhstan the state language is Kazakh.

2.   Russian shall be employed officially in state bodies and local government bodies on a par with Kazakh.

3.   The state shall take care to create conditions for the study and development of the languages of the people of Kazakhstan.

Article 8

The Republic of Kazakhstan respects the principles and rules of international law. It pursues a policy of co-operation and good-neighbourly relations between states, of equality between them, of non-interference in one other's internal affairs and of peaceful resolution of international disputes; and it renounces the first use of armed force.

Article 9

The Republic of Kazakhstan has state symbols: a flag, coat of arms and national anthem. The description of these and the procedure for their official use shall be established by constitutional law.

Section 2 – Man and citizen

Article 10

1.   Citizenship of the Republic of Kazakhstan shall be acquired and terminated in accordance with the law and shall be uniform and equal, regardless of the grounds on which it was acquired.

2.   Under no circumstances may a citizen of the republic be stripped of citizenship or the right to change his citizenship, nor may he be expelled from Kazakhstan.

3.   Citizenship of another state will not be recognised for any citizen of the republic.

Article 11
1.   A citizen of the Republic of Kazakhstan may not be extradited to a foreign state unless otherwise stipulated by international treaties of the republic.
2.   The republic shall guarantee its citizens protection and patronage outside its own borders.

Article 12
1.   The rights and liberties of the individual shall be recognised and guaranteed in the Republic of Kazakhstan in accordance with the Constitution.
2.   The rights and liberties of the individual belong to everyone from birth, they are deemed absolute and inalienable and they determine the content and application of laws and other regulatory legal documents.
3.   A citizen of the republic has rights and obligations by virtue of citizenship.
4.   Foreigners and stateless persons in the republic shall enjoy the rights and liberties and bear the obligations established for citizens unless otherwise specified by the constitution, laws and international treaties.
5.   The exercise of human and civil rights and liberties must not violate the rights and liberties of other persons or endanger the constitutional system or public morality.

Article 13
1.   Every person shall be entitled to recognition of his legal identity as a person and shall have the right to defend his rights and liberties in all ways, including justifiable defence, that do not contravene the law.
2.   Everyone shall have the right to judicial defence of his rights and liberties.
3.   Everyone shall be entitled to obtain qualified legal aid. In cases specified by law, legal aid shall be rendered free of charge.

Article 14
1.   Everyone is equal before the law and the courts.
2.   No one may be subjected to any discrimination on grounds of origin, of social, official or property status, of sex, race, ethnic origin, language, religious views, beliefs, place of residence or any other circumstance.

Article 15
1.   Everyone has the right to life.
2.   No one shall be entitled to deprive a person of his life arbitrarily. The death penalty is established by law as an exceptional measure of punishment for especially grave crimes, with the convicted party accorded the right to appeal for mercy.

Article 16
1.   Everyone shall be entitled to personal liberty.
2.   Arrest and custody shall be permitted only in those instances specified by law and only by sanction of a court or prosecutor, with the arrested party

accorded the right of judicial appeal. A person may be held in detention for a period of no more than 72 hours without sanction of a prosecutor.
3.   Every detainee, arrested person and person charged with having committed a crime shall be entitled to avail himself of the assistance of a lawyer (defence attorney) from the time of his detention, arrest or the referral of charges, respectively.

Article 17
1.   The dignity of the individual is inviolable.
2.   No one may be subjected to torture, violence or other treatment or punishment which is cruel or degrading to human dignity.

Article 18
1.   Everyone shall have the right to inviolability of private life, personal and family secrecy and defence of personal honour and dignity.
2.   Everyone shall have the right to secrecy of personal deposits and savings, correspondence, telephone conversations and postal, telegraph and other communications. Qualification of this right shall be permitted only in the instances and according to the procedure directly established by law.
3.   State bodies, public associations, officials and the media shall be required to ensure that every citizen has an opportunity to familiarise himself with documents, decisions and sources of information which concern his rights and interests.

Article 19
1.   Everyone shall be entitled to decide and to indicate or not indicate his ethnic, party and religious affiliation.
2.   Everyone shall be entitled to use his native language and culture and to freely choose his language of communication, education, tuition and creative work.

Article 20
1.   Freedom of speech and creativity are guaranteed. Censorship is prohibited.
2.   Everyone shall have the right freely to obtain and disseminate information in any way that is not prohibited by law. The list of information which constitutes state secrets of the Republic of Kazakhstan shall be defined by law.
3.   Propaganda of, or campaigning for, a forcible change of the constitutional system, violation of the integrity of the republic, undermining of the state's security, war, or social, racial, ethnic, religious, class or tribal superiority, and also the cult of brutality and violence, are banned.

Article 21
1.   Everyone who is legitimately on the territory of the Republic of Kazakhstan shall be entitled to unrestricted movement around its territory and unrestricted choice of place of residence, except in instances stipulated by law.
2.   Everyone shall be entitled to travel out of the republic. Citizens of the republic shall have the right of unimpeded return to the republic.

Article 22
1.   Everyone shall have the right to freedom of conscience.
2.   Exercise of the right to freedom of conscience must not condition or limit general human and civil rights and obligations to the state.

Article 23
1.   Citizens of the Republic of Kazakhstan shall be entitled to freedom of association. The activity of public association shall be regulated by law.
2.   Servicemen, employees of the national security bodies and the law enforcement organisations and judges must not be members of parties and trade unions or act in support of any political party.

Article 24
1.   Everyone shall have the right to freedom of labour and freedom of choice of mode of activity and occupation. Forced labour shall be permitted only in accordance with a court sentence or under the conditions of a state of emergency or martial law.
2.   Everyone shall have the right to working conditions that are in keeping with safety and hygiene requirements, to compensation for labour without any discrimination and to social protection against unemployment.
3.   The right to individual and collective labour disputes using the ways of resolving them established by law, including the right to strike, is recognised.
4.   Everyone shall be entitled to rest. Persons employed on a work contract shall have a guaranteed length of working week, days off, holidays and paid annual leave established by law.

Article 25
1.   The home is inviolable. Deprivation of a home, other than by a court ruling, is not permitted. Entry into a home and inspections and searches of homes are permitted only in the instances and according to the procedure established by law.
2.   Conditions shall be created in the Republic of Kazakhstan for providing citizens with housing. Housing shall be made available to those categories of citizens specified in law who are in need of housing, for an affordable payment, out of the available public housing stock in accordance with the rules established by law.

Article 26
1.   Citizens of the Republic of Kazakhstan may privately own any property that has been acquired legitimately.
2.   Ownership, including the right of inheritance, is guaranteed by law.
3.   No one may be deprived of his property other than by a court ruling. Property may be subject to compulsory sequestration for official needs in exceptional cases specified by law on condition that equivalent compensation is provided.
4.   Everyone shall be entitled to freedom of entrepreneurial activity and to unrestricted use of his property for any legitimate entrepreneurial activity. Monopoly activity shall be regulated and limited by law. Unfair competition is prohibited.

Article 27
1.   Marriage and the family, maternity, paternity and children are under the protection of the state.
2.   The care and upbringing of children are the natural right and obligation of parents.
3.   Adult, able-bodied children are required to care for parents who are inca- pacitated for work.

Article 28
1.   A citizen of the Republic of Kazakhstan shall be guaranteed a minimum wage, a pension and social security in old age and in the event of illness, dis- ability, loss of breadwinner and other legal grounds.
2.   Voluntary social insurance, the creation of supplementary forms of social security and charity are encouraged.

Article 29
1.   Citizens of the Republic of Kazakhstan shall have the right to health-care protection.
2.   Citizens of the republic shall be entitled to obtain free of charge the guar- anteed amount of medical assistance established by law.
3.   Paid medical assistance in state-owned and private medical establish- ments and also from persons engaged in private medical practice shall be obtained on the grounds and according to the procedure established by law.

Article 30
1.   Citizens shall be guaranteed free secondary education in state educa- tional institutions. Secondary education is compulsory.
2.   A citizen shall be entitled to obtain, on a competitive basis, free higher education in a state higher educational institution.
3.   Paid education in private educational institutions shall be obtained according to the terms and procedures established by law.
4.   The state sets general compulsory standards of education. The activities of all educational institutions must meet these standards.

Article 31
1.   The state seeks to protect the environment so that it is conducive to human life and health.
2.   Officials who conceal facts and circumstances that are a threat to human life and health shall be liable under the law.

Article 32
Citizens of the Republic of Kazakhstan shall be entitled to assemble and to hold meetings, rallies, demonstrations, marches and picket lines peacefully and without weapons. Enjoyment of this right may be restricted by law in the interests of state security, public order, and safeguarding the health of other persons or defending their rights and liberties.

Article 33
1.   Citizens of the Republic of Kazakhstan shall be entitled to participate in the administration of the affairs of state in a direct manner and via

representatives, to appeal in person, and to address individual and group appeals to state and local government bodies.

2.   Citizens of the republic shall be entitled to vote for and be elected to state and local government bodies and also to participate in republican referendums.

3.   Citizens found incapable by a court or held in places of imprisonment in accordance with a court sentence shall not be entitled to vote, be elected or take part in a republican referendum.

4.   Citizens of the republic shall enjoy equal rights to join the civil service. The requirements placed on applicants for civil service positions shall be determined only by the nature of official duties, and shall be established by law. A civil servant may not be more than 60 years of age, or in exceptional cases 65.

Article 34
1.   Everyone shall be required to comply with the constitution and legislation of the Republic of Kazakhstan and to respect the rights, liberties, honour and dignity of other persons.

2.   Everyone shall be required to respect the state symbols of the republic.

Article 35
It is the duty and obligation of everyone to pay legally established taxes, levies and other compulsory payments.

Article 36
1.   Defence of the Republic of Kazakhstan is the sacred duty and obligation of each of its citizens.

2.   Citizens of the republic shall perform military service according to the procedures and forms established by law.

Article 37
Citizens of the Republic of Kazakhstan shall be required to display concern for the preservation of the historical and cultural heritage and to take care of historical and cultural monuments.

Article 38
Citizens of the Republic of Kazakhstan shall be required to preserve the natural environment and to treat natural resources with care.

Article 39
1.   The rights and liberties of man and citizen [human and civil rights and liberties] may be restricted only by law and only to the extent that is necessary to defend the constitutional system and to safeguard public order, human rights and liberties, and the health and morals of the populace.

2.   Any action capable of disrupting inter-ethnic accord shall be deemed unconstitutional.

3.   Restriction of civil rights and liberties on political grounds is not permitted in any form. Under no circumstances may there be any restriction of those

rights and liberties specified by Articles 10, 11, 13-15; Clause 1 of Article 16; Article 17; Article 19; Article 22; or Clause 2 of Article 26 of the constitution.

Section 3 – The President

Article 40
1.   The President of the Republic of Kazakhstan is the head of state and its highest official, who determines the main areas of the state's domestic and foreign policy and represents Kazakhstan within the country and in international relations.
2.   The president of the republic is symbol and guarantor of the unity of people and state power, the permanency of the Constitution and human and civil rights and liberties.
3.   The president of the republic ensures that all branches of state power act in concerted fashion and that the authorities are answerable to the people.

Article 41
1.   The President of the Republic of Kazakhstan shall be elected for a five-year term in accordance with constitutional law by a secret ballot of the adult citizens of the republic, on the basis of general, equal and direct suffrage.
2.   A citizen of the republic by birth who is at least 35 years of age and no older than 65, has a fluent command of the state language, and has lived in Kazakhstan for no less than 15 years may be elected president of the republic.
3.   Regular elections of president of the republic shall be held on the first Sunday in December and may not coincide with the time of elections to a new parliament of the republic.
4.   Extraordinary elections of the president of the republic shall be held in the instances and within the frame of time established by Clause 1 of Article 48 of the Constitution.
5.   Elections shall be considered valid if more than 50% of the electorate take part in voting. A candidate who musters more than 50% of votes of the electorate who took part in the ballot shall be considered elected. In the event of no candidate mustering the said number of votes, a run-off between the two candidates who mustered the largest number of votes shall be conducted. The candidate who musters the larger number of votes of the electorate who took part in the ballot shall be considered elected in the run-off.

Article 42
1.   The President of the Republic of Kazakhstan shall assume office from the moment he swears the following oath to the people: "I solemnly swear to faithfully serve the people of Kazakhstan, abide strictly by the constitution and the laws of the Republic of Kazakhstan, guarantee civil rights and liberties and conscientiously discharge the high obligations of President of the Republic of Kazakhstan entrusted to me".
2.   The oath shall be administered on the second Wednesday in January at a ceremony attended by deputies of parliament and members of the Constitutional Council, judges of the Supreme Court and also all former presidents

of the republic. If a president is elected at extraordinary elections, the oath shall be administered within one month of publication of the election results.

3. The powers of the president of the republic shall terminate the moment that a newly-elected president of the republic assumes office, and also in the event of the early release, dismissal from office or death of the president. All former presidents of the republic, except for those dismissed from office, shall have the title of Former President of the Republic of Kazakhstan.

4. The powers of a president of the republic elected at extraordinary elections shall be exercised up to the assumption of office of a president of the republic elected at regular presidential elections, which are to be held on the first Sunday in December five years after extraordinary elections.

5. One and the same person may not be elected president of the republic more than twice in succession.

Article 43

1. The President of the Republic of Kazakhstan is not entitled to be a deputy of a representative body, hold other paid positions or engage in entrepreneurial activity.

2. For the period of the exercise of his authority the president of the republic shall suspend his activity in any political party.

Article 44

The President of the Republic of Kazakhstan:

1. shall address an annual message to the people of Kazakhstan on the situation in the country and the main areas of domestic and foreign policy of the republic;

2. shall schedule regular and extraordinary elections to the Parliament of the Kazakh republic; convene the first session of parliament and administer the oath of its deputies to the people of Kazakhstan; convene extraordinary joint sittings of the chambers of parliament; sign within 15 working days a law submitted by the parliamentary Senate, promulgate this law or send it or certain of its articles back for further discussion and a vote;

3. shall, with the consent of parliament, appoint the prime minister of the republic to office and relieve him of office; on the representation of the Prime Minister, determine the structure of the government of the republic, appoint its members to office and relieve them of office, and form, abolish and reorganise central executive bodies of the republic which do not form part of the government; administer the oath to members of the government with submitting bills to the parliamentary Majlis; shall cancel or suspend fully or partially acts of the government and of the akims [heads of administration] of regions, cities of republican significance and the capital of the republic;

4. shall, with the consent of parliament, appoint to office the chairman of the National Bank of the Republic of Kazakhstan, and relieve him of office;

5. shall, with the consent of the parliamentary Senate, appoint to and relieve of office the Prosecutor-General and the chairman of the National Security Committee of the republic;

6. shall appoint and recall the heads of diplomatic missions of the republic;

7. shall appoint to office for a five-year term the chairman of the Accounts Committee for Supervising the Administration of the Republican Budget;

8.	shall confirm state programmes of the republic;

9.	shall, on the representation of the Prime Minister of the republic, confirm a uniform system of financing and labour compensation for all bodies maintained by the state budget of the republic;

10.	shall take the decision to hold a republican referendum;

11.	shall negotiate and sign international treaties of the republic; sign instruments of ratification; receive the credentials and letters of recall of diplomatic and other representatives of foreign states accredited to him;

12.	is supreme commander-in-chief of the armed forces of the republic and appoints and replaces the top command of the armed forces;

13.	shall bestow state awards of the republic and confer honours, senior military and other ranks, grades, diplomatic ranks and qualification classes;

14.	shall resolve matters of citizenship of the republic and of granting political asylum;

15.	shall grant pardons to citizens;

16.	in the event that the democratic institutions, independence, territorial integrity and political stability of the republic, and the safety of its citizens, come under grave and immediate threat, and, that the normal functioning of the constitutional authorities of the state is disrupted, he shall adopt, following official consultations with the Prime Minister and the chairmen of the chambers of parliament of the republic, measures dictated by the said circumstances, including the imposition throughout Kazakhstan, or in certain areas of it, of a state of emergency and the use of the armed forces of the republic, with parliament to be notified of this immediately;

17.	shall, in the event of aggression against the republic or of a direct external threat to its security, impose martial law on the territory of the republic or in specific areas, announce a partial or general mobilisation, and immediately notify the republic's parliament of this;

18.	shall form a Presidential Bodyguard Service and a Republican Guard under his jurisdiction;

19.	shall appoint to and relieve from office the State Secretary of the Republic of Kazakhstan, define his status and authorities; and form the office of the president of the republic;

20.	shall form the Security Council, the Supreme Judicial Council and other consultative and advisory bodies;

21.	shall exercise other authorities in accordance with the Constitution and laws of the republic.

Article 45

1.	On the basis and in execution of the Constitution and laws, the president of the republic shall issue decrees and directives which are binding throughout the republic.

2.	In the instance specified by Subclause 4 of Article 53 of the Constitution, the president of the republic shall issue laws and in the instance specified in Clause 2 of Article 61 of the constitution, he shall issue decrees carrying the force of laws of the republic.

3.	Acts of parliament signed by the president of the republic and acts of the president issued on the initiative of the government shall be initially sealed by the signatures of the Chairman of each chamber of parliament or of the Prime

Minister, as appropriate, who shall bear legal responsibility for the constitutionality and legality of the said acts.

Article 46
1. The President of the Republic of Kazakhstan and his honour and dignity are sacrosanct.
2. The support, service and protection of the president of the republic and his family shall be undertaken at the expense of the state.
3. The provisions of this article shall extend to former presidents of the republic.

Article 47
1. The President of the Republic of Kazakhstan may be relieved of office early if he exhibits a consistent incapacity to carry out his obligations owing to illness. In this case parliament shall form a commission consisting of an equal number of deputies from each chamber and specialists in the corresponding fields of medicine. A decision on early release shall be adopted at a joint sitting of the chambers of parliament by a majority of no less than three-quarters of the total number of deputies of each chamber, based on the findings of the commission and Constitutional Council findings that the established constitutional procedures have been complied with.
2. The president of the republic shall be made answerable for activities performed while in office only in the event of his having committed treason and may be dismissed from office by parliament for this. A decision to indict and investigate him may be adopted by a majority of the total number of deputies of the Majlis on the initiative of no less than one-third of its deputies. The investigation of a charge shall be organised by the Senate, and its results shall be a majority vote of the total number of deputies of the Senate be submitted for consideration by a joint sitting of the chambers of parliament. A final decision on this matter shall be adopted at a joint sitting of the chambers of parliament by a majority of not less than three-quarters of the total number of votes of members of each chamber, if accompanied by Supreme Court findings that there is substance to the charge and Constitutional Council findings that the established constitutional procedures have been complied with. Failure to produce a final decision within two months of the indictment being brought shall result in the indictment against the president of the republic being dismissed. Dismissal of a treason indictment against the president of the republic at any stage shall result in the early termination of the powers of the Majlis members who initiated the consideration of this matter.
3. The question of dismissal of the President of the Republic of Kazakhstan from office may not be raised at the same time as he is considering early termination of the authority of parliament.

Article 48
1. In the event of the early release or dismissal from office of the President of the Republic of Kazakhstan, or of his death, the discharge of the obligations of president shall pass temporarily to the Chairman of the parliamentary Senate. If it is not possible for the Chairman of the Senate to assume the obligations of the president, they shall pass to the Prime Minister of the republic.

Extraordinary elections of the president of the republic must be held within two months of the early termination of the authority of the president of the republic.

2. The acting president of the republic shall not be entitled to dissolve the parliament of the republic, terminate the powers of the government of the republic, schedule a republican referendum, or submit proposals concerning revisions and addenda to the Constitution of the republic.

Section 4 – Parliament

Article 49

1. Parliament is the supreme representative body of the republic, exercising legislative functions.

2. Parliament's term is four years. The term of parliament begins with the opening of its first session and ends with the start of business of the first session of the new parliament.

3. Parliament's term may be ended early in line with the instances and procedures specified by the constitution.

4. The organisation and activity of parliament and the legal position of its deputies shall be determined by constitutional law.

Article 50

1. Parliament consists of two chambers, the Senate and the Majlis, on a standing basis.

2. The Senate shall be formed by two deputies each from every region, city of republican significance and the capital of the Republic of Kazakhstan. They will be elected at a joint sitting of the deputies of all representative bodies of the regions, cities of republican significance, and the capital of the republic, respectively. Seven deputies of the Senate shall be appointed by the president of the republic for the duration of parliament's term.

3. The Majlis shall consist of 67 deputies elected from single-mandate territorial constituencies which are formed in line with the administrative-territorial arrangement of the republic and which contain approximatively equal numbers of voters.

4. A deputy of parliament may not be a member of both chambers simultaneously.

Article 51

1. Deputies of parliament shall be elected by secret ballot on the basis of general, equal and direct suffrage. Regular elections of deputies of the Majlis shall be held no later than two months prior to the end of the term of the current parliament.

2. Deputies of the Senate shall be elected by secret ballot on the basis of indirect suffrage. One-half of the deputies in the Senate shall be subject to election every two years. Elections [to the Senate] shall be held here no later than two months prior to the end of these [outgoing] deputies' term.

3. Extraordinary elections of deputies of parliament shall be held within two months of the early termination of the powers of parliamentary deputies.

4. Any citizen of the Republic of Kazakhstan who has held citizenship for no less than five years, has reached 30 years of age, has higher education and

an employment record of no less than five years, and who has been a permanent resident of the corresponding region, city of republican significance, or republican capital for no fewer than three years, can become a deputy of the Senate. A citizen of the republic who has reached the age of 25 can become a deputy of the Majlis.

5.   Elections shall be considered valid if more than 50% of the electorate take part in the ballot. A candidate who musters more than 50% of the votes of the electorate who took part in the ballot shall be deemed elected. In the event of no candidate mustering the said number of votes, a repeat vote involving the two candidates who mustered the largest number of votes shall be held. The candidate who musters the larger number of votes of the electorate who took part in the [repeat] ballot shall be deemed elected.

6.   A parliamentary deputy shall swear an oath to the people of Kazakhstan.

Article 52

1.   A deputy of parliament shall not be bound by any imperative mandate.

2.   Deputies of parliament shall be required to take part in the work of the Parliament. Deputies may vote in parliament only in person. If a deputy is absent from sittings of the chambers or their bodies more than three times without valid reason or transfers his vote to someone else, he shall be subject to penalties established by law.

3.   A parliamentary deputy is not entitled to be a deputy of another representative body, hold other paid posts except teaching, academic and other creative activity, engage in entrepreneurial activity or be a member of the management or supervisory board of a commercial organisation. Violation of this rule shall result in the deputy's powers being terminated. A parliament deputy is not guaranteed that his former job (office) or an equivalent job (office) will be held open until his term is terminated or has expired.

4.   A parliamentary deputy may not during his term be arrested, brought in for questioning, subjected to judicially imposed administrative penalties, or arraigned on a criminal charge without the consent of the corresponding chamber, other than in cases of detention at the scene of the crime or the perpetration of grave crimes.

5.   A parliamentary deputy's mandate ceases in cases where he tenders his resignation or is deemed incapable, where parliament is dissolved, and in other instances specified by the Constitution. A deputy loses his mandate when a court conviction against him comes into effect or if he moves to a place of permanent residence outside the republic of Kazakhstan.

6.   The Central Election Commission of the Republic of Kazakhstan shall be responsible for preparing the material for applying punitive measures against deputies, their observance of the requirements of Clause 3 of this article, the ethical rules for deputies, and also for the discontinuation of the deputies' powers and deprivation of their powers and immunity.

Article 53

At joint sittings of its chambers, parliament shall:

1.   as moved by the president of the republic, introduce amendments and addenda to the constitution, pass constitutional laws and introduce amendments and addenda to them;

2.   approve the republican budget and the reports which the government and the Accounts Committee for Supervising the Administration of the Republican Budget make on its implementation, and submit and addenda to the budget;

3.   hold a repeat debate and vote on laws that evoke the objections of the president of the republic within one month from the time the objections are forwarded. Failure to observe this time-frame shall signify approval of the president's objections. If parliament upholds, by a two-thirds majority vote of the total number of deputies in each chamber, the decision it adopted earlier, then the president shall sign the law within seven days. If the president's objections are not overridden, the law shall be deemed not to have been passed or else deemed to have been passed in the version proposed by the president;

4.   have the right to delegate legislative power to the president for a period not exceeding one year, on the president's initiative, by a two-thirds vote of the total number of deputies in each chamber;

5.   consent to the president's appointment of the Prime Minister of the republic and the Chairman of the National Bank of the republic;

6.   hear the Prime Minister's report on the government programme and approve or reject the programme. The programme may be rejected for a second time by a two-thirds majority vote of the total number of deputies in each chamber, and this shall signify a vote of no confidence in the government. The absence of such a majority shall signify approval of the government programme;

7.   express a vote of no confidence in the government by a two-thirds majority vote of the total number of deputies in each chamber, on the initiative of no less than one-fifth of the total number of deputies of parliament, or in the cases set out in the constitution;

8.   decide matters of war and peace;

9.   as moved by the president of the republic, take the decision to use the armed forces of the republic to fulfil international peacekeeping and security commitments;

10. take the initiative to hold a republican referendum;

11. hear annual messages from the Constitutional Council of the republic on the state of constitutional legality in the republic;

12. form joint commissions of its chambers, elect their chairmen and relieve them of office and hear reports on the activity of the commissions;

13. exercise the other powers entrusted to parliament by the Constitution.

Article 54

At separate sittings of its chambers, whereby issues are considered first in the Majlis and subsequently in the Senate, parliament shall:

1.   pass laws;

2.   discuss the republican budget, reports on its implementation, and amendments and additions to the budget, and establish and abolish state taxes and levies;

3.   establish the procedure for resolving matters of the administrative-territorial structure of the Republic of Kazakhstan;

4.   institute state awards, establish honours, military and other ranks, grades.

and diplomatic ranks of the republic, and define the state symbols of the republic;
5.   decide questions of state loans and the republic's rendering of economic and other assistance;
6.   promulgate acts of amnesty for citizens;
7.   ratify and denounce international treaties of the republic.

Article 55
Under the exclusive jurisdiction of the Senate are:
1.   on representation from the President of the Republic of Kazakhstan, the election and release from office of the Chairman of the Supreme Court and the board chairman and judges of the Constitutional Council of the republic, and the administration of the oath to them;
2.   consent to the appointment by the President of the Republic of Kazakhstan of the Prosecutor-General and the Chairman of the National Security Committee of the republic;
3.   deprivation of the immunity of the Prosecutor-General and of the chairman and judges of the Supreme Court of the republic;
4.   early termination of the powers of local representative bodies in accordance with the legislation of the republic;
5.   the delegation of two deputies to the Supreme Judicial Council of the Republic of Kazakhstan;
6.   examination of an issue raised by the Majlis concerning the dismissal of the President of the Republic from office and submission of the results of this examination for consideration by a joint sitting of the chambers.
[The remainder of this item will be published at a later date.]

Constitution of Kazakhstan
Second part of constitution

The following is the second part of the Constitution of the Republic of Ka-zakhstan, which was published in the Vecherniy Almaty *newspaper. For the first part of the constitution, see SWB issue SU/2429, section S1. Subhead-ings are as published.*

Article 56
Under the exclusive jurisdiction of the Majlis are:
1.   acceptance for consideration, and the actual consideration, of bills;
2.   the draft of proposals on objections filled by the President of the Repub-lic of Kazakhstan to laws passed by the republic's parliament;
3.   on the representation of the president of the republic, the election and release from office of the chairman, deputy chairman, secretary and members of the Central Election Commission of the republic;
4.   the announcement of regular elections of the president of the republic and the scheduling of extraordinary presidential elections;
5.   the delegation of two deputies to the Justice Qualifications Board;
6.   the referral of an indictment of treason against the president of the republic.

Article 57
Each chamber of parliament shall independently, without the involvement of the other chamber:
1.   appoint to a five-year term of office two members of the Accounts Com-mittee for Supervising the Administration of the Republican Budget;
2.   delegate half the members of the commission formed by parliament in the instance specified by Clause 1 of Article 47 of the Constitution;
3.   elect half the members of joint commissions of the chambers;
4.   terminate the powers of deputies and also, on the representation of the Prosecutor-General of the Republic of Kazakhstan, decide questions of deputies of the chambers being stripped of their immunity;
5.   conduct parliamentary hearings on matters lying within their jurisdiction;
6.   on the initiative of no less than one-third of the total number of their deputies, have the right to hear reports from members of the government of the republic on their activity, and by a two-thirds majority vote of the total number of deputies of the chamber, adopt an appeal to the president of the republic on releasing a member of the government from office if he has failed to execute the laws of the republic;
7.   form co-ordinating and working bodies of the chambers;

8.   adopt the standing regulations for its activity and other decisions on matters relating to the organisation and standard procedures of the chambers.

Article 58
1.   The chambers shall be headed by chairmen who have a fluent command
of the state language and who are elected by the Senate and the Majlis from
the ranks of their deputies by secret ballot, by a majority vote of the total
number of deputies of the chambers. Nominations for the office of Chairman
of the Senate shall be made by the President of the Republic of Kazakhstan.
Nominations for the office of Chairman of the Majlis shall be made by the
deputies of that chamber.
2.   The Chairmen of the chambers may be recalled from office, and also
have the right to tender their resignations if a majority of the total number of
deputies of the chambers vote in favour of this.
3.   The Chairmen of the chambers of parliament shall:
      i.   convene and chair sittings of the chambers;
      ii.   exercise overall management of the preparation of questions sub-
mitted for consideration by the chambers;
      iii.   ensure that the activity of the chambers complies with the stand-
ing regulations;
      iv.   direct the activities of the co-ordinating bodies of the chambers;
      v.   sign acts issued by the chambers;
      vi.   each appoint two members of the Constitutional Council of the
Republic of Kazakhstan;
      vii.   carry out other duties charged to them by the parliamentary reg-
ulations.
4.   The chairman of the Majlis shall:
      i.   open sessions of parliament;
      ii.   convene regular joint sittings of the chambers and chair regular
and extraordinary joint sittings of the chambers;
5.   The Chairmen of the chambers shall issue directives on matters within
their jurisdiction.

Article 59
1.   Sessions of parliament shall be held in the form of joint and separate sittings of its chambers.
2.   The first session of parliament shall be convened by the President of the
Republic of Kazakhstan no later than 30 days following publication of the
election results.
3.   Regular sessions of parliament shall be conducted once a year, lasting
from the first working day of September until the last working day of June.
4.   A session of parliament shall be opened by the president of the republic
and closed at joint sittings of the Senate and the Majlis. In the period between
sessions of parliament, the President of the Republic of Kazakhstan may, on
his own initiative or at the proposal of the chairmen of the chambers or of no
less than one-third of the total number of deputies of parliament, convene a
special joint sitting of the chambers. This may consider only those matters for
which it was convened.

5.   Joint and separate sittings of the chambers shall be held on the precondition that no less than two-thirds of the total number of deputies of each chamber are present at them.

6.   The joint and separate sittings of the chambers shall be open. Closed sessions may be held in the instances specified by standing regulations. The president of the republic, the Prime Minister and members of the government, the Chairman of the National Bank, the Prosecutor-General and the Chairman of the National Security Committee shall be entitled to attend and speak at any sitting.

Article 60

1.   The chambers shall form standing committees, not exceeding seven per chamber.

2.   The Senate and the Majlis shall be entitled to form joint commissions on a parity basis to resolve matters relating to the joint activity of the chambers.

3.   Committees and commissions shall issue decrees on matters falling within their jurisdiction.

4.   The procedures for setting up committees and commissions, their powers, and the organisation of their activities, shall be determined by law.

Article 61

1.   The right of legislative initiative belongs to deputies of the Parliament of the Republic of Kazakhstan and to the government of the republic and shall be realised exclusively in the Majlis.

2.   The president of the republic shall be entitled to define the priority for the consideration of a bill as an urgent matter, this signifying that parliament must consider this bill within one month from the day it was submitted. If parliament fails to meet this requirement, the president of the republic shall be entitled to issue a decree carrying the force of a law, which shall remain valid until a new law is issued by parliament in the manner prescribed by the Constitution.

3.   Parliament shall be entitled to issue laws that regulate the most important social relations and to establish fundamental principles and norms concerning:

   i.   the legal identity of natural and legal persons, civil rights and liberties, and the obligations and responsibility of natural and legal persons;

   ii.   systems of ownership and other material rights;

   iii.   the foundations for the organisation and work of state bodies, local government bodies, the civil service and military service;

   iv.   taxation and the establishment of levies and other compulsory payments;

   v.   the republican budget;

   vi.   matters concerning the judicial system and judicial procedure;

   vii.   education, health care and social protection;

   viii.   the privatisation of enterprises and their assets;

   ix.   environmental protection;

   x.   the administrative-territorial structure of the republic;

   xi.   the defence and security of the state. All other relations shall be regulated by legally binding acts.

4.   A bill that is considered and approved by a majority of votes of the total number of Majlis deputies shall be passed to Senate, where it shall be discussed within no more than 60 days. A bill approved by a majority vote of the total number of Senate deputies shall become law and it shall be submitted to the president for signing within 10 days. A bill that is rejected in total by a majority vote of the total number of Senate deputies shall be returned to the Majlis. If the Majlis, by a two-thirds majority vote of the total number of deputies, once again approves the bill, it shall be passed to the Senate for a repeat debate and vote. A bill that is rejected twice may not be re-submitted in the course of the same session.

5.   Amendments and addenda to a bill made by a majority vote of the total number of Senate deputies shall be forwarded to the Majlis. If by a majority vote of the total number of its deputies the Majlis agrees to the proposed amendments and addenda, the law shall be considered adopted. If, however, the Majlis objects by that same majority vote to the amendments and addenda expressed by the Senate, the differences between the chambers shall be resolved by way of conciliation procedures.

6.   Bills specifying a reduction in state revenues or an increase in state spending may be submitted only if accompanied by positive findings produced by the government of the republic.

7.   If a bill submitted by the government is rejected, the Prime Minister shall be entitled to raise the question of confidence in the government at a joint sitting of the chambers of parliament. A vote on this shall be held no sooner than 48 hours after the moment the no confidence issue was presented. If the no confidence motion fails to muster the number of votes required by the Constitution, the bill shall be considered to have been passed without a vote. However, the government may not avail itself of this right more than twice a year.

Article 62

1.   Parliament shall pass legislative acts in the form of laws of the Republic of Kazakhstan, resolutions of parliament, and resolutions of the Senate and the Majlis, which are binding on the territory of the whole republic.

2.   Laws of the republic shall take effect after they are signed by the president of the republic.

3.   Amendments and addenda to the Constitution shall be introduced by a majority of no less than three-quarters of the votes of the total number of deputies of each chamber.

4.   Constitutional laws shall be passed on matters specified by the Constitution by a majority of no less than two-thirds of the votes of the total number of deputies of each chamber.

5.   Legislative acts of parliament and its chambers shall be passed by a majority vote of the total number of deputies of the chambers, unless otherwise specified by the Constitution.

6.   Issues of amendments and addenda to the constitution and the adoption of constitutional laws, or amendments and addenda to these, must have two readings.

7.   Laws of the republic and resolutions of parliament and its chambers must not contravene the constitution. Resolutions of parliament and its chambers must not contravene laws.

8.   The procedure for drafting, submitting, debating, executing and publishing legislative and other regulatory legal acts of the republic shall be regulated by a special law and by the regulations of parliament and its chambers.

Article 63
1.   The President of the Republic of Kazakhstan may dissolve parliament in the following cases: if parliament passes a vote of no confidence in the government; if parliament refuses to consent to the appointment of a Prime Minister; if there is a political crisis resulting from insurmountable disagreements between the chambers of parliament, or between parliament and other branches of state power.
2.   Parliament may not be dissolved in the period of a state of emergency or martial law, in the last six months of a presidential term, and also for one year following a previous dissolution.

Section 5 – The Government

Article 64
1.   The government exercises the executive power of the Republic of Kazakhstan, it stands at the head of the system of executive bodies and it manages their activities.
2.   The government shall be responsible in all its activity to the president of the republic and also accountable to the parliament of the republic in the instance specified by Clause 6 of Article 53.
3.   Members of the government shall be accountable to the chambers of parliament in the instance specified by Clause 6 of Article 57 of the Constitution.
4.   The competence of the government and its organisational and operational procedures shall be determined by constitutional law.

Article 65
1.   The government shall be formed by the President of the Republic of Kazakhstan in line with the procedures specified by the Constitution.
2.   Proposals concerning the structure and composition of the government shall be submitted to the president of the republic by the Prime Minister of the republic within 10 days of the appointment of the Prime Minister.
3.   Members of the government shall take an oath to the people and the President of Kazakhstan.

Article 66
The government of the Republic of Kazakhstan shall:
1.   draft the main areas of the state's socio-economic policy, defence capability, security and public order, and organise their implementation;
2.   draft the republican budget and the report on its implementation and present them to parliament, and ensure that the budget is implemented;
3.   submit bills to the Majlis and provide for the execution of laws;
4.   organise the management of state property;

5.   formulate measures for the pursuit of the foreign policy of the republic;
6.   direct the activity of ministries, state committees and other central and local executive bodies;
7.   revoke or suspend fully or in part the effect of acts of ministries, state committees and other central and local executive bodies of the republic;
8.   appoint to and release from office the leaders of central executive bodies which are not part of the government;
9.   appoint for a five-year term four members of the Accounts Committee for Supervising the Administration of the Republican Budget;
10. perform other functions entrusted to it by the Constitution, laws and presidential acts.

Article 67

The Prime Minister of the Republic of Kazakhstan shall:
1.   organise and direct the activity of the government and be personally responsible for its work;
2.   within a month of appointment, present a report on the government programme to parliament, and in the event that this is rejected, present a second report on the programme within two months;
3.   sign government resolutions;
4.   report to the president on the main areas of the government's activity and on all of its most important decisions;
5.   perform other functions connected with organisation and management of the government's activity.

Article 68

1.   Members of the government shall be collectively responsible for decisions adopted by the government – even if they have not voted for their adoption – if they do not state their disagreement immediately.
2.   Members of the government shall not be entitled to be deputies of a representative body, hold other paid posts except teaching, academic and other creative activities, engage in entrepreneurial activity, or be a member of the board of management or supervisory board of a commercial organisation.

Article 69

1.   The government of the Republic of Kazakhstan shall issue resolutions that are binding throughout the republic on matters which fall within its jurisdiction.
2.   The Prime Minister of the republic shall issue directives that are binding throughout the republic.
3.   Government resolutions and directives of the Prime Minister must not contravene the Constitution, legislative acts or decrees and directives of the president of the republic.

Article 70

1.   The government shall relinquish its powers to the newly-elected President of the Republic of Kazakhstan.

2. The government and any member of it shall be entitled to tender their resignations to the president of the republic if they deem it impossible to continue performing the functions entrusted to them.
3. The government shall tender its resignation to the president of the republic if parliament passes a vote of no confidence in the government.
4. The president of the republic shall within 10 days consider whether to accept or reject the resignation.
5. Acceptance of the resignation shall signify the cessation of the term of office of the government or the member of it, respectively. Acceptance of the Prime Minister's resignation shall signify the cessation of the term in office of the entire government.
6. If the resignation of the government or a member of it is rejected, the president shall instruct them to continue to discharge their obligations. If the government tenders its resignation after a parliamentary vote of no confidence in it, but this resignation is rejected, the president shall have the right to dissolve parliament.
7. The president of the republic shall be entitled, on his own initiative, to take the decision to end the term of office of the government or any member thereof. Cessation of the term of office of the Prime Minister shall signify and end to the term of the entire government.

Section 6 – Constitutional Council

Article 71
1. The Constitutional Council of the Republic of Kazakhstan consists of seven members whose term in office is six years. Former presidents of the republic shall by right be life members of the Constitutional Council.
2. The Chairman of the Constitutional Council shall be appointed by the president of the republic and has the casting vote when there is an equal split of votes.
3. Two members of the Constitutional Council shall be appointed by the president of the republic, two by the Chairman of the Senate and two by the Chairman of the Majlis.
Half the members of the Constitutional Council shall be replaced every three years.
4. The offices of Chairman and member of the Constitutional Council are incompatible with possession of a deputy's mandate, with tenure of other paid offices except teaching, academic and other creative creativity; with entrepreneurial activity and with membership of a management body or supervisory board of a commercial organisation.
5. During their term of office the chairman and members of the Constitutional Council may not be arrested, brought in for questioning, subjected to judicially imposed administrative penalties or arraigned on a criminal charge without the consent of parliament, other than in cases of detention at the scene of the crime or the perpetration of serious crimes.
6. The organisation and activity of the Constitutional Council shall be regulated by constitutional law.

Article 72
1. On application by the President of the Republic of Kazakhstan, the

Chairman of the Senate, the Chairman of the Majlis, no less than one-fifth of the total number of deputies in parliament, or the Prime Minister, the Constitutional Council shall:

    i.   if a dispute arises, decide the issue of whether it is correct to hold elections of the president of the republic or of parliamentary deputies, or a republican referendum;

    ii.   prior to signature by the president, examine laws passed by Parliament for compliance with the constitution of the republic;

    iii.   prior to ratification, examine international treaties of the republic for their compliance with the constitution;

    iv.   produce official interpretations of the standards set by the Constitution;

    v.   present its findings in the instances specified in Clauses 1 and 2 of Article 47 of the Constitution.

2.   The Constitutional Council shall consider appeals by courts in the instances established by Article 78 of the constitution.

Article 73

1.   If a case is taken to the Constitutional Council concerning the issues listed in Article 72, Clause 1, Subclause i. of the constitution, then the assumption of office by the president, the registration of deputies elected to parliament or the collation of the results of a republican referendum shall be suspended.

2.   If a case is taken to the Constitutional Council concerning the issues listed in Article 72, Clause 1, Subclauses ii. and iii. of the constitution, then the time-scale for signing or ratifying the said acts shall be frozen.

3.   The Constitutional Council shall announce a ruling within one month of the day the appeal is submitted. This time-span may be reduced to 10 days at the demand of the president of the republic if the issue brooks no delay.

4.   A Constitutional Council ruling may wholly or in part be subject to objections raised by the president of the republic, which shall be overridden by a two-third vote of all members of the Constitutional Council. If the president's objections are not overridden, the Constitutional Council ruling shall be deemed not to have been adopted.

Article 74

1.   Laws and international treaties deemed not to conform to the Constitution of the Republic of Kazakhstan may not be signed or ratified, respectively, or put into effect.

2.   Laws and other regulatory legal documents deemed to encroach on the human and civil rights and liberties established by the Constitution shall be annulled and are not to be applied.

3.   Constitutional Council rulings shall come into force the day that they are adopted and shall be deemed binding throughout the republic, final and not subject to appeal.

Section 7 – Courts and justice

Article 75

1.   Justice in the Republic of Kazakhstan shall be administered only by the courts.

2. Judicial authority shall be exercised by means of civil, criminal and other forms of judicial procedure established by law.

3. The courts of the republic are the Supreme Court and the local courts established by law.

4. The judicial system of the republic is established by the constitution of the republic and constitutional law. The establishment of special or emergency courts under any name is prohibited.

Article 76

1. Judicial authority shall be exercised in the name of the Republic of Kazakhstan and have as its purpose the protection of the rights, liberties and legitimate interests of citizens and organisations and the guaranteed execution of the constitution, laws, other regulatory legal documents and international treaties of the republic.

2. Judicial authority shall extend to all cases and disputes arising out of the constitution, laws, other regulatory legal documents and international treaties of the republic.

3. The judgements, sentences and other decisions of the courts shall be binding throughout the Republic of Kazakhstan.

Article 77

1. Judges are independent in the administration of justice and shall be subordinate only to the constitution and the law.

2. Any interference in the courts' administration of justice is inadmissible and shall entail liability according to the law. Judges are not accountable in respect of specific cases.

3. In the application of the law a judge must be guided by the following principles:

    i. a person is considered innocent of a crime until his guilt is recognised by a court sentence coming into force;

    ii. no-one may be made criminally or administratively liable for one and the same offence more than once;

    iii. the jurisdiction specified for a party by law may not be changed without his consent;

    iv. in court, everyone has the right to be heard;

    v. laws establishing or increasing liability, placing new obligations on citizens, or to the detriment of their position, are not retroactive. If, after an offence has been committed, the liability for it is revoked or mitigated by law, the new law shall apply;

    vi. the accused shall not be required to prove his innocence;

    vii. no-one shall be required to testify against himself, his wife (her husband) or close relatives, the list of which shall be determined by law. Members of the clergy shall not be required to bear witness against those who have confided confessions in them;

    viii. any doubts as to a party's innocence shall be interpreted in favour of the accused;

    ix. evidence obtained illegally has no legal force. No-one may be convicted merely on the basis of his own confession;

    x. the application of criminal law by analogy is not permitted.

4.   The principles of justice established by the Constitution shall be common and indivisible for all courts and judges in the republic.

Article 78
1.   The courts are not entitled to apply laws or other regulatory legal documents which infringe upon the rights and liberties of man and a citizen established by the Constitution. If a court discerns that an applicable law or other regulatory legal document infringes upon the human and civil rights and liberties established by the Constitution, it shall suspend proceedings and submit an application to the Constitutional Council of the Republic of Kazakhstan for this act to be deemed unconstitutional.

Article 79
1.   Courts shall consist of permanent judges whose independence is protected by the Constitution and the law. A judge's authority may be terminated or suspended only on the grounds established by law.
2.   A judge may not be arrested, brought in for questioning, subjected to judicially imposed administrative penalties or arraigned on a criminal charge without the consent of the President of the Republic of Kazakhstan, based on the findings of the Supreme Judicial Council of the republic, or without the consent of Senate in the instance established in Clause 3 of Article 55 of the Constitution; other than in cases of detention at the scene of the crime or the perpretration of serious crimes.
3.   Citizens of the republic who have reached the age of 25, who possess a higher legal education, who have worked in the legal profession for not less than two years and who have passed the qualifying examination may become judges. Additional requirements for judges of the republic's courts may be established by law.
4.   The office of judge is incompatible with possession of a deputy's mandate, with tenure of another paid office, except for teaching, academic and other creative activity, with entrepreneurial activity and with membership of a management body or supervisory board of a commercial organisation.

Article 80
The courts shall be financed and judges provided with housing out of republican budgetary funds and this should ensure that full and independent administration of justice is possible.

Article 81
The Supreme Court of the Republic of Kazakhstan is the highest judicial body for civil, criminal, and other cases subject to the jurisdiction of general courts. It supervises their activity in the procedural forms specified by the law and it provides clarifications on questions of judicial practice.

Article 82
1.   The chairman of the Supreme Court, the chairmen of the board and the judges of the Supreme Court of the Republic of Kazakhstan shall be elected

by the Senate on the representation of the president of the republic based on recommendations from the Supreme Judicial Council of the republic.

2.   The chairmen of regional courts and courts which are equated with them, the chairmen of boards and judges of regional courts and courts equated with them shall be appointed to office by the president of the republic on the recommendation of the Supreme Judicial Council of the republic.

3.   Chairmen and judges of other courts of the republic shall be appointed to office by the president of the republic on a representation from the Minister for Justice based on the recommendations of the Justice Qualification Board.

4.   The Supreme Judicial Council shall be headed by the president of the republic and shall consist of the Chairman of the Constitutional Council, the chairman of the Supreme Court, the prosecutor-general, the Minister for Justice, deputies of the Senate, judges and other persons appointed by the president of the republic. The Justice Qualification Board is an autonomous, independent institution formed from deputies of the Majlis, judges, prosecutors, law teachers, legal scholars and employees of the justice authorities.

5.   The status of the Supreme Judicial Council and the Justice Qualification Board and the procedures for forming them and organising their work shall be determined by law.

Article 83
1.   In the name of the state, the Prosecutor-General's Office exercises supreme supervision over the accurate and uniform application of laws, decrees of the President of the Republic of Kazakhstan and other regulatory legal documents on the territory of the republic, and over the legality of operational investigate activity, preliminary inquiries and investigations, and administrative and executive proceedings; it takes measures to identify and put a stop to breaches of legality and it lodges appeals against laws and other regulatory legal documents which contravene the Constitution and laws of the republic. The Prosecutor-General's Office represents the interests of the state in court and pursues criminal prosecutions in the instances, according to the procedures and within the limits established by the law.

2.   The Prosecutor-General's Office of the republic constitutes a single centralised system with local prosecutors subordinate to their higher counterparts and the Prosecutor-General of the republic. It exercises its authority independently of other state bodies and officials and is accountable only to the president of the republic.

3.   Within his term in office, the Prosecutor-General may not be arrested, brought in for questioning, subjected to judicially imposed administrative penalties or arraigned on a criminal charge without the consent of Senate, other than in cases of detention at the scene of the crime or the perpretration of serious crimes. The term in office of the Prosecutor-General is five years.

4.   The powers of the Prosecutor-General's Office of the republic and the organisation of and procedures for its activity shall be determined by law.

Article 84
1.   Inquiries and preliminary investigations into criminal cases shall be carried out by special bodies and are separated from the court and the Prosecutor-General's Office.

2.   The powers of the inquiry and investigating authorities, the organisation of and procedures for their activity, and questions of operational investigative activity in the Republic of Kazakhstan are regulated by law.

Section 8 – Local state administration and local government

Article 85
Local state administration is exercised by local representative and executive bodies which are responsible for the state of affairs on their own territory.

Article 86
1.   The local representative authorities – the councils [Kazakh: maslikhat] – express the will of the population of the corresponding administrative-territorial units and, bearing in mind the overall state interest, define the measures necessary to realise this will and monitor the way these are implemented.
2.   Councils are elected for a four-year term by a secret ballot of the public on the basis of general, equal and direct suffrage.
3.   Any citizen of the Republic of Kazakhstan who has reached the age of 20 may be elected a deputy of a council. A citizen of the republic may be a deputy of only one council.
4.   Under the jurisdiction of the councils are:
    i.   approval of plans, of economic and social development programmes for the territory, of the local budget, and of the reports on their implementation;
    ii.   the resolution of those matters relating to the local administrative-territorial structure which lie within their jurisdiction;
    iii.   consideration of reports by the leaders of the local executive authorities on matters which legally fall within the given council's jurisdiction;
    iv.   the formation of standing commissions and other working council bodies, the hearing of reports on their activity and the resolution of other matters relating to the organisation of the work of the council;
    v.   in line with the legislation of the Republic of Kazakhstan, the exercise of other powers to safeguard the rights and legitimate interests of citizens.
5.   The term of a council shall be ended early by the Senate on grounds and according to the procedures established by law, and also if it decides to dissolve itself.
6.   The competence of councils, the procedures for their organisation and activity and the legal position of their deputies are established by law.

Article 87
1.   The local executive bodies are part of the unified system of executive bodies of the Republic of Kazakhstan and ensure that the general state policy of the executive authority is implemented in co-ordination with the interests and development needs of the corresponding territory.
2.   Under the jurisdiction of the local executive bodies are:
    i.   the drafting of plans, economic and social development programmes for the territory, and the local budget, and support for their implementation;

 ii. the administration of municipal property;
 iii. the appointment to and release from office of the leaders of local executive authorities and the resolution of other matters relating to organising the work of the local executive bodies;
 iv. in the interests of local state administration, the exercise of other powers that are entrusted to the local executive bodies by the legislation of the republic.
3. The local executive body shall be headed by the akim of the corresponding administrative-territorial unit, who is the representative of the president and government of the republic.
4. The akim of regions, cities of republican significance and the capital shall be appointed to and released from office by the president of the republic on the representation of the Prime Minister. The akims of other administrative-territorial units shall be appointed by the akims superior to them. The president of the republic shall be entitled to relieve akims from office at his own discretion.
5. A council shall be entitled to pass a vote of no confidence in the akim by a two-thirds vote of the total number of its deputies and to put the issue of his release from office to the president of the republic or a superior akim, as appropriate. The term of the akim of regions, cities of republican significance and the capital shall end when a newly elected president of the republic assumes office.
6. The competence of the local executive authorities and the organisation of and procedures for their activity shall be established by law.

Article 88
1. On matters falling within their jurisdiction, councils shall adopt decisions and akims shall adopt decisions and directives that are binding on the territory of the corresponding administrative-territorial unit.
2. Draft decisions of councils providing for a reduction in local budget revenue or an increase in local budgetary expenditure may be submitted for consideration only if accompanied by positive findings from the akim.
3. Decisions of councils which do not conform to the constitution and legislation of the Republic of Kazakhstan may be judicially revoked.
4. Decisions and directives of the akim may be revoked by the president and government of the Republic of Kazakhstan or by the superior akim, as appropriate, and also judicially.

Article 89
1. Local government which allows the public to resolve matters of local importance independently is recognised in the Republic of Kazakhstan.
2. Local government shall be exercised by the public directly via elections, and also via elected and other local government bodies in rural and urban local communities encompassing territories that are densely populated.
3. The procedures for the organisation and activity of local government bodies shall be determined by the citizens themselves within the limitations established by law.
4. The independence of local government bodies, within the limits of their authority established by law, is guaranteed.

Section 9 – Final and transitional provisions

Article 90

1.   The Constitution of the Republic of Kazakhstan, adopted at a republican referendum, shall take effect the day the referendum results are officially published, and the term of the previous Constitution of the Republic of Kazakhstan shall simultaneously end.

2.   The day the Constitution is adopted by a republican referendum shall be declared a state holiday: Constitution Day of the Republic of Kazakhstan.

Article 91

1.   Amendments and addenda to the Constitution of the Republic of Kazakhstan may be made only by a republican referendum conducted in accordance with a decision by the president of the republic, taken either on his own initiative or at the proposal of parliament or government. Draft amendments and addenda to the Constitution shall not be put to a republican referendum if the president decides to submit them for consideration by parliament. In this case, parliament shall adopt a decision according to the procedure established by the Constitution.

2.   The unitary character, territorial integrity and form of government of the republic which are established by the Constitution may not be changed.

Article 92

1.   Constitutional laws must be adopted within one year of the Constitution coming into force. If laws which the Constitution cites as constitutional or acts carrying the same force were adopted prior to it [the Constitution] coming into force, they shall be brought into line with the Constitution and regarded as constitutional laws of the Republic of Kazakhstan.

2.   Other laws cited in the Constitution must be adopted according to the procedures and within the time-frame determined by parliament, but no later than two years after the Constitution comes into force.

3.   Decrees which the president of the republic issues within a period when he is exercising additional powers in accordance with the Law on Temporary Delegation of Additional Powers to the President of the Republic of Kazakhstan and Heads of Local Administrations of the Republic of Kazakhstan issued on 10 December 1993, and which carry the force of law, may be amended, supplemented or revoked only according to the procedures specified for amending, supplementing or revoking laws of the republic. Decrees which the president of the republic issues within a period when he is exercising additional powers on matters specified by Clauses 12-15, 18 and 20 of Article 64 of the Constitution of the Republic of Kazakhstan, which was adopted on 28 January 1993, shall not be subject to approval by the parliament of the republic.

4.   The legislation of the Republic of Kazakhstan which is in force at the time the constitution comes into force shall apply where it does not contravene the Constitution and must be brought into line with it within two years of the adoption of the Constitution.

Article 93

With the aim of fulfilling Article 7 of the Constitution, the government and the local representative and executive bodies are required to create all the necessary organisational, material and technical conditions for all citizens of the Republic of Kazakhstan to acquire a fluent command of the state language free of charge, in accordance with a special law.

Article 94
1. The President of the Republic of Kazakhstan, who has been elected in accordance with the legislation of the Republic of Kazakhstan which is in force at the time the Constitution takes effect, shall assume those powers of President of the Republic of Kazakhstan which the constitution establishes and exercise these for the period established by the decision which was adopted at the republican referendum on 29 April 1995.
2. The Vice-President of the Republic of Kazakhstan, who has been elected in accordance with the legislation of the Republic of Kazakhstan in force at the time the Constitution takes effect, shall retain his powers until the term for which he was elected expires.

Article 95
One-half of the deputies of the Senate in its first convocation shall be elected for a four-year term and the other half for a two-year term, according to the procedures established by a constitutional law.

Article 96
On the day that the Constitution takes effect, the Cabinet of Ministers of the Republic of Kazakhstan shall assume the rights, obligations and responsibilities of the government of the Republic of Kazakhstan.

Article 97
1. The first composition of the Constitutional Council of the Republic of Kazakhstan shall be formed in the following manner: the president of the republic, the Chairman of the parliamentary Senate and the Chairman of the parliamentary Majlis shall each appoint one member of the Constitutional Council for a three-year term and one member of the Constitutional Council for a six-year term. The chairman of the Constitutional Council shall be appointed by the president of the republic for a six-year term.

Article 98
1. The justice and investigatory authorities specified by this Constitution shall be formed according to the procedures and within the time-frame specified by the corresponding laws. Until they are formed, the existing justice and investigatory authorities shall retain their authorities.
2. Judges of the Supreme Court, the Supreme Court of Arbitration and the local courts of the Republic of Kazakhstan shall retain their authority until the courts specified by the Constitution have been formed. Vacant posts of judges shall be filled according to the procedure established by the Constitution.

Kyrghyzstan

Chronology

1989

September 24: The Supreme Soviet adopts a law making Kirghiz the state language. Russian is retained as the official language.

1990

February 22: Following violent unrest in Dushanbe, the capital of Tadjikistan, due to fears about Armenian refugees fleeing there, similar demonstrations broke out in Kyrghyzstan. In order to ease the tension, the Presidium of the Supreme Soviet issues a decree prescribing legal penalties for making written or verbal statements containing "a threat to public order or calls for pogroms".

February 25: Elections of local Soviets and of the Supreme Soviet are held.

April 10: The newly elected Supreme Soviet elects Absamat Masaliyev, the first secretary of the Communist Party (CP), to the post of Chairman.

June 4: The Presidium of the Supreme Soviet declares a state of emergency because of ethnic violence between Kirghiz and Uzbeks.

July: The clashes between Kirghiz and Uzbeks continue. Most serious incidents occur in Uzgen, where the Uzbek population is subjected to a pogrom by gangs of Kirghiz.

October 28: After several rounds the Supreme Soviet elects from a field of six candidates a new executive President, Aksar Akayev, the President of the Academy of Sciences, from a field of six candidates.

December 13: The name "Republic of Kyrghyzstan" is proclaimed by the Supreme Soviet.

1991

January 22: The Supreme Soviet replaces the Council of Ministers with a Cabinet attached to the President. Nasirdin Isanov is elected as head of the Cabinet.

March 17: Kyrghyzstan holds the all-union referendum on the preservation of the Soviet Union. 94.6% of the population vote for the preservation of the Soviet Union and 4.0% vote against. The turnout is 92.9%.

April 23: President Mikhail Gorbachev signs, with nine of the fifteen union republics including Kyrghyzstan, a pact aimed at achieving stable relations between the central government and governments of the republics. It sets out a timetable for major political changes, starting with the signing of the new Union Treaty. No longer than six months after signature of the Treaty a new Union constitution will be promulgated, followed by elections to the Congress of People's Deputies.

April 6: The plenum of the CP central committee elects Dzhumgalbek Aman-bayev as first secretary. He replaces Absamat Masaliyev.

August 19: Attempted *coup d'état* in Moscow.

August 28: The Supreme Council declares the country independent. President Akayev leaves the Communist Party of the Soviet Union (CPSU), and resigns from the Kirghiz CP politburo and secretariat. Party property is nationalised and funds frozen.

August 30: The CP's activities are suspended for six months.

October 12: In the first popular Kirghiz presidential elections, the sole candidate, Aksar Akayev is elected with 95.3 % of vote for a five-year term, limited to two consecutive terms. Turnout is estimated at 90 %.

November 29: President Akayev replaces Prime Minister Nasirdin Isanov, who died in a car accident.

December 8: Belarus, the Russian Federative Republic and Ukraine sign the Minsk agreement, establishing a Commonwealth of Independent States (CIS).

December 12: Kyrghyzstan signs the Alma Ata Agreement, thus joining the CIS.

December 21: The CIS formally replaces the Soviet Union, grouping eleven republics with the exception of Georgia. The Russian Federative Republic takes over many of the former Union functions, including its seat in the UN Security Council.

1992

June 10: Kyrghyzstan signs a friendship treaty with Russia.

June 22: A constituent congress of the Communist Party of Kyrghyzstan is held, chaired by the dismissed former first secretary Absamat Masaliyev.

December 8: After having failed to win parliamentary support for a draft version of the Constitution in the summer, Akayev accepts a re-draft of the Constitution with amendments shifting the balance of power away from the President. The Constitution describes the President as head of the state and the

Prime Minister as head of the executive. Deputies vote to rename the Supreme Soviet the *Uluk Kenesh.*

1993

April 3: Several centrist parties announce that they agree to form a bloc for the sake of political stability because strong government and state regulation of a market economy is demanded.

May 5: The first Constitution is formally adopted approved by the Parliament. The Constitution transfers the responsibilities of the head of government to the Prime Minister and the current terms of office of the President, Vice-President and members of the Parliament will expire in 1995.

May 10: A new currency, the *som,* is adopted and replaces the rouble.

June 2: Delegates of the Democratic Movement of Kyrghyzstan vote to transform the organisation, founded in 1991 to co-ordinate the activities of a range of democratic groups, into a political party.

July 7: The Social Democratic Party holds its constituent conference in Bishkek. Akayev is one of the Party's principal supporters.

December 13: President Akayev dismisses the government because Prime Minister Chyngyshev fails to win a vote of confidence in the *Uluk Kenesh.*

December 17: The *Uluk Kenesh* approves a new government and appoints Apas Jumagulov as the new Prime Minister, after his predecessor's failure to win a vote of confidence.

1994

January 30: A reform programme established by President Akayev in a confidence referendum is approved by 96.2% from a turnout of 95.9%. The vote strengthens his position *vis-à-vis* the conservative-dominated parliament.

May 28: Sheraly Sadykov is elected as Chairman of the Communist Party of Kyrghyzstan.

June 15: President Akayev issues a decree ordering the recognition of Russian as an official language. The decree aims at halting the migration of Russian-speakers from Kyrghyzstan, applies to all districts with a predominantly Russian population, and to some sectors of the national economy, including science, technology and public health. Akayev also requests a delay in the changeover to Kirghiz as an official language to secure a fair representation of the Russian-speaking population in the state administration.

September 2: 143 pro-reform deputies in the 350-seat *Uluk Kenesh* announce a boycott of the Kenesh on its next scheduled session on 27 September, thereby rendering it inquorate and thus effectively suspended. They declare that the Kenesh lost its prestige and call for elections in January 1995 as well as for the establishment of a strong presidency.

September 5: The pro-reform President Aksar Akayev decrees that legislative elections scheduled for February or March 1995 will be held before the end of 1994. He also announces that a referendum will be held on 22 October on a package of constitutional amendments enhancing the powers of the presidency and abolishing the Kenesh in favour of a bicameral parliament with around 100 full-time deputies. Simultaneously, Akayev reveals a package designed to reform the social security and tax systems. The pro-reform Government of Apas Jumagulov resigns claiming that the government is paralysed because of political games in the parliament.

September 13: An attempt to hold an emergency session fails when conservatives muster only 125 deputies and the Kenesh is ruled inquorate.

October 22: A referendum approves the proposed constitutional amendments, abolishing the 350-member *Uluk Kenesh,* in favour of a new, smaller, bicameral parliament. Voters also favour that all future constitutional changes shall be sanctioned by referendum.

October 27: Akayev announces the formation of a constitutional commission to prepare the amendments approved by the referendum. The work on the preparation of the amendments will be completed by the end of December and submitted to the Constitutional Court by 1 March 1995.

1995

February 5 and 19: First general elections are held since independence. Results: 82 seats of the 105 are filled, sufficient to achieve a quorum. The Communist Party won 2 seats, the Nationalist Ata Meken Party, 4 seats; the Social Democratic Party, 3 seats; the multi-ethnic Kyrghyzstan Unity won 2 seats, the other party affiliations have not been disclosed. Turnout 61.55%. According to the ITAR-TASS press agency, 78 out of the 105 seats of the parliament are filled. Of the elected deputies, 64 are ethnic Kirghiz, 5 are Russians, 7 are Uzbeks, one is German and one is Karachay.

April 5: Apas Jumagulov is reappointed as Prime Minister.

June 15: A new Agrarian Labour Party is founded.

September 6: The *Adilet* (justice) Civic Movement Party is launched.

September 20: The Legislative Assembly votes against a proposal to hold a referendum on the extension of the tenure of the President. Such a referendum would be unconstitutional, whereas the President can only be elected through a direct alternative election.

December 24: Presidential election is held. President Aksar Akayev is reelected for a second five-year term by 71.6%. (Absamat Masaliyev 24.4%, Medetkan Sherimkulov 1.7%) Turnout: 82%.

1996

February 10: A referendum endorses a constitutional amendment granting the President extensive new powers, including the right to appoint all senior officials with the exception of the Prime Minister whose nomination will require parliamentary approval.

February 26: President Akayev accepts the resignation of the government of the Prime Minister Apas Jumagulov, clearing the way for a new government appointed directly by the President.

March 1: Apas Jumagulov is confirmed as Prime Minister by the *Zhogorku Kenesh.*

March 4: President Akayev appoints Jumagulov's new Cabinet.

March 11: Based on a decree of June 1994 by President Akayev, the Kenesh agrees to award the Russian language official status, allowing its use in workplaces and in Russian-majority areas. Kirghiz remains the official state language.

November 25: President Akayev signs a decree allowing the private ownership of land, effective on 1 January.

Constitution of the Kyrghyz Republic[1, 2]

Adopted by the Soviet Supreme of the Kyrghyz Republic, 5 May 1993

Preamble

We, people of the Kyrghyz Republic,
in order to secure national revival of the Kyrghyz, the defence and development of interests of representatives of all nationalities who form together with the Kyrghyz the people of Kyrghyzstan, guided by the ancestors' precepts to live in unity, peace and concord;
to confirm our adherence to human rights and freedoms and the idea of national statehood;
full of determination to develop the economy, political and legal institutions, culture in order to ensure worthy standards of living for everybody;
announcing our adherence to universal human principles, and moral values of national traditions;
full of desire to establish ourselves among the people of the world as a free and democratic civil society;
in our role as authorised representatives do enact the present Constitution.

Chapter 1 – The Kyrghyz Republic

Section 1 – General principles

Article 1
1. The Kyrghyz Republic (Kyrghyzstan) shall be a sovereign unitary democratic republic created on the basis of a legal secular state.
2. Sovereignty of the Kyrghyz Republic shall not be limited and shall extend throughout its territory.
3. People of the Kyrghyz Republic shall bear sovereignty and shall be the only source of state power in the Kyrghyz Republic.
4. People of the Kyrghyz Republic shall exercise their power directly and through the system of state bodies on the basis of this Constitution and laws of the Kyrghyz Republic.

---

1. European Commission for Democracy through Law
2. Translation provided by the Kyrghyz authorities.

Only the Jogorku Kenesh and the President of the Kyrghyz Republic elected by the people of Kyrghyzstan shall have the right to act on behalf of the people of Kyrghyzstan.

5.   Laws and other issues of State life, in order to reveal the will of the people, may be put to a referendum. The basis and procedure of holding a referendum shall be established by the Constitutional Act.

6.   Citizens of the Kyrghyz Republic shall elect the President, Deputies of the Jogorku Kenesh and their representatives to bodies of local self-government. Elections shall be free and shall be held on the basis of universal equal and direct suffrage by secret ballot. To participate in the election a citizen must have attained the age of 18.

Article 2

1.   The State and its bodies shall serve the whole society, and not a particular group.

2.   No group of people, no organisation, nor any person shall have the right to assume power in the State. The usurpation of state power shall be a felony.

Article 3

1.   The territory of the Kyrghyz Republic within its present boundaries shall be inviolable and indivisible.

2.   The territory of the Kyrghyz Republic shall be divided into administrative territorial units established by law for the purposes of the organisation of state government.

Article 4

1.   In the Kyrghyz Republic there may be state and private property.
The Kyrghyz Republic shall guarantee the diversity of property tires and their equal protection by law.

2.   In the Kyrghyz Republic the land, its subsoil, water, air space, fauna and flora and all natural resources shall be the property of the State.

3.   Plots of land, in the procedure and size provided by law of the Kyrghyz Republic may be given to citizens and their associations for private possession. The purchase and sale of land shall not be allowed.

4.   The Kyrghyz Republic shall defend the right of its citizens and legal entities to own property, and shall defend citizens' and governmental property located on the territories of other states.

Article 5

1.   The official language of the Kyrghyz Republic shall be the Kyrghyz language.

2.   The Kyrghyz Republic shall guarantee preservation, equal and free development and functioning of the Russian language and all other languages which are used by the population of the Republic.

3.   Infringement of the citizens' rights on the ground of absence of knowledge and command of the official language shall not be allowed.

Article 6

The state symbols of the Kyrghyz Republic are the state flag, emblem and anthem. The capital of the Kyrghyz Republic is the city of Bishkek.

Section 2 – The structure and activity of the State

Article 7
1. State power in the Kyrghyz Republic shall be based on the following principles:
    –   the division of power into legislative, executive and judicial branches;
    –   nation-wide elections of the head of the State – the President of the Kyrghyz Republic, who shall be the guarantor of the stability of the Constitution and unity of the State;
    –   the division between national power and local self-government.
2. State power in the Kyrghyz Republic shall be vested in and exercised by:
    the legislative power, by the Jogorku Kenesh;
    the executive power, by the Government and local state administration;
    The Judicial power, by the Constitutional Court, the Supreme Court, the Supreme Economic Court, courts and judges of the system of justice.
Bodies of legislative, executive and judicial power shall function independently and in co-operation with each other. They shall have no right to exceed their powers established by the Constitution of the Kyrghyz Republic.

Article 8
1. Political parties, trade unions and other public associations may be organised in the Kyrghyz Republic on the bases of free will and unity of interests. The State shall guarantee the rights and lawful interests of public associations.
2. Political parties may participate in state affairs only in the following forms:
    –   to nominate their candidates for the election to the Jogorku Kenesh, state posts and to bodies of local self-government;
    –   to form factions in representative bodies.
3. In the subject of religion all sects shall be separated from the State.
4. The following shall not be allowed in the Kyrghyz Republic:
    –   the amalgamation of state and party institutions, as well as subordination of State activity to party programmes and decisions;
    –   the formation and activity of party organisations in state institutions and establishments. Officials shall have the right to carry out their party activities outside their working hours;
    –   membership and activity in support of any political party by military men, officials in the organs of internal affairs, national security, justice, procuracy and courts;
    –   organisation of political parties on religious grounds.
Religious organisations shall not pursue political aims and tasks;
    –   interference by members of religious organisations and sects with the activity of state bodies;
    –   the activity of political parties of foreign countries.

Article 9
1. The Kyrghyz Republic shall not pursue the policy of expansion, aggression and claim to territorial extent performed by means of military force.

It shall reject any kind of militarisation of national life, subordination of the government or its activity for the purposes of war. The military forces of Kyrghyzstan shall be organised in accordance with the principles of self-defence and defensive sufficiency.

2.   The right to go to war shall not be acknowledged except in cases of aggression against Kyrghyzstan or other countries coming under the obligations to collective defence. The permission in each case when a military unit crosses over the borders of Kyrghyzstan must be received in the form of a decision of the Jogorku Kenesh approved by not less than two-thirds of the total number of Deputies.

3.   The use of military force for the solution of internal political issues shall be prohibited. Military personnel may be called upon in case of natural disasters and in other similar cases prescribed directly by law.

4.   The Kyrghyz Republic shall seek universal and just peace, mutual co-operation, solution of global and regional problems by peaceful measures, and shall observe universally recognised principles of international law.

Actions aimed at disturbing the peaceful communal life of the people, propaganda and encouragement of ethnic clashes shall be unconstitutional.

Article 10

1.   A state of emergency in Kyrghyzstan may be imposed only in case of natural disaster, direct threat to the constitutional structure, breach of public order accompanied by violence and menace to human life, as well as under the circumstances and for limited periods, as provided for in the Constitutional Law.

2.   A state of emergency throughout the territory of the Kyrghyz Republic may be imposed only by the Jogorku Kenesh. A state of emergency may be imposed by the President in limited locations under circumstances requiring immediate action; the President shall inform the Jogorku Kenesh the same day. The Jogorku Kenesh shall confirm the act of the President within not more than three days.

If such a confirmation has not been made within the indicated time, the state of emergency shall be annulled.

3.   Martial law in the Kyrghyz Republic may be introduced by the Jogorku Kenesh only in case of aggression against the Kyrghyz Republic.

4.   A recess of the session of the Jogorku Kenesh shall not be allowed during a state of emergency and martial law. In those cases when the Jogorku Kenesh is not in session and a state of emergency has been imposed by the President, the Jogorku Kenesh shall call a special session not later than the day following the introductions of the state of emergency.

5.   Referendums, elections to state bodies as well as any changes in the structure, functions and power of state bodies established by the Constitution shall not be allowed during a state of emergency and martial law.

Article 11

1.   The state budget of the Kyrghyz Republic shall consist of the republican budget and local budgets, comprising all expenditures and revenues of the state. The republican budget shall be approved by the Jogorku Kenesh upon presentation by the Government.

2.   Revenue in the republican budget shall be derived from taxes established by law, other liabilities, income from state property and other incomes.

A single system of taxation shall function in the territory of the Kyrghyz Republic. The right to impose taxes shall belong to the Jogorku Kenesh of the Kyrghyz Republic.

3.   The Jogorku Kenesh shall have the right to establish extra-budgetary dedicated financial funds. The sources of income for these extra-budgetary funds may be attracted assets.

4.   The report on the execution of the republican budget and extra-budgetary funds shall be approval by the Jogorku Kenesh.

Article 12

1.   The Constitution shall have supreme legal force and direct effect in the Kyrghyz Republic.

2.   Laws and other normative acts shall be adopted on the basis of the Constitution.

3.   International treaties and other norms of international law which have been ratified by the Kyrghyz Republic shall be a component and directly applicable part of legislation of the Kyrghyz Republic.

Chapter 2 – Citizens

Section 1 – Citizenship

Article 13

1.   The belonging of a citizen to the Kyrghyz Republic and his status shall be determined by citizenship.

A citizen of the Kyrghyz Republic shall observe the Constitution and laws of the republic, and shall respect the rights, freedoms, honour and dignity of other people.

2.   Citizenship of other countries shall not be recognised for citizens of the Kyrghyz Republic.

3.   No citizen of the Kyrghyz Republic shall be deprived of his citizenship or the right to change his citizenship.

4.   The Kyrghyz Republic shall guarantee defence and protection of its citizens when outside its territory.

Article 14

1.   Every citizen of the Kyrghyz Republic by virtue of his citizenship shall enjoy rights and perform obligations.

2.   Foreign citizens and stateless persons when in Kyrghyzstan shall enjoy the rights and freedoms of citizens and perform duties on the bases, under the terms and in the procedure prescribed by law, of international treaties and agreements.

Section 2 – The rights and freedoms of the individual

Article 15

1.   The dignity of an individual in the Kyrghyz Republic shall be absolute and inviolable.

2.   The basic human rights and freedoms shall belong to every person from birth. They shall be recognised as absolute, inalienable and protected by law and the courts from infringement by any other person.

3.   All persons in the Kyrghyz Republic are equal before law and the court. No person shall be subject to any kind of discrimination, violation of his rights and freedoms on the ground of ethnic origin, sex, race, nationality, language, religion, political and religious convictions, as well as under other conditions and circumstances of private or social nature.

4.   Human rights and freedoms are valid in the Kyrghyz Republic. Such rights shall determine the meaning, content and application of the laws, shall be respected by the legislative and executive branches and local self-government, and shall be guaranteed by the judicial system.

5.   In the Kyrghyz Republic, the State shall encourage folk customs and traditions which do not contravene the Constitution and human rights and freedoms.

Article 16

1.   In the Kyrghyz Republic the basic human rights and freedoms shall be recognised and guaranteed in accordance with universally accepted norms and principles of international law, international treaties and agreements on the issues of human rights which have been ratified by the Kyrghyz Republic.

2.   Every person in the Kyrghyz Republic shall enjoy the right:
   –   to life, physical and moral immunity;
   –   to personal freedom and security;
   –   to freedom of personal development;
   –   to freedom of conscience, spirit and worship;
   –   to free expression and dissemination of his thoughts, ideas, opinions, freedom of literary, artistic, scientific and technical creative work, freedom of the press, transmission and dissemination of information;
   –   to freedom of movement and freedom to choose his place of residence throughout the territory of Kyrghyzstan, and the right to travel abroad and return home;
   –   to freedom of assembly;
   –   to associate peacefully without weapons, to hold meetings and demonstrations;
   –   to inviolability of the home;
   –   to dignity, freedom of private life, personal and family secrecy;
   –   to secrecy of post, telephone and telegraphic communications;
   –   to have property, to possess, use and administer it on his own account;
   –   to economic freedom, free use of his abilities and property for any type of economic activity;
   –   to freedom of labour, and free choice of his type of activity and occupation.

The enumeration of rights and freedoms in the Constitution shall not be interpreted as negating or infringing upon other universally recognised human rights and freedoms.

Article 17

1.   In the Kyrghyz Republic no laws shall be enacted which abolish or infringe on human rights and freedoms.
2.   Restrictions on the exercise of rights and freedoms shall be allowed by the Constitution and laws of the Kyrghyz Republic only for the purposes of guaranteeing rights and freedoms of other persons providing public safety and constitutional order. In such cases, the essence of the constitutional rights and freedoms shall not be effected.

Article 18

1.   Limitations of physical and moral inviolability shall be allowed only on the basis of law by the decision of a court as punishment for a crime committed. No one may be tortured, subjected to ill-treatment or inhuman degrading punishment.
2.   Medical, biological, and physiological experiments on people shall be prohibited without a voluntary agreement properly expressed and confirmed by the person participating in the experiment.
3.   No one may be subjected to arrest or detention except on the basis of law. Any actions aimed at imposing responsibility for a crime on a person before the sentence has been passed by the court shall not be allowed, and shall be grounds for material and moral compensation to the victim by the court.
4.   Capital punishment may be imposed only in exceptional cases under the sentence of a court. Any person sentenced to capital punishment shall have the right to appeal for pardon.

Article 19

1.   Private property in the Kyrghyz Republic shall be recognised and guaranteed as an inalienable human right, as a natural source of his welfare, business and creative activity, and as a guarantor of his economic and personal independence.
2.   Property shall be inviolable. No person can be deprived of his property, and its deprivation against the will of its owner shall be allowed only by the decision of a court.
3.   In the Kyrghyz Republic the right of inheritance shall be guaranteed and protected by law.

Article 20

The Kyrghyz Republic may grant political asylum to foreign citizens and stateless persons in response to human rights violations.

Section 3 – The rights and duties of a citizen

Article 21

1.   Citizens of the Kyrghyz Republic, and their organisations, shall be allowed to engage in any action or activity, except those prohibited or restricted by the present Constitution and laws of the Kyrghyz Republic.

2.   The enjoyment of the rights and freedoms by a citizen of the Kyrghyz Republic shall be inseparable from his duties as are necessary for the security of private and national interests.

Article 22
Laws of the Kyrghyz Republic concerning the rights and freedoms of citizens shall be equally applied to all citizens and shall not bestow on anyone privileges and preferences, except those provided by the Constitution and laws for the social protection of citizens.

Article 23
Citizens of the Kyrghyz Republic shall participate in governing both directly and through their representatives, in the discussion and adoption of laws, decisions of republican and local significance, and they shall have equal access to governmental services.

Article 24
Citizens of the Kyrghyz Republic shall have the right and duty to defend the Motherland. Citizens shall perform military service within the limits and in the forms established by law.

Article 25
Citizens of the Kyrghyz Republic are obliged to pay taxes and fees in accordance with legislation.

Article 26
1.   The family shall be the fundamental unit of society; family, fatherhood, motherhood and childhood shall be the subject of concern for the whole society and subject to preferable protection by law; childcare and upbringing shall be the natural right and civic duty of the parents. Children are obliged to render help to their parents.
2.   The government shall provide material assistance, upbringing and education for orphans and children deprived of parental support.
3.   Respect for old people and support for relatives shall be a sacred tradition of the people of Kyrghyzstan.

Article 27
1.   In the Kyrghyz Republic social maintenance at the expense of the government shall be guaranteed in old age, in sickness and in the event of complete or partial disability or loss of the breadwinner.
2.   Pensions and social maintenance in accordance with economic resources of the society shall provide a standard of living not below the minimum wage established by law.
3.   Voluntary social insurance and the establishment of additional forms of security and charity shall be encouraged.

Article 28
1.   Citizens of the Kyrghyz Republic shall have the right to protection of labour in all its forms and ways, including the right to working conditions

which comply with norms of security and hygiene, as well as the right to social protection against unemployment.

2.   The government shall provide for professional training and improvement of professional skills of citizens, and shall encourage and promote international agreements and international organisations which have the aim of consolidating and securing the right of work.

3.   The forced labour of citizens shall be prohibited, except in cases of war, natural disaster, epidemic, or in other extraordinary circumstances, as well as in the execution of punishment upon sentence of the court.

Article 29

Citizens of the Kyrghyz Republic working under labour agreement (contract) shall have the right to fair remuneration not below the minimum wage established by the government.

Article 30

Citizens of the Kyrghyz Republic shall have the right to strike.
The procedure and conditions for holding strikes shall be prescribed by law.

Article 31

1.   Citizens of the Kyrghyz Republic shall have the right to rest.

2.   The maximum duration of working hours, minimum weekly rest and annual paid leave as well as other terms of exercise of the right to rest shall be prescribed by law.

Article 32

1.   Every citizen of the Kyrghyz Republic shall have the right to education.

2.   General secondary education shall be compulsory and free of charge. Every person shall have the right to obtain it at national educational institutions.
Every citizen shall have the right to obtain free education at national educational institutions.

3.   The State shall provide for every person, in accordance with individual aptitude, accessibility to vocational, special secondary and higher education.

4.   Paid education for citizens at national and other educational institutions shall be allowed on the basis and in the procedure established by legislation.

5.   The State shall exercise control over the activity of educational institutions.

Article 33

Citizens of the Kyrghyz Republic shall have the right to housing.
The State promotes the fulfilment of the right to housing by giving and selling state-owned housing, and by encouragement of individual house building.

Article 34

1.   Citizens of the Kyrghyz Republic shall enjoy the right to protection of health, to benefit freely from the network of state public health institutions.

2. Paid medical service shall be allowed on the basis and in the procedure established by law.

Article 35
1. Citizens of the Kyrghyz Republic shall have the right to a healthy safe environment and to compensation for the damage caused to their health and property by the activity in the sphere of environmental exploitation.
2. The protection of the environment, natural resources and historical monuments shall be the sacred duty of every citizen.

Article 36
1. Culture, art, literature, science and the mass media shall be free.
2. The State shall protect historical monuments, care and provide the necessary conditions for the development of literature, art, science, the mass media and sports.
3. Citizens shall have the right to enjoy cultural benefits, to study art and science.

Article 37
The social activity of the State shall not be substituted by state care limiting economic freedom and activity or the opportunity of a citizen to achieve economic welfare for himself and his family.

Article 38
1. It is the duty of the state and all its bodies and officials to provide for full, absolute and immediate protection of the rights and freedoms of citizens, to prevent the infringement of rights in this sphere and to restore any provision which is violated.
2. The Kyrghyz Republic shall guarantee judicial defence of all the rights and freedoms of citizens established by the Constitution and laws.

Article 39
1. A citizen charged with an offence shall be presumed innocent until found guilty by sentence of the court.
2. The State shall guarantee everyone defence from arbitrary and unlawful interference with his private and family life, infringement of one's honour and dignity, or breach of secrecy of correspondence and telephone conversations.
3. No one shall have the right to enter a dwelling except in cases when it is necessary to conduct a sanctioned search or seizure of property, to secure public order, to arrest a criminal, or to save the life, health or property of a person.

Article 40
Every citizen in the Kyrghyz Republic shall be guaranteed effective legal assistance and defence of the rights and freedoms provided for by the Constitution.

Article 41
The publication of laws and other normative legal acts concerning the rights, freedoms and duties of an individual and a citizen shall be a compulsory condition for their application.

Chapter 3 – President

Article 42
1.   The President of the Kyrghyz Republic shall be the head of State and shall represent the Kyrghyz Republic inside the country and in foreign relations.
2.   The President of the Kyrghyz Republic shall secure the unity of the state and stability of the Constitutional order, he shall act in the capacity of the guarantor of the Constitution and laws, the rights and freedoms of citizens of the Kyrghyz Republic and shall provide for the co-ordinated functioning and interaction of national bodies.

Section 1 – The election of the President

Article 43
1.   The President of the Kyrghyz Republic shall be elected for a term of five years.
2.   The same person shall not be elected President for more than two terms running.
3.   A citizen of the Kyrghyz Republic may be elected President of the Kyrghyz Republic if he is not younger than 35 years of age and is not older than 65 years of age, who has command of the official language and has been a resident of the republic for not less than 15 years before the nomination of his candidature to the office of President.
4.   The President of the Kyrghyz Republic shall not be a Deputy of the Jogorku Kenesh, shall not hold other posts and engage in free enterprise activity.
5.   The President of the Kyrghyz Republic shall suspend his activity in political parties and organisations during the term of office till the beginning of a new election for President of the Kyrghyz Republic.

Article 44
1.   A new election for the office of President of the Kyrghyz Republic shall be held two months before the date on which the powers of the President of the Kyrghyz Republic expire.
2.   The President of the Kyrghyz Republic shall be elected by citizens of the Kyrghyz Republic by a majority of actual votes cast; elections shall be held on the basis of universal equal and direct suffrage by secret ballot.
3.   The number of candidates for the office of President of the Kyrghyz Republic shall not be limited. Any person who has registered and has obtained not less than 50 000 voter signatures may be a candidate for President of the Kyrghyz Republic.
4.   The election of the President shall be considered valid if more than 50% of all votes in the republic have taken part in the election.
In the first ballot, a candidate shall be considered elected to the office of President if he has obtained more than half of those votes cast in the election.

If none of the candidates obtains more than half of the votes cast in the first ballot, only the two candidates who have obtained the largest number of votes shall be appear on the second ballot.

A candidate who obtains more than half of the votes cast in the second ballot shall be considered elected if not less than 50% of all voters have taken part in the second ballot.

Article 45

1.   The results of the elections for President of the Kyrghyz Republic shall be confirmed by the Constitutional Court of the Kyrghyz Republic not later than seven days after the date of the election.

2.   After the Chairman of the Supreme Court of the Kyrghyz Republic announces the results of voting, the President shall take the oath of office within 30 days.

3.   Upon entry into office, the President of the Kyrghyz Republic shall take an oath before the people of Kyrghyzstan:

    "I,...., taking on the obligations of President of the Kyrghyz Republic, before my people and the sacred Motherland of Ala-Too do swear:

    to observe and protect the Constitution and laws of the Kyrghyz Republic; to guard the sovereignty and independence of the Kyrghyz State; to respect and guarantee the rights and freedoms of all citizens of the Kyrghyz Republic; to perform faithfully the high duties of the President of the Kyrghyz Republic entrusted to me by the confidence of all the people!".

4.   The term of the Presidential mandate shall become effective from the moment of taking the oath of office. The powers of the President shall terminate upon the moment a newly-elected President enters office.

Section 2 – The powers of the President

Article 46

1.   The President of the Kyrghyz Republic shall:

    i.   determine the structure of the Government of the Kyrghyz Republic and submit it to confirmation by the Jogorku Kenesh;

    ii.   appoint the Prime Minister of the Kyrghyz Republic with the consent of the Jogorku Kenesh;

    iii.   appoint members of the Government upon presentation by the Prime Minister and with the consent of the Jogorku Kenesh;

    iv.   relieve of their posts members of the Government and heads of administrative departments of the Kyrghyz Republic;

    v.   accept the resignation of the Government; on his own initiative with the consent of the Jogorku Kenesh shall take a decision on withdrawal of the powers of the Government before the date the powers of the Government expire.

2.   The President of the Kyrghyz Republic shall:

    i.   appoint with the consent of the Jogorku Kenesh the Procurator-General of the Kyrghyz Republic;

    ii.   appoint with the consent of the Jogorku Kenesh the Chairman of the Board of the National Bank of the Kyrghyz Republic;

iii.   appoint upon presentation by the Prime Minister and with the consent of the corresponding local Keneshs heads of state administrations of oblasts and the city of Bishkek;

iv.   approve heads of regional and city state administrations nominated by the Prime Minister with the consent of local Keneshs upon presentation by the heads of state administrations of regions and the city of Bishkek;

v.   present to the Jogorku Kenesh the candidatures for the office of Chairman of the Constitutional Court of the Kyrghyz Republic, Deputy Chairman and seven judges of the Constitutional Court of the Kyrghyz Republic;

vi.   present to the Jogorku Kenesh the candidatures for the offices of Chairman of the Supreme Court, the Supreme Economic Court of the Kyrghyz Republic, Deputy Chairmen and judges of the Supreme Court and the Supreme Economic Court of the Kyrghyz Republic;

vii.   appoint with the consent of the Jogorku Kenesh Chairmen, deputy Chairmen and judges of regional courts, the court of the city of Bishkek, district and city courts, regional economic courts as well as military tribunals of the Kyrghyz Republic and remove them from office in the events prescribed by the Constitution and laws;

viii.   appoint with the consent of the Jogorku Kenesh heads of diplomatic missions of the Kyrghyz Republic in foreign countries and to international organisations;

ix.   receive the Letters of Credence and Recall of diplomatic missions of foreign countries and representatives of international organisations accredited to him;

x.   confer high military ranks, diplomatic ranks, class ranks and other special titles.

3.   The President of the Kyrghyz Republic shall:

i.   decide the matters concerning granting citizenship of the Kyrghyz Republic;

ii.   award honorary ranks and state bonuses of the Kyrghyz Republic.

4.   The President of the Kyrghyz Republic shall:

i.   on his own initiative submit bills to the Jogorku Kenesh;

ii.   sign within a two-week term laws after their adoption by the Jogorku Kenesh or refer them to the Jogorku Kenesh with his remarks for a second consideration. If the Jogorku Kenesh confirms the previously taken decision by a majority of two-thirds from the total number of Deputies, the President of the Kyrghyz Republic shall sign the law; if the President does not express his attitude to the law within a two-week term and does not demand its second consideration, he shall be obliged to sign that law;

iii.   address the people with an annual report on the situation in the Republic announced in the Jogorku Kenesh;

iv.   conduct international negotiations and sign international treaties of the Kyrghyz Republic; submit them for ratification to the Jogorku Kenesh;

v.   have the right to protest to the Constitutional Court of the Kyrghyz Republic against a law adopted by the Jogorku Kenesh or an international treaty ratified by the Jogorku Kenesh;

vi.   abolish or suspend the effect of acts of the Government of the Kyrghyz Republic, Ministries, state committees and administrative departments of the Kyrghyz Republic, heads of local state administration in case they contravene the Constitution and Laws of the Kyrghyz Republic.

5. The President of the Kyrghyz Republic shall have the right to:
    i.   convene an extraordinary session of the Uluk Kenesh;
    ii.   submit issues of state life to a public referendum;
    iii.   dissolve the Jogorku Kenesh before the date on which its powers
expire in accordance with the results of a public referendum and set up the
date of a new election to the Jogorku Kenesh.
6. The President of the Kyrghyz Republic shall notify a possibility of introduction of a state of emergency with the existence of grounds envisaged by
law and in case of necessity shall impose it in separate localities without preliminary announcement and immediately notify the Jogorku Kenesh.
7. The President of the Kyrghyz Republic shall declare universal or partial
mobilisation, declare a state of war in case of military aggression against the
Kyrghyz Republic and shall immediately submit this issue to the consideration
by the Jogorku Kenesh; he shall proclaim martial law in the interests of
defence of the country and security of the population and shall immediately
submit this issue to the consideration by the Jogorku Kenesh.

Article 47
The President of the Kyrghyz Republic shall be the Commander-in-Chief of
the armed forces, he shall appoint and replace the Commander-in-Chief of
the armed forces of the Kyrghyz Republic.

Article 48
1. The President of the Kyrghyz Republic shall issue within his powers on
the basis and for the implementation of the Constitution of the Kyrghyz
Republic decrees binding upon the whole territory of the country.
2. The President of the Kyrghyz Republic shall issue resolutions and instructions on separate matters referred to his competence.

Article 49
The President of the Kyrghyz Republic may delegate the execution of his
powers envisaged in subpoint 9 of point 2 and in subpoint 4 of point 4 of Article 46 to the Toroga of the Jogorku Kenesh.

Article 50
The President of the Kyrghyz Republic shall enjoy the right of integrity and
immunity.

Article 51
1. The powers of the President may be stopped as a result of his retirement
by a resignation sent to the Jogorku Kenesh, inability to discharge his powers
in the event of illness, in case of his death as well as in the event of removal
from office in the events envisaged in the present Constitution.
2. In case the President of the Kyrghyz Republic is unable to discharge his
powers on the account of illness, the Jogorku Kenesh shall on the basis of the
conclusion of an independent medical commission decide on the removal of
the President of the Kyrghyz Republic before the date on which the powers
of the President expire; a majority of not less than two-thirds of votes from

the total number of Deputies of the Jogorku Kenesh shall be required to remove the President.

Article 53
1. In case of inability of the President of the Kyrghyz Republic to exercise his powers for any reason they shall be delegated to the Toroga of the Jogorku Kenesh pending the election of a new President. In case the Toroga of the Jogorku Kenesh is unable to discharge the powers of the President, they shall be delegated to the Prime Minister.
2. The election of a new President of the Kyrghyz Republic in this case shall be held within three months.

Chapter 4 – The Jogorku Kenesh

Section 1 – The election of the Jogorku Kenesh

Article 54
1. The Jogorku Kenesh of the Kyrghyz Republic shall be the highest standing representative body. The legislative power and functions of control shall be vested in the Jogorku Kenesh.
2. The Jogorku Kenesh shall consist of 105 Deputies who shall be elected for a term of five years. The procedure of election of the Deputies shall be determined by the Constitutional act.

Article 55
1. Deputies of the Jogorku Kenesh shall be elected from electoral districts on the basis of universal, equal and direct suffrage by secret ballot.
2. A voter from every electoral district shall have one vote. Voters shall take part in the election directly and on equal grounds.

Article 56
1. A citizen of the Kyrghyz Republic may be elected a Deputy of the Jogorku Kenesh if he has attained the age of 25 and permanently resided in the Republic for not less than five years.
2. A Deputy of the Jogorku Kenesh shall be a representative of the people of Kyrghyzstan, shall be subordinate to the Constitution of the Kyrghyz Republic and his conscience.
3. A Deputy of the Jogorku Kenesh shall have the right to integrity and immunity. He may not be persecuted for his statements expressed in accordance with his activity of a Deputy and for the results of his voting in the Jogorku Kenesh. A Deputy shall not be detained or arrested, subject to search or individual examination except when he is caught in the act. Provisional commissions of the Jogorku Kenesh shall examine the validity of measures taken by the competent bodies and if these measures have not been taken by a court, the Jogorku Kenesh shall invalidate them. A Deputy may be prosecuted for criminal or administrative activity only with the consent of the Jogorku Kenesh.
4. A Deputy of the Jogorku Kenesh shall have no right to hold any posts in state service, judicial bodies or engage in business activity.

5.   A Deputy of the Jogorku Kenesh may be deprived of his mandate only in case of his resignation, commitment of a crime, confirmation of disability, or otherwise only by an international resolution of the Jogorku Kenesh.

Article 57
A Deputy of the Jogorku Kenesh shall have the right to address inquiries to bodies and officials of state administration, who are obliged to respond to the inquiry at the session of the Jogorku Kenesh.

Section 2 – The powers of the Jogorku Kenesh

Article 58
The following powers shall be vested in the Uluk Kenesh:
1.   to amend and change the Constitution of the Kyrghyz Republic in accordance with the procedure established by the Constitution;
2.   to adopt laws of the Kyrghyz Republic; to amend laws and to exercise control over their fulfilment;
3.   to make official interpretation of the adopted normative acts;
4.   to determine the guidelines of domestic and foreign policy;
5.   to approve the republican budget of the Kyrghyz Republic and the report on its execution;
6.   to determine the monetary system in the Kyrghyz Republic;
7.   to change the boundaries of the Kyrghyz Republic;
8.   to decide the matters concerning administrative territorial structure of the republic;
9.   to set up the date of election for President of the Kyrghyz Republic;
10.   to organise the Central Commission on election and referendums;
11.   upon presentation by the President of the Kyrghyz Republic to elect the Chairman of the Constitutional Court of the Kyrghyz Republic, Deputy Chairman and seven judges of the Constitutional Court of the Kyrghyz Republic;
12.   upon presentation by the President of the Kyrghyz Republic to elect the Chairman of the Supreme Court, the Chairman of the Supreme Economic Court of the Kyrghyz Republic, Deputy Chairmen and judges of the Supreme Court and the Supreme Economic Court of the Kyrghyz Republic;
13.   to determine the structure of the Government of the Kyrghyz Republic;
14.   to give consent to the appointment of the Prime Minister of the Kyrghyz Republic and the composition of the Government of the Kyrghyz Republic, the Procurator-General of the Kyrghyz Republic and the Chairman of the Board of the National Bank;
15.   to give consent to the appointment of heads of diplomatic missions of the Kyrghyz Republic to foreign countries and international organisations;
16.   to give consent to the dissolution of the Government before the date on which the powers of the Government expire;
17.   upon presentation by the Toroga of the Jogorku Kenesh to appoint the Chairman and Deputy Chairmen of the Supervisory Chamber of the Jogorku Kenesh;
18.   to ratify and denounce international treaties; to decide issues of war and peace;

19. to institute military ranks, diplomatic ranks, class ranks and other special titles of the Kyrghyz Republic;

20. to establish state awards and honorary titles of the Kyrghyz Republic;

21. to issue acts of amnesty;

22. to impose a state of emergency or to confirm and abolish the act of the President of the Kyrghyz Republic on this issue; the resolution of the Jogorku Kenesh approving the decision of the President to impose a state of emergency shall be adopted by a majority of not less than two-thirds from the total number of Deputies of the Jogorku Kenesh;

23. to proclaim martial law, announce a state of war and to issue a resolution concerning their declaration by the President of the Kyrghyz Republic;

24. to decide on the use of the contingent of armed forces of the republic when it is necessary to support peace and security in accordance with intergovernmental treaty obligations;

25. to hear reports of the bodies formed or elected by it as well as reports of officials appointed or elected by it; in case when it is necessary, to decide the question of confidence in the Government of the republic or its individual members by a majority of two-thirds from the total number of Deputies by secret ballot;

26. to submit the matters of state life to a referendum;

27. to decide the matter concerning the removal of officials in the events specified in Article 52 and point 1 of Article 81 of the present Constitution.

Article 59
1. The Jogorku Kenesh shall elect the Toroga and Deputy Toroga from among Deputies, form committees, Supervisory Chamber and provisional commissions.
2. The Toroga of the Jogorku Kenesh shall be elected by secret ballot. He shall be accountable to the Jogorku Kenesh and may be relieved from his office by the decision of the Jogorku Kenesh taken by a majority of not less than two-thirds of the total number of the Deputies.
3. The Toroga of the Jogorku Kenesh shall preside at the sessions of the Jogorku Kenesh, exercise general control over the preparation of the matters liable to consideration at the sessions of the Jogorku Kenesh and its Presidium and shall be responsible for their internal order, sign resolutions and decisions adopted by the Jogorku Kenesh and its Presidium and shall exercise other powers vested in it by the Constitution and laws of the Kyrghyz Republic.
4. Deputy Torogas of the Jogorku Kenesh shall be elected by secret ballot, they shall carry out on the commission of the Toroga his separate functions and act as Toroga in case of his absence or inability to discharge his powers.

Article 60
1. The Toroga, Deputy Torogas, and Chairmen of committees shall form the Presidium of the Jogorku Kenesh.
2. The Presidium of the Jogorku Kenesh shall be accountable to the Jogorku Kenesh and shall provide the organisation of its activity.
3. The Presidium shall prepare the sittings of the Jogorku Kenesh, co-ordinate the activity of committees and provisional commissions, organise nationwide discussion of draft laws of the Kyrghyz Republic and other important issues of state life.

4.   The Presidium shall publish texts of laws of the Kyrghyz Republic and other acts adopted by the Jogorku Kenesh.

Article 61
Committees and provisional commissions of the Jogorku Kenesh shall work on draft laws, make a preliminary consideration of questions referred to the competence of the Jogorku Kenesh and supervise the implementation of adopted laws and decisions.

Article 62
The Procedure of activity of the Jogorku Kenesh shall be determined by rules.

Article 63
The Jogorku Kenesh may be dissolved before the date on which its powers expire by the decision taken by not less than two-thirds of the total number of Deputies or on the results of a nation-wide referendum.

Section 3 – The legislative activity of the Jogorku Kenesh

Article 64
The right to initiate laws shall be vested in Deputies of the Jogorku Kenesh, the President of the Kyrghyz Republic, the Government of the Kyrghyz Republic, the Supreme Court of the Kyrghyz Republic, the Supreme Economic Court of the Kyrghyz Republic and in the electorate by means of a petition of at least 30 000 electors.

Article 65
A bill submitted to the Jogorku Kenesh shall be discussed in committee after which the bill shall be referred to the Presidium which shall send it for consideration to the Jogorku Kenesh.

Article 66
1.   A bill shall be considered passed if it has been voted for by a majority of the total number of Deputies of the Jogorku Kenesh.
2.   In the case of amending or changing the Constitution of the Kyrghyz Republic, adoption of the constitutional acts and amending them not less than two-thirds of votes from the total number of Deputies of the Jogorku Kenesh shall be required.
3.   Amending the Constitution and constitutional acts shall be prohibited during a state of emergency and martial law.

Article 67
A law shall become effective from the moment of its publication if not indicated otherwise in the law itself or in the resolution of the Jogorku Kenesh on the procedure of its implementation.

Article 68
A referendum shall be held by the proposal of not less than 300 000 of electors or one-third of the total number of Deputies of the Jogorku Kenesh.

Chapter 5 – The executive power

Article 69

The executive power in the Kyrghyz Republic shall be vested in the Government of the Kyrghyz Republic, and the ministries, state committees, administrative departments, local state administration accountable to it.

Section 1 – The Government

Article 70

1.   The Government of the Kyrghyz Republic shall be the highest executive body of state power in the Kyrghyz Republic.

2.   The activity of the Government of the Kyrghyz Republic shall be headed by the Prime Minister of the Kyrghyz Republic. The Government of the Kyrghyz Republic shall consist of the Prime Minister of the Kyrghyz Republic, Vice-Prime Ministers, Ministers and Chairmen of state committees of the Kyrghyz Republic.

3.   The structure of the Government shall be determined by the President of the Kyrghyz Republic upon presentation of the Prime Minister and shall be approved by the Jogorku Kenesh.

Article 71

The Prime Minister of the Kyrghyz Republic shall:

    –   present to the President the candidatures for the office of members of the Government;

    –   form and abolish administrative departments of the Kyrghyz Republic;

    –   appoint heads of administrative departments;

    –   present to the President the candidatures for the office of heads of regional state administrations upon presentation by heads of state administration of regions and the city of Bishkek and remove them from office.

The decisions by the Prime Minister concerning appointment and removal shall become effective after they have been approved by the President of the Kyrghyz Republic.

Article 72

1.   The President of the Kyrghyz Republic shall exercise control over the work of the Government of the Kyrghyz Republic.

The President shall have the right to preside at the sitting of the Government.

2.   The annual report on the work of the Government shall be submitted to the Jogorku Kenesh by the Prime Minister. The Jogorku Kenesh shall have the right to demand the report from the Government or its individual members.

Article 73

1.   The Government of the Kyrghyz Republic shall decide all matters of state governing except for those administrative and supervisory authorities vested in the President of the Kyrghyz Republic and the Jogorku Kenesh by the Constitution.

2.   The Government of the Kyrghyz Republic shall:

–   prepare the republican budget, submit it to the Jogorku Kenesh and provide its implementation;
–   pursue budgetary financial, tax and price policy;
–   organise and manage state property;
–   take measures on the defence of the country, state security and the implementation of foreign policy of the Kyrghyz Republic;
–   take measures to provide the rule of law, the rights and freedoms of citizens, the protection of property and public order and the fight with criminality.
3.   The Government of the Kyrghyz Republic and the National Bank of Kyrghyzstan shall provide for a sole monetary, credit and currency policy.

Article 74
The Government of the Kyrghyz Republic shall issue decrees and ordinances binding throughout the territory of the Kyrghyz Republic for all bodies, organisations, officials and citizens and organise, supervise and secure their fulfilment.

Article 75
1.   The Government of the Kyrghyz Republic shall guide the activity of ministries, state committees, administrative departments and bodies of local state administration.
2.   Ministries, state committees and administrative departments shall issue within their competence decrees and ordinances on the basis and for the implementation of the Constitution, laws of the Kyrghyz Republic, resolutions of the Jogorku Kenesh, acts of the President and organise, verify and secure their implementation.
3.   The Government shall hear reports of the heads of local state administration, invalidate the acts of the heads of local state administration which contravene the legislation with further notice to the President.

Article 76
The Procuracy of the Kyrghyz Republic shall within its competence supervise the precise and universal observation of legislative acts.
The bodies of the Procuracy shall exercise criminal pursuit and participate in judicial proceedings in cases in the procedure prescribed by law.

Section 2 – Local state administration

Article 77
1.   The executive power in regions, districts and towns shall be vested in local state administration directed by the heads of the local state administration.
2.   The executive power in ails and settlements shall be vested in the chairmen of the corresponding ail and settlement keneshs.

Article 78
1.   The heads of local state administration and the chairmen of ail and settlement keneshs shall act under the guidance of the Government.

2.   Decisions reached by the heads of local state administration or by the chairmen of ail and settlement keneshs within their competence shall be binding throughout the corresponding territory.

Chapter 6 – Court and justice

Article 79
1.   Justice in the Kyrghyz Republic shall be administered only by the courts.
2.   In the Kyrghyz Republic there shall be the following courts: the Constitutional Court of the Kyrghyz Republic, the Supreme Court of the Kyrghyz Republic, the Supreme Economic Court of the Kyrghyz Republic and local courts (regional courts, courts of the city of Bishkek, district and municipal courts, regional economic courts, military tribunals as well as courts of elders and courts of arbitration).
The creation and establishment of extraordinary or special courts and judicial positions shall not be allowed.
3.   The status of courts and judges in the Kyrghyz Republic shall be specified by the constitutional laws. The organisation of and procedure for court operation shall be specified by law.
4.   Judges shall be subordinate only to the Constitution and the Law. Judges shall enjoy the right to integrity and immunity and in accordance with their status shall be provided with social, material and other guarantees of their independence.

Article 80
1.   A citizen of the Kyrghyz Republic may serve as a judge on the Constitutional Court, the Supreme Court or the Supreme Economic Court of the Kyrghyz Republic if he is not younger than 35 years of age and not older than 70 years of age, and has higher legal education and not less than ten years' experience in the legal profession.
Judges of the Constitutional Court of the Kyrghyz Republic shall be elected for a term of fifteen years by the Jogorku Kenesh upon presentation by the President of the Kyrghyz Republic.
Judges of the Supreme Court and the Supreme Economic Court of the Kyrghyz Republic shall be elected for a term of ten years by the Jogorku Kenesh upon presentation by the President of the Kyrghyz Republic.
2.   A citizen of the Kyrghyz Republic may serve as a judge on a local court if he is not older than 65 years of age, has higher legal education and not less than five years of experience in the legal profession.
Judges of local courts shall be appointed by the President of the Kyrghyz Republic with the consent of the Jogorku Kenesh; the first term shall be for three years, and subsequent terms shall be for seven years.

Article 81
1.   Judges of the Constitutional Court, the Supreme Court and the Supreme Economic Court of the Kyrghyz Republic may be removed from office for treason and other offences by the Jogorku Kenesh on the basis of the judgement of the Constitutional Court of the Kyrghyz Republic; a majority of not less than two-thirds of the votes of the total number of Deputies shall be required to remove a judge from office.

2.   Judges of local courts may be removed from office on the basis of their health, at their personal request, according to the results of examinations, for the violation of law or dishonorable conduct incompatible with their high position as well as on the basis of a binding court judgment.

A judge of a local court may be prosecuted for criminal activity with the consent of the Constitutional Court of the Kyrghyz Republic.

Article 82

1.   The Constitutional Court shall be the highest body of judicial power for the protection of the Constitution of the Kyrghyz Republic.

2.   The Constitutional Court shall consist of the Chairman, the Deputy Chairman and seven judges of the Constitutional Court.

3.   The Constitutional Court shall:

    i.   declare laws and other normative legal acts unconstitutional in the event that they contravene the Constitution;

    ii.   decide disputes concerning the effect, application and interpretation of the Constitution;

    iii.   determine the validity of the elections for President of the Kyrghyz Republic;

    iv.   issue a judgment concerning the removal from office of the President of the Kyrghyz Republic as well as judges of the Constitutional Court, the Supreme Court and the High Court of Arbitrage of the Kyrghyz Republic;

    v.   give its consent for the criminal prosecution of judges of local courts;

    vi.   issue a judgment concerning the removal from office of the President of the Kyrghyz Republic as well as judges of the Constitutional Court and the Supreme Court and the High Court of Arbitrage of the Kyrghyz Republic;

    vii.   annul the decisions of bodies of local self-government which contravene the Constitution of the Kyrghyz Republic;

    viii.   render decisions concerning the constitutionality of practices in the application of laws which affect the constitutional rights of citizens.

4.   A decision of the Constitutional Court shall be final and no appeal will be heard.

If the Constitutional Court declares laws or other acts unconstitutional, such laws or acts shall no longer be in effect on the territory of the Kyrghyz Republic; such a finding shall also annul normative and other acts which are based on the act declared unconstitutional.

Article 83

1.   The Supreme Court of the Kyrghyz Republic shall be the highest body of judicial power in the sphere of civil, criminal and administrative court action.

2.   The Supreme Court of the Kyrghyz Republic shall supervise the operation of the court of the city of Bishkek, regional, municipal courts and military tribunals of the Kyrghyz Republic.

Article 84

1.   The Supreme Economic Court of the Kyrghyz Republic and regional economic courts shall form a single system of economic courts of the Kyrghyz Republic.

2.   Economic Courts shall decide economic disputes between objects of economy based on different forms of property.
3.   The Supreme Economic Court of the Kyrghyz Republic shall supervise the operation of regional economic courts of the Kyrghyz Republic.

Article 85
1.   Courts of elders and courts of arbitration may be established on the territory of ails, settlements and cities by the decision of citizens' meetings from among elder people and other citizens held in respect and authority.
2.   Courts of elders and courts of arbitration shall consider property, family disputes and other cases envisaged by law referred to them by the arguing parties with the purpose of conciliation and passing a just decision which does not contravene the law.
3.   The decisions of courts of elders and courts of arbitration may be appealed against to the corresponding regional and municipal courts of the Kyrghyz Republic.

Article 86
1.   The decisions of courts of the Kyrghyz Republic which have come into force shall be binding upon all state bodies, economic objects, public organisations, officials and citizens on the territory of the republic.
2.   Non-execution of court decisions which came into force as well as interference with the activity of courts shall lead to responsibility established by law.

Article 87
1.   A court shall have no right to adopt a normative act which contravenes the Constitution of the Kyrghyz Republic.
2.   If in the process of consideration of a case in any judicial instance, there arises a doubt on the constitutionality of a law or any other act on which the decision of the case depends, the court shall send an inquiry to the Constitutional Court of the Kyrghyz Republic.

Article 88
1.   A citizen shall have the right to defence of his dignity and rights in trial in case of any public or any other accusation; under no circumstances shall he be denied such court defence.
2.   Defence shall be an inalienable right of a person at any stage of consideration of a case.
Citizens without financial means shall be given legal assistance and defence at the expense of the Government.
3.   Every participant of a trial shall have the right to be heard.

Article 89
1.   The burden of proving guilt on criminal and administrative cases is on the procurator.
2.   Evidence obtained illegally shall not be admitted; reference to it in trial shall not be allowed.

Article 90
Principles of justice established by the Constitution shall be universal and uniform for all courts and judges in the Kyrghyz Republic.

Chapter 7 – Local self-government

Article 91
Matters of life of the population of ails, towns, districts and regions which are of local significance shall be decided on the basis of local self-government operating along with the state power.

Article 92
Local self-government in ails, settlements, districts and regions shall be exercised by local keneshs, elected by the population of the corresponding territorial units.

Article 93
Laws of the Kyrghyz Republic shall establish the fundamentals of the organisation and functioning of local self-government as well as regulating the relationship between local self-government and bodies of local state administration.

Article 94
Chairmen of ail and settlement keneshs shall be heads of local self-government and shall perform the functions of the local state administration.

Article 95
1.   Local keneshs shall:
     –   approve and exercise control over the programmes of social and economic development on the territory and for the social protection of the population;
     –   approve the local budget and report on its implementation as well as hearing information on the use of extra-budgetary funds.
2.   Local keneshs of districts, towns and regions shall have the right to take a vote of no confidence to the head of local state administration of the corresponding territorial unit.
3.   Local keneshs shall operate irrespective of local state administration.
4.   Local keneshs within their powers shall adopt acts binding throughout their territory.

Chapter 8 – The procedure for amendments and additions to the Constitution of the Kyrghyz Republic

Article 96
1.   Amendments and additions to the present Constitution shall be adopted by the Jogorku Kenesh upon presentation by the President of the Kyrghyz Republic by a majority of not less than one-third of the Deputies of the Jogorku Kenesh of the Kyrghyz Republic or not less than 300 000 citizens of the Kyrghyz Republic.

2.   Proposals concerning amending and changing the Constitution of the Kyrghyz Republic shall be considered by the Jogorku Kenesh of the Kyrghyz Republic on receipt of the judgment of the Constitutional Court of the Kyrghyz Republic not earlier than in three months and not later than six months since the date of their registration.

3.   The wording of amendments and additions to the Constitution of the Kyrghyz Republic may not be changed in the course of their discussion by the Jogorku Kenesh.

Article 97

1.   Amendments and additions to the Constitution of the Kyrghyz Republic shall be deemed adopted if they have received two-thirds of votes of the total number of Deputies of the Jogorku Kenesh.

2.   The proposal which has not been passed may not be re-submitted for a second consideration within one year.

Moldova

Chronology

1989

August 31: The Supreme Soviet of the south-western republic of Moldova passes a law giving the Moldovan language the status of state language. Another law reinstates the use of Latin script instead of the Cyrillic script imposed following annexation by the Soviet Union in 1940. The laws adopted, by 321 votes in favour and 11 against, include a compromise retaining Russian and a guarantee of the protection of the Gagauz language.

1990

January 8: The Gagauz minority demands creation of its own autonomous republic.

January 10: The Presidium of the Supreme Soviet appoints Pyotr Paskar as Prime Minister. He replaces Ivan Kalin, who is to take up a diplomatic post.

January 28: A referendum called by the city soviet in Tiraspol, declares greater autonomy for the Tiraspol district and supports the potential declaration of Tiraspol and neighbouring Russian-populated towns as an autonomous republic.

January 31: The Presidium of the Supreme Soviet declares the Tiraspol referendum invalid. At an emergency session, the Presidium declares a six-month moratorium on "all political events which are likely to cause inter-ethnic strife". This means a ban on all unauthorised rallies, marches and ballots, and a greater legal supervision of registered public organisations such as the nationalist Moldovan Popular Front (MPF) and rival groups representing the Russian and other minority populations in the republic.

February 25: Elections for the local soviets and the Supreme Soviet are held. There is a marked division of voting along ethnic lines. The strong showing for candidates affiliated to the nationalist MPF appears to have been matched by an equally strong showing for the rival *Yedvinstvo* (unity) movement, backed by Russian and Ukrainian minority communities. Neither group competes as a political party in the elections, but gives its backing to independent candidates. Many independents are Moldovan Communist Party (CP) members and also enjoy the party's backing. According to the results given in *Izvestiya*, the USSR central government newspaper, all but 10 of the 380 seats of the Moldovan Supreme Soviet are filled. Eighty per cent of the elected deputies are identified as communists, while both the MPF and *Yedinstvo* are reported each to be represented by approximately 20% of these deputies.

April 27: The new republic's official flag the red, yellow and blue tricolour of Romania, instead of the variation on the Soviet red flag previously in use is adopted. The Supreme Soviet elects Mircea Snegur, backed by the MPF, as its President. He defeats the leader of the CP, Petru Lucinschi.

May 24: Pyotr Paskar resigns as Prime Minister in response to criticism of his government voiced in the Supreme Soviet.

May 25: Mircea Druk, a reformist, is elected Prime Minister.

June 23: The Supreme Soviet adopts a sovereignty declaration proclaiming that land, mineral and other resources on the republic's territory as well as the entire economic, scientific, technical, financial potential and national valuables are the exclusive property of Moldova. It establishes the supremacy of the Moldovan constitution and legislation throughout the country. Additionally, the Supreme Soviet endorses a report by a special parliamentary commission, declaring illegal the 1940 Soviet annexation from Romania of Bessarabia (most of which now forms Soviet Moldova) and other territories.

August 19: A congress of representatives of Moldova's Gagauz minority announces the foundation of a separate "Republic of Gagauzia" comprising areas of southern Moldova. It requests recognition from President Gorbachev and from the USSR and Supreme Soviets in the other USSR republics.

August 20: The government rules these secession moves unconstitutional.

August 22: The government outlaws the Gagauz Khalky (People's) movement.

August 25: The Supreme Council declares Moldova independent.

September 2: The leaders of the majority Russian population in the Dnestr valley, in east Moldova, proclaim secession from Moldova and the creation of the Dnestr Soviet Republic.

September 3: The post of executive President is created as a result of the deteriorating social and political situation in the republic caused by the Dnestr Russians' proclamation and the similar move by the Gagauz minority in August. Mircea Snegur is elected unopposed to the new post. He is empowered to introduce direct presidential rule in regions not obeying the Moldovan constitution.

October 26: The Supreme Soviet declares a state of emergency in the Gagauz districts.

October 31: The new Gagauz Supreme Soviet convenes in the town of Komrat and elects Stepan Topal as Gagauzia's President.

November 3: Gorbachev threatens to declare a state of emergency if law and order are not restored immediately; conflicts can only be resolved in accordance with the USSR and Moldovan Constitutions.

November 4: On Snegur's recommendation, the Moldovan Supreme Soviet passes a resolution ordering the disbanding of all voluntary militia, confiscation of their firearms, and lifting of blockades. It also sets up a "conciliation commission".

November 25: The Russian population in the Dnestr valley hold constituent elections to the Supreme Soviet of the "Transdnestr Republic" (Turnout: 81%).

December 6: The state of emergency, in force since late October in the Gagauz populated districts, is lifted.

December 22: President Mikhail Gorbachev issues a decree ordering the normalisation of the situation in Moldova.

December 30: Fearing that direct rule might be imposed by the USSR, the Supreme Soviet votes to endorse a decree ordering the authorities to ensure the observance of USSR legislation in the republic, to review its August 1989 language law and to adopt legislation ensuring equal rights for all citizens. In order to disband all voluntary militia, it declares invalid the Gagauz and Dnestr Russian independence declarations and also a Moldovan resolution of 23 June, concerning the illegality of Moldova's 1940 annexation by the Soviet Union.

1991

February 4: The Communist Party elects Grigory Yeremey as first secretary and he thus becomes a member of the politburo of the Communist Party of the Soviet Union (CPSU).

February 21: President Mircea Snegur tenders his resignation because of attacks by the Communist Party and of his inability to work with the Prime Minister Mircea Druk. The Supreme Soviet refuses his resignation and forms a commission to formulate proposals to reform executive power in Moldova.

March 17: Moldova holds the all-union referendum on the preservation of the Soviet Union. 98.3% of the Moldovan population vote in favour of the preservation of the Soviet Union and 1.3% vote against. The turnout is 83.3%.

April 23: President Mikhail Gorbachev signs, with nine of the fifteen union republics including Moldova, a pact aimed at achieving stable relations between the central government and the governments of the republics. It sets out a timetable for major political changes, starting with the signing of the new Union Treaty. No longer than six months after signature of the Treaty a new Union constitution would be promulgated, followed by elections to the Congress of People's Deputies.

May 22: The Prime Minister, Mircea Druk, is removed from office following a vote of no confidence by the Supreme Soviet.

May 23: The adjectives Soviet and Socialist are dropped from the republic's formal name, now the Moldovan Republic. The Supreme Soviet renames itself the Moldovan Parliament.

May 28: Valery Muravsky replaces Mircea Druk as Prime Minister.

August 19: Attempted *coup d'état* in Moscow.

August 22: The first secretary of the Moldovan CP, Grigory Yeremy, resigns from the CPSU politburo.

August 23: President Snegur bans the Communist party.

August 27: The Parliament declares the country independent.

September 2: The Congress of People's Deputies of the "Dnestr Soviet Republic" adopts a constitution, confirms as its flag the former flag of the Moldovan SSR (Moldova having adopted the flag of Romania) and decides to form its own armed forces.

September 4: President Snegur takes control of customs posts and border troops, since with the independence declarations of Moldova and Ukraine, no borders with the Soviet Union exist.

December 1: A National Council of Reunification between Moldova and Romania is established, consisting of 28 Moldovan and 37 Romanian parliamentarians. The Dnestr Republic holds its own presidential elections together with a referendum on independence for the region. Igor Smirnov is elected President and 98% of the 78% turnout vote for independence. In the Gagauz region, 95.4% of the 85.1% turnout vote for independence. Stepan Topol is elected President of the Gagauz region.

December 8: Mircea Snegur is elected President of Moldova by 98.17% of the votes, with a turnout of 82.88%.

December 8: The Russian Federative Republic, Belarus and Ukraine sign the Minsk Agreement, establishing a Commonwealth of Independent States (CIS).

December 11: Moldovan leaders declare the referendums of Dnestr and Gagauz illegal.

December 12: Moldova signs the Alma Ata Agreement thus joining the CIS.

December 21: The CIS formally replaces the Soviet Union, grouping eleven republics, including Moldova. The Russian Federative Republic takes over many of the former Union functions, including its seat in the UN Security Council.

1992

March 28: President Snegur imposes a state of emergency and direct presidential rule on the self-proclaimed Dnestr republic.

March 30: The Dnestr republic's Supreme Council condemn the emergency decree and urges measures to ensure the Dnestr republic's security.

April 6: The Foreign Ministers of Russia, Moldova, Ukraine and Romania agree on a ceasefire with effect from 7 April.

June 6: A summit meeting of the CIS heads of state take place in Moscow with the result of establishing peacemaking forces in Moldova.

June 9: The Parliament convenes, attended by some deputies from Dnestr. Snegur announces the resignation of the government, except the Security, Defence and Interior ministers.

July 1: 185 out of 244 deputies vote to appoint Andrei Sangheli, member of the Agrarian Democratic Party (ADP), as Prime Minister.

July 21: The Russian President Yeltsin and President Snegur sign a deployment agreement envisaging special status for the Dnestr region and a right to self-determination in case of Moldova's reunification with Romania.

July 29-August 4: The Parliament approves the new "government of national accord", said to include four portfolios for Dnestr representatives.

July 29: A joint Russian, Moldovan and Dnestr peacekeeping force is deployed to halt the fighting after the agreement signed on July 21.

September 8: The Supreme Council of Dnestr region approves a new government structure including 13 ministries, 12 committees and directorates and a law on languages recognizing Moldovan, Russian and Ukrainian as official languages of equal status. Moldovan will continue to be written in the Cyrillic alphabet.

1993

January 20: The Parliament defeats a proposal by President Snegur to hold a referendum on reunification with Romania. The referendum plan which needs the backing of more than 50% of deputies, fails by one vote. Opposition deputies are backed by the parliamentary leadership and take advantage of absentees to block the referendum.

February 4: Petru Lucinschi (ADP) is elected Speaker of Parliament.

February 5: Moldova is granted special guest status by the Council of Europe.

August 3: During an extraordinary session of the Parliament, President Snegur is granted more powers in order to facilitate economic reform. Snegur is given a mandate to rule by decree until July 1994, to reorganise the structure of government and after consultation with the Prime Minister, to appoint and dismiss Cabinet ministers.

August 4: The Parliament fails to ratify Moldova's membership of the CIS, after supporters of ratification fall four votes short of the 50% required by the constitution.

August 10: After the failure of ratification, the motion for the dissolution of the Parliament and the holding of early elections is supported by Snegur and the Speaker of Parliament Lucinschi.

September 9: The Parliament votes to legalise the Moldovan Communist Party, which was banned following the August 1991 Soviet coup attempt.

September 12: Alexandr Lebed, commander of the Russian 14th Army, is elected a deputy of the Supreme Council of the separatist Dnestr region.

November 29: Moldova introduces the leu (plural: lei).

December 4: The rouble is phased out.

1994

January 21: Eight members of the government including Prime Minister Andrei Sangheli and Deputy Prime Ministers Kunev and Oliinik are temporarily dismissed by President Snegur, pending legislative elections due in February.

February 1: Moldova approves a plan envisaging a high degree of autonomy for the Dnestr region but not granting federal status, devised by the Conference on Security and Co-operation in Europe for resolving the Dnestr conflict.

February 27: Elections to the legislature result in gains for the country's largest political party, the ADP, and losses for the pro-Romanian opposition. A second round is due on 14 March.

March 6: A national plebiscite shows over 95% support for Moldovan independence. Of a turnout of 75.1%, 95.4% are in favour, 2% are against, with 2.6% of votes invalid.

March 14: Second round of legislative elections. Final results: 43.21% vote for the ADP (56 seats), 21.77% for the Socialist Party and Yedinstvo Movement (28 seats), 9.2% for Peasants and Intellectuals bloc (11 seats) and 7.31% for the Christian Democratic People's Front (9 seats). The remaining parties fail to achieve the 4% minimum.

March 29: Petru Lucinschi is re-elected Speaker of Parliament by 57 votes to 43 and Dimitru Motpan (ADP) and Nicolae Andronic (ADP) are elected Vice-Presidents.

March 31: The new Parliament elects Andrei Sangheli (ADP) as Prime Minister, by 97 votes to 15.

April 5: The Parliament approves a reorganised, reduced government with a pro-reform make-up.

April 8: The Parliament ratifies membership of the CIS and of the CIS Economic Union but rules out the participation in CIS military alliances and in monetary union.

July 28: A new constitution is adopted by the parliament and comes into force on 27 August. The constitution proclaims a "Parliamentary Republic" based on political pluralism and the preservation, development and expression of ethnic and linguistic identity and permanent neutrality.

September 23: The Ministry of Justice suspends the opposition National-Christian Party citing its failure either to disclose the minutes of its meetings or to register its members.

October 21: In Moscow, Prime Minister Sangheli and Prime Minister of Russia Viktor Chernomyrdin sign an agreement providing for the withdrawal of the Russian 14th army based in Moldova.

1995

May: A splinter group of the ADP, supported by Petru Lucinschi, sets up a new political party: the Party of Social Progress of Moldova (PPSM).

April 16: Local elections are held and the ruling ADP gains 49.9% of the seats, the Alliance of Democratic Forces gains 20% of the seats, the Communist Party 16.6% of the seats and the remaining seats are distributed among the remaining parties. The Dnestr Republic boycotts the elections by supporting the Patriotic Bloc.

June 26: President Snegur resigns from the ADP, accusing the party of pursuing an "anti-presidential policy and trying to reduce the power of the head of state" and gets elected as chair of the Party of Revival and Harmony.

July 13: Moldova becomes a member of the Council of Europe.

September 13: Talks between the President and Dnestr leader Igor Smirnov, on the status of Dnestr, end in deadlock.

October 16: The leading opposition group United Democratic Congress (CDU) is formally constituted as the Moldovan Party for Democratic Forces (PMFD).

December 24: A referendum with a turnout of 62% is held in Dnestr; 82.7% approves the Constitution, proclaiming the region an "independent state" and 89.7% approves it joining the CIS.

1996

May 17: The Party of Socialist Action holds its constituent congress. Aurel Cepoi, a member of the Socialist Union group in parliament, is elected chair of the new party.

November 21: The first round of presidential elections is held. (Turnout: 68%) Mircea Snegur wins 38.74% of the votes, Petru Lucinschi, Speaker of parliament, 27.91%.

December 1: The second round of the presidential elections are held. Petru Lucinschi is elected as the new President. He gains 54.02% of the vote in the second round and his opponent Mircea Snegur gains 45.98% (Turnout: 71,62%).

December 3: The Parliament accepts the resignation of the cabinet.

December 14: President Lucinschi emphasizes that Moldova will not be joining any military blocs, either Nato or such structures in the CIS.

December 22: Igor Smirnov, the President of the Dnestr region, is re-elected for a second term at the elections for the head of the self-proclaimed Dnestr Moldovan Republic. Smirnov gains 71.9% of the votes and his rival, Vladimir Malakhov, receives 19.8%. Smirnov wants the establishment of relations with Moldova on a treaty basis with equal rights. He favours the strengthening of the Dnestr region's independence, its integration into the CIS and the retention of Russian troops on the region's territory as a guarantee of peace.

The Constitution of the Republic of Moldova

Adopted by the Parliament on 29 July 1994, and entered into force on 27 August 1994

We, the plenipotentiary representatives of the people of the Republic of Moldova, members of Parliament,
Starting from the age-old aspirations of our people to live in a sovereign country, and fulfilling those aspirations in proclaiming the independence of the Republic of Moldova,
Considering that while growing into a nation the Moldovan people has given strong evidence of historical and ethnic continuity in its statehood,
Striving to satisfy the interests of those of its citizens that, while being of a different ethnic origin, are, together with the Moldovans, forming the Moldovan people,
Judging the rule of law, the civic peace, democracy, human dignity, the rights and freedoms of man, the free development of human personality, justice and political pluralism to be supreme political values,
Being aware of our responsibility and duties towards the past, present and future generations,
Reasserting our devotion to overall human values, and our wish to live in peace and harmony with all the peoples of this world, in accordance with the unanimously acknowledged principles and norms of international law,
we herewith adopt for our country this Constitution, and proclaim it to be the Supreme Law of Our Society and State.

Title 1 – General principles

Article 1 – The State of the Republic of Moldova
1.   The Republic of Moldova is a sovereign, independent, unitary and indivisible state.
2.   The form of government of the State is the republic.
3.   Governed by the rule of law, the Republic of Moldova is a democratic State in which the dignity of people, their rights and freedoms, the open development of human personality, justice and political pluralism represent supreme values, that shall be guaranteed.

Article 2 – Sovereignty and State Power
1.   National sovereignty resides with the people of the Republic of Moldova, who shall exercise it directly and through its representative bodies in the ways provided for by Constitution.

2. No private individual, national segment of population, social grouping, political party or public organisation may exercise state power on its own behalf. The usurpation of state power constitutes the gravest crime against the people.

Article 3 – The territory
1. The territory of the Republic of Moldova is inalienable.
2. The frontiers of the country are sanctioned by an organic law under the observance of unanimously recognised principles and norms of international law.

Article 4 – Human rights and freedoms
1. Constitutional provisions for human rights and freedoms shall be understood and implemented in accordance with the Universal Declaration of Human Rights, and with other conventions and treaties endorsed by the Republic of Moldova.
2. Wherever disagreements appear between conventions and treaties signed by the Republic of Moldova and its own national laws, priority shall be given to international regulations.

Article 5 – Democracy and political pluralism
1. Democracy in the Republic of Moldova is exercised under conditions of political pluralism, which are incompatible with dictatorship or totalitarianism.
2. No ideology may be pronounced as an official ideology of the State.

Article 6 – Separation and co-operation of powers
The Legislative, the Executive and the Judicial Powers are separate and co-operate in the exercise of their prerogatives in accordance with the provisions of the Constitution.

Article 7 – The Constitution as the supreme law
The Constitution of the Republic of Moldova is the supreme law of the country. No laws or other legal acts and regulations in contradiction with the provisions of the Constitution may have any legal power.

Article 8 – Observance of international law and international treaties
1. The Republic of Moldova pledges to respect the Charter of the United Nations and the treaties to which it is a party, to observe in its relations with other states the unanimously recognised principles and norms of international law.
2. The coming into force of an international treaty containing provisions contrary to the Constitution shall be preceded by a revision of the latter.

Article 9 – The fundamental principles regarding property
1. Property can be public or private, and it can consist of material and intellectual goods.
2. No property may be used to encroach upon or damage the rights, liberty and dignity of people.

3.   The national economy is based on the interaction of market forces, also on free economic initiative and fair competition.

Article 10 – The unity of the nation and the right to national identity
1.   The national unity of the Republic of Moldova constitutes the foundation of the State. The Republic of Moldova is the common and indivisible motherland of all its citizens.
2.   The State recognises and guarantees all its citizens the right to preserve, develop and express their ethnic, cultural, linguistic and religious identity.

Article 11 – The Republic of Moldova as a neutral State
1.   The Republic of Moldova proclaims its permanent neutrality.
2.   The Republic of Moldova will not admit the stationing of any foreign military troops on its territory.

Article 12 – National symbols
1.   The Republic of Moldova has its own flag, coat of arms and anthem.
2.   The State flag of the Republic of Moldova is a tricolour. The colours are arranged vertically in the following order from the flagpole: blue, yellow, red. The coat of arms is printed on the central yellow stripe of the tricolour.
3.   Moldova's coat of arms consists of a shield divided horizontally into two parts: the upper part is red, and the lower part is blue with a superimposed auroch's head showing between its horns an eight-pointed star. On its right the auroch's head is flanked by a five-petalled rose, and on its left by a slightly rotated crescent. All heraldic elements present on the shield are of golden (yellow) colour. The shield is laid on the breast of a natural eagle holding in its beak a golden cross, in its right claw a green olive-tree branch and in its left claw a golden sceptre.
4.   Moldova's State anthem shall be established by organic law.
5.   The flag, the coat of arms and the anthem are State symbols of the Republic of Moldova, and are protected by law as such.

Article 13 – The national language, use of other languages
1.   The national language of the Republic of Moldova is Moldovan, and its writing is based on the Latin alphabet.
2.   The Moldovan State acknowledges and protects the right to preserve, develop and use the Russian language and other languages spoken within the national territory of the country.
3.   The State will encourage and promote studies of foreign languages enjoying widespread international usage.
4.   The use of languages in the territory of the Republic of Moldova will be established by organic law.

Article 14 – The capital
The city of Chisinau is the capital of the Republic of Moldova.

Title 2 – Fundamental rights, freedoms and duties

Chapter 1 – General Provisions

Article 15 – Universality
The Constitution in conjunction with other laws grants the citizens of the Republic of Moldova their rights and freedoms and also lays down their duties upon them.

Article 16 – Equality of rights
1.   It is the foremost duty of the State to respect and protect the human person.
2.   All citizens of the Republic of Moldova are equal before the law and the public authorities, without any discrimination as to race, nationality, ethnic origin, language, religion, sex, political choice, personal property or social origin.

Article 17 – Citizenship of the Republic of Moldova
1.   The citizenship of the Republic of Moldova can be acquired, retained or lost only under the conditions provided for by the organic law.
2.   No one may be deprived arbitrarily of his/her citizenship or the right to change it.
3.   No citizen of the Republic of Moldova can be extradited or expelled from his/her country.
4.   Foreign or stateless citizens may be extradited only in compliance with an international agreement or under conditions of reciprocity in consequence of a decision a court of law.

Article 18 – Citizenship restrictions and state protection for its nationals
1.   Except in those cases where international accords adhered to by the Republic of Moldova have different provisions, no citizen of the Republic of Moldova may be simultaneously a citizen of another country.
2.   The citizens of the Republic of Moldova shall enjoy the protection of their State both at home and abroad.

Article 19 – Rights and duties of aliens and stateless persons
1.   Except in cases where the law has different rulings, aliens and stateless persons shall enjoy the same rights and shall have the same duties as the citizens of the Republic of Moldova.
2.   The right to asylum shall be granted and denied by rule of law in compliance with those international treaties the Republic of Moldova is a party to.

Article 20 – Free access to justice
1.   Every citizen has the right to obtain effective protection from competent courts of jurisdiction against actions infringing on his/her legitimate rights, freedoms and interests.
2.   No law may restrict access to justice.

Article 21 – Presumption of innocence
Any person accused of having committed an offence shall be presumed innocent until found guilty on legal grounds, brought forward in a public trial in the course of which all guarantees for necessary defence will have been taken.

Article 22 – Non-retroactivity of law
No-one may be sentenced for actions or omissions which did not constitute an offence at the time they were committed. Also, no punishment may be given that is harsher than that applicable at the time when the offence was committed.

Article 23 – The right to know one's rights and duties
1.   Everyone has the right to an acknowledged legal status.
2.   The State ensures the right of everybody to know his/her rights and duties. For that purpose the State shall publish all its laws and regulations and make them accessible to everybody.

Chapter 2 – Fundamental rights and freedom

Article 24 – The right to life and physical and mental integrity
1.   The State guarantees everybody the right to life, and to physical and mental integrity.
2.   No one may be subjected to torture or to cruel, inhuman or degrading punishment or treatment.
3.   Until its final prohibition, capital punishment may be applied only if it is based on a sentence passed in a court of justice, as foreseen by law.

Article 25 – Individual freedom and personal security
1.   Individual freedom and personal security are declared to be inviolable.
2.   Searching, detaining in custody or arresting a person shall be permitted only if based on the authority of law.
3.   The period of detention in custody may not exceed 24 hours.
4.   Persons may be arrested only under warrant issued by a magistrate for a maximum time limit of 30 days. The arrested person may contest the legality of the warrant and lay a complaint before a court judge who is bound to reply by way of a motivated decision. The time limit of detention may be extended to six months and in exceptional cases, if approved by decision of Parliament, to twelve months.
5.   The person detained in custody or arrested shall be informed without delay of the reasons for his/her detention or arrest, as well as of the charges made against him/her, which may take place only in the presence of a lawyer, either chosen by the defendant or appointed *ex officio*.
6.   If the reasons for detention in custody or arrest have ceased to exist, the release of the person concerned must follow without delay.

Article 26 – Right of defence
1.   The right of defence is guaranteed.

2.   Everybody has the right to respond independently by appropriate legitimate means to an infringement of his/her rights and freedoms.
3.   Throughout the trial the parties have the right to be assisted by a lawyer, either chosen or appointed *ex officio.*
4.   Any interference with the activity of those carrying out the defence within legally established confines shall be punished by authority of law.

Article 27 – The right to free movement
1.   The right to move freely within the boundaries of one's native country is guaranteed.
2.   Every citizen of the Republic of Moldova is guaranteed the right to choose his/her place of residence anywhere within the national territory, to travel in and out of the country and also to emigrate at will.

Article 28 – Private and family life
The State shall respect and protect private and family life.

Article 29 – Inviolability of domicile
1.   The domicile is inviolable. No one may enter upon or stay on the premises of a domicile without the owner's consent.
2.   The law shall allow for derogation from the provisions of paragraph (1) under the following circumstances.
    a.   for executing an arrest warrant or a decision of a court of law;
    b.   for forestalling imminent danger threatening the life, physical integrity or the property of a person;
    c.   for preventing the spread of an epidemic disease.
3.   Searches and questioning in a domicile may be ordered and carried out only in accordance with the rule of law.
4.   Except for cases where an obvious offence has been committed, night searches are forbidden.

Article 30 – Privacy of correspondence
The State shall ensure the privacy of letters, telegrams, other postal despatches or telephone conversations and the use of other legal means of communication.

Article 31 – Freedom of conscience
1.   Freedom of conscience is guaranteed, and its manifestations should be in a spirit of tolerance and mutual respect.
2.   Freedom of religious worship is guaranteed and religious bodies are free to organise themselves according to their own statutes under the rule of law.
3.   In their mutual relationships religious cults are forbidden to use, express or incite to hatred or enmity.
4.   Religious cults are autonomous *vis-à-vis* the State and shall enjoy the latter's support, including that aimed at providing religious assistance in the army, in hospitals, prisons, homes for the elderly and orphanages.

Article 32 – Freedom of opinion and expression
1.   All citizens are guaranteed freedom of opinion as well as freedom of publicly expressing their thoughts and opinions by way of word, image or any other means possible.
2.   Freedom of expression may not harm the honour, dignity or the rights of other people to have and express their own opinions or judgements.
3.   The law shall forbid and prosecute all actions aimed at denying and slandering the State or the people. Likewise shall be forbidden and prosecuted the instigation to sedition, war, aggression, ethnic, racial or religious hatred, the incitement to discrimination, territorial separation, public violence, or other actions threatening constitutional order.

Article 33 – Freedom to create
1.   The freedom to create scientific and artistic works is guaranteed. Creative work may not be submitted to censorship.
2.   The law shall protect the rights of citizens to their intellectual property, and to the material and moral interests related to various forms of intellectual creation.
3.   The State shall support the preservation, development and propagation of national and world achievements in culture and science.

Article 34 – The right of access to information
1.   Having access to any information of public interest is the right of everybody which may not be curtailed.
2.   According to their established level of competence, public authorities shall ensure that citizens are correctly informed both on public affairs and matters of personal interest.
3.   The right of access to information may not prejudice either the measures taken to protect citizens or national security.
4.   The State and private media are obliged to ensure that correct information reaches public opinion.
5.   The public media shall not be submitted to censorship.

Article 35 – The right of access to education
1.   The right of access to education is put into effect through the compulsory comprehensive public school system, local (public secondary school) and vocational education, as well as the higher education system, and other forms of instruction and training.
2.   The State will enforce under the law the right of each person to choose his/her language in which teaching will be effected.
3.   In all forms of educational institutions the study of the country's official language will be ensured.
4.   State public education is free.
5.   All educational institutions, including those that are not financed by the state, shall be established and function under the rule of law.
6.   Higher education institutions have the right to be autonomous.
7.   The access to local, vocational and higher education is equally open to all and is based on personal merit.

8.	The State ensures under the law the freedom of religious education. The State ensures a lay education.
9.	The priority right of choosing an appropriate educational background for children lies with the parents.

Article 36 – The right of health security
1.	The right of health security is guaranteed.
2.	The State shall provide a minimum health insurance, which is free.
3.	Organic laws will establish the structure of the national health security system and the means necessary for protecting individual physical and mental health.

Article 37 – The right to live in a healthy environment
1.	Every human being has the right to live in an environment that is ecologically safe for life and health, to obtain healthy food products and harmless household appliances.
2.	The State guarantees every citizen the right of free access to truthful information regarding the state of the natural environment, living and working conditions, and the quality of food products and household appliances.
3.	Non-disclosure or falsification of information regarding factors detrimental to human health constitute offences punishable by law.
4.	Private individuals and legal entities shall be held responsible before the law for any damages they may cause to personal health and property due to an ecological offence.

Article 38 – The right of voting and being elected
1.	The foundation of State power is the will of the people made known through free elections held at regular intervals and based on universal, equal, direct, and free suffrage.
2.	Except for the persons banned from voting by law, all the citizens of the Republic of Moldova having attained the age of 18 on or by the voting day inclusively have the right to vote.
3.	The right of being elected is granted to all citizens of the Republic of Moldova enjoying the right of voting.

Article 39 – The right of administering
1.	The citizens of the Republic of Moldova have the right of participating in the administration of public affairs, either directly or through their representatives.
2.	The access to a public office or position is guaranteed by law to all citizens of the Republic of Moldova.

Article 40 – Freedom of assembly
All meetings, demonstrations, rallies, processions or any other assemblies are free, and they may be organised and take place only peacefully and without the use of weapons.

Article 41 – Freedom of political association
1.	All citizens are free to associate in parties and other social and political organisations. These organisations contribute to the definition and expression

of public political will, and under the rule of law take part in the electing process.

2.   All parties and other social/political organisations are equal before the law.

3.   The State shall ensure the protection of the rights and legitimate interests of parties and other social/political organisations.

4.   Parties and social/political organisations are declared unconstitutional if by their aims or activities they are engaged in fighting against political pluralism, the principles of the rule of law, the sovereignty and independence or territorial integrity of the Republic of Moldova.

5.   Secret associations are forbidden.

6.   The activity of parties consisting of foreign nationals is forbidden.

7.   The organic law shall establish those public offices whose holders may not join political parties.

Article 42 – The right of establishing and joining trades unions

1.   Any employee has the right to establish and join a trade union in order to defend his/her interests.

2.   Trades unions are founded and carry on their activities in accordance with their statutes under the law. They make their contribution to the defence of employees' professional, economic and social interests.

Article 43 – The right of working and of access to work

1.   Every person has the right to freely choose his/her work, and to benefit from equitable and satisfactory working conditions, as well as to be protected against unemployment.

2.   All employees have the right of work protection. In this respect the protective measures will bear upon work security and hygiene, working conditions for women and young people, the introduction of minimum wages across the national economy, the weekly period of rest, paid holidays, difficult working conditions, as well as other specific situations.

3.   The length of the working week shall not exceed 40 hours.

4.   The right of collective bargaining is guaranteed, and so is the legal enforceability of collective agreements.

Article 44 – Prohibition of forced labour

1.   Forced labour is prohibited.

2.   Not to be regarded as forced labour are the following:

     a.   military-like duty or the activities designed to replace it, carried out by those who under the law are exempted from compulsory military service;

     b.   work done by a convicted person under normal conditions, in custody or on conditional release;

     c.   services such as those required to deal with calamities or other dangers or as considered under the law to be a part of the normal obligations of civilians.

Article 45 – The right to strike

1.   The right to strike is acknowledged. Strikes may be started only if aimed at defending the economic, social and professional interests of employees.

2.   The law will establish the conditions requested in the exercise of this right, as well as the responsibility involved in the illegal start of strikes.

Article 46 – The right of private property and its protection

1.   The right to possess private property and the debts incurred by the State are guaranteed.
2.   No one may be expropriated except for reasons dictated by public necessity, as established by law and against just and appropriate compensation made in advance.
3.   No assets legally acquired may be confiscated. The effective presumption is that of legal acquirement.
4.   Goods destined for, used or resulted from crimes or offences may be confiscated only as established by law.
5.   The right of private property carries with it the duty to observe the rules regarding the protection of the environment, the maintenance of good neighbourly relations and the observance of all the other duties that have to be fulfilled by owners of private property under the law.
6.   The right to inherit private property is guaranteed.

Article 47 – The right of receiving social assistance and protection

1.   The State is obliged to take action aimed at ensuring that every person has a decent standard of living, whereby good health and welfare, based on available food, clothing, shelter, medical care, and social services are secured for that person and his/her family.
2.   All citizens have the right to be insured against such adversities as: unemployment, disease, disability, widowhood, old age or other situations where, due to causes beyond one's control one loses the source or means of obtaining the necessities of life.

Article 48 – Family

1.   The family is the natural and fundamental constituent of society, and as such has the right to be protected by the State and by society.
2.   The family is founded on the freely consented marriage of husband and wife, on the spouses equality of rights and on the duty of parents to ensure their children's upbringing and education.
3.   The law shall establish under what conditions a marriage may be concluded, terminated or annulled.
4.   Children have a duty to look after their parents and help them in need.

Article 49 – Protection of family and orphaned children

1.   By economic and other actions the State shall support the formation and development of families, and the fulfilment of their duties.
2.   The State shall protect motherhood, the children and the young and promote the development of the institutions required to put that protection into effect.
3.   All efforts aimed at maintaining, bringing up and educating orphaned children and those children deprived of parental care constitute the responsibility of the State and of society. The state promotes and supports charitable activities for the benefit of these children.

Article 50 – Protection of mothers, children and young people
1.   Mothers and children have the right of receiving special protection and care. All children, including those born out of wedlock, shall enjoy the benefits of the same social assistance.
2.   Children and young people enjoy a special form of assistance in the enforcement of their rights.
3.   The State shall grant the required allowances for children and the aid needed for the care of sick or disabled children. The law shall provide for other forms of social assistance for children and the young.
4.   Both the exploitation of minors and their misuse in activities endangering their health, moral conduct, life or normal development are forbidden.
5.   It is the duty of the public authorities to establish the conditions enabling the young people to take part freely in the social, economic, cultural and sporting life of the country.

Article 51 – Protection of disabled persons
1.   The disabled persons shall enjoy a special form of protection from the whole of society. The State shall ensure that normal conditions exist for medical treatment and rehabilitation, education, training and social integration of disabled persons.
2.   Except for those cases that are provided for under the law nobody may be submitted to forced medical treatment.

Article 52 – Right of petitioning
1.   All citizens have the right to apply to public authority by way of petitions formulated on behalf of the applicants.
2.   Legally established organisations may petition exclusively on behalf of the associations or bodies they represent.

Article 53 – Rights of persons aggrieved by public authority
1.   Any person, whose rights have been trespassed upon in any way by public authority through an administrative ruling or lack of timely legal reply to an application, is entitled to obtain acknowledgement of those rights, the cancellation of the ruling and payment of damages.
2.   The State is under patrimonial liability as foreseen by the law for any prejudice or injury caused in lawsuits through errors of the police or the judiciary.

Article 54 – Restricting the exercise of certain rights or freedoms
1.   The exercise of certain rights or freedoms may be restricted only under the law and only as required in cases like: the defence of national security, of public order, health or morals, of citizens rights' and freedoms, the carrying-out of investigations in criminal cases, preventing the consequence of a natural calamity or of a technological disaster.
2.   The restrictions enforced must be in proportion to the situation that caused it, and may not affect the existence of that right or liberty.

Chapter 3 – Fundamental duties

Article 55 – Exercise of rights and freedoms as part of an integrated system.
1.   Every citizen has to perform certain duties towards State and society, and these duties are such as derive directly from the rights and freedoms that are guaranteed to him/her.
2.   Respect is due to all legitimate rights and interests and to the dignity of other citizens.

Article 56 – Allegiance to the country
1.   Allegiance and loyalty to the country are sacred.
2.   Citizens entrusted with the holding of public office, as well as the military, are under the responsibility to fulfil faithfully their duties towards the State, and in given situations shall also take the oath as requested by law.

Article 57 – Defence of motherland
1.   It is the right and the sacred duty of every citizen to defend the motherland.
2.   The national armed forces constitute the framework for performing military services, for national defence, guarding the borders, and maintaining public order under the law.

Article 58 – Financial contributions
1.   All citizens are under obligation to contribute by way of taxes and financial impositions to public expenditure.
2.   The system of legal taxation must ensure a just distribution of fiscal burdens over the population.
3.   All taxation other than that established by law is forbidden.

Article 59 – Protection of environment and public monuments
It is the duty of every citizen to protect the natural environment, and to preserve and protect the country's historical and cultural sites and monuments.

Title 3 – Public authorities

Chapter 4 – Parliament

First section – Structure and functioning

Article 60 – Parliament as the supreme representative body and legislative authority
1.   Parliament is the supreme representative body of the people and the sole legislative authority of the State in the Republic of Moldova.
2.   Parliament consists of 101 members.

Article 61 – Parliamentary elections
1.   The members of Parliament are elected by voting based on universal, equal direct, secret and freely expressed suffrage.

2. The organic law shall establish the way of organising and holding elections.

3. The election of Parliament members will be started not later than three months from the end of the previous mandate or from the dissolution of the previous Parliament.

Article 62 – Validation of members'mandates
On a proposal submitted by the Central Electoral Board the Constitutional Court will decide upon the validation or invalidation of a member of Parliament's mandate, whenever electoral legislation has been transgressed.

Article 63 – Duration of mandate
1. The members of Parliament are elected for a four year-term, which may be extended by organic law, and in the event of war or a national disaster.

2. Parliament shall be convened in session by the President of the Republic of Moldova within at most 30 days from election day.

3. The mandate of the current Parliament may be extended until the structure of the new Parliament has been completed and the latter can meet in full session. During this period no amendments may be brought to the Constitution, and no organic law may be adopted, changed or abrogated.

4. The legislative projects and proposals contained in the agenda of the previous Parliament will be carried over onto the agenda of the new Parliament.

Article 64 – Internal structure
1. The structure, organisation and functioning of Parliament are established by internal regulations. The Parliament approves the national budget and, with it, its own financial resources.

2. The President of Parliament is elected by secret ballot based on the majority of votes cast by members for a term of office equal to that of Parliament. The Parliament may revoke the President at any time by secret ballot based on a two-thirds majority of votes cast by members.

3. On consultations with parliamentary factions the President of Parliament calls for the election of Parliament's Vice-Presidents.

Article 65
1. Parliament's sessions are public.

2. The Parliament may decide to hold certain sessions behind closed doors.

Article 66 – Basic powers
The following are Parliament's basic powers:
    a.   to pass laws, decisions and motions;
    b.   to declare the holding of referendums;
    c.   to provide legislative interpretations and ensure the legislative unity of regulations throughout the country;
    d.   to approve the main directions of the state's internal and external policy;
    e.   to approve the state's military doctrine;

f.   to exercise parliamentary control over executive power in the ways and within the limits provided for by the Constitution;

g.   to ratify, denounce, suspend and abrogate the action of the international treaties concluded by the Republic of Moldova;

h.   to approve and control the national budget;

i.   to supervise and control the allocation of State loans, the aid of an economic or other nature granted to foreign countries, the conclusion of agreements concerning State loans or credits obtained from foreign sources;

j.   to elect and nominate State officials as foreseen by law;

k.   to approve the orders, medals and awards of the Republic of Moldova;

l.   to declare partial or general mobilisation of the armed forces;

m.   to declare the states of national emergency, martial law, and war;

n.   to initiate investigations and hearings concerning any matters touching upon the interests of society;

o.   to suspend the activity of local institutions of public administration under the law;

p.   to pass bills of amnesty;

q.   to exercise other powers, as provided for by the Constitution and the Law.

Article 67 – Parliamentary sessions
1.   Parliament meets in two ordinary sessions per year. The first parliamentary session starts in February and may not go beyond the end of July. The second parliamentary session starts in September and may not go beyond the end of December.
2.   Parliament may also meet in extraordinary or special meetings at the specific request of the President of the Republic of Moldova, of the President of Parliament or of a third of the members.

Second section – The Status of Members of Parliament

Article 68 – Representational mandate
1.   In the exercise of their power the Members of Parliament are in the service of the people.
2.   Imperative mandates shall be null and void.

Article 69 – Mandate of Members of Parliament
1.   The Members of Parliament shall enter upon the exercise of their mandate under condition of prior validation.
2.   The powers ascribed to any Member of Parliament cease with the lawful assembly of the newly-elected Parliament, on resignation on the part of that member, on mandate suspension, as well as in cases of incompatibility or death.

Article 70 – Incompatibility and immunities
1.   The equality and rights ascribed to Members of Parliament are incompatible with the holding of other remunerated positions.

2. Other possible incompatibilities shall be established by organic law.
3. Except in cases of flagrant infringement of law, Members of Parliament may not be detained for questioning, put under arrest, searched or put on trial without Parliament's assent, after prior hearing of the Members in question.

Article 71 – Independence of opinion
Members of Parliament may not be prosecuted or tried by law for their votes or opinions expressed in the exercise of their mandate.

Third section – Legislation and Acts of Parliament

Article 72 – Classification of laws
1. Parliament is endowed with the powers to pass constitutional, organic and ordinary laws.
2. Constitutional laws are aimed at revising the Constitution.
3. The purpose of the organic laws is to direct and control:
    a. the working of the electoral system;
    b. the organisation and carrying out of referendums;
    c. the organisation and functioning of Parliament;
    d. the organisation and functioning of Government;
    e. the organisation and functioning of the Constitutional Court, the Higher Magistrates Council, the judiciary and courts of administrative judicature;
    f. the organisation of local administration, of the national territory, and the general functioning of local autonomy;
    g. the organisation and functioning of political parties;
    h. the manner of selecting exclusive economic zones;
    i. the legal status of private property and inheritance;
    j. the general implementation of the working relations and social protection, and the functioning of trades unions;
    k. the general organisation of the educational system;
    l. the general status of religious worship;
    m. the states of national emergency, martial law and war;
    n. criminal offences, the punishments requested, and the ways of executing the latter;
    o. the granting of amnesty and pardon;
    p. other provinces where the Constitution provides for the necessity of passing organic laws;
    q. other provinces where Parliament recommends the passing of organic laws.
4. Basically, social relations are the province of ordinary law, excepting those for whose regulation constitutional and organic laws have been appointed.

Article 73 – Legislative initiative
The right to initiate legislation belongs to Members of Parliament, the President of the Republic of Moldova and the Government.

Article 74 – The passing of laws and resolutions
1.   Organic laws shall be passed by majority vote based on at least two ballots.
2.   Ordinary laws and resolutions shall be passed by the majority of the votes cast by the Members present in session.
3.   The laws passed shall be submitted to the President of the Republic of Moldova for promulgation.

Article 75 – The referendum
1.   Problems of utmost gravity or urgency confronting the Moldovan society or State shall be resolved by referendum.
2.   The decisions passed in consequence of the results produced by the republican referendum have supreme judicial power.

Article 76 – The coming into force of laws
Laws shall be published in the "Monitorul Oficial" of the Republic of Moldova and shall come into force either on their publication date or on the date mentioned in their original text. Unless published, the law is non-existent.

Chapter 5 – The President of the Republic of Moldova

Article 77 – The President of the Republic of Moldova – the Head of the State
1.   The President of the Republic of Moldova is the head of State.
2.   The President of the Republic of Moldova represents the State and is the guarantor of national sovereignty, independence, and of the unity and territorial integrity of the nation.

Article 78 – The election of the President
1.   The President of the Republic of Moldova is elected by freely expressed, universal, equal, direct, and secret suffrage.
2.   Any citizen of the Republic of Moldova over 35 years of age who has been living in the country for at least ten years and speaks the State language can run for the office of President of the Republic of Moldova. The appropriate organic law shall determine the manner of selecting the candidates aspiring to this office.
3.   The candidate obtaining at least half the votes cast in the presidential election shall be proclaimed as the new President.
4.   If after the first ballot no candidate shall have obtained the above-mentioned majority of votes, a second ballot shall be held to choose from the first-places two candidates, in the order of the number of votes cast for them in the first ballot. On condition that the number of the votes cast for him be bigger than the number of the votes cast against him, the candidate obtaining most of the votes cast in the second ballot shall be proclaimed as the new President.
5.   The office of the President of the Republic of Moldova may be held by the same person for not more than two consecutive terms.

Article 79 – Mandate validation and taking of the oath
1.   The Constitutional Court will validate the results of the presidential election.
2.   Within 45 days from the date when elections were completed the successful presidential candidate shall take the following oath before Parliament and the Constitutional Court:
"I solemnly swear to devote all my personal strength and abilities to the advancement and prosperity of the Republic of Moldova, to always abide by the Constitution and the laws of the country to defend democracy, the fundamental rights and freedoms of the Republic of Moldova and the sovereignty, independence, unity and territorial integrity of Moldova."

Article 80 – Term of office
1.   The President of the Republic of Moldova takes office on the oath-taking day and his term has a duration of 4 years.
2.   The President of the Republic of Moldova exercises his mandate until the next President is sworn in.
3.   By organic law the mandate of the President of the Republic of Moldova may be prolonged in the event of war or catastrophe.

Article 81 – Incompatibilities and immunities
1.   The office of the President of the Republic of Moldova is incompatible with holding another remunerated position.
2.   The President of the Republic of Moldova will enjoy immunity from civil action for any personal opinions expressed while in the execution of his mandate.
3.   Based on the majority of at least two-thirds of the votes cast by its members, Parliament may decide to indict the President of the Republic of Moldova if the latter commits an offence. In such a case it is the Supreme Court of Justice which has the competence to sue under the rule of law, and the President will be removed from office on the very day that the court sentence convicting him has been passed as definitive.

Article 82 – Nomination of government
1.   On consultation with the parliamentary majority, the President of the Republic of Moldova will designate a candidate for the office of Prime Minister and will make use of the vote of confidence given him by Parliament to nominate the Government.
2.   In cases of cabinet reshuffling or vacancies the President may, on proposals submitted to him by the Prime Minister, revoke and renominate certain members of Government.

Article 83 – Participation in government meetings. Consultation with the government
1.   The President of the Republic of Moldova can take part in Government meetings, in which case he will preside over them.
2.   The President of the Republic of Moldova can consult the Government on matters of special importance and urgency.

Article 84 – Messages
1.   The President of the Republic of Moldova can take part in Parliament's proceedings and debates.
2.   The President of the Republic of Moldova will address to Parliament messages concerning the main issues of national interest.

Article 85 – Dissolution of Parliament
1.   In cases where an impossibility has been reached in forming the Government or a situation has been encountered whereby the passing of new legislation has been deadlocked for three consecutive months, the President of the Republic of Moldova, on consultations with parliamentary groups, may dissolve Parliament.
2.   If within 45 days from a first presidential request for a vote of confidence to form a new government a second such request been also rejected by Parliament, the President may dissolve the Parliament.
3.   The Parliament may be dissolved only once in the course of a year.
4.   The Parliament may not be dissolved either during the President's last six months of office or during a state of emergency martial law or war.

Article 86 – Powers regarding foreign policy
1.   The President of the Republic of Moldova is empowered to enter official discussions, take part in negotiations, conclude in the name of the Republic of Moldova the international treaties resulting therefrom, and submit those treaties to Parliament for ratification.
2.   On specific proposals submitted to him by Government, the President of the Republic of Moldova can accredit and revoke the Republic of Moldova's diplomatic representatives, as well as approve the establishment, disestablishment, and ranking of diplomatic missions abroad.
3.   The President of the Republic of Moldova receives letters of accreditation or revocation of foreign diplomatic envoys to Moldova.

Article 87 – Powers regarding national defence
1.   The President of the Republic of Moldova is the Commander-in-Chief of the armed forces.
2.   On prior approval from Parliament the President of the Republic of Moldova can declare partial or general mobilisation of the armed forces.
3.   In the event of armed aggression against the country, the President of the Republic of Moldova takes the steps required to repel aggression, and to declare a state of war, and informs Parliament without delay of the situation. If Parliament is not in session, the President convenes by right the Parliament within 24 hours from the time when the aggression was launched.
4.   In order to ensure national security and public order the President of the Republic of Moldova can under the rule of law also take other steps.

Article 88 – Other powers
The President of the Republic of Moldova is also empowered to:
    a.   award medals and titles of honour;
    b.   award such supreme military ranks as provided for by the law;

c.   find solutions to problems concerning the rights of citizenship of the Republic of Moldova and grant political asylum;

d.   appoint public officials under the law;

e.   grand individual pardon or amnesty;

f.   request the citizens of the Republic of Moldova to express their will by way of referendum on matters of national interests;

g.   award diplomatic ranks;

h.   award higher ranks to officials holding positions with Magistrates' Courts and Civil Courts, and to other civil servants;

i.   suspend those Acts of Government that run against existing legislation until a final decision has been passed by the Constitutional Court;

j.   exercise other powers as foreseen by the law.

Article 89 – Suspension from office
1.   In the event where the President of the Republic of Moldova commits grave offences infringing upon constitutional provisions, he may be suspended from office by Parliament if two-thirds of the members cast their votes in support of suspension.
2.   The motion requesting the suspension from office may be initiated by at least one-third of the members, and it must be brought to the knowledge of the President without delay. The President may give explanations of the actions for which he is being censured before Parliament.
3.   If the motion requesting suspension from office meets with approval, a national referendum shall be organised within 30 days for removing the President from office.

Article 90 – Vacancy of office
1.   The office of the President of the Republic of Moldova may become vacant in consequence of the expiry of the presidential mandate, on resignation from office, removal from office, definite impossibility of executing his duties, or death.
2.   The request to remove the President of the Republic of Moldova from office will be brought forward in Parliament, which will pass a decision on that request.
3.   Within three months from the date when the presidential office was announced as vacant elections for a new President will be held in accordance with the law.

Article 91 – Interim office
When the office of the President of the Republic of Moldova becomes vacant or the President has been suspended from office, or finds himself in the temporary impossibility of discharging his duties, the responsibility of the office shall devolve *ad interim* on the President of Parliament or the Prime Minister, in that order of priority.

Article 92 – Responsibility of interim President
Should the person acting as interim President of the Republic of Moldova commit grave offences infringing upon constitutional provisions Article 89 Paragraph (1) and Article 91 will apply.

Article 93 – Promulgation of laws
1.	The President of the Republic of Moldova promulgates the laws.
2.	The President of the Republic of Moldova has the right, whenever he objects to a given law, to submit it within at most two weeks to Parliament for re-examination. Should Parliament stick to its previously passed decision, then the President must promulgate the law.

Article 94 – Presidential acts
1.	In the exercise of his powers the President of the Republic of Moldova issues decrees whose execution is compulsory throughout the entire territory of the State. These decrees shall be published in the "Monitorul Oficial" of the Republic of Moldova.
2.	Those decrees issued by the President that fall under the provisions of Article 86 paragraph (2) and Article 87 Paragraphs (2), (3) and (4) must also be countersigned by the Prime Minister also.

Article 95 – Budget of Presidential institution. Compensation and other rights
1.	The budget of the presidential institution shall be submitted to Parliament for approval and shall be included in the budget.
2.	The law will determine the level of compensation and the other rights the President is entitled to.

Chapter 6 – The Government

Article 96 – The role of Government
1.	It is the role of government to carry out the domestic and foreign policy of the State and to apply general control over the work of public administration.
2.	A specific programme of activities approved by Parliament will constitute the guidelines which Government will use in the exercise of its powers.

Article 97 – Structure of Government
The Government consists of a Prime Minister, a First Vice-Prime Minister, Vice-Prime Ministers, of Ministers and other members as determined by organic law.

Article 98 – Investiture
1.	The President of the Republic of Moldova designates a candidate for the office of Prime Minister.
2.	Within 15 days from his designation, the candidate for the office of Prime-Minister will request a vote of confidence for Parliament regarding his work programme and the entire list of Government members.
3.	Parliament will debate in joint session both the programme and the list of Government members and will grant Government the requested vote of confidence based on majority vote.
4.	Government enters into the execution of its powers on the very day when its members take the oath before the President of the Republic of Moldova.

Article 99 – Incompatibilities
1.   The office of government member is incompatible with the holding of another remunerated position.
2.   Other incompatibilities will be specified by organic law.

Article 100 – Termination of Government membership
The office of a government member ends in cases of resignation, removal from office, incompatibility or death.

Article 101 – The Prime Minister
1.   The Prime Minister leads the Government and co-ordinates the activity of its members, while respecting the powers delegated to them. He keeps informed the President of the Republic of Moldova on matters of special importance.
2.   Whenever the Prime Minister finds himself in one of the situations described under Article 100 or in the impossibility of discharging his duties, the President of the Republic of Moldova shall designate another Government member as an interim Prime Minister to fulfil the duties of the latter until the formation of a new Government. Should the Prime Minister resume his activity within the Government structure in the interim period, then the temporary character of his inability to fulfil his duties also ceases.
3.   A resignation on the part of the Prime Minister leads to the resignation of the whole Government.

Article 102 – Acts of Government
1.   The Government issues decisions and orders that are published in the "Monitorul Oficial" of the Republic of Moldova.
2.   The decisions and orders are issued by way of legal execution and are signed by the Prime Minister.
3.   Under the rule of law certain orders may be countersigned by the Ministers bearing the responsibility of putting them into effect.

Article 103 – Termination of mandate
1.   The Government is empowered to exercise its mandate up to the date that has been officially sanctioned for the holding of parliamentary elections.
2.   In cases where Parliament has passed a vote of no confidence in the current Government, or the Prime Minister has been removed from office, or as provided for by paragraph (1) above, the Government shall only control the administration of the public affairs until the new Government has been sworn in.

Chapter 7 – The Parliament – Government Interrelationship

Article 104 – Reporting to Parliament
1.   The Government is responsible before Parliament, its committees and its individual members for supplying them with all information and documents that may be requested.

2. The access of Government members to parliamentary proceedings is ensured, and their presence may be obligatory if so requested.

Article 105 – Questioning and interpellating
1. Both the Government as a whole and each one of its members are obliged to reply to the questions and interpellation raised by Parliament members.
2. Parliament may pass a motion to substantiate its position *vis-à-vis* the issue that has caused an interpellation.

Article 106 – Motion of no confidence
1. If initiated by at least a quarter of the members present in session and based on their majority vote, Parliament may carry a motion of no confidence in the Government.
2. The initiative to carry a motion of no confidence in the Government will be examined within three days from the date when it was brought before Parliament.

Chapter 8 – Public Administration

Article 107 – Specialised central public administration
1. Ministries constitute the State's specialised agencies. They put into practice under the law the Government's policy, decisions and orders, exercise control over their areas of competence and are answerable for their activities.
2. In order to manage, co-ordinate and control the national economy, as well as other areas outside the direct responsibility of ministries, other administrative authorities may be set up in accordance with the law.

Article 108 – The armed forces
1. The armed forces are subordinated solely to the will of the nation, and their purpose is to safeguard the sovereignty, independence, unity and territorial integrity of the country, as well as the constitutional democracy.
2. The structure of the national defence system will be determined by organic law.

Article 109 – Basic principles of local public administration
1. Public administration as manifested in the administrative/territorial units is based on the principles of local autonomy, of decentralisation of public services, of the eligibility of local public administration authorities and of consulting the citizenry on local problems of special interest.
2. The concept of autonomy encompasses both the organisation and functioning of local public administration, as well as the management of the communities represented by that administration.
3. The enforcement of the principles described above may not detract from the unitary character of the State.

Article 110 – Administrative/territorial organisation
From the administrative point of view the territory of the Republic of Moldova is structured in districts, towns and villages. Certain towns may under the law be declared municipalities.

Article 111 – Special autonomy statutes
1.   The places on the left bank of the Nistru river, as well as certain other places in the south of the Republic of Moldova may be granted special forms of autonomy according to special statutory provisions of organic law.
2.   The organic laws establishing special statutes for the places mentioned under paragraph (1) above may be amended if three-fifths of the Parliament members support such amendments.

Article 112 – Village and town authorities
1.   At village and town level the public administration authorities through which local autonomy is executed are represented by the elected local councils and mayors.
2.   The local councils and the mayors operate under the law as autonomous administrative authorities and are assigned the task of solving public affairs in villages and towns.
3.   The ways of electing local councils and mayors, as well as their powers and competencies, shall be established by law.

Article 113 – Districts councils
1.   The district council co-ordinates the activity of the village and town councils to achieve public service at district level.
2.   The district council will be elected and will work in accordance with the law.
3.   The interrelationships of public authorities are based on the principles of autonomy, legality and co-operation in solving common problems.

Chapter 9 – Judicial authority

First Section – Courts of Law

Article 114 – Administration of justice
Justice shall be administered in the name of the law by courts of law only.

Article 115 – Courts of Law
1.   Justice shall be administered by the Supreme Court of Justice, the Court of Appeal, by tribunals and the courts of law.
2.   To hear certain categories of cases special courts may be set up under the law.
3.   It is forbidden to set up courts of exception.
4.   The structure of the courts of law, their areas of competence and the corresponding judicial procedures shall be established by organic law.

Article 116 – Status of judges
1.   Judges sitting in the courts of law are independent, impartial and irremovable under the law.
2.   The judges sitting in the courts of law are appointed by the President of the Republic of Moldova following a proposal submitted to him by the Higher Magistrates Council. Those judges who have passed the judicature entry

test are appointed in their positions at first for a five-year term, and subsequently for a ten-year term. After fifteen years judges will be appointed for a term of office which expires with their reaching the age limit.

3.   Both the President and the members of the Supreme Court of Justice shall be appointed by Parliament following a proposal submitted by the Higher Magistrates Council. They must provide evidence of work experience in courts of law that is not less than fifteen years long.

4.   Judges may be promoted or transferred at their own consent only.

5.   Judges may be punished as provided for under the rule of law.

6.   The office of judge is incompatible with holding any other public or private remunerated position, except in the area of teaching or academic research.

Article 117 – Public character of legal proceedings

Legal hearings in all courts of law are public. Cases may be heard behind closed doors only as stipulated by law in compliance with all established legal procedures.

Article 118 – Language used in hearings and right to use an interpreter

1.   Legal cases will be heard in the Moldovan language.

2.   Those persons who do not know or are unable to speak Moldovan have the right to take knowledge of all documents and items on file and to talk to the court through an interpreter.

3.   In accordance with the law, legal hearings may also be conducted in a language that is found to be acceptable by the majority of the persons participating in the hearing.

Article 119 – Appealing

The parties involved in a case and the state authorities may appeal against sentences pronounced in courts of law in accordance with the law.

Article 120 – Compulsory character of sentences and of other final legal rulings

It is compulsory to abide by the sentences and the other final legal rulings pronounced in courts of law and to co-operate with the latter at their specific request during trials, the execution of sentences and other final rulings of justice.

Article 121 – The budget of the Courts of Law, compensation and other rights

1.   The budget of the courts of law is approved by Parliament and is included in the national budget.

2.   The compensation and other rights of judges are established by law.

3.   The courts of law have control over the police forces placed at their disposal.

Second Section – The Higher Magistrates' Council

Article 122 – Composition
1.   The Higher Magistrates' Council is composed of eleven magistrates whose mandate is valid for five years.
2.   The following belong by right to the Higher Magistrates' Court: the Minister of Justice, the President of the Supreme Court of Justice, the President of the Court of Appeal, the President of the Court of Business Audit, the Prosecutor-General.
3.   Furthermore, the reunited colleges of the Supreme Court of Justice select by secret ballot three more magistrates, and another three are selected by Parliament from amongst accredited university professors.

Article 123 – Powers
The Higher Magistrates' Council in accordance with regulations established in the organisation of the judiciary performs the appointments, transfers, promotions of judges, as well as the disciplinary actions against them.

Third Section – The Public Prosecution Office

Article 124 – Powers and structure
1.   The Prosecutor-General and the public prosecutors under him exercise control over the exact and uniform enaction of laws by public administration authorities, by juridical and physical entitles and their associations, while defending legal order, the rights and freedoms of citizens and supporting the enforcement of justice under the law.
2.   The public prosecution system is composed of the General Prosecution Office, territorial prosecution offices and specialised prosecution offices.
3.   The structure, powers and activities of the prosecution offices are established by law.

Article 125 – Mandate of public prosecutors
1.   The Prosecutor-General is appointed by Parliament following a proposal submitted to the latter by its President.
2.   The other public prosecutors are subordinated to the Prosecutor-General, and appointed by him.
3.   The public prosecutors receive their mandate for a period of five years.
4.   The office of public prosecutor is incompatible with holding any other remunerated position, be it public or private, except in teaching or academic research.
5.   In exercising their powers public prosecutors may submit only to the law.

Title 4 – National economy and public finance

Article 126 – Economy
1.   The economy of the Republic of Moldova is a socially-orientated market economy based on the co-existence of freely competing private and public properties.
2.   The State must ensure:

a. the regulation of economic activity, and the administration of the public property belonging to the State under the law;

b. the freedom of trading and of entrepreneurial activity, the protection of legal competition, the setting-up of an appropriate framework for developing all factors capable of stimulating production;

c. the protection of the national interests involved in economic, financial and currency exchange activities;

d. the promotion of national scientific research;

e. the national exploitation of the soil and of other natural resources, in harmony with the national interests;

f. the restoration and protection of the environment, and the maintenance of ecological balance;

g. the increase in the number of the people employed, the establishment of conditions adequate for improving the quality of life;

h. the inviolability of investments made by physical and juridical entitles, including those from abroad.

Article 127 – Property

1. The State protects property.
2. The State guarantees everybody the right to possess property in any such form as requested by the owner, as long as that form of property does not conflict with the interests of society.
3. Public property belongs to the State or to the administrative/territorial units.
4. All underground resources, the air space, the waters and forests used for the benefit of the public at large, the natural resources of given economic regions and of the continental shelf, the communication ways, as well as other assets stipulated by law, constitute the exclusive province of public property.

Article 128 – Property of aliens and stateless persons

1. In the Republic of Moldova the property of other states, of international organisations, of foreign citizens and of stateless persons is protected by law.
2. The law determines the manner and conditions under which the right of property can be exercised by physical and juridical entities of foreign extraction, and by stateless persons throughout the territory of the Republic of Moldova.

Article 129 – External economic activities

1. Parliament approves the main directions of external economic activities, the principles guiding the utilisation of foreign loans and credits.
2. The Government ensures the protection of national interests involved in external economic activities, and depending on the demands of national interest ensures either a free-trade policy or a protectionist one.

Article 130 – Financial system and crediting

1. The law specifies the formation, administration, utilisation and control of the State's financial resources, of the administrative/territorial units, and of public institutions.

2.   The national currency of the Republic of Moldova is the Moldovan leu (pl. lei).

3.   The National Bank of the Republic of Moldova has the exclusive right of mintage. The minting of a money issue can be effected by act of Parliament only.

Article 131 – National public budget

1.   The national public budget is made up of the national budget, the national social security budget, and the local budgets of districts, towns and villages.

2.   The Government issues an annual draft of the national budget, and of the social security budget, which it submits separately to Parliament for approval. Supplementary budgets formed in addition to the national budget shall also be submitted to Parliament for approval.

3.   If the national budget and the national social security budget have not been approved by at least three days before expiry of the current budget exercise, both the national and the national social security budgets continue to apply until the new budgets have been approved.

4.   The budgets of districts, towns and villages shall be issued, approved and executed in accordance with the law.

5.   No budget expenditure may be approved without prior identification of a corresponding source of funding for it.

Article 132 – Fiscal system

1.   All taxes, duties, and other revenue of the national budget, including the national social security budget, also the district, town and village budgets shall be established under the law by the representative agencies, as required.

2.   Any other types of taxation are forbidden.

Article 133 – Court of Audit

1.   The Court of Audit controls the ways of creating administering and utilising public financial resources.

2.   The Court of Audit is composed of seven members.

3.   The President of the Court of Audit is appointed for a five-year term by Parliament on proposal submitted by the President of Parliament.

4.   The Court of Audit submits annually to Parliament a report on the administration and utilisation of public financial resources.

5.   The Court of Audit's other powers, as well as its structure and functioning will be established by organic law.

Title 5 – Constitutional Court

Article 134 – Statute

1.   The Constitutional Court is the sole authority of constitutional judicature in the Republic of Moldova.

2.   The Constitutional Court is independent of any other public authority and obeys only the Constitution.

3.   The Constitutional Court guarantees the supremacy of the Constitution, enforces the practical implementation of the principle regarding the

separation of the State powers into the legislative, executive and judicial powers, and guarantees the responsibility of State towards the citizen, and also of the citizen towards the State.

Article 135 – Powers
1.   The Constitutional Court:
    a.   enforces on notification constitutionality control over laws, regulations and orders of Parliament, Presidential decrees, decisions and orders of Government, as well as international treaties endorsed by the Republic of Moldova;
    b.   explains and clarifies the Constitution;
    c.   formulates its position on initiatives aimed at revising the Constitution;
    d.   confirms the results of republican referendums;
    e.   confirms the results of parliamentary and presidential elections in the Republic of Moldova;
    f.   ascertains the circumstances justifying the dissolution of Parliament, the suspension from office of the President of the Republic of Moldova or the interim office of the President of the Republic of Moldova;
    g.   solves exceptional cases of non-constitutionality of judicial acts, as signalled by the Supreme Court of Justice;
    h.   decides over matters dealing with the constitutionality of parties.
2.   The Constitutional Court carries out its activities on initiatives started by the legal entities mentioned in the law regarding the Constitutional Court.

Article 136 – Structure
1.   The Constitutional Court is composed of six judges, who are appointed for a six-year mandate.
2.   The Parliament, the President of the Republic of Moldova and the Higher Magistrates' Council appoint two judges each.
3.   The judges of the Constitutional Court elect its president by secret ballot.

Article 137 – Independence
For the duration of their mandate the judges of the Constitutional Court are irremovable, independent, and obey only the Constitution.

Article 138 – Appointment qualifications
The judges of the Constitutional Court must possess outstanding judicial knowledge, high professional competence and long (at least fifteen years) experience in judicature positions, in law education or academic research.

Article 139 – Incompatibilities
The office of Constitutional Court judge is incompatible with holding any other remunerated public or private position, except in education and research.

Article 140 – Decisions of the Constitutional Court
1.   Laws and other regulations or parts thereof become null and void from the moment that the Constitutional Court passes the appropriate decisions to that effect.

2. The decisions of the Constitutional Court are final and cannot be appealed against.

Title 6 – Revising the Constitution

Article 141 – Initiatives for Constitutional revision
1. A revision of the Constitution may be initiated by:
    a. an number of at least 200 000 voting citizens of the Republic of Moldova. The citizens initiating a revision of the Constitution must cover with the number of their listed residences at least a half of the nation's districts and municipalities, and in their turn each of those districts and municipalities must be represented by at least 5 000 registered signers in support of the said initiative;
    b. no less than a third of the members of Parliament;
    c. the President of the Republic of Moldova;
    d. the Government.
2. Constitutional law projects shall be submitted to Parliament on condition that the Constitutional Court issues the appropriate recommendation support by at least four judges.

Article 142 – Limits of revision
1. The provisions regarding the sovereignty, independence and unity of the State, as well as those regarding the permanent neutrality of the State may be revised only by referendum based on a majority vote of registered voting citizens.
2. No revision shall be allowed if it results in the suppression of the fundamental rights and freedoms of citizens, or of the guarantees of those rights and freedoms.
3. The Constitution may not be revised under a state of national emergency, martial law or war.

Article 143 – The Law on Constitutional Revision
1. Parliament has the right to pass a law for revising the Constitution after no less than six months from the date when the revising initiative was submitted. This law has to be passed by a two-thirds majority.
2. If within one year from the date when the revising initiative was submitted Parliament has not passed the appropriate constitutional law, the initiative shall be considered null and void.

Title 7 – Final and transitory provisions

Article 1
1. This Constitution shall be endorsed by Parliament and the President of the Republic of Moldova shall promulgate it within three days from that endorsement.
2. The Constitution of the Republic of Moldova comes into force on 27 August 1994. On that same date the Constitution of the Republic of Moldova of 15 April 1978, including all its subsequent revisions and amendments, shall be abrogated in its entirety.

Article 2
1.   The laws and other regulations retain their force only to the extent to which they do not transgress on the Constitution.
2.   Within one year from the coming into force of the present Constitution the permanent parliamentary committees, and the Government shall examine the compliance of legislation with the Constitution, and submit adequate proposals in that respect to Parliament.

Article 3
1.   All State institutions in existence as of the date marking the coming into force of this Constitution retain their functionality until new institutions are established.
2.   Parliament is made up of 104 members elected by freely expressed, universal, equal, direct and secret suffrage within the framework of political and party pluralism in accordance with the law passed on 14 October 1993. As such, Parliament remains in operation until its mandate expires, except in those cases provided for by this Constitution.
3.   The President of the Republic of Moldova is elected by freely expressed, universal, equal, direct and secret suffrage within the framework of political and party pluralism for a five-year term, as provided for by the law of 18 September 1991 concerning presidential elections in the Republic of Moldova. As such, the President remains in office until his mandate expires, except in those cases provided for by this Constitution.
4.   Government is invested by Parliament, and retains its powers until the expiry of its mandate, except in those cases provided for by the Constitution.
5.   Local authorities of state power and national administration remain in operation until the expiration of their mandate, except in those cases provided for by this Constitution.
6.   Judges who on the coming into force of this Constitution have been employed in courts of justice for not less than fifteen years come under the protection of the principle of irremovability in accordance with Article 116, paragraph (1) by presidential decree, on proposal submitted by the Minister of Justice and the President of the Supreme Court of Justice.
7.   Within two years from the coming into force of this Constitution, the system of the courts of jurisdiction will be reorganised by law in accordance with Article 115.

Article 4
The provisions of Article 25, paragraph (4) regarding the terms of detention in custody will have no bearing until 1 January 1995 on those persons who have committed major offences under Article 7, paragraph (1) of Criminal Law.

Article 5
1.   Within six months from the coming into force of this Constitution a Constitutional Court and a Court of Audit shall be established.
2.   For the first formation of the Constitutional Court the judges representing the Higher Magistrates' Council are appointed by the general assembly of the people's judges and the members of the Supreme Court of Justice.

Article 6

Until the establishment of the Constitutional Court all cases stipulated under Article 135 of this Constitution may be solved on Parliament's initiative by the Supreme Court of Justice.

Article 7

1.   The law of 1 September 1989 regarding the use of languages spoken throughout the territory of the Republic of Moldova stays in force to the extent that it does not trespass on this Constitution.

2.   The above-named law may be amended over the seven years ensuing from the date when this Constitution has come into force, if it has been passed by a two-thirds majority.

Article 8

1.   Title 7, Final and Transitory Provisions is considered to be an integral part of this Constitution and has the purpose of solving those problems that are linked with its coming into force.

Mongolia

Chronology

1989

December 22: The People's Great Hural officially recognises the Mongolian Democratic Union (MDU), chaired by Sanjaasurengiyn Dzorig, as a political party.

1990

February 17: Members of the MDU found the Mongolian Democratic Party (MDP).

February: Three more opposition groups are founded: the New Progressive Association, the Social Democratic Party (SDP) and the Mongolian Students Association.

March 12: The General Secretary, Jambyn Batmonh, of the ruling Mongolian People's Revolutionary Party (MPRP) resigns. After persistent pressure by the opposition parties, the seven-member politburo also resigns. Gombojavyn Ochirbat is elected as the new MPRP General Secretary.

March 21: Opening of the Great Hural. Jambyn Batmonh resigns as Chairman of the Great Hural's Presidium, i.e. head of state. Deputy Chairman Dumaagiyn Sodnom, *de facto* Prime Minister, also resigns. Punsalmaagiyn Ochirbat, former Minister of External Economic Relations, is elected Chairman of the Great Hural's Presidium, i.e. head of state and Sharavyn Gungaadorj, former Minister of Agriculture, is elected Deputy Chairman, i.e. Prime Minister.

March 23: The People's Great Hural approves the removal from the Constitution of Article 82, which sets out the role of the MPRP in the Government, and approves by 324 votes in favour, with 10 abstentions a new electoral law allowing for multi-candidate elections.

May 11: The People's Great Hural approves: (i) legislation which legally entrenches the multiparty system; (ii) the formation of a standing parliament, the Little Hural, to be filled partly through popular election and (iii) the creation of the post of President.

July 29: Mongolia's first multiparty elections are held to (i) the 430-member People's Great Hural, (ii) the 53-member Little Hural and (iii) the municipal and provisional People's Hurals. Turnout 91.9 %. In the People's Great

Hural, the MPRP wins 357 seats; the pro-MPRP Mongolian Revolutionary Youth, nine seats; the MDP, 20 seats; the SDP, four seats; the National Progress Party, 6 seats; and 29 seats go to independents. In the Little Hural, the MPRP wins 33 seats, the MDP, 13 seats; the SDP, 4 seats; and the National Progressive Party, 3 seats.

September 3: The People's Great Hural elects, by 372 votes against 54, Punsalmaagiyn Ochirbat, MPRP, as Mongolia's first President.

September 7: The People's Great Hural elects Radnaasumbereliyn Gonchigdorj, SDP, as Vice-President.

September 11: The People's Great Hural elects MPRP central committee member Dashiyn Byambasuren as Prime Minister.

October 5: The Little Hural confirms the new Mongolian Cabinet, which is drawn from all four represented political parties: the ruling MPRP, the MDP, the National Progress Party and the Mongolian Green Party.

1991

December 2: A new party, the Party for Mongolian Renaissance, is created by a faction of the ruling, former communist party, the MPRP.

1992

January 13: The People's Great Hural adopts a new Constitution by 382 votes to 1, with 2 abstentions. The new Constitution renounces socialism, describing Mongolia as a republic with a parliamentary democracy and a directly elected president. The 76-member unicameral parliament, the People's Great Hural, is elected by a simple majority vote with a participation of at least 50% of the electors in each constituency.

January 16: Prime Minister, Dashiyn Byambasuren, tenders his resignation to the Great Hural proposing a government reshuffle. The Great Hural votes by 186 votes to 129 not to accept his resignation.

June 28: General elections take place. The MPRP takes 56.9% of the votes and wins 70 of the 76 seats in the People's Great Hural. A coalition of three opposition parties, made up of the National Progress party, the MDP and the Mongolian United Party, receives 17.5% of the vote and four seats. The SDP with 10.1% secures one seat and an independent MPRP candidate wins the remaining seat.

July 7: The Little Hural is disbanded and gives its place to the Great Hural to act as the country's new single-chamber legislative body.

July 21: Puntsagiyn Jarsay, MPRP, is elected as the new Prime Minister, by an overwhelming majority in the People's Great Hural.

October 27: Four major opposition parties (the MDP, the National Progress Party, the Mongolian United Party and the Party for Mongolian Renaissance) merge to form the Mongolian National Democratic Party (MNDP). Davaadorjiyn Ganbold is elected as chairman.

1993

April 10: The MPRP chooses Lodongiyn Tudev, editor of the official party newspaper, as its candidate for the direct presidential elections, to be held in June, in preference to Punsalmaagiyn Ochirbat.

April 16: The incumbent President Punsalmaagiyn Ochirbat, contests the presidential elections, supported by the MNDP and the SDP coalition.

June 6: Mongolia's first direct presidential elections take place. The incumbent President Punsalmaagiyn Ochirbat receives 57.8% of the votes and his sole opponent Lodongiyn Tudev 38.7%. Turnout 92.7%.

June 18: Ochirbat is formally sworn in as President.

1994

October 24: The government stays in office after a parliamentary vote of confidence on its performance since 1992.

1996

June 30: General parliamentary elections are held to the People's Great Hural. The Democratic Union coalition composed by the MNDP and the SDP defeats the MPRP, by winning 45 of the 76 seats. The final results: the MNDP gains 33 seats, the MPRP 25 seats, the SDP 12 seats, the Mongolian United Party one seat and 5 seats go to the remaining parties. Turnout 87.38%.

July 18: The People's Great Hural elects Radnaasumbereliyn Gonchigdorj, leader of the SDP, as its chair.

July 19: The People's Great Hural elects Mendsayhany Enhsayhan, leader of the Democratic Union coalition and former Minister for Culture, as Prime Minister and entrusts him with forming a new government.

July 30: The People's Great Hural approves the composition of the new government.

September: The Democratic Union coalition appoints Davaadorjiyn Ganbold, Chair of the MNDP, as its General Secretary, replacing Mendsayhany Enhsayhan.

Constitution of Mongolia[1]

Adopted by the People's Great Hural, 13 January 1992

A. The Constitution of Mongolia, January 1992

We, the people of Mongolia:
consolidating the independence and sovereignty of the nation,
cherishing human rights and freedoms, justice and national unity,
inheriting the traditions of national statehood, history and culture,
respecting the accomplishments of human civilisation,
aspiring to the supreme objective of building a humane and democratic civil
society in the country,
Hereby, proclaim the Constitution of Mongolia.

Chapter 1 – Sovereignty of the State

Article 1
1.   Mongolia is an independent, sovereign republic.
2.   The fundamental principles of the activities of the State shall be democracy, justice, freedom, equality and national unity and respect for the law.

Article 2
1.   By virtue of its state structure, Mongolia is a unitary State.
2.   The territory of Mongolia shall be divided into administrative units only.

Article 3
1.   State power shall be vested in the people of Mongolia. The people shall exercise it through their direct participation in State affairs as well as through the representative bodies of State power elected by them.
2.   Illegal seizure of State power or any attempt to do so shall be prohibited.

Article 4
1.   The territorial integrity and frontiers of Mongolia shall be inviolable.
2.   The frontiers of Mongolia shall be fixed and safeguarded by law.

---

1. Association of Secretaries General of Parliaments, Inter-Parliamentary Union

3.   The stationing of foreign troops in the territory of Mongolia and their crossing of State borders for the purpose of passing through the country's territory shall be prohibited unless an appropriate law is adopted.

Article 5
1.   Mongolia shall have an economy based on different forms of property and in accordance with both universal trends of world economic development and specific national characteristics.
2.   The State recognises all forms of both public and private property and shall protect the rights of the owner by law.
3.   The owner's rights shall be restricted exclusively by the law.
4.   The State shall regulate the economy of the country with a view to ensuring the nation's economic security, the development of all sectors of the economy and the social development of the population.
5.   Livestock is a national asset subject to State protection.

Article 6
1.   The land, its subsoil, forests, water, fauna and flora and other natural resources shall be subject to national sovereignty and State protection.
2.   The land, except that privately owned by citizens, as well as the subsoil with its mineral wealth, forests, water resources and game, shall be the property of the State.
3.   Apart from grazing land and areas under public and special use, the State may give plots of land for private ownership only to citizens of Mongolia. This provision shall not apply to ownership of the subsoil.
Citizens shall be prohibited from transferring the land in their possession to foreign nationals and stateless persons by way of selling, bartering, donating or pledging as well as transferring to others for exploitation without permission from competent State authorities.
4.   The State shall have the right to hold responsible the landowners in connection with the manner the land is used, to exchange or take it over with compensation on the grounds of special public need, or confiscate the land if it is used in a manner adverse to the health or the population, the interests of environmental protection and national security.
5.   The State may allow foreign nationals, legal persons and stateless persons to lease land for a specified period of time under conditions and procedures as provided for by law.

Article 7
1.   The historical, cultural, scientific and intellectual heritage of the Mongolian people shall be under State protection.
2.   Intellectual property produced by the citizens are the property of their authors and the national wealth of Mongolia.

Article 8
1.   The Mongolian language is the official language of the State.
2.   Section 1 of this Article shall not affect the right of national minorities of other tongues to use their native languages in education and communication and in the pursuit of cultural, artistic and scientific activities.

Article 9

1.   The State shall respect the Church and the Church shall honour the State.
2.   State institutions shall not engage in religious activities and religious institutions shall not pursue political activities.
3.   The relationship between the State and religious institutions shall be regulated by law.

Article 10

1.   Mongolia shall adhere to the universally recognised norms and principles of international law and pursue a peaceful foreign policy.
2.   Mongolia shall fulfil in good faith its obligations under national treaties to which it is a party.
3.   The international treaties to which Mongolia is a party shall become effective as domestic legislation upon the entry into force of the laws on their ratification or accession.
4.   Mongolia shall not abide by any international treaty or other instrument incompatible with its Constitution.

Article 11

1.   Securing the country's independence and ensuring national security and public order shall be the duty of the State.
2.   Mongolia shall have armed forces for self-defence. The structure and organisation of the armed forces and the rules of military service shall be determined by law.

Article 12

1.   The symbols of the independence and sovereignty of Mongolia are the State emblem, standard, flag, seal and the anthem.
2.   The State emblem, standard, flag and the anthem shall express the historical tradition, aspiration, unity, justice and the spirit of the people of Mongolia.
3.   The State emblem shall be based on the white lotus of purity. The outer frame shall be the "Tumen Nasan" of eternity in the shape of a blue sphere symbolising the eternal sky.
In the centre shall be a combination of the Golden Soyombo and the Treasured Steed, an expression of the independence, sovereignty and spirit of Mongolia.
In the upper part is the Chandmani which grants wishes and symbolises the past, present and future.
In the lower part shall be a green background of mountains representing Mother Earth and the Wheel of Destiny. Mixed in with the Wheel of Destiny shall be a khadag-a scarf symbolising welcome.
4.   The traditional great white standard representing the unified Mongolian State is a State ceremonial attribute.
5.   The State flag shall be divided vertically into three equal parts coloured red, blue and red. The three stripes, of identical width, shall be blue for the eternal sky in the middle, and red, the symbol of progress and prosperity, for the two stripes on either side. The Golden Soyombo shall be depicted in the

centre of the red stripe nearest to the flag-pole. The ratio of the width to length of the flag shall be 1:2.

6.   The State seal, having a lion-shaped handle, shall be square in form. It shall have the State Emblem in the centre and the words "Mongol Uls" (Mongolia) written on both sides. The holder of the State seal shall be the President.

7.   The procedure for the ceremonial use of the State symbols and the text and melody of the State anthem shall be prescribed by law.

Article 13

1.   The capital of the State shall be the city in which the State Supreme bodies sit on a permanent basis. The capital city of Mongolia is the city of Ulaanbaatar.

2.   The legal status of the capital city shall be determined by law.

Chapter 2 – Human rights and freedoms

Article 14

1.   All persons lawfully residing within Mongolia are equal before the law and the courts.

2.   No person shall be discriminated against on the basis of ethnic origin, language, race, age, sex, social origin and status, property, occupation and post, religion, opinion and education. Every person shall be a subject before the law.

Article 15

1.   The grounds and procedure for Mongolian nationality and the acquisition or loss of citizenship shall be defined only by law.

2.   Deprivation of Mongolian citizenship, exile and extradition of citizens of Mongolia shall be prohibited.

Article 16

The citizens of Mongolia shall enjoy the following fundamental rights and freedoms:

1.   the right to life. Deprivation of human life shall be strictly prohibited unless capital punishment, constituted by Mongolian penal law for the most serious crimes, is imposed by a competent court as its final decision.

2.   the right to a healthy and safe environment, and to be protected against environmental pollution and ecological imbalance.

3.   the right to fair acquisition, possession and inheritance of movable and immovable property. Illegal confiscation and requisitioning of the private property of citizens shall be prohibited. If the State and its bodies appropriate private property on the basis of exclusive pubic need, they shall make due compensation and payment.

4.   the right to free choice of employment, suitable conditions of work, remuneration, rest and private enterprise. No-one shall be unlawfully forced to work.

5.   the right to material and financial assistance in old age, disability, childbirth and childcare and in other cases provided for by law.

6. the right to protection of health and medical care. The procedure and conditions of free medical aid shall be determined by law.

7. the right to education. The State shall provide universal general education free of charge. Citizens may establish and operate private schools if these meet the requirements of the State.

8. the right to engage in creative work in cultural, artistic and scientific fields and to benefit therefrom. Copyrights and patents shall be protected by law.

9. the right to take part in the government of the country directly or through representative bodies. The right to vote and to stand for election to State bodies. The right to vote shall be enjoyed from the age of 18 years and the minimum age for membership shall be determined by law according to the requirements in respect of the bodies or posts concerned.

10. the right to freedom of association in political parties or other voluntary organisations on the basis of social and personal interests and opinion. Political parties and other mass organisations shall uphold public order and State security, and abide by the law. Discrimination against or persecution of a person for joining a political party or other associations or for being a member thereof shall be prohibited. Party membership of some categories of State employees may be suspended.

11. men and women shall enjoy equal rights in political, economic, social, cultural fields and in marriage. Marriage shall be based on the equality and mutual consent of the spouses who have reached the age determined by law. The State shall protect the interests of the family, motherhood and the child.

12. the right to submit a petition or a complaint to State bodies and officials. State bodies and officials shall be obliged to respond to the petitions or complaints of citizens in conformity with law.

13. the right to personal liberty and safety. No one shall be searched, arrested, detained, prosecuted or restricted of liberty save in accordance with procedures and grounds determined by law. No one shall be subjected to torture, inhuman, cruel or degrading treatment. When a person has been arrested he/she, his/her family and counsel shall be notified within a period of time established by law of the reasons for and grounds of the arrest. Privacy of citizens, their families, correspondence and homes shall be protected by law.

14. the right to appeal to the court to protect his/her rights if he/she considers that the rights or freedoms as spelt out by Mongolian law or an international treaty have been violated; to be compensated for the damage illegally caused by others; not to testify against himself/herself, his/her family, or parents and children; to defence; to receive legal assistance; to have evidence examined; to a fair trial; to be tried in his/her presence; to appeal against a court decision; to seek pardon. Compelling a person to testify against himself/herself shall be prohibited. Every person shall be presumed innocent until proved guilty by a court by due process of law. The penalities imposed on the convicted shall not be applicable to his/her family members and relatives.

15. freedom of conscience and religious belief.

16. freedom of thought, opinion and expression, speech, press, assembly and peaceful demonstration. Procedures for organising demonstrations and other assemblies shall be determined by law.

17. the right to seek and receive information except that which the State and its bodies are legally bound to protect as secret. Information which is not subject to disclosure shall be classified and protected by law in order to protect human rights and the dignity and reputation of persons and to ensure national defence, security and public order.

18. the right to freedom of movement and residence within the country, to travel and reside abroad and to return to the home country. The right to travel and reside abroad may be limited exclusively by law for the purpose of ensuring the security of the country and population and protecting public order.

Article 17

1. Citizens of Mongolia, while upholding justice and humanism, shall fulfil in good faith the following basic duties:
    1. to respect and abide by the Constitution and other laws;
    2. to respect the dignity, reputation, rights and legitimate interests of others;
    3. to pay taxes levied by law;
    4. to defend the motherland and serve in the army according to the law.
2. working, protecting his/her health, bringing up and educating his/her children and protecting nature and the environment shall be a sacred duty for every citizen.

Article 18

1. The rights and duties of aliens residing in Mongolia shall be regulated by Mongolian law and by the treaties concluded with the State of the person concerned.
2. Mongolia shall adhere to the principle of reciprocity in determining the rights and duties of foreign nationals when concluding international treaties.
3. The rights and duties of stateless persons within the territory of Mongolia shall be determined by Mongolian law.
4. Aliens or stateless persons persecuted for their convictions, political or other activities in pursuit of justice, may be granted asylum in Mongolia on the basis of their well-founded request.
5. In allowing the foreign nationals and stateless persons under the jurisdiction of Mongoia to exercise the basic rights and freedoms provided for in Article 16 of this Constitution, the State of Mongolia may establish necessary restrictions upon the rights other than the inalienable rights spelt out in the international instruments to which Mongolia is a party, out of a concern to ensure the security of the country and population, and public order.

Article 19

1. The State shall be responsible to the citizens for the creation of economic, social, legal and other guarantees ensuring human rights and freedoms, for the prevention of violations of human rights and freedoms and the restoration of infringed rights.
2. In case of a state of emergency or martial law, the human rights and freedoms defined by the Constitution and other laws shall be subject to limitation

only by a law. Such a law shall not affect the right to life, freedom of opinion, conscience and religion, as well as the right not to be subjected to torture, inhuman and cruel treatment.

3.   In exercising his/her rights and freedoms, a person may not infringe national security or the rights and freedoms of others or violate public order.

Chapter 3 – Structure of the State

I.   The State Great Hural

Article 20
The State Great Hural is the highest organ of State power, and legislative power shall be vested solely therein.

Article 21
1.   The State Great Hural shall have one chamber and consist of 76 members.
2.   The members of the State Great Hural shall be elected by citizens qualified to vote, on the basis of universal, free, direct suffrage by secret ballot for a term of four years.
3.   Citizens of Mongolia who exercise their electoral rigths and have reached the age of 25 shall be eligible for election to the State Great Hural.
4.   The procedure for the election of members of the State Great Hural shall be determined by law.

Article 22
1.   If extraordinary circumstances arising from sudden calamities in the whole or part of the country or imposition of martial law or outbreak of public disorder prevent the holding of regular general elections, the State Great Hural shall retain its mandate until the extraordinary circumstances cease to exist and the newly elected members of the State Great Hural have been sworn in.
2.   The State Great Hural may decide on its dissolution if not less than two-thirds of its members consider that it is unable to carry out its mandate, or if the President, in consultation with the Chairman of the State Great Hural, proposes to do so for the same reason. In the event of such a decision, the State Great Hural shall exercise its powers until its newly elected members have been sworn in.

Article 23
1.   A member of the State Great Hural shall be an envoy of the people, and shall represent and uphold the interests of all the citizens and the State.
2.   The mandate of a member of the State Great Hural shall begin with an oath taken before the State Emblem and shall expire when newly elected members of the State Great Hural are sworn in.

Article 24
1.   The Chairman and Vice-Chairman of the State Great Hural shall be nominated and elected from among the members of that body by secret ballot.

2. The term of office of the Chairman and Vice-Chairman of the State Great Hural shall be four years. They can be relieved of or removed from their posts before the expiry to their terms for reasons defined by law.

Article 25

1. The State Great Hural may consider on its own initiative any issue pertaining to domestic and foreign policies of the country. It shall be the sole competent body for the following questions:

    1. adopting, supplementing and amending laws;
    2. determining the basis of the State's domestic and foreign policies;
    3. setting and announcing the dates of elections of President, the State Great Hural and its members;
    4. determining and changing the structure and composition of the Standing Committees of the State Great Hural, the Government and other bodies directly accountable to it under the law;
    5. passing a law validating the election of the President and recognising his powers, releasing him from his duties or recalling him;
    6. appointing, replacing or removing the Prime Minister, members of the Government and other bodies responsible and accountable to the State Great Hural as provided for by law;
    7. defining the State's financial, credit, tax and monetary policies, laying down basic guidelines for the country's economic and social development, approving the Government's programme of action, the State budget and the report on its execution;
    8. supervising the implementation of laws and other decisions of the State Great Hural;
    9. defining the State's borders;
    10. determining the structure, composition and powers of the National Security Council of Mongolia;
    11. approving and changing the administrative and territorial division of the country at the suggestion of the Government;
    12. determining the legal basis of the system, structure and activities of local self-governing and administrative bodies;
    13. instituting titles, orders, medals and higher military ranks, determining the table of ranks in some special fields of State service;
    14. issuing acts of amnesty;
    15. ratifying and denouncing international agreements to which Mongolia is a party, establishing and severing diplomatic relations with foreign States at the suggestion of the Government;
    16. holding national referendums, verifying the validity of a referendum in which the majority of eligible citizens has taken part, and considering the question which has obtained a majority vote as decided;
    17. declaring a state of war in the event that the sovereignty and independence of the State are threatened by armed actions on the part of a foreign power, and ending it;
    18. declaring a state of emergency or martial law in the whole or some parts of the country in special circumstances described in Sections 2 and 3 of this Article, and approving or nullifying the President's decree to that effect.

2. Under the following extraordinary circumstances the State Great Hural

may declare a state of emergency to eliminate the consequences thereof and to restore the life of the population and society to the norm:

1.   natural disasters or other unforeseen dangers which directly threaten or may threaten the life, health, well-being and security of the population in the whole or a part of the country's territory;

2.   if the public authorities are not able within legal limits to cope with public disorders caused by organised, violent, illegal actions of an organisation or a group of people threatening the constitutional order and the existence of the legitimate social system.

3.   The State Great Hural may declare martial law if public disorders in the whole or a part of the country's territory result in armed conflict or create a real threat of an armed conflict, or if there is an armed aggression or a real threat of such aggression by a foreign State.

4.   The other powers, organisation and the procedures of the State Great Hural shall be defined by law.

Article 26

1.   The President, members of the State Great Hural and the Government shall have the right of legislative initiative.

2.   Citizens and other organisations shall forward their suggestions on draft laws to those entitled to initiate a law.

3.   National laws shall be subject to official promulgation through pubication and, if the law does not provide otherwise, shall enter into force ten days after the date of publication.

Article 27

1.   The State Great Hural shall exercise its powers through its sessions and other organisational forms.

2.   Regular sessions of the State Great Hural shall be convened once every six months. Each session shall last not less than 75 working days.

3.   Special sessions may be convened at the demand of more than one-third of the members of the State Great Hural, and/or on the initiative of the President and the Chairman of the State Great Hural.

4.   The President shall convene constitutent sessions of the State Great Hural within 30 days following the elections. Other sessions shall be convened by the Chairman of the State Great Hural.

5.   Should the President proclaim a state of emergency or war, the State Great Hural shall be convened for a special session within 72 hours without prior announcement.

6.   The presence of an overwhelming majority of members of the State Great Hural shall be required to consider a session valid, and decisions shall be taken by a majority of all members present if the Constitution and other laws do not provide otherwise.

Article 28

1.   The State Great Hural shall establish the Standing Committees it needs to carry out its activities.

2.   The State Great Hural shall determine the competence, organisation, and procedures of the Standing Committees.

Article 29

1. Members of the State Great Hural shall be remunerated from the State budget during their tenure. They shall not concurrently hold any posts and employment other than those assigned by law.
2. Immunity of members of the State Great Hural shall be protected by law.
3. The State Great Hural, meeting in plenary, shall debate questions concerning the involvement of one of its members in a crime to decide on the suspension of his/her mandate. If a court rules that the member is guilty, it shall end his/her term of office.

2. The President

Article 30

1. The President shall be the Head of State and embodiment of the unity of the Mongol people.
2. A citizen born a Mongol who has attained the age of 45 years, and has permanently resided as a minimum for the last five years in Mongolia, shall be eligible for election to the post of President for a term of four years.

Article 31

1. Presidential elections shall be conducted in two stages.
2. Political parties which have obtained seats in the State Great Hural shall nominate individually or collectively presidential candidates, with one candidate per party or coalition of parties.
3. At the primary stage of the elections, citizens eligible to vote shall participate in electing the President on the basis of universal, free and direct suffrage by secret ballot.
4. The State Great Hural shall consider the candidate who has obtained a majority of all votes cast in the first voting as elected the President, and shall pass a law recognising his/her powers.
5. If none of the candidates obtains a majority of votes in the first round, voting shall take place a second time involving the two candidates who have obtained the largest number of votes in the first round. The candidate who wins a majority of all votes cast in the second ballot shall be considered as elected, and the State Great Hural shall pass a law recognising his/her powers.
6. If neither of the candidates wins in the second ballot, presidential elections shall be held anew.
7. The President shall only be eligible for re-election once.
8. The President shall not be Prime Minister, a member of the State Great Hural or a member of the Government. Nor shall he hold concurrently any other posts or pursue any occupation not relating to his duties assigned by law. If the President holds another office or a post, he/she shall be relieved of it from the date on which he/she is inaugurated.

Article 32

1. The mandate of the President shall become effective with an oath taken by him/her and shall expire with an oath taken by the newly elected President.

2.   Within 30 days after the election the President shall take an oath before the State Great Hural: "I swear to guard and defend the independence and sovereignty of Mongolia, freedom of the people and national unity and to uphold and observe the Constitution and faithfully perform the duties of President".

Article 33
1.   The President enjoys the following prerogatives:
    1.   to veto, wholly or partially, laws and other decisions adopted by the State Great Hural. The laws or decisions shall remain in force if two thirds of the members of the State Great Hural present do not accept the President's veto;
    2.   to propose to the State Great Hural the name of a candidature for appointment to the post of Prime Minister in consultation with the majority party or parties in the State Great Hural if none of them has obtained a majority, as well as to propose to the State Great Hural the dissolution of the Government;
    3.   to instruct the Government on issues within his competence. If the President issues a relevant decree it shall become effective upon signature by the Prime Minister;
    4.   to represent the Mongolian State in foreign relations and, in consultation with the State Great Hural, to conclude international treaties on behalf of Mongolia;
    5.   to appoint and recall heads of plenipotentiary missions to foreign countries in consultation with the State Great Hural;
    6.   to receive the letters of accreditation or recall of heads of diplomatic missions of foreign States;
    7.   to confer State titles and higher military ranks and award orders and medals;
    8.   to grant pardon;
    9.   to decide matters related to the granting and withdrawing of Mongolian citizenship and the granting of asylum;
    10. to head the National Security Council of Mongolia;
    11. to declare general or partial conscription;
    12. to declare a state of emergency or martial law on the whole or a part of the national territory and to order the deployment of armed forces when extraordinary circumstances described in Sections 2 and 3 of Article 25 of this Constitution arise and the State Great Hural, in between two sessions, cannot be summoned at short notice. The State Great Hural shall consider within seven days the presidential decree declaring a state of emergency or martial law and shall approve or disapprove it. If the State Great Hural does not take a decision on the matter, the presidential decree shall become null and void.
2.   The President shall be the Commander-in-Chief of the Armed Forces of Mongolia.
3.   The President may address messages to the State Great Hural and/or to the people; he may at his own discretion attend sessions of the State Great Hural, report on and submit proposals concerning vital issues of domestic and foreign policies of the country.
4.   Other specific powers may be vested in the President only by law.

Article 34

1.   The President within his powers shall issue decrees in conformity with the law.

2.   If a presidential decree is incompatible with the law, the President himself or the State Great Hural shall invalidate it.

Article 35

1.   The President shall be responsible to the State Great Hural.

2.   If the event of a violation of the Constitution and/or abuse of power in breach of his oath, the President may be removed from his post on the basis of the findings of the Constitutional Court by an overwhelming majority of members of the State Great Hural present and voting.

Article 36

1.   The person, residence and transport of the President shall be inviolable.

2.   The dignity and immunity of the President shall be protected by law.

Article 37

1.   In the temporary absence of the President, his powers shall be exercised by the Chaiman of the State Great Hural.

2.   In the event of the resignation, death or voluntary retirement of the President, his powers shall be exercised by the Chairman of the State Great Hural pending the inauguration of the newly elected President. In such a case, the State Great Hural shall announce and hold presidential elections within four months.

3.   The procedure for the discharge of presidential duties by the Chairman of the State Great Hural shall be determined by law.

3.   The Government

Article 38

1.   The Government is the highest executive body of the State.

2.   Carrying out the State laws and directing the economic, social and cultural development of the country, the Government shall exercise the following powers:

    1.   to organise and ensure nationwide implementation of the Constitution and other laws;

    2.   to work out a comprehensive policy on science and technology, basic guidelines for economic and social development, the State budget, credit and fiscal plans and to submit these to the State Great Hural and to execute decisions taken thereon;

    3.   to elaborate and implement comprehensive measures on sectoral, intersectoral, as well as regional development;

    4.   to undertake measures on the protection of the environment and on the rational use and restoration of natural resources;

    5.   to head central state administrative bodies and to direct the activities of local administrations;

    6.   to strenghten the country's defence capabilities and to ensure national security;

7.   to take measures for the protection of human rights and freedoms, enforcement of public order and prevention of crime;

8.   to implement the State's foreign policy;

9.   to conclude and implement international treaties with the consent of and subsequent ratification by the State Great Hural as well as to conclude and abrogate intergovernmental treaties.

3.   The specific powers, structure and procedure of the Government shall be determined by law.

Article 39

1.   The Government shall comprise the Prime Minister and members.

2.   The Prime Minister shall, in consultation with the President, submit his/her proposals on the structure and composition of the Government and on the changes in these to the State Great Hural.

3.   The State Great Hural shall discuss individually each of the candidatures proposed on the structure and composition of the Government and on the changes in these to the State Great Hural.

4.   The State Great Hural shall discuss individually each of the candidatures proposed by the Prime Minister and take decisions on their appointment.

Article 40

1.   The term of the mandate of the Government shall be four years.

2.   The term of office of the Government shall start from the day of the appointment of the Prime Minister by the State Great Hural and terminate upon the appointment of a new Prime Minister.

Article 41

1.   The Prime Minister shall lead the Government and shall be responsible to the State Great Hural for the implementation of State laws.

2.   The Government shall be accountable for its work to the State Great Hural.

Article 42

1.   Personal immunity of the Prime Minister and members of the Government shall be protected by law.

Article 43

1.   The Prime Minister may tender his/her resignation to the State Great Hural before the expiry of his/her term of office if he/she considers that the Government is unable to exercise its powers.

2.   The Government shall step down in its entirely upon the resignation of the Prime Minister or if half of the members of the Government resign at the same time.

3.   The State Great Hural, after having taken the initiative to dissolve the Government, having received a proposal from the President of the Republic to this effect or having received a statement or notice of resignation from the Prime Minister, shall debate the matter and decide in favour thereof or against within fifteen days.

4.   The State Great Hural shall consider and take a decision on the dissolution of the Government if not less than one-fourth of the members of the State Great Hural officially propose the dissolution of the Government.

Article 44
If the Government submits a draft resolution requesting a vote of confidence, the State Great Hural shall proceed with the matter in accordance with Section 3 of Article 43.

Article 45
1.   The Government shall, in conformity with legislation, issue decrees and ordinances which shall be signed by the Prime Minister and the Minister responsible for their application.
2.   If these decrees and ordinances are incompatible with laws and regulations, the Government itself or the State Great Hural shall invalidate them.

Article 46
1.   Ministries and other government offices shall be constituted in accordance with law.
2.   State employees shall be Mongolian nationals. They shall strictly abide by the Constitution and other laws and work for the benefit of the people and in the interests of the State.
3.   The work conditions and social guarantees of State employees shall be determined by law.

4.   The judiciary

Article 47
1.   In Mongolia, the judicial power shall be vested exclusively in courts.
2.   Regardless of the circumstances, unlawful constitution of courts and exercise of judicial power by any other organisation but courts shall be prohibited.
3.   Courts shall be constituted solely under the Constitution and other laws.

Article 48
1.   The judicial system shall consist of the Supreme Court, Aimag (province) and capital city courts, Soum (provincial district), intersoum and Düüreg (city district) courts. Specialised courts such as criminal, civil, and administrative courts may be formed. The activities and decisions of these specialised courts shall not be removed from the supervision of the Supreme Court.
2.   The structure of courts and the legal basis of their activities shall be defined by law.
3.   The courts shall be financed from the State budget. The State shall provide an economic guarantee of the courts' activities.

Article 49
1.   Judges shall be independent and subject only to the law.

2. Neither any private person nor the President, Prime Minister, members of the State Great Hural or the Government, officials of political parties or other voluntary organisations shall interfere with the way in which judges exercise their duties.

3. So as to ensure the independence of the judiciary, a General Council of Courts shall function.

4. The General Council of Courts, without interfering in the activities of courts and judges, shall deal exclusively with the selection of judges from among lawyers, protection of their rights and other matters pertaining to the ensurance of conditions guaranteeing the independence of the judiciary.

5. The organisation and procedures of the General Council of Courts shall be defined by law.

Article 50

1. The Supreme Court shall be the highest judicial organ. It shall exercise the following powers:

    1. to try at first instance criminal cases and legal disputes under its jurisdiction;

    2. to examine decisions of lower-instance courts through appeal and supervision;

    3. to examine and take decision on matters related to the protection of law and human rights and freedoms therein and transferred to it by the Constitutional Court and the Prosecutor-General;

    4. to provide official interpretations for correct application of all other laws except the Constitution;

    5. to make judgments on all other matters assigned to it by law.

2. Decision taken by the Supreme Court shall be a final judiciary decision and shall be binding upon all courts and other persons. If a decision taken by the Supreme Court is incompatible with law, the Supreme Court itself shall have to repeal it. If an interpretation made by the Supreme Court is incompatible with a law, the latter shall have precedence.

3. The Supreme Court and other Courts shall have no right to apply laws that are unconstitutional or have not been promulgated.

Article 51

1. The Supreme Court shall comprise the Erönhii Shüügch (Chief Justice) and judges.

2. The President shall appoint the judges of the Supreme Court upon their presentation to the State Great Hural by the General Council of Courts.

3. A Mongolian national who has reached 35 years of age with a higher education in law and a professional career of not less than ten years may be appointed a judge of the Supreme Court. A Mongolian national of 25 years of age with a higher education in law and a professional career of not less than three years may be appointed a judge of the other courts.

4. Removal of a judge of a court of any instance shall be prohibited except in cases where he/she is relieved at his/her own request or removed on the grounds provided for in the Constitution and/or the law on the Judiciary and by a valid court decision.

Article 52

1.   Courts of all instances shall consider and pass judgment on cases and disputes on the basis of collective decision-making.

2.   In passing a collective decision on cases and disputes, the courts of first instance shall allow representatives of citizens to participate in the proceedings in accordance with the procedures prescribed by law.

3.   A judge alone may take a decision on certain cases which are specifically singled out by law.

Article 53

1.   Court trials shall be conducted in the Mongolian language.

2.   A person who does not know Mongolian shall be acquainted with all the facts of the case through translation and shall have the right to use his/her native language at the trial.

Article 54

Courts trials shall be open to the public except in cases specifically singled out by law.

Article 55

1.   The accused shall have the right to defend himself.

2.   The accused shall be accorded legal assistance according to law and at his/her request.

Article 56

1.   The prosecutor shall exercise supervision over the inquiry into the investigation of cases and the execution of punishment, and shall participate in the court proceedings on behalf of the State.

2.   The President shall appoint the Prosecutor-General and his/her deputies in consultation with the State Great Hural for a term of six years.

3.   The system, structure and legal basis of the activities of the Prosecutor's Office shall be determined by law.

Chapter 4 – Administrative and territorial units and their governing bodies

Article 57

1.   The territory of Mongolia shall be divided administratively into Aimags and a capital city; Aimags shall be subdivided into Soums; Soums into Baghs (provincial subdistrict); the capital city shall be divided into Düüregs and Düüregs into Horoos (city subdistrict).

2.   The legal status of towns and other settlements located on the territories of administrative divisions shall be defined by law.

3.   Revision of an administrative and territorial unit shall be considered and decided by the State Great Hural on the basis of an opinion by a respective local Hural and local population, and with account taken of the country's economic structure and the distribution of the population.

Article 58

1.   Aimags, the capital city, Soums and Düüregs are administrative, territorial and economic and social complexes with their functions and administrations provided for by law.

2.   The borders of Aimags, the capital city, Soums and Düüregs shall be approved by the State Great Hural at the suggestion of the Government.

Article 59
1.   Governance of administrative and territorial units of Mongollia shall be organised on the basis of a combination of the principles of both self-government and central government.
2.   The self-government bodies in Aimags, the capital city, Soums and Düüregs shall be Hurals (Assemblies) of representatives of the citizens of respective territories; in Baghs and Horoos, general meetings of citizens. In between the sessions of the Hurals and general meetings their Presidiums shall assume administrative functions.
3.   Hurals of Aimags and the capital city shall be elected for a term of four years. The memberships of these Hurals, as well as those of Soums and districts, and the procedure of their election shall be determined by law.

Article 60
1.   State power shall be exercised on the territories of Aimags, the capital city, Soums, Düüregs, Baghs and Horoos by the Zasag Darga (governor) of these territories.
2.   Candidates for Zasag Darga are nominated by the Hurals of respective Aimags, the capital city, Soums, Düüregs, Baghs and Horoos, Zasag Darga of the respective Aimags and the capital city are appointed by the Prime Minister; Soum and Düüreg Zasag Darga by the Zasag Darga of Aimags and the capital city; Zasag Dargas of Baghs and Horoos by the Zasag Dargas of Soums and respectively for a term of four years.
3.   If a gubernatorial nominee is not accepted by the Prime Minister or a Zasag Darga of a higher level, the previously appointed Zasag Darga shall exercise his/her mandate pending the appointment of a new Zasag Darga in the manner prescribed in Section 2 of this Article.

Article 61
1.   While working for the implementation of the decisions of a respective Hural, a Zasag Darga, as a representative of State power, shall be responsible to the Government and the Zasag Darga of higher instance for proper observance of national laws and fulfilment of the decisions of the Government and the respective superior body in his/her territory.
2.   Zasag Darga shall have a right to veto decisions of the respective Aimag, capital city, Soum, Düüreg, Bagh or Horoo Hurals.
3.   If a Hural by a majority vote overrides the veto, the Zasag Darga may tender his/her resignation to the Prime Minister or to the Zasag Darga of higher instance if he/she considers that he/she is not able to implement the decision concerned.
4.   Zasag Dargas of Aimags, the capital city, Soums and Düüregs shall have secretariat/Offices of the Seal. The Government shall determine the structure and sizes of these offices individually or by a uniform standard.

Article 62
1.   Local self-governing bodies, besides making independent decisions on matters concerning the economic and social life of the respective Aimag, the

capital city, Soum, Düüreg, Bagh and Horoo, shall organise the participation of the population in solving problems of larger territorial divisions and those of a national scale.

2.   Authorities of higher instance shall not take decision on matters coming under the jurisdiction of local self-governing bodies. If law and decisions of respective superior State organs do not specifically deal with definite local matters, local self-governing bodies can decide upon them independently in conformity with the Constitution.

3.   If the State Great Hural and the Government deem it necessary, they may refer some matters within their competence to the Aimag and capital city Hurals and Zasag Darga for them to solve.

Article 63
1.   Hurals of Aimag, the capital city, Soums, Düüregs, Baghs and Horoos shall adopt resolutions and Governors shall issue ordinances within their competence.

2.   Resolutions of the Hurals and ordinances of the Zasag Darga shall be in conformity with Presidential decrees and decisions of the Government and shall be binding within their respective territories.

3.   Administrative and territorial units, and the powers, structure and procedure of their governing bodies shall be determined by law.

Chapter 5 – Ündsen Huuliin Tsets (The Constitutional Court)

Article 64
1.   The Constitutional Court shall be an organ exercising supreme supervision over the implementation of the Constitution, handing down conclusions on the violation of its provisions and resolving constitutional disputes. It shall be the guarantee for the strict observance of the Constitution.

2.   The Constitutional Court and its members in the execution of their duties shall be subject to the Constitution only and shall be independent of any organisation, official or any other person.

3.   The independence of the members of the Constitutional Court shall be ensured by the guarantees set out in the Constitution and other laws.

Article 65
1.   The Constitutional Court shall consist of nine members, Members of the Constitutional Court shall be appointed by the State Great Hural for a term of six years, with three of them to be nominated by the State Great Hural, three by the President and the remaining three by the Supreme Court.

2.   A member of the Constitutional Court shall be a Mongolian national who has reached 40 years of age and has high political and legal qualifications.

3.   The Chairman of the Constitutional Court shall be elected from among nine members for a term of three years by a majority vote of the members of the Constitutional Court. He is eligible for re-election once.

4.   If the Chairman or a member of the Constitutional Court violates the law, he/she may be withdrawn by the State Great Hural on the basis of the decision of the Constitutional Court and on the opinion of the institution which nominated him/her.

5. The President, members of the State Great Hural, the Prime Minister, members of the Government and members of the Supreme Court shall not be nominated to serve on the Constitutional Court.

Article 66
1.   The Constitutional Court shall examine and settle constitutional disputes on its initiative on the basis of petitions and information received from citizens or at the request of the State Great Hural, the President, the Prime Minister, the Supreme Court and the Prosecutor-General.
2.   The Constitutional Court, in accordance with Section 1 of this Article, shall give its conclusions to the State Great Hural on:
    1.   the conformity of laws, decrees and other decisions by the State Great Hural and the President, as well as Government decisions and international treaties signed by Mongolia with the Constitution;
    2.   the constitutionality of decisions of the central election authorities on national referendums and the elections of the State Great Hural and its members as well as presidential elections;
    3.   breaches of law by the President, Chairman and members of the State Great Hural, the Prime Minister, members of the Government, the Chief Justice and the Prosecutor-General;
    4.   the well-foundedness of the grounds for the removal of the President, Chairman of the State Great Hural and the Prime Minister and for the recall of members of the State Great Hural.
3.   If a conclusion submitted in accordance with Clauses 1 and 2 of Section 2 of this Article is not accepted by the State Great Hural, the Constitutional Court shall re-examine it and take a final decision.
4.   If the Constitutional Court decides that the laws, decrees and other decisions of the State Great Hural and the President as well as Government decisions and international treaties concluded by Mongolia are incompatible with the Constitution, the laws, decrees, instruments of ratification and decisions in question shall be considered invalid.

Article 67
Decisions of the Constitutional Court shall enter into force immediately.

Chapter 6 – Amendment of the Constitution

Article 68
1.   Amendments to the Constitution may be initiated by organisations and officials enjoying the right to legislative initiative and/or proposed by the Constitutional Court to the State Great Hural.
2.   A national referendum on constitutional amendment may be held on the concurrence of not less than two-thirds fo the members of the State Great Hural. The referendum shall be held in accordance with the provisions of Clause 16, Section 1, Article 25 of the Constitution.

Article 69
1.   The Constitution and any amendments thereto shall be adopted by a vote of not less than three-fourths of all members of the State Great Hural.

2.   A draft amendment to the Constitution which has twice failed to win three-fourths of the votes of all members of the State Great Hural may not be reconsidered until the State Great Hural has been reconvened with its new members following regular general elections.
3.   The State Great Hural shall not undertake amendment of the Constitution within the six months prior to the next general elections.
4.   Amendments which have been adopted shall have the same force as the Constitution.

Article 70
1.   Laws, decrees and other decisions of State bodies, and activities of all other organisations and citizens must be in conformity with the Constitution.
2.   This Constitution of Mongolia shall enter into force at 12.00 hours on 12 February 1992, i.e. at the hour of the Horse on the prime and benevolent ninth day of the Yellow Horse of the first spring month of the Black Tiger, in the year of the Water Monkey of the Seventeenth 60-year Cycle.

Learn the Constitution and Abide by it

The Great People's Hural
of the
Mongolian People's Republic

Ulaanbaatar
11.35 a.m., 13 January 1992

B. Provisional Law annexed to the Constitution of Mongolia, January 1992

On the transition from the Constitution of the MPR to the Constitution of Mongolia

Article 1 – Re-organisation of supreme legislative and executive bodies in accordance with the Constitution of Mongolia
1.   Following the elections for the State Great Hural to be held in June 1992 in accordance with the provisions of the Constitution of Mongolia, the State Great Hural of Mongolia shall be established and shall form the Government of Mongolia.
2.   The Great People's Hural and the State Baga Hural of the MPR shall retain their mandates until the State Great Hural and the Government of Mongolia are formed and they start to exercise their powers. During this period:
    1.   the Great People's Hural may on its own initiative consider and decide any matters pertaining to either domestic or foreign policy and may elect, relieve and/or remove the President and Vice-President, introduce changes in the composition of the State Baga Hural and appoint, replace and/or remove the Prime Minister in accordance with Clauses 6, 7 of Section 1 of Article 25 of the Constitution of Mongolia, determine the basic guidelines of the economic and social development of the country, and also exercise the powers provided by Article 69 of the Constitution of Mongolia.
    2.   the State Baga Hural shall exercise full powers provided for by the Constitution of Mongolia in the capacity of the Supreme Legislature except in matters specifically assigned by this Annexed Law to the jurisdiction of the Great People's Hural. It shall further take decisions to appoint and/or relieve the Prime Minister in between sessions of the Great People's Hural, subject to subsequent confirmation by the latter.
    3.   the Government of the MPR shall retain its mandate until the State Great Hural forms a new Government, during which period it shall exercise its full powers provided for by the Constitution of Mongolia.

Article 2 – Exercise of power by the President
1.   In accordance with the provisions of the Constitution of Mongolia, the first President of the MPR shall exercise the powers of the President of the Republic until a new President has been elected and sworn in. From the day the Constitution of Mongolia enters into force, the President shall be called the President of Mongolia.
2.   The election of the President of Mongolia shall be held in June 1993.

Article 3 – Exercise of judicial power (reorganisation of courts and prosecution)
1.   As provided for by the Constitution of Mongolia, judges of all instances and people's assessors shall exercise their full powers in conformity with the Constitution of Mongolia until the General Council of Courts has been formed and judges of appropriate instances have been appointed by the President of Mongolia.

2.   The Prosecutor-General appointed by the Great People's Hural and sub-ordinate Prosecutors shall exercise their powers in conformity with the Constitution of Mongolia until a law on the Prosecution has been enacted and the President of Mongolia has appointed the Prosecutor-General.

3.   The reorganisation of the system of courts and prosecution as provided for by the Constitution of Mongolia, shall be carried out by the end of 1993.

4.   The Constitution Court (Tsets) shall be formed within thirty days following the day on which an appropriate law comes into effect.

Article 4 – Implementation of Constitutional provisions on administrative and territorial units of Mongolia and their governing bodies

1.   Until Hurals of representatives of citizens of Aimags, the capital city, Soums and districts have been formed and Zasag Darga (governors) have been appointed, the People's Hurals of all instances and their Presidiums, executive authorities and their subordinate bodies shall exercise their full powers in accordance with the laws on People's Hurals and other relevant laws.

2.   As provided for by the Constitution of Mongolia, the forming of local self-governing bodies, administrative integration of towns of local status situated in the territories of some Aimags, of Horoos and Düüregs in the territories of other Soums into respective Aimags and Soums, the reorganisation of existing districts in the capital city into new districts and Horoos as well as forming of Baghs in rural areas shall be carried out by 1993.

3.   Until the legal status of towns and urban areas has been determined by law and their local governments have been set up accordingly, the towns of Darhan, Choyr and Erdenet shall have on their present territories administrative and territorial structures comparable to those of Aimags.

Article 5 – Verification of the Constitutionality of legislation

1.   All laws in effect prior to the enactment of the Constitution of Mongolia shall be further observed as having force if they do not contradict this Constitution.

2.   Relations to be regulated only by law as prescribed by the Constitution of Mongolia, shall be subject to regulation, until a new law has been enacted to that effect, by the provisions of laws and other legal instruments which have governed such relations before. Consequently, laws provided for by the Constitution shall be adopted in 1993 in accordance with the timetable worked out by the State Baga Hural.

3.   From the day the Constitution of Mongolia enters into force, the laws and other legal instruments and their provisions incompatible with this Constitution shall be regarded as void.

4.   The alignment of legislation with the Constitution of Mongolia shall be completed by the end of 1996.

Article 6 – The Constitution of Mongolia and international treaties of Mongolia

1.   International treaties to which the MPR has been a Party prior to the entry into force of the Constitution of Mongolia shall be further abided by if they do not contradict this Constitution.

2.   If an international treaty of the MPR is not contrary to the Constitution of Mongolia but is in contradiction to the provisions of other laws of Mongolia, the provisions of the respective international treaty shall have precedence.
3.   If international treaties of the MPR or their provisions are contrary to the Constitution of Mongolia, the question of their alignment with this Constitution shall be resolved in 1993 in accordance with the universally recognised principles of international law and the conditions and procedures set out by the respective treaties.

Article 7 – The Constitution of Mongolia and human rights
1.   All persons who were nationals of the MPR on the day the Constitution of Mongolia entered into force shall remain citizens of Mongolia.
2.   Until relevant laws have been enacted, issues relating to the withdrawal of Mongolian citizenship and granting this citizenship to aliens and stateless persons shall be resolved in accordance with the "Law on the citizenship of the MPR", and the "Law on the rights and duties of aliens residing in the MPR", in conformity with the substance of the Constitution of Mongolia.
3.   Application of laws and international treaties of the MPR and their provisions which degrade human rights spelt out in the Constitution of Mongolia shall be prohibited once the Constitution of Mongolia has come into effect. If the provisions of a law of Mongolia or of an international treaty which are not contrary to the Constitution of Mongolia contradict human rights, the latter shall have precedence.

Article 8 – Miscellaneous provisions
1.   The text and music of the State Anthems shall be approved by the State Baga Hural before 10 July 1992. Pending this approval, the text and music of the current Anthem shall remain in use.
2.   The State emblem, standard, flag and seal shall be used from the day the Constitution of Mongolia enters into force. The Government shall gradually and in due time replace the seals and stamps of central and local State bodies as the respective institutions are reorganised.
3.   From the day the Constitution of Mongolia comes into effect, the words "Mongolian People's Republic" in the names of all State institutions shall be replaced with the words "Mongol Uls" (Mongolia).

Article 9 – Enforcement of the law
1.   This annexed law shall have the same force as the Constitution of Mongolia.
2.   This annexed law of the Constitution of Mongolia shall become effective on 12 February 1992.
3.   On the day the Constitution of Mongoia comes into effect (12 February 1992) the Constitution of the MPR (1960) and its annexed law shall cease to serve as having completed their historic mission.

The Great People's Hural
of the
Mongolian People's Republic

Ulaanbaatar
9.38 a.m., 19 January, 1992

Russian Federation

Chronology

1990

May 4: The Social Democratic Party of Russia holds its constituent congress.

May 29: The Congress of People's Deputies of the Russian Soviet Federative Socialist Republic (RSFSR) elects Boris Yeltsin as Chairman of the Supreme Soviet, making him *de facto* President of the RSFSR.

June 9: The newly elected Supreme Soviet elects Ivan Silayev as Prime Minister.

June 12: The Congress declares the RSFSR a sovereign state.

June 21: The Communist Party (CP) of the RSFSR, chaired by Ivan Polozkov, is formally founded.

July 12: Boris Yeltsin resigns his party membership, because of dissatisfaction with the Communist Party of the Soviet Union's (CPSU) policy.

1991

March 17: In an all-union referendum 71.3% vote in favour of the preservation of the USSR (Turnout 75.4%).

April 2: The Congress rejects a motion of no confidence against Boris Yeltsin by 767 votes to 121.

April 5: The Congress approves a proposal by Boris Yeltsin on the establishment of a directly elected executive President, by 608 votes to 228 with 100 abstentions.

April 23: President Mikhail Gorbachev signs, with nine of the fifteen union republics including the RSFSR, a pact aimed at achieving stable relations between the central government and the governments of the republics. It sets out a timetable for major political changes, starting with the signing of the new Union Treaty. No longer than six months after signature of the Treaty a new Union constitution would be promulgated, followed by elections to the Congress of People's Deputies.

June 12: Boris Yeltsin is elected President of the RSFSR by gaining 57.3% of the votes cast. The new Vice-President is Aleksandr Rutskoi (Turnout 74.66%).

August 19: Attempted *coup d'état* in Moscow.

October 29: A Constitutional Court is elected in order to supervise the constitutionality of Russian laws and treaties with foreign states.

November 6: Yeltsin takes the post of Prime Minister, replacing Ivan Silayev. He also issues a decree banning the CPSU and the RCP (Russian Communist Party).

November 28: The Supreme Soviet passes a law giving citizenship to Russians living outside the borders of the Russian Federative Republic.

December 8: The Russian Federative Republic, Belarus and Ukraine sign the Minsk Agreement, establishing a Commonwealth of Independent States (CIS).

December 10: The Supreme Soviet ratifies the CIS declaration.

December 21: The CIS formally replaces the Soviet Union, grouping eleven republics with the exception of Georgia. The Russian Federative Republic takes over many of the former Union functions, including its seat in the UN Security Council.

December 25: The Supreme Soviet changes the Republic's name from the Russian Soviet Federative Socialist Republic to the Russian Federation.

1992

January 14: The Parliamentary Assembly of the Council of Europe grants the Russian Parliament its Special Guest Status.

March 31: Eighteen of the twenty autonomous republics within the Russian Federation sign the Federation Treaty which defines the demarcation of powers between the federation and the constituent republics.

April 12: The government resigns following a resolution adopted by the Congress, criticising the economic reforms.

April 15: The Congress adopts, by 578 to 203 votes with 64 abstentions, a declaration on support of the economic reforms and the President refuses the resignation of the governement.

April 17: The Congress adopts, by 759 votes to 77 with 30 abstentions, a proposal to change the name of the state to Russia.

April 22: Former communists and nationalist groups form a new opposition bloc: the Russian Unity bloc.

May 21: The Supreme Soviet votes to annul the 1954 decree ceding the Crimea from Russia to Ukraine.

May 25: The Ukrainian Ministry of Foreign Affairs states that the status of Crimea is an internal Ukrainian matter, which cannot be subjected to external interference.

June 2: The Ukrainian Parliament issues a statement rejecting the Russian Supreme Soviet rescission of the 1954 decree.

June 4: The Supreme Soviet passes a law on the formation of the Ingush Republic within the Russian Federation, splitting the Chechen-Ingushetia Republic as the Chechens have already demanded their independence from the Russian Federation in November 1991.

June 15: Yeltsin, having held the post of Prime Minister since November 1991, appoints Yegor Gaidar as his successor.

June 21: The opposition group "Civic Union" holds its constituent congress. This group comprises the People's Party of Free Russia led by Rutskoi, the Democratic Party of Russia and the Union of Renewal.

July 4: A new pro-Yeltsin political bloc is established: the Democratic Choice.

August 11: The Ministry of Justice bans the Liberal Democratic Party (LDPR), chaired by Vladimir Zhirinovsky, on the grounds of alleged falsification of the party's membership list.

October 16: Senior Ministers warn foreign journalists of a possible conservative-led coup against Yeltsin and his reform policy, accusing Ruslan Khasbulatov, Chairman of the Supreme Soviet of heavy involvement.

October 28: A presidential decree bans the neo-communist and nationalist alliance, the National Salvation Front (NSF), shortly after its constitution.

November 30: The Constitutional Court announces its verdict on the banning of the CPSU and the RCP by Yeltsin in November 1991: the imposed ban on the "leading and organisational structure" is constitutional, but not the banning of "primary organisations formed on a territorial basis".

December 9: The Congress of People's Deputies rejects Gaidar as Prime Minister by 486 votes to 467.

December 14: The Congress elects Viktor Chernomyrdin as Prime Minister by 721 votes in a confirmatory ballot.

1993

March 20: Yeltsin announces that he has signed decrees introducing a "special regime", by which the Congress of People's Deputies will cease to exist under a new constitution.

March 23: The Constitutional Court rules that the decrees on the "special régime" signed by the President are unconstitutional and violate the Federation Treaty.

March 28: The Congress moves to a motion to dismiss the President. Although the voting results in 617 votes to 268 in favour of the dismissal, it is not binding as the two-thirds majority of 1033 deputies is not reached.

April 21: The Constitutional Court rules that in the forthcoming referendum only the questions concerning early elections should require an approval of more than 50% of the electorate.

April 25: A referendum is held, containing four questions: (i) Do you have confidence in President Boris Yeltsin? 58.7% of the votes cast are in favour, (ii) Do you approve of the socio-economic policies carried out by the President? 53.0% of the votes cast are in favour, (iii) Do you consider it necessary to hold early presidential elections? 31.7% of the electorate vote in favour and (iv) Do you consider it necessary to hold elections for the Congress of People's Deputies? 43.1% of the electorate vote in favour. Turnout 64.5%.

April 30: The President unveils a new draft Constitution, by which a popular elected President will serve as head of state and head of the government and a new bicameral parliament will be established.

June 5: A constitutional conference to finalise and adopt a new constitution embarks.

June 15: Yegor Gaidar, Aleksandr Yakovlev and Mikhail Gorbachev found the Democratic Block of Reformist Forces "Russia's Choice".

July 9: The Supreme Soviet passes a resolution declaring Russian sovereignty over the Ukrainian port of Sebastopol (Crimea). The Ukrainian President describes the resolution as an interference in Ukraine's internal affairs.

September 1: Yeltsin suspends Vice-President Aleksandr Rutskoi, on account of the growing political discord between them.

September 21: President Yeltsin issues a decree on constitutional reform, declaring the suspension of all legislative, administrative and control functions of the Parliament and calling parliamentary elections on 11 and 12 December 1993 in order to settle the political stalemate, between the pro-reform President and the conservative President of the Supreme Soviet, Ruslan Khasbulatov. The Constitutional Court decides in an emergency meeting that Yeltsin's statements are in violation of the Constitution and form the basis for an impeachment.

September 24: The Congress of People's Deputies, the supreme legislative body, votes to impeach Yeltsin and confirms Aleksandr Rutskoi, who has been sworn in on 21 September, as the new President.

September 27: Troops seal off the Parliament. Telephone links and electricity supply have already been cut.

October 3: Armed clashes take place between forces loyal to the President and rebels protesting against the suspension of the parliament. The

Parliament is seized by the rebelling party and Yeltsin dismisses Aleksandr Rutskoi as Vice-President.

October 4: The rebel leaders surrender by coming out of the burning parliament building.

October 7: Yeltsin suspends the Constitutional Court on the grounds of "placing the country on the brink of civil war by its hasty actions and decisions".

October 15: Aleksandr Rutskoi and Ruslan Khasbulatov are charged with "organising mass disorder".

October 18: Yeltsin lifts the state of emergency that which was declared on 3 October.

November 10: Registration of parties for general elections starts. Among the new parties are Russia's Choice and *Yabloko,* a pro-reform bloc.

December 7: Yeltsin orders the close-down of the Russian-Chechen border. The Chechen leader Dzhakar Dudayev states that this amounts to a declaration of war.

December 12: A referendum on the draft constitution results in 58.4% of the votes in favour of the draft, with a turnout of 54.8%. The new constitution increases the powers of the President, according him the right to veto parliamentary legislation and abolishing the post of vice-president. The Parliament will consist of two houses: a 178-member Federation Council, to which each of the 89 regions and republics are to elect two members and a 450-member State Duma, in which 225 seats are to be filled according to proportional representation on a party list basis, and 225 are to be elected in single-member constituencies.

December 12: Elections to the new Parliament are held, resulting in a victory for the ultra-nationalist LDPR, led by Vladimir Zhirinovsky, securing 22.8% of the party preference votes and a total of 66 seats in the State Duma. Results of the remaining parties: Russia's Choice, 15.4% of the votes and 103 seats, the Communist Party, 12.4% and 62 seats; Women of Russia, 8.1% and 25 seats; Agrarian Party 7.9% and 49 seats; *Yabloko,* 7.8% and 28 seats; the Party of Russian Unity and Accord, 6.8% and 29 seats; and Democratic Party of Russia, 5.5% and 17 seats. Five other parties have not achieved the threshold on the party list seats, the Independents gain 35 seats, 30 seats are won by the remaining parties and 6 remain unfilled.
The results of the elections and the referendum are contested by a panel of experts, members of the presidential administration.

1994

January 13: The New Regional Policy bloc is formed in the Parliament, consisting of 65 independent deputies.

April 28: 245 social and political organisations sign the Treaty on Civil Accord, committing the parties not to engage in activities undermining the civil peace.

April 28: 39 State Duma deputies form a new radical reform parliamentary faction: the Liberal Democratic Union.

May 23: Aleksandr Rutskoi's People's Party of Free Russia renames itself as the Russian Social Democratic People's Party (RSDP).

June 12-13: The Federal Assemby's pro-reform bloc Russia's Choice formally reconstitutes itself as a party: Russia's Democratic Choice.

November 29: Yeltsin issues an ultimatum to the Dudayev regime in Chechenya, warning that a Russian military intervention will be used to quell the conflict.

December 11: Russian troops officially launch an offensive against the rebel forces in Chechenya, with the aim of restoring central control.

1995

January 5: Valentin Kovalyev, appointed as Justice Minister, is the first member of the Communist Party to serve in a government under Yeltsin.

January: Russian forces gain control of most of Grozny. The first attempt in the beginning of January failed. The second invasion took almost two weeks and was accompanied by great loss of life. There is suspicion of mass murdering of civilians and parts of the troops are out of control.

February 6: The board of the RSDP party dismisses its Chair Aleksandr Rutskoi.

March 10: The State Duma passes a vote of no confidence in Viktor Yerin, the Interior Minister.

April 5: Foundation of the centrist United Industrial Party (ROPP), chaired by Arkady Volsky.

May 12: Prime Minister Viktor Chernomyrdin founds a new pro-Yeltsin political movement: Our Home is Russia.

May 15: The Agrarian Party and the Agrarian Union of Russia support the constitution of the leftist Accord bloc: *Soglasiye*.

June 21: The Chechen conflict spreads to Russian territory and Russian troops fail to end the situation. The State Duma approves by 241 votes to 72 a motion of no confidence in the Russian government over the handling of this situation. A second motion of no confidence within three months would constitutionally require the President to dissolve the parliament or to appoint a new government.

July 1: With 193 votes in favour, a second motion of no confidence in the Government on account of the Chechen conflict is not accepted by the State Duma, since 226 votes are required for acceptance.

October 11: The State Duma passes a law by which the Upper House, the Council of the Federation, should consist of the heads of local executives and parliaments.

October 25: The Council of the Federation rejects this law, because more than half of the current members do not represent local bodies.

October 27: The State Duma overrides this rejection by 309 votes to 1 and tries to reach a compromise with the President.

October 29: The Election Commission rejects the registration of *Yabloko* and former Vice-President Aleksandr Rutskoi's *Derzhava* movement for the elections to the State Duma on 17 December. Both groups immediately make appeals to the Supreme Court against this rejection.

November 1: The Supreme Court orders the Election Commission to reverse its earlier decision denying the registration of two mainstream parties for the legislative elections.

November 1: The Chechen Supreme Soviet unanimously elects Moscow-backed Prime Minister Doku Zavgaev as "head of state" of the republic, a post created in an attempt to facilitate stability in Chechenya.

November 8: Some deputies call for modification of the electoral law, as it seems by opinion polls that the communist and nationalist candidates could win two-thirds of the seats in the new Duma.

November 20: The Constitutional Court states that it will not consider the constitutionality of the election law and that the contest should take place as scheduled.

November 11: Yeltsin vetoes the law adopted by the State Duma on October 11 on the Council of the Federation.

November 15: The Council of the Federation decides unanimously that presidential elections should be held on 16 June 1996.

December 14: Elections are held in Chechenya. Turnout 74.8%. Almost half of the votes go to "Our Home is Russia". In simultaneous elections for the President of the Republic, Prime Minister Doku Zavgayev wins 93% of the votes cast.

December 17: The Communist Party wins the elections to the State Duma, with a total of 157 seats (22.30%) in the 450-member parliament. Our Home is Russia gains 55 seats (10.13%), the LDPR 51 seats (11.18%) and *Yabloko* 45 seats (6.89%). The other parties do not attain the 5% threshold in the proportional representation system. Results for the other parties are: Agrarian Party, 20 seats (3.78%); Russia's Democratic Choice, 9 seats (3.86%); Power to the People, 9 seats (1.61%); Congress of Russian Communities, 5 seats (4.31%); Women of Russia, 3 seats (4.61%); Forward Russia, 3 seats (1.94); Rybkin Bloc, 3 seats (1.11%); the remaining parties, 12 seats (15.19%); and the Independents, 78 seats. Turnout 64.38%.

1996

January 5: Andrei Kozyrev resigns as Minister of Foreign Affairs, because of the criticism of being too pro-western.

February 15: Yeltsin formally announces his candidature for the June Presidential elections.

February 28: Russia accedes to the Council of Europe as a full member.

March 15: The State Duma passes a resolution in order to "deepen the integration of the peoples previously united in the USSR". This resolution revokes the 1991 agreement which established the CIS, and the Supreme Soviet's resolution of 12 December 1991 which abrogates the treaty on the formation of the USSR. The Duma also adopts a resolution upholding the legal validity of the results of the 17 March 1991 referendum on the future of the USSR.

March 31: Yeltsin announces an unilateral ceasefire, concerning the Chechen situation.

April 16: Eleven presidential candidates register with the Central Electoral Commission. Among them are Boris Yeltsin, Gennady Zyuganov (leader of the Communist Party), Vladimir Zhirinovsky, General Aleksandr Lebed and Mikhail Gorbachev.

April 21: The Chechen separatist leader Dzhokhar Dudayev is killed by a rocket.

April 22: Zelimkhan Yandarbiev replaces Dudayev as the Chechen separatist leader.

June 16: President Yeltsin narrowly wins the presidential elections by 35.28%. Gennady Zyuganov gains 32.04% of the votes, General Aleksandr Lebed 14.52% and the remaining 18.16% goes to the other candidates. Turnout 69.82%. A run-off election is scheduled to take place on 3 July.

June 17: Boris Yeltsin and General Aleksandr Lebed forge an alliance.

June 18: Yeltsin appoints Lebed as Secretary of the Security Council.

July 3: Boris Yeltsin defeats Gennady Zyuganov in the second round of presidential elections by gaining 53.82% of the votes, with a turnout of 68.89%.

August 7: The Communist Party and the Agrarian Party form a new alliance, the Popular-Patriotic Union of Russia (PPUR), by joining with several smaller nationalist and leftist groups.

Russian Federation

August 9: Yeltsin is sworn in as President of the Russian Federation. Immediately after his inauguration he formally reappoints Viktor Chernomyrdin as Prime Minister.

August 10: The State Duma approves the nomination of Viktor Chernomyrdin by 314 votes to 85 with three abstentions.

August 31: General Lebed and Chechen military leader Aslan Maskhadov sign a peace agreement in the city of Khasavyurt, providing for the withdrawal of Russian troops.

October 8: The Federation Council approves the Khasavyurt agreement, though concluding that Chechenya remains an integral part of the Russian Federation.

October 17: Yeltsin dismisses Lebed as Secretary of the Security Council and Presidential National Security Adviser after allegations, made by the Interior Minister Kulikov, that Lebed was planning to launch a coup in the country, by secretly recruiting Chechen rebels. However, Prime Minister Chernomyrdin dismisses the allegations of coup plotting.

October 18: Aslan Maskhadov is nominated Prime Minister and Minister of Defence of Chechenya.

November 5: Boris Yeltsin undergoes a multiple heart bypass operation.

November 23: Prime Minister Chernomyrdin and Chechen Prime Minister Maskhadov sign an agreement, based upon the 31 August Khasavyurt Agreement.

December 27: General Aleksandr Lebed sets up the Russian Republican Party, as a "third force" reuniting all who do not consider themselves communists or as belonging to the party in power.

Constitution of the Russian Federation[1]

*Adopted by the nationwide vote of 12 December 1993
and in force since 25 December 1993*

We, the multinational people of the Russian Federation, united by a common destiny on our land, confirming the rights and freedoms of man and civil peace and harmony,
preserving the historically established state unity,
proceeding from the universally recognised principles of legal equality and self-determination of the peoples,
revering the memory of our ancestors who passed down to us love and respect for the fatherland and faith in good and justice,
reviving the sovereign statehood of Russia and confirming the unshakeability of its democratic foundation,
seeking to ensure the well-being and prosperity of Russia,
proceeding from responsibility for our homeland to present and future generations,
recognising ourselves as part of the world community,
adopt the Constitution of the Russian Federation.

Section 1

Chapter 1 – The Foundations of the Constitutional system

Article 1
1.   The Russian Federation/Russia is a democratic federative law-based state with a republican form of administration.
2.   The names Russian Federation and Russia are identical.

Article 2
The individual and his rights and freedoms are the highest value. Recognition, observance and protection of the rights and freedoms of man and citizen is an obligation of the state.

---

1. Instituut voor Oosteuropees Recht en Ruslandkunde

Article 3

1.   The multinational people of the Russian Federation is the bearer of sovereignty and the sole source of power within the Russian Federation.
2.   The people exercises its power directly as well as through organs of state power and organs of local self-government.
3.   A referendum and free elections are the highest direct expression of people's power.
4.   Nobody can arrogate power in the Russian Federation. The seizure of power or arrogation of state powers will be prosecuted under a federal law.

Article 4

1.   The sovereignty of the Russian Federation extends throughout its territory.
2.   The Constitution of the Russian Federation and federal laws have supremacy throughout the territory of the Russian Federation.
3.   The Russian Federation ensures the integrity and inviolability of its territory.

Article 5

1.   The Russian Federation consists of republics, territories, provinces, cities of federal significance, an autonomous province and autonomous areas which are legally equal subjects of the Russian Federation.
2.   A republic (state) has its constitution and legislation. A territory, province, city of federal significance, autonomous province or autonomous area has its charter and legislation.
3.   The federal structure of the Russian Federation is based on its state integrity, unity of the system of state power between organs of state power of the Russian Federation and organs of state power of the subjects of the Russian Federation, and legal equality and self-determination of the peoples in the Russian Federation.
4.   All subjects of the Russian Federation have mutually equal rights in their interrelationships with federal organs of state power.

Article 6

1.   Citizenship of the Russian Federation is acquired and terminated in accordance with a federal law and is uniform and equal irrespective of the grounds of its acquisition.
2.   Each citizen of the Russian Federation possesses all rights and freedoms on its territory and bears equal obligations provided by the Constitution of the Russian Federation.
3.   A citizen of the Russian Federation cannot be deprived of his citizenship or of the right to change it.

Article 7

1.   The Russian Federation is a social state whose policy is aimed at creating conditions ensuring a dignified life and the free development of man.
2.   In the Russian Federation labour and health of the people are protected; a guaranteed minimum wage is established; state support is ensured for the

family, mothers, fathers, children, invalids and elderly citizens; a system of social services is developed; and state pensions, allowances and other guarantees of social protection are established.

Article 8

1. In the Russian Federation the unity of the economic space, the free movement of goods, services and financial resources, support of competition and freedom of economic activity are guaranteed.
2. In the Russian Federation private, state, municipal, and other types of ownership are equally recognised and protected.

Article 9

1. In the Russian Federation land and other natural resources are utilised and protected as the basis of life and activity of the peoples inhabiting the corresponding territory.
2. Land and other natural resources can be in private, state, municipal or other types of ownership.

Article 10

State power in the Russian Federation is exercised on the basis of separation in legislative, executive and judicial power. The organs of legislative, executive or judicial power are independent.

Article 11

1. The President of the Russian Federation, the Federal Assembly (the Council of the Federation and the State Duma), the Government of the Russian Federation and the courts of the Russian Federation exercise the power of the state in the Russian Federation.
2. The organs of state power founded by the subjects of the Russian Federation exercise the state power in them.
3. The delimitation of areas of jurisdiction and powers between the organs of state power of the Russian Federation and the organs of state power of the subjects of the Russian Federation is effected by this Constitution, and Federative and other agreements concerning the delimitation of areas of jurisdiction and of powers.

Article 12

In the Russian Federation local self-government is recognised and guaranteed. Within the limits of its powers local self-government is independent. Organs of local self-government do not belong to the system of organs of state power.

Article 13

1. In the Russian Federation ideological diversity is recognised.
2. No ideology may be established as a state or compulsory ideology.
3. In the Russian Federation political diversity and a multiparty system are recognised.

4.   Social associations are equal before the law.
5.   The creation and activity of social associations whose aims and actions are directed towards the alteration of the foundations of the constitutional system by violence and the violation of the integrity of the Russian Federation, the undermining of the security of the state, the creation of armed formations, or the stirring-up of social, racial, national or religious dissension are prohibited.

Article 14
1.   The Russian Federation is a secular state. No religion may be established as a state or compulsory religion.
2.   Religious associations are separated from the state and equal before the law.

Article 15
1.   The Constitution of the Russian Federation has the highest legal force, is directly operative and applies throughout the territory of the Russian Federation. Laws and other legal enactments adopted in the Russian Federation may not contravene the Constitution of the Russian Federation.
2.   Organs of state power, organs of local self-government, officials, citizens and their associations are obliged to observe the Constitution of the Russian Federation and its laws.
3.   Laws are subject to official publication. Unpublished laws are not applicable. Any normative legal enactments affecting rights, freedoms and obligations of man and citizen cannot be applied unless they have been officially published for universal information.
4.   Universally recognised principles and norms of international law and the international treaties of the Russian Federation are a constituent part of its legal system. If an international treaty of the Russian Federation establishes rules other than those provided by a law, the rules of the international treaty apply.

Article 16
1.   The provisions of the present Chapter of the Constitution constitute the foundations of the constitutional system of the Russian Federation and cannot be amended except by the procedure laid down by this Constitution.
2.   No other provision of this Constitution can contravene the foundations of the constitutional system of the Russian Federation.

Chapter 2 – The rights and freedoms of man and citizen

Article 17
1.   In the Russian Federation the rights and freedoms of man and citizen are guaranteed in accordance with the universally recognised principles and norms of international law and in conformity with this Constitution.
2.   The basic rights and freedoms of man are inalienable and belong to everybody from birth onwards.
3.   The exercise of rights and freedoms of man and citizen must not violate the rights and freedoms of others persons.

Article 18
The rights and freedoms of man and citizen are directly operative. They determine the meaning, content and application of laws and the activity of the legislative and executive powers and of local self-government and are safeguarded by the judiciary.

Article 19
1.   All are equal before the law and the court.
2.   The state guarantees equality of rights and freedoms of man and citizen regardless of sex, race, nationality, language, origin, property and official position, place of residence, attitude towards religion, convictions, membership of social associations as well as other circumstances. Any forms of restriction of rights of citizens on grounds of social, racial, national, linguistic or religious affiliation are prohibited.
3.   Men and women have equal rights and freedoms and equal opportunities to exercise them.

Article 20
1.   Everybody has the right to life.
2.   Until its abolition the death penalty can be prescribed by federal law as an extraordinary penalty for particularly grave crimes against life, the accused having the right to have his case considered by a court with the participation of sworn assessors.

Article 21
1.   The dignity of the individual is protected by the state. Nothing may be grounds to encroach on it.
2.   No one may be subjected to torture, violence or other brutal or inhuman degrading treatment or punishment. No one may be subjected to medical, scientific or other experiments without voluntary consent.

Article 22
1.   Everybody has the right to liberty and personal inviolability.
2.   Arrest, taking into custody and keeping in custody are permitted only by judicial decision. Pending a court decision a person cannot be detained for a period of more than 48 hours.

Article 23
1.   Everybody has the right to inviolability of his private life, personal and family secrecy, and defence of his honour and good name.
2.   Everybody has the rights to secrecy of correspondence, telephone conversations and postal, telegraph and other communications. Restriction of this right is permitted only on the basis of a court decision.

Article 24
1.   The collection, storage, utilisation and dissemination of information about a person's private life without his consent are not permitted.

2.   Organs of state power and organs of local self-government and their officials are obliged to ensure that everybody has the opportunity to get acquainted with documents and materials directly affecting his rights and freedoms unless otherwise provided by law.

Article 25
The home is inviolable. No-one is entitled to enter a home against the will of the persons residing therein except in cases provided by federal law or on the basis of a court decision.

Article 26
1.   Everybody is entitled to determine and indicate his national affiliation. No-one may be compelled to determine and indicate his national affiliation.
2.   Everybody has the rights to use his native language and to the free choice of language of communication, upbringing, receiving instruction and creativity.

Article 27
1.   Everybody who is legally present on the territory of the Russian Federation has the right to travel freely and choose his place of stay and residence.
2.   Everybody may freely leave the Russian Federation. A citizen of the Russian Federation has the right to return freely to the Russian Federation.

Article 28
Everybody is guaranteed freedom of conscience and freedom of religion, including the right to profess any religion individually or together with others or not to profess any, and freely to choose, hold and disseminate religious and other convictions and to act upon them.

Article 29
1.   Everybody is guaranteed freedom of thought and speech.
2.   Propaganda or agitation exciting social, racial, national or religious hatred and hostility is not permitted. Propaganda of social, racial, national, religious or linguistic superiority is prohibited.
3.   No-one may be compelled to express his opinions and convictions or to renounce them.
4.   Everybody has the right freely to seek, receive, transmit, produce and disseminate information by any lawful method. The list of information constituting a state secret is determined by federal law.
5.   The freedom of mass information is guaranteed. Censorship is prohibited.

Article 30
1.   Everybody has the right of association, including the right to create trade unions to protect his interests. The freedom of activity of social associations is guaranteed.
2.   No-one may be compelled to join or to remain in any association.

Article 31

Citizens of the Russian Federation have the right to assemble peacefully without weapons and to hold assemblies, meetings, and demonstrations, marches and pickets.

Article 32

1.   Citizens of the Russian Federation have the right to take part in the administration of the affairs of the state both directly as well as through their representatives.
2.   Citizens of the Russian Federation have the right to vote and to be elected to organs of state power and organs of local self-government, as well as to participate in a referendum.
3.   Citizens declared incapable by a court and also those detained in places of deprivation of freedom upon a court sentence do not have the right to vote and to be elected.
4.   Citizens of the Russian Federation have equal access to state service.
5.   Citizens of the Russian Federation have the right to take part in the administration of justice.

Article 33

Citizens of the Russian Federation have the right to appeal personally, as well as to send individual and collective addresses, to state organs and organs of local self-government.

Article 34

1.   Everybody has the right to make free use of his capacities and property for entrepreneurial activity and other economic activity not prohibited by law.
2.   Economic activity directed towards monopolisation and unfair competition is not permitted.

Article 35

1.   The right of private ownership is protected by law.
2.   Everybody is entitled to own property and to possess, use and dispose of it both individually and together with other persons.
3.   No-one may be deprived of his property except by court decision. The compulsory expropriation of property for state needs may be carried out only under condition of equivalent advance-compensation.
4.   The right to inheritance is guaranteed.

Article 36

1.   Citizens and their associations are entitled to have land in private ownership.
2.   Owners freely possess, use and dispose of land and other natural resources provided that this does not damage the environment and violate the rights and lawful interests of other persons.
3.   The conditions and procedure for the utilisation of land are defined on the basis of a federal law.

Article 37

1.   Labour is free. Everybody has the right freely to dispose of his abilities to work and to choose type of activity and occupation.
2.   Forced labour is prohibited.
3.   Everybody has the right to work in conditions meeting the requirements of safety and hygiene and to receive remuneration for labour without any form of discrimination and of not less than the minimum wage established by a federal law, and also the right to protection against unemployment.
4.   The right is recognised to individual and collective labour disputes utilising the methods of solving them established by a federal law, including the right to strike.
5.   Everybody has the right to leisure. Persons working on the basis of an employment agreement are guaranteed working hours, days off, holidays and paid annual leave, established by federal law.

Article 38

1.   Maternity and childhood and the family are under the state's protection.
2.   The care for children and their upbringing are the equal right and duty of the parents.
3.   Children who are able to work and have reached the age of 18 years must take care of disabled parents.

Article 39

1.   Everybody is guaranteed social security on the basis of age, in the event of sickness, disability or loss of breadwinner, for the raising of children, and in other cases provided by law.
2.   State pensions and social allowances are established by law.
3.   Voluntary social insurance, the creation of additional forms of social security and charity are encouraged.

Article 40

1.   Everybody has the right to housing. No-one may be arbitrarily deprived of his housing.
2.   Organs of state power and organs of local self-government encourage housing construction and create conditions for exercise of the right to housing.
3.   Housing is provided free of charge or at affordable payment to low-income and other citizens mentioned in the law who are in need of housing, from state, municipal and other housing funds in accordance with norms established by law.

Article 41

1.   Each person has the right to health care and medical assistance. Medical assistance in state and municipal health care institutions is provided to citizens free of charge by means of funds from the relevant budget, insurance contributions and other revenues.
2.   In the Russian Federation federal programmes to protect and strengthen the population's health are financed, measures to develop state,

municipal and private health care systems are taken, and activities furthering the strengthening of people's health, the development of physical culture and sport, and ecological, sanitary and epidemiological well-being are encouraged.
3.   The concealment by officials of facts and circumstances creating a threat to people's lives and health entails liability in accordance with federal law.

Article 42
Everybody has the right to a decent environment, reliable information about the state of the environment and compensation for damage caused to his health or property by ecological breaches of the law.

Article 43
1.   Everybody has the right to education.
2.   The general access to free of charge pre-school, elementary general and secondary professional education in state or municipal educational institutions and in enterprises is guaranteed.
3.   Everybody is entitled on a competitive basis to receive higher education free of charge in state or municipal educational institutions or in enterprises.
4.   Elementary general education is compulsory. Parents or their surrogates ensure that children receive elementary general education.
5.   The Russian Federation establishes federal state educational standards and supports various forms of education and self-education.

Article 44
1.   Everybody is guaranteed freedom of literary, artistic, scientific, technical and other types of creativity, and of teaching. Intellectual property is protected by law.
2.   Everybody has the right to participate in cultural life, use institutions of culture and to have access to cultural values.
3.   Everybody is bound to take care to preserve the historical and cultural heritage and look after historical and cultural monuments.

Article 45
1.   The state protection of rights and freedoms of man and citizen in the Russian Federation is guaranteed.
2.   Everybody is entitled to protect his rights and freedoms by any methods not prohibited by law.

Article 46
1.   Everybody is guaranteed judicial protection of his rights and freedoms.
2.   Decisions and actions (or inactions) of organs of state power, organs of local self-government, social associations, and officials can be appealed against in court.
3.   In accordance with the international treaties of the Russian Federation everybody is entitled to appeal to interstate organs for the protection of rights and freedoms of man, if all available means of juridical protection inside the state have been exhausted.

Article 47

1.   No-one can be deprived of the right to have his case heard by the court or the judge to whose jurisdiction it is assigned by federal law.
2.   In cases provided by federal law, everybody accused of having committed a crime has the right to have his case heard by a court with the participation of sworn assessors.

Article 48

1.   Everybody is guaranteed the right to receive qualified juridical assistance. Juridical assistance is rendered free of charge in the instances provided by law.
2.   Each person who is detained, held in custody or accused of having committed a crime has the right to use the assistance of a lawyer (defence counsel) from the moment of his detention, placing in custody, or the indictment respectively.

Article 49

1.   Everybody accused of having committed a crime is presumed innocent until his guilt is proved in the procedure provided by federal law and established by means of a final court sentence.
2.   The accused is not obliged to prove his innocence.
3.   Any irremovable doubts regarding the individual's guilt are interpreted in the accused's favour.

Article 50

1.   No-one can be tried a second time for one and the same crime.
2.   The use of any evidence acquired in violation of a federal law is not permitted in the administration of justice.
3.   Everybody sentenced for a crime has the right to have his sentence reviewed by a higher court in the procedure provided by federal law, as well as the right to appeal for pardon or a reduction of the penalty.

Article 51

1.   No one is obliged to testify against himself or against his spouse or close relatives, the range of the latter being defined by federal law.
2.   Other instances when the obligation to give evidence as witness is lifted can be established by federal law.

Article 52

The rights of the victims of crimes or of abuses of power are protected by law. The state guarantees the victims' access to justice and to compensation for damage caused.

Article 53

Everybody has the right to compensation from the state for damage caused by the unlawful actions (or inactions) of organs of state power or their officials.

Article 54
1.   A law establishing or mitigating liability does not have retroactive force.
2.   No-one can be held liable for any behaviour which, at the time it was committed, was not considered to be a breach of the law. If liability for a breach of the law is abolished or mitigated after the behaviour, the new law is applied.

Article 55
1.   The listing of the basic rights and freedoms in the Constitution of the Russian Federation must not be interpreted as negating or diminishing other universally recognised rights and freedoms of man and citizen.
2.   Laws abolishing or diminishing rights and freedoms of man and citizen must not be issued in the Russian Federation.
3.   Rights and freedoms of man and citizen can be restricted by federal law only to the extent to which this may be necessary for the aim of protecting the foundations of the constitutional system, morality and the health, rights and lawful interests of other persons, or of ensuring the country's defence and the state's security.

Article 56
1.   Certain restrictions of rights and freedoms can be introduced, with an indication of their extent and duration, in a state of emergency in order to ensure the citizens' security and the defence of the constitutional system in accordance with a federal constitutional law.
2.   A state of emergency may be introduced throughout the territory of the Russian Federation or in individual localities thereof given the circumstances and according to the procedure provided by a federal constitutional law.
3.   The rights and freedoms contained in Articles 20, 21, 23.1, 24, 28, 34.1, 40.1, and 46-54 of the Constitution of the Russian Federation may not be restricted.

Article 57
Everybody is obliged to pay lawfully established taxes and duties. Laws introducing new taxes or worsening the position of taxpayers cannot be retroactive.

Article 58
Everybody is obliged to protect nature and the environment and to look after the natural wealth.

Article 59
1.   The protection of the fatherland is a duty and obligation of citizens of the Russian Federation.
2.   Citizens of the Russian Federation perform military service in accordance with federal law.
3.   In the event that the convictions or religious beliefs of a citizen of the Russian Federation are at odds with the performance by him of military service, as well as in other instances established by federal law, the citizen has the right to its substitution by alternative civil service.

Article 60
A citizen of the Russian Federation can independently exercise his rights and obligations in full from the age of 18 years.

Article 61
1.   A citizen of the Russian Federation cannot be expelled from the Russian Federation or extradited to another state.
2.   The Russian Federation guarantees defence and protection of its citizens abroad.

Article 62
1.   A citizen of the Russian Federation can hold citizenship of a foreign state (dual citizenship) in accordance with federal law or an international treaty of the Russian Federation.
2.   The fact that a citizen of the Russian Federation holds citizenship of a foreign state does not diminish his rights and freedoms or exempt him from the obligations stemming from Russian citizenship, unless otherwise provided by federal law or an international treaty of the Russian Federation.
3.   Foreign citizens and stateless persons in the Russian Federation enjoy equal rights and bear equal obligations with the citizens of the Russian Federation, except when otherwise provided by federal law or an international treaty of the Russian Federation.

Article 63
1.   The Russian Federation offers political asylum to foreign citizens and stateless persons in accordance with universally recognised norms of international law.
2.   The Russian Federation does not permit the extradition to other states of persons persecuted for political beliefs or for actions (or inactions) which are not considered a crime in the Russian Federation. The extradition of persons accused of having committed a crime, or the extradition of sentenced persons to serve their sentence in other states, is performed on the basis of a federal law or an international treaty of the Russian Federation.

Article 64
The provisions of this Chapter constitute the foundations of the legal status of the individual in the Russian Federation and cannot be amended except by the procedure laid down by the present Constitution.

Chapter 3 – The Federation structure

Article 65
1.   The Russian Federation comprises the following subjects of the Russian Federation: the Republic Adygeia (Adygeia), the Republic Altai, the Republic Bashkortostan, the Republic Buriatia, the Republic Dagestan, the Ingush Republic, the Kabardino-Balkar Republic, the Republic Kalmykia – Khal'mg Tangch, the Karachai-Cherkes Republic, the Republic Karelia, the Republic

Komi, the Republic Mari El, the Republic Mordovia, the Republic Sakha (Iaku-tia), the Republic North Ossetia, the Republic Tatarstan (Tatarstan), the Republic of Tuva, the Udmurt Republic, the Republic Khakasia, the Chechen Republic, the Chuvash Republic – *Chavash respubliki;*
the Altai territory, Krasnodar territory, Krasnoiarsk territory, Primor'e territory, Stavropol' territory, Khabarovsk territory, the Amur province, Arkhangel'sk province, Astrakhan' province, Belgorod province, Briansk province, Vladimir province, Volgograd province, Vologda province, Voronezh province, Ivano-vo province, Irkutsk province, Kaliningrad province, Kaluga province, Kam-chatka province, Kemerovo province, Kirov province, Kostroma province, Kurgan province, Kursk province, Leningrad province, Lipetsk province, Mag-adan province, Moscow province, Murmansk province, Nizhnii Novgorod province, Novgorod province, Novosibirsk province, Omsk province, Oren-burg province, Orel province, Penza province, Perm' province, Pskov province, Rostov province, Riazan' province, Samara province, Saratov province, Sakhalin province, Sverdlovsk province, Smolensk province, Tam-bov province, Tver' province, Tomsk province, Tula province, Tiumen' province, Ulianovsk province, Cheliabinsk province, Chita province, Iaroslavl' province;
the cities of federal significance: Moscow, St. Petersburg;
the Jewish autonomous province;
the Aga-Buriat autonomous area, the Perm-Komi autonomous area, the Kori-ak autonomous area, the Nentsy autonomous area, the Taimyr (Dolgany-Nentsy) autonomous area, the Ust'-Orda-Buriat autonomous area, the Khan-ty-Mansi autonomous area, the Chukchi autonomous area, the Evenki autonomous area, the Iamal-Nentsy autonomous area.
2.   The admission to the Russian Federation and the creation within the Russian Federation of a new subject are carried out according to the proce-dure laid down by federal constitutional law.

Article 66
1.   The status of a republic is determined by the Constitution of the Russian Federation and by the constitution of the republic.
2.   The status of a territory, province, city of federal significance, autonomous province and autonomous area is determined by the Constitu-tion of the Russian Federation and the charter of the territory, province, city of federal significance, autonomous province and autonomous area adopted by the legislative (representative) organ of the relevant subject of the Russ-ian Federation.
3.   A federal law on the autonomous province or an autonomous area can be adopted upon submission by the legislative and executive organs of the autonomous province or autonomous area.
4.   The relations of autonomous areas that belong to a territory or province can be regulated by a federal law and an agreement between the organs of state power of the autonomous area and the organs of state power of the ter-ritory or province, respectively.
5.   The status of a subject of the Russian Federation can be changed by mutual consent of the Russian Federation and the subject of the Russian Fed-eration in accordance with a federal constitutional law.

Article 67
1. The territory of the Russian Federation includes the territories of its subjects, inland waters and the territorial sea and the airspace over these.
2. The Russian Federation possesses sovereign rights and exercises jurisdiction over the continental shelf and within the exclusive economic zone of the Russian Federation in accordance with the procedure defined by federal law and the norms of international law.
3. The borders between subjects of the Russian Federation can be changed with their mutual consent.

Article 68
1. The Russian language is the state language of the Russian Federation throughout its territory.
2. Republics are entitled to establish their state languages. They are used alongside the state language of the Russian Federation in the organs of state power, organs of local self-government and state institutions of the republics.
3. The Russian Federation guarantees all its people the right to retain their native language and to create conditions for its study and development.

Article 69
The Russian Federation guarantees the rights of small indigenous peoples in accordance with the universally recognised principles and norms of international law and the international treaties of the Russian Federation.

Article 70
1. The state flag, emblem and anthem of the Russian Federation, the description of these, and the procedure for their official use are established by a federal constitutional law.
2. The city of Moscow is the capital of the Russian Federation. The status of the capital is established by federal law.

Article 71
To the jurisdiction of the Russian Federation belong:
    a. adopting and amending the Constitution of the Russian Federation and federal laws, supervision of their observation;
    b. the federative structure and the territory of the Russian Federation;
    c. regulation and defence of rights and freedoms of man and citizen; citizenship in the Russian Federation; regulation and defence of the rights of national minorities;
    d. the establishment of the system of federal organs of legislative, executive and judicial power, the manner of their organisation and operation; the composition of the federal organs of state power;
    e. federal state ownership and its management;
    f. the establishment of the fundamentals of federal policy and federal programmes in the area of state, economic, ecological, social, cultural, and national development of the Russian Federation;
    g. the establishment of the legal foundations of a single market; financial, currency, credit and customs regulation, the issue of money and the

foundations of price policy; federal economic services, including federal banks;

    h.   the federal budget; federal taxes and duties; federal funds for regional development;

    i.   the federal systems of energy, nuclear energy, fissionable materials; the federal transport, railways, information and communications; space activities;

    j.   foreign policy and international relations of the Russian Federation and the international treaties of the Russian Federation; questions of war and peace;

    k.   foreign economic relations of the Russian Federation;

    l.   defence and security; the defence industry; the determination of the manner of sale and purchase of arms, ammunition, military technology and other military goods; the production of poisonous substances, narcotic means and the manner of their utilisation;

    m. the determination of the status and protection of the state border, territorial sea, airspace, exclusive economic zone and continental shelf of the Russian Federation;

    n.   judicial organisation; the procuracy; criminal, criminal-procedure and criminal-executive legislation; amnesty and granting of pardons; civil, civil procedural and arbitral procedural legislation; legal regulation of intellectual property;

    o.   federal law of conflicts;

    p.   the meteorological service, standards and standard weights and measurements, the metrical system and calculation of time; geodesy and cartography; names of geographic objects; official statistics and accountancy;

    q.   state awards and honorary ranks of the Russian Federation;

    r.   the federal state service.

Article 72

1.   To the joint jurisdiction of the Russian Federation and the subjects of the Russian Federation belong:

    a.   ensuring the conformity of the constitutions and laws of republics, and the charters, laws and other normative legal enactments of territories, provinces, cities of federal significance, the autonomous province and autonomous areas with the Constitution of the Russian Federation and federal laws;

    b.   the defence of rights and freedoms of man and citizen; defence of the rights of national minorities; the safeguarding of legality, the legal order and public security; the regime of border zones;

    c.   questions of the possession, use and disposal of land, mineral wealth, water and other natural resources;

    d.   delimitation of state property;

    e.   the utilisation of nature; environmental protection and safeguarding ecological security; special natural conservation sites; protection of historical and cultural monuments;

    f.   general issues of upbringing, education, science, culture, physical culture and sport;

g.   the co-ordination of questions of health protection; the defence of the family, motherhood, fatherhood and infancy; social protection, including social security;

h.   the realisation of measures to counteract catastrophes, natural disasters and epidemics and the elimination of their consequences;

i.   the establishment of general principles of levying taxes and duties in the Russian Federation;

j.   administrative, administrative-procedural, labour, family, housing, land, water, and forestry legislation, and legislation on mineral resources and on protection of the environment;

k.   staffing of judicial and law-enforcement organs; lawyers and notaries;

l.   the protection of the indigenous dwelling place and traditional way of life of small ethnic communities;

m.   the establishment of the general principles for the organisation of the system of organs of state power and local self-government;

n.   co-ordination of the international and foreign economic relations of subjects of the Russian Federation and fulfilment of the international treaties of the Russian Federation.

2.   The provisions of this Article extend in equal measure to the republics, territories, provinces, cities of federal significance, the autonomous province and autonomous areas.

Article 73

Outside the boundaries of the jurisdiction of the Russian Federation and of the powers of the Russian Federation in the areas of the joint jurisdiction of the Russian Federation and the subjects of the Russian Federation, the subjects of the Russian Federation possess all fullness of state power.

Article 74

1.   The establishment of customs' borders, duties, or levies, and any other hindrances to the free movement of goods, services, and financial assets within the territory of the Russian Federation is not permitted.

2.   Restrictions on the movement of goods and services can be introduced in accordance with a federal law if this is essential for ensuring safety, the protection of the life and health of people, and the protection of nature and cultural values.

Article 75

1.   The rouble is the monetary unit in the Russian Federation. The issue of money is carried out exclusively by the Central Bank of the Russian Federation. The introduction and issue of other currencies is not permitted in the Russian Federation.

2.   The protection and the guaranteeing of the stability of the rouble is the basic function of the Central Bank of the Russian Federation, which carries out this task independently of the other organs of state power.

3.   The system of taxes levied for the federal budget and the general principles of levying taxes and duties in the Russian Federation are established by federal law.

4.   State loans are issued in the manner determined by federal law and are floated on a voluntary basis.

Article 76

1.   With regard to the areas of the jurisdiction of the Russian Federation federal constitutional laws and federal laws are adopted, which operate directly throughout the territory of the Russian Federation.
2.   With regard to the areas of joint jurisdiction of the Russian Federation federal laws and – adopted in accordance with them – laws and other normative legal enactments of the subjects of the Russian Federation are promulgated.
3.   Federal laws cannot contravene federal constitutional laws.
4.   Outside the boundaries of the jurisdiction of the Russian Federation and the joint jurisdiction of the Russian Federation and the subjects of the Russian Federation, the republics, territories, provinces, cities of federal significance, the autonomous province and the autonomous areas exercise their own legal regulation, including the adoption of laws and other normative legal enactments.
5.   The laws and other normative legal enactments of the subjects of the Russian Federation cannot contravene federal laws adopted in conformity with the first and second sections of this Article. In the event of conflict between a federal law and another enactment promulgated in the Russian Federation, the federal law prevails.
6.   In the event of a discrepancy between the federal law and a normative legal enactment of a subject of the Russian Federation promulgated in accordance with the fourth section of this Article, the normative legal enactment of the subject of the Russian Federation prevails.

Article 77

1.   The system of organs of state power of the republics, territories, provinces, cities of federal significance, the autonomous province and autonomous areas is established by the subjects of the Russian Federation independently in accordance with the foundations of the constitutional system of the Russian Federation and the general principles of the organisation of representative and executive organs of state power established by federal law.
2.   Within the boundaries of the jurisdiction of the Russian Federation and the powers of the Russian Federation in the areas of the joint jurisdiction of the Russian Federation and the subjects of the Russian Federation, the federal organs of executive power and the organs of executive power of the subjects of the Russian Federation constitute the unitary system of executive power in the Russian Federation.

Article 78

1.   In order to exercise their powers, federal organs of executive power can create their own territorial organs and appoint the officials concerned.
2.   By agreement with the organs of executive power of the subjects of the Russian Federation federal organs of executive power can transfer to them

the implementation of a part of their powers provided that this does not conflict with the Constitution of the Russian Federation and federal laws.
3.   By agreement with the federal organs of executive power the organs of executive power of the subjects of the Russian Federation can transfer to them the implementation of a part of their powers.
4.   The President of the Russian Federation and the Government of the Russian Federation ensure, in accordance with the Constitution of the Russian Federation, the exercise of the powers of federal state power throughout the territory of the Russian Federation.

Article 79
1.   The Russian Federation can participate in interstate associations and hand over to them part of its powers in accordance with international treaties unless this entails the restriction of rights and freedoms of man and citizen and unless it contravenes the foundations of the constitutional system of the Russian Federation.

Chapter 4 – The President of the Russian Federation

Article 80
1.   The President of the Russian Federation is the head of state.
2.   The President of the Russian Federation is the guarantor of the Constitution of the Russian Federation and of the rights and freedoms of man and citizen. Within the procedure established by the Constitution of the Russian Federation, he adopts measures to safeguard the sovereignty of the Russian Federation and its independence and state integrity and ensures the harmonised functioning and collaboration of the organs of state power.
3.   The President of the Russian Federation, in compliance with the Constitution of the Russian Federation and the federal laws, determines the basic guidelines of the state's domestic and foreign policy.
4.   In his capacity as head of state, the President of the Russian Federation represents the Russian Federation within the country and in international relations.

Article 81
1.   The President of the Russian Federation is elected for four years by citizens of the Russian Federation on the basis of general, equal and direct voting rights by secret ballot.
2.   A citizen of the Russian Federation who is at least 35 years of age and has been permanently resident in the Russian Federation for at least ten years can be elected President of the Russian Federation.
3.   One and the same person may not hold the office of President of the Russian Federation for more than two consecutive terms.
4.   The manner of election of the President of the Russian Federation is established by federal law.

Article 82
1.   When entering into office the President of the Russian Federation takes the following oath to the people: "In exercising the powers of the President

of the Russian Federation I swear to respect and protect the rights and free-doms of man and citizen, to observe and defend the Constitution of the Russ-ian Federation, to defend the state's sovereignty and independence and its security and integrity, and faithfully to serve the people."
2.   The oath is administered in a ceremonial atmosphere in the presence of members of the Council of the Federation, deputies of the State Duma and justices of the Constitutional Court of the Russian Federation.

Article 83
The President of the Russian Federation:
    a.   appoints the chairman of the Government of the Russian Federation with the consent of the State Duma;
    b.   is entitled to chair sessions of the Government of the Russian Feder-ation;
    c.   adopts the decision on dismissal of the Government of the Russian Federation;
    d.   submits to the State Duma the candidacy for appointment to the office of chairman of the Central Bank of the Russian Federation; raises before the State Duma the question of removing from office the chairman of the Central Bank of the Russian Federation;
    e.   at the proposal of the chairman of the Government of the Russian Federation appoints and removes from office the Deputy-Chairmen of the Government of the Russian Federation and federal ministers;
    f.   submits to the Council of the Federation the candidacy for appoint-ment to the office of justices of the Constitutional Court of the Russian Fed-eration, the Supreme Court of the Russian Federation, and also the candida-cy for the Procurator-General of the Russian Federation; submits to the Council of the Federation the proposal on removing from office the Procura-tor-General of the Russian Federation; appoints the judges of other federal courts;
    g.   composes and heads the Security Council of the Russian Federation, whose status is defined by federal law;
    h.   approves the military doctrine of the Russian Federation;
    i.   composes the Administration of the President of the Russian Feder-ation;
    j.   appoints and removes plenipotentiary representatives of the Presi-dent of the Russian Federation;
    k.   appoints and removes the high command of the armed forces of the Russian Federation;
    l.   appoints and recalls, following consultations with the relevant com-mittees or commissions of the chambers of the Federal Assembly, diplomatic representatives of the Russian Federation in foreign states and international organisations.

Article 84
The President of the Russian Federation:
    a.   schedules elections to the State Duma in accordance with the Con-stitution of the Russian Federation and federal law;
    b.   dissolves the State Duma in the instances and the manner provided by the Constitution of the Russian Federation;

    c.   schedules referendums according to the procedure prescribed by a federal constitutional law;
    d.   submits draft laws to the State Duma;
    e.   signs and promulgates federal laws;
    f.   delivers to the Federal Assembly annual messages on the state of the country and on the basic guidelines of the state's domestic and foreign policy.

Article 85

1.   The President of the Russian Federation may use conciliation procedures to resolve disagreements between organs of state power of the Russian Federation and organs of state power of subjects of the Russian Federation, and also between organs of state power of subjects of the Russian Federation. In the event of failure to reach an agreed solution he may refer the resolution of the dispute for examination by the appropriate court.

2.   Pending a resolution of the matter by the appropriate court, the President of the Russian Federation is entitled to suspend the operation of enactments by organs of executive power of subjects of the Russian Federation if these enactments contravene the Constitution of the Russian Federation and federal laws or the Russian Federation's international obligations or violate rights and freedoms of man and citizen.

Article 86

The President of the Russian Federation:
    a.   exercises guidance over the foreign policy of the Russian Federation;
    b.   conducts talks and signs international treaties of the Russian Federation;
    c.   signs instruments of ratification;
    d.   accepts the credentials and letters of recall of diplomatic representatives accredited to him.

Article 87

1.   The President of the Russian Federation is the highest Commander-in-chief of the armed forces of the Russian Federation.

2.   In the event of aggression against the Russian Federation or a direct threat of aggression the President of the Russian Federation introduces martial law on the territory of the Russian Federation or in individual localities of its territory and immediately notifies the Council of the Federation and State Duma of this.

3.   The regime of martial law is defined by a federal constitutional law.

Article 88

Under the circumstances and in the manner laid down by a federal constitutional law, the President of the Russian Federation introduces a state of emergency on the territory of the Russian Federation or in individual localities of its territory and immediately notifies the Council of the Federation and State Duma of this.

Article 89

The President of the Russian Federation:

    a.   resolves questions of citizenship of the Russian Federation and of granting political asylum;

    b.   grants state awards of the Russian Federation and awards honorary ranks of the Russian Federation and higher military and higher special ranks;

    c.   grants pardons.

Article 90

1.   The President of the Russian Federation issues edicts and resolutions.

2.   Edicts and resolutions of the President of the Russian Federation are mandatory and to be abided by throughout the territory of the Russian Federation.

3.   Edicts and resolutions of the President of the Russian Federation may not contravene the Constitution of the Russian Federation and federal laws.

Article 91

The President of the Russian Federation enjoys inviolability.

Article 92

1.   The President of the Russian Federation begins exercising his powers from the moment he swears the oath and ceases exercising them upon the expiry of his term of office from the moment that the newly elected President of the Russian Federation swears the oath.

2.   The President of the Russian Federation ceases to exercise his powers early in the event of his resignation, persistent inability to exercise his powers for reasons of health, or removal from office. Furthermore, the election of a President of the Russian Federation must take place no later than three months after the early cessation of the exercise of his powers.

3.   In all instances where the President of the Russian Federation is unable to perform his duties, they are temporarily carried out by the Chairman of the Government of the Russian Federation. An acting President of the Russian Federation does not have the right to dissolve the State Duma, schedule a referendum or submit proposals on amendments to and the revision of the provisions of the Constitution of the Russian Federation.

Article 93

1.   The President of the Russian Federation can only be removed from office by the Council of the Federation on the basis of a charge of high treason or commission of another grave crime, filed by the State Duma and confirmed by an opinion of the Supreme Court of the Russian Federation that actions of the President of the Russian Federation contain the elements of a crime and an opinion of the Constitutional Court of the Russian Federation on the observation of the procedure established for filing the charge.

2.   The decision by the State Duma on filing the charge and the decision by the Council of the Federation on removing the President from office must be adopted by a vote of two-thirds of the total membership of each chamber on the initiative of at least one-third of the deputies of the State Duma and on the basis of a conclusion of a special commission formed by the State Duma.

3.   The decision by the Council of the Federation on removing the President of the Russian Federation from office must be adopted within three months after filing the charge against the President by the State Duma. If the decision by the Council of the Federation is not adopted within this period of time, the charge against the President is deemed rejected.

Chapter 5 – The Federal Assembly

Article 94
The Federal Assembly – the parliament of the Russian Federation – is the representative and legislative organ of the Russian Federation.

Article 95
1.   The Federal Assembly consists of two chambers: the Council of the Federation and the State Duma.
2.   The Council of the Federation consists of two representatives from each subject of the Russian Federation: one each from the representative and the executive organ of state power.
3.   The State Duma consists of 450 deputies.

Article 96
1.   The State Duma is elected for a term of four years.
2.   The procedure for composing the Council of the Federation and the manner of electing deputies of the State Duma are established by federal laws.

Article 97
1.   A citizen of the Russian Federation who has attained the age of 21 years and has the right to participate in elections can be elected a deputy of the State Duma.
2.   One and the same person cannot simultaneously be a member of the Council of the Federation and a deputy of the State Duma. A deputy of the State Duma cannot be a deputy of any other representative organs of state power or organs of local self-government.
3.   Deputies of the State Duma work full time and on a professional basis. Deputies of the State Duma cannot be in state service or engage in any other paid activity, apart from teaching, scientific or other creative activity.

Article 98
1.   Members of the Council of the Federation and deputies of the State Duma enjoy inviolability for the duration of the entire term of their mandate. They cannot be detained, arrested or subjected to a search unless detained at the scene of a crime, nor can they be subjected to a body search except in instances provided by federal law in order to guarantee other people's safety.
2.   Any question concerning the lifting of inviolability is decided by the appropriate chamber of the Federal Assembly upon a proposal by the Procurator-General of the Russian Federation.

Article 99
1.   The Federal Assembly is a permanently functioning organ.
2.   The State Duma meets for its first session on the thirtieth day after its election. The President of the Russian Federation can convene a session of the State Duma prior to this date.
3.   The first session of the State Duma is opened by the oldest deputy.
4.   From the moment that the work of a newly elected State Duma begins, the powers of the previous State Duma are terminated.

Article 100
1.   The Council of the Federation and the State Duma hold separate sessions.
2.   Sessions of the Council of the Federation and the State Duma are open. In instances stipulated by the standing orders of a chamber it is entitled to conduct closed sessions.
3.   Chambers may convene jointly to hear messages from the President of the Russian Federation, messages from the Constitutional Court of the Russian Federation and speeches by leaders of foreign states.

Article 101
1.   The Council of the Federation elects from its members the Chairman of the State Duma and his deputies.
2.   The Chairman of the Council of the Federation and his deputies, and the Chairman of the State Duma and his deputies chair the sessions and control the internal procedures of the chamber.
3.   The Council of the Federation and the State Duma create committees and commissions and conduct parliamentary hearings in the matters under their jurisdiction.
4.   Each of the chambers adopts its own standing orders and decides matters relating to the internal procedure governing its activity.
5.   In order to supervise the observation of the federal budget the Council of the Federation and the State Duma create an audit chamber, whose composition and manner of work are determined by federal law.

Article 102
1.   To the jurisdiction of the Council of the Federation belongs:
     a.   confirming alterations to borders between subjects of the Russian Federation;
     b.   confirming an edict of the President of the Russian Federation on the introduction of martial law;
     c.   confirming an edict of the President of the Russian Federation on the introduction of a state of emergency;
     d.   resolving the question of the possibility of the utilisation of Russian Federation Armed Forces outside the borders of the territory of the Russian Federation;
     e.   scheduling elections for the President of the Russian Federation;
     f.   removing the President of the Russian Federation from office;
     g.   appointing justices of the Constitutional Court of the Russian Federation, the Supreme Court of the Russian Federation and the Supreme Arbitration Court of the Russian Federation;

h.   appointing and removing from office the Procurator-General of the Russian Federation;

i.   appointing and removing from office the deputy chairman of the Audit Chamber and half of its staff of auditors.

2.   The Council of the Federation adopts decrees on matters referred to its jurisdiction by the Constitution of the Russian Federation.

3.   Decrees of the Council of the Federation are adopted by a majority of the votes of the total membership of the Council of the Federation unless another procedure for adopting a decision is provided by the Constitution of the Russian Federation.

Article 103

1.   To the jurisdiction of the State Duma belongs:

a.   giving consent to the President of the Russian Federation for the appointment of the Chairman of the Government of the Russian Federation;

b.   resolving the question of confidence in the Government of the Russian Federation;

c.   appointing and removing from office the Chairman of the Central Bank of the Russian Federation;

d.   appointing and removing from office the Chairman of the Audit Chamber and half of its staff of auditors;

e.   appointing and removing from office the Commissioner for Human Rights, who operates in compliance with a federal constitutional law;

f.   declaring an amnesty;

g.   filing a charge against the President of the Russian Federation to remove him from office.

2.   The State Duma adopts decrees on matters referred to its jurisdiction by the Constitution of the Russian Federation.

3.   Decrees of the State Duma are adopted by a majority of the votes of the total number of deputies of the State Duma unless another procedure for adopting a decision is provided by the Constitution of the Russian Federation.

Article 104

1.   The right of legislative initiative is vested in the President of the Russian Federation, the Council of the Federation, members of the Council of the Federation, deputies of the State Duma, the Government of the Russian Federation and the legislative (representative) organs of subjects of the Russian Federation. The right of legislative initiative is also vested in the Constitutional Court of the Russian Federation, the Supreme Court of the Russian Federation and the High Arbitration Court of the Russian Federation in matters under their jurisdiction.

2.   Draft laws are submitted to the State Duma.

3.   Draft laws on the introduction or abolition of taxes, exemption from the payment of taxes, the issue of state loans, the alteration of the financial obligations of the state and other draft laws envisaging expenditure funded out of the state budget can be submitted only together with an opinion of the Government of the Russian Federation.

Article 105

1.   Federal laws are adopted by the State Duma.

2.   Federal laws are adopted by a majority of the votes of the total number of deputies of the State Duma unless otherwise provided by the Constitution of the Russian Federation.

3.   Federal laws adopted by the State Duma are passed to the Council of the Federation within five days for examination.

4.   A federal law is deemed to have been approved by the Council of the Federation if more than half of the total membership of this chamber have voted for it or if it has not been examined by the Council of the Federation within fourteen days. In the event of the rejection of a federal law by the Council of the Federation the chambers may form a conciliation commission to overcome differences which have arisen, after which the federal law is subject to a second examination by the State Duma.

5.   In the event of disagreement by the State Duma with a decision of the Council of the Federation, a federal law is deemed to have been adopted if at least two-thirds of the total number of deputies of the State Duma vote for it in the second vote on it.

Article 106
Federal laws adopted by the State Duma are subject to compulsory examination in the Council of the Federation when they concern questions of:
    a.   the federal budget;
    b.   federal taxes and duties;
    c.   financial, currency, credit and customs regulation and issue of money;
    d.   ratification and denunciation of international treaties of the Russian Federation;
    e.   the status and protection of the state border of the Russian Federation;
    f.   war and peace.

Article 107
1.   An adopted federal law is submitted within five days to the President of the Russian Federation for signing and promulgation.

2.   The President of the Russian Federation signs and promulgates a federal law within fourteen days.

3.   If the President of the Russian Federation, within fourteen days of receiving the federal law, rejects it, the State Duma and the Council of the Federation examine the said law anew in the manner laid down by the Constitution of the Russian Federation. If, after the second examination, the federal law is approved by a majority of not less than two-thirds of the votes of the total number of members of the Council of the Federation and deputies of the State Duma in the wording previously adopted, it is to be signed by the President of the Russian Federation within seven days and promulgated.

Article 108
1.   Federal constitutional laws are adopted on matters provided by the Constitution of the Russian Federation.

2.   A federal constitutional law is deemed to be adopted if it is approved by a majority of the votes of at least three-quarters of the total membership of

the Council of the Federation and at least two-thirds of the total number of deputies of the State Duma. A federal constitutional law that has been adopted is to be signed by the President of the Russian Federation and promulgated within fourteen days.

Article 109
1.   The State Duma may be dissolved by the President of the Russian Federation in the circumstances provided in Articles 111 and 117 of the Constitution of the Russian Federation.
2.   In the event of a dissolution of the State Duma, the President of the Russian Federation sets the date of elections so as to ensure that the newly elected State Duma is convened not later than four months from the date of dissolution.
3.   The State Duma may not be dissolved on the grounds stipulated in Article 117 of the Constitution of the Russian Federation for one year following its election.
4.   The State Duma may not be dissolved from the moment it files a charge against the President of the Russian Federation, until the adoption of the decision in the question by the Council of the Federation.
5.   The State Duma may not be dissolved during the period of operation of a state of martial law or state of emergency on the whole territory of the Russian Federation, or within the six months preceding the expiry of the term of office of the President of the Russian Federation.

Chapter 6 – The Government of the Russian Federation

Article 110
1.   Executive power in the Russian Federation is exercised by the Government of the Russian Federation.
2.   The Government of the Russian Federation consists of the Chairman of the Government of the Russian Federation, the deputy Chairmen of the Government of the Russian Federation and the federal ministers.

Article 111
1.   The Chairman of the Government of the Russian Federation is appointed by the President of the Russian Federation with the consent of the State Duma.
2.   A proposal on the candidacy for the Chairman of the Government of the Russian Federation is submitted no later than two weeks following the entry into office of a newly elected President of the Russian Federation or the resignation of the Government of the Russian Federation or within a week following the rejection of a candidacy by the State Duma.
3.   The State Duma examines the candidacy for the Chairman of the Government of the Russian Federation submitted by the President of the Russian Federation within a week of the day the proposal is submitted.
4.   Following three rejections by the State Duma of candidacies submitted for the Chairman of the Government of the Russian Federation, the President of the Russian Federation appoints a Chairman of the Government of the Russia Federation, dissolves the State Duma and schedules new elections.

Article 112

1.   The Chairman of the Government of the Russian Federation, no later than one week following his appointment, submits to the President of the Russian Federation proposals on the structure of the federal organs of executive power.

2.   The Chairman of the Government of the Russian Federation proposes to the President of the Russian Federation candidacies for the posts of deputy Chairmen of the Government of the Russian Federation and federal ministers.

Article 113

The Chairman of the Government of the Russian Federation, in accordance with the Constitution of the Russian Federation, federal laws and edicts of the President of the Russian Federation, defines the basic guidelines for the activity of the Government of the Russian Federation and organises its work.

Article 114

1.   The Government of the Russian Federation:

   a.   drafts the federal budget, submits it to the State Duma and ensures its implementation; submits to the State Duma a report on the implementation of the federal budget;

   b.   ensures the implementation of a uniform fiscal, credit and monetary policy in the Russian Federation;

   c.   ensures the implementation of a uniform state policy in the Russian Federation in the sphere of culture, education, health, social security and ecology;

   d.   administers federal ownership;

   e.   implements measures to ensure the defence of the country, state security and the realisation of the foreign policy of the Russian Federation;

   f.   implements measures to ensure legality, the rights and freedoms of the citizens, the protection of ownership and public order, and the struggle against crime;

   g.   exercises other powers vested in it by the Constitution of the Russian Federation, federal laws and edicts of the President of the Russian Federation.

2.   The manner of work of the Government of the Russian Federation is defined by a federal constitutional law.

Article 115

1.   On the basis of and in implementation of the Constitution of the Russian Federation, federal laws and normative edicts of the President of the Russian Federation, the Government of the Russian Federation issues decrees and orders and ensures their implementation.

2.   Decrees and resolutions of the Government of the Russian Federation are mandatory to be abided in the Russian Federation.

3.   Decrees and resolutions of the Government of the Russian Federation, in the event that they are at variance with the Constitution of the Russian Federation, federal laws or edicts of the President of the Russian Federation, may be rescinded by the President of the Russian Federation.

Article 116
The Government of the Russian Federation surrenders its powers to a newly elected President of the Russian Federation.

Article 117
1.   The Government of the Russian Federation may offer its resignation, which is accepted or rejected by the President of the Russian Federation.
2.   The President of the Russian Federation may adopt a decision on the discharge of the Government of the Russian Federation.
3.   The State Duma may express no confidence in the Government of the Russian Federation. A decree of no confidence in the Government of the Russian Federation is adopted by a majority of votes of the total number of deputies of the State Duma. Following an expression of no confidence by the State Duma in the Government of the Russian Federation, the President of the Russian Federation is entitled to announce the dismissal of the Government of the Russian Federation or to disagree with the decision of the State Duma. In the event that the State Duma expresses no confidence in the Government of the Russian Federation for a second time within three months, the President of the Russian Federation announces the dismissal of the Government or dissolves the State Duma.
4.   The Chairman of the Government of the Russian Federation may submit to the State Duma a motion of confidence in the Government of the Russian Federation. If the State Duma refuses its confidence, the President adopts a decision within seven days on the dismissal of the Government of the Russian Federation or on the dissolution of the State Duma and the holding of new elections.
5.   In the event of its resignation or the surrender of its powers, the Government of the Russian Federation, on the instructions of the President of the Russian Federation, continues to act until the formation of a new Government of the Russian Federation.

Chapter 7 – The Judicial Branch

Article 118
1.   Justice in the Russian Federation is exercised only by the court.
2.   Judicial power is exercised by means of constitutional, civil, administrative and criminal court proceedings.
3.   The system of courts of the Russian Federation is established by the Constitution of the Russian Federation and by a federal constitutional law. The creation of extraordinary courts is not permitted.

Article 119
Citizens of the Russian Federation who have attained the age of 25 and have higher legal education and at least five years'experience in the legal profession may become judges. Additional requirements may be established by federal law for the judges of the courts of the Russian Federation.

Article 120
1.   Judges are independent and are subordinate only to the Constitution of the Russian Federation and to federal law.

2.   The court, having determined in the course of examining a case that an enactment of a state organ or other organ is not in conformity with a law, adopts a ruling in accordance with the law.

Article 121
1.   Judges may not be removed.
2.   A judge's mandate may not be terminated or suspended except in accordance with the procedure and on the grounds laid down by federal law.

Article 122
1.   Judges are inviolable.
2.   A judge may not be subjected to criminal proceedings except in accordance with the procedure defined by federal law.

Article 123
1.   The examination of cases in all courts is open. Hearing a case in closed session is permitted in circumstances stipulated in federal law.
2.   The *in absentia* examination of criminal cases in the courts is not permitted, except in circumstances provided in federal law.
3.   Court proceedings are carried out on the basis of the adversarial system and the equality of the rights of the parties.
4.   In instances provided in federal law, court proceedings take place with the participation of juror assessors.

Article 124
The financing of courts is effected solely from the federal budget and must ensure the possibility of the complete and independent exercise of justice in accordance with federal law.

Article 125
1.   The Constitutional Court of the Russian Federation consists of 19 judges.
2.   The Constitutional Court of the Russian Federation, on the application of the President of the Russian Federation, the Council of the Federation, the State Duma, one-fifth of the members of the Council of the Federation or deputies of the State Duma, the Government of the Russian Federation, the Supreme Court of the Russian Federation or the High Arbitration Court of the Russian Federation, or organs of legislative and executive power of the subjects of the Russian Federation, resolves cases relating to the compliance with the Constitution of the Russian Federation of:
   a.   federal laws and normative enactments of the President of the Russian Federation, the Council of the Federation, the State Duma or the Government of the Russian Federation;
   b.   the constitutions of republics and charters as well as the laws and other normative acts of subjects of the Russian Federation in matters falling within the jurisdiction of organs of state power of the Russian Federation or the joint jurisdiction of organs of state power of the Russian Federation and organs of state power of subjects of the Russian Federation;

     c.   agreements between organs of state power of the Russian Federation and organs of state power of subjects of the Russian Federation and agreements between organs of state power of subjects of the Russian Federation;

     d.   international treaties of the Russian Federation that have not yet entered into force.

3.   The Constitutional Court of the Russian Federation resolves competence disputes;

     a.   between federal organs of state power;

     b.   between organs of state power of the Russian Federation and organs of state power of subjects of the Russian Federation;

     c.   between the highest state organs of subjects of the Russian Federation.

4.   The Constitutional Court of the Russian Federation, at complaints on the violation of constitutional rights and freedoms of citizens and at the request of courts, verifies the constitutionality of the law that has been applied or had to be applied in the specific case, in accordance with the procedure laid down by federal law.

5.   The Constitutional Court of the Russian Federation provides an interpretation of the Constitution of the Russian Federation at a request of the President of the Russian Federation, the Council of the Federation, the State Duma, the Government of the Russian Federation or organs of legislative power of subjects of the Russian Federation.

6.   Enactments or individual provisions thereof that are declared unconstitutional lose their force; international treaties of the Russian Federation that are not compatible with the Constitution of the Russian Federation shall not enter into force or be subject to application.

7.   The Constitutional Court of the Russian Federation, on the application of the Council of the Federation, issues an opinion on the observation of the manner established for filing the charge against the President of the Russian Federation of high treason or the commission of another grave crime.

Article 126

The Supreme Court of the Russian Federation is the highest judicial organ for civil, criminal, administrative and other cases under the jurisdiction of courts of general jurisdiction, exercises judicial supervision over their activity within the procedural forms provided by federal law and gives explanations on questions of judicial practice.

Article 127

The High Arbitration Court of the Russian Federation is the highest judicial organ for the resolution of economic disputes and other cases examined by the courts of arbitration, exercises judicial supervision over their activity within the procedural forms provided by federal law and gives explanations on questions of judicial practice.

Article 128

1.   Judges of the Constitutional Court of the Russian Federation, the Supreme Court of the Russian Federation and the High Arbitration Court of

the Russian Federation are appointed by the Council of the Federation on the proposal of the President of the Russian Federation.
2.   Judges of other federal courts are appointed by the President of the Russian Federation in the manner laid down by federal law.
3.   The powers and the manner of formation and work of the Constitutional Court of the Russian Federation, the Supreme Court of the Russian Federation, the High Arbitration Court of the Russian Federation and other federal courts are laid down by a federal constitutional law.

Article 129
1.   The Procuracy of the Russian Federation is a unitary centralised system in which lower-level procurators are subordinate to higher-level procurators and to the Procurator-General of the Russian Federation.
2.   The Procurator-General of the Russian Federation is appointed and dismissed from office by the Council of the Federation on the proposal of the President of the Russian Federation.
3.   The procurators of subjects of the Russian Federation are appointed by the Procurator-General of the Russian Federation in agreement with these subjects.
4.   Other procurators are appointed by the Procurator-General of the Russian Federation.
5.   The powers and the organisation and manner of operation of the Procuracy of the Russian Federation are defined by federal law.

Chapter 8 – The local self-government

Article 130
1.   Local self-government in the Russian Federation ensures the independent resolution of questions of local significance by the population and the possession, utilisation and disposal of municipal property.
2.   Local self-government is exercised by citizens by means of a referendum, elections and other forms of direct expression of will and through elected and other organs of local self-government.

Article 131
1.   Local self-government in urban and rural settlements and other territories is exercised taking into account the historical and other local traditions. The structure of local self-government organs is independently determined by the population.
2.   Changes to the borders of territories wherein local self-government is exercised are permitted taking into account the opinion of the population of the territories concerned.

Article 132
1.   Organs of local self-government independently administer municipal property, formulate, approve and implement the local budget, establish local taxes and duties, implement the protection of public order as well as resolve their questions of local significance.

2.   Individual state powers can be vested by law in organs of local self-government with the transfer of the material and financial means necessary to exercise them. The exercise of the transferred powers is supervised by the state.

Article 133
Local self-government in the Russian Federation is guaranteed by the right to judicial protection, compensation for additional expenditure arising as a result of decisions adopted by organs of state power, and the prohibition of the restriction of the rights of local self-government established by the Constitution of the Russian Federation and federal laws.

Chapter 9 – Constitutional amendments and revision of the Constitution

Article 134
Proposals to correct or revise provisions of the Constitution of the Russian Federation can be submitted by the President of the Russian Federation, the Council of the Federation, the State Duma, the Government of the Russian Federation, legislative (representative) organs of subjects of the Russian Federation, and also by a group comprising at least one-fifth of members of the Council of the Federation or deputies of the State Duma.

Article 135
1.   The provisions of Chapters 1, 2 and 9 of the Constitution of the Russian Federation cannot be revised by the Federal Assembly.
2.   If a proposal to revise the provisions of Chapters 1, 2 and 9 of the Constitution of the Russian Federation is supported by a vote of three-fifths of the total number of members of the Council of the Federation and deputies of the State Duma a Constitutional Assembly is convened in accordance with federal constitutional law.
3.   The Constitutional Assembly either confirms the immutability of the Constitution of the Russian Federation or elaborates a draft of a new Constitution of the Russian Federation which is adopted by the Constitutional Assembly by a vote of two-thirds of its total membership or is submitted to a nationwide vote. If a nationwide vote is held, the Constitution of the Russian Federation is considered adopted if votes for it are cast by more than one-half of the voters taking part in the ballot, provided that more than one-half of the electorate have cast their votes.

Article 136
Corrections to Chapters 3-8 of the Constitution of the Russian Federation are adopted by the procedure envisaged for the adoption of a federal constitutional law and come into force after they have been approved by the organs of legislative power of at least two-thirds of the subjects of the Russian Federation.

Article 137
1.   Amendments to Article 65 of the Constitution of the Russian Federation, which determines the composition of the Russian Federation, are submitted

on the basis of a federal constitutional law relating to admission to the Russian Federation, and the formation of a new subject of the Russian Federation within it or to the alteration of the constitutional-legal status of a subject of the Russian Federation.

2.   In the event of changes to the name of a republic, territory, province, city of federal significance, autonomous province or autonomous area, the new name of the subject of the Russian Federation is to be incorporated in Article 65 of the Constitution of the Russian Federation.

Section 2 – Concluding and transitional provisions

1.   The Constitution of the Russian Federation comes into force on the day of its official publication upon the basis of the results of the nationwide vote. The day of the nationwide vote, 12 December 1993, is deemed the day of the adoption of the Constitution of the Russian Federation.

The Constitution (Basic law) of the Russian Federation-Russia, adopted on 12 April 1978 with its subsequent amendments and additions, simultaneously ceases to be in force.

In the event of non-compliance with provisions of the Constitution of the Russian Federation of provisions of the Federative Agreement – the Agreement on the delimitation of areas of jurisdiction and of powers between federal organs of state power of the Russian Federation and organs of state power of sovereign republics within the Russian Federation, the Agreement on the delimitation of areas of jurisdiction and of powers between federal organs of state power of the Russian Federation and organs of state power of territories, provinces and the cities of Moscow and St. Petersburg in the Russian Federation, the Agreement on the delimitation of areas of jurisdiction and of powers between federal organs of state power of the Russian Federation and organs of state power of the autonomous province and autonomous areas of the Russian Federation, as well as other agreements between federal organs of state power of the Russian Federation and organs of state power of subjects of the Russian Federation, and agreements between organs of state power of subjects of the Russian Federation – the provisions of the Constitution of the Russian Federation shall prevail.

2.   Laws and other legal enactments which were in force on the territory of the Russian Federation prior to the entry into force of the present Constitution are applied to the extent to which they do not contravene the Constitution of the Russian Federation.

3.   From the day the present Constitution comes into force, the President of the Russian Federation, elected in accordance with the Constitution (Basic Law) of the Russian Federation-Russia, exercises the powers laid down by the present Constitution until the expiry of the term for which he was elected.

4.   From the day the present Constitution comes into force, the Council of Ministers-Government of the Russian Federation acquires the right, obligations and responsibility of the Government of the Russian Federation established by the Constitution of the Russian Federation and is thereafter called the Government of the Russian Federation.

5.   Courts in the Russian Federation administer justice in compliance with their powers laid down by the present Constitution.

After the Constitution has come into force, the judges of all courts in the Russian Federation retain their powers until the expiry of the term for which they were elected. Vacancies are filled according to the procedure established by the present Constitution.

6.   Pending the entry into force of the federal law laying down the procedure for the hearing of cases by a court with the participation of sworn assessors, the existing procedure for judicial examination of such cases is retained. The existing procedures for the arrest, holding in custody and detention of persons suspected of having committed a crime are retained until such time as the criminal procedure legislation of the Russian Federation is brought into line with the provisions of the present Constitution.

7.   The first Council of the Federation and the first State Duma are elected for a term of two years.

8.   The Council of the Federation will convene for its first session on the thirtieth day following its election. The first session of the Council of the Federation will be opened by the President of the Russian Federation.

9.   A deputy of the first State Duma can simultaneously be a member of the Government of the Russian Federation. The provisions of the present Constitution on deputies' inviolability for actions (or inactions) associated with the performance of official duties do not extend to deputies of the State Duma who are members of the Government of the Russian Federation.

The deputies of the first Council of the Federation perform their duties on a non-permanent basis.

Tadjikistan

Chronology

1989

July 22: The Supreme Soviet gives legal status to the Tadjik language; Russian remains as the official language for communication between nationalities within Tadjikistan.

December 24: The elections for the local soviets are held.

1990

February 12: The Tadjik Communist Party (CP) headquarters are besieged. The Supreme Soviet declares a state of emergency and a night-time curfew in Dushanbe.

February 14: The CP first secretary Kakhar Makhkamov, the President of the Supreme Soviet Presidium Gaibnazar Pallayev and Prime Minister Izatullo Khayeyev offer their resignation at a meeting with the unofficial Vaadad ("Unity") People's Committee, formed shortly after the outbreak of the Dushanbe violence and uniting government representatives and activists from the Popular Front-style Rastokhez (Rebirth) organisation.

February 16: At an extraordinary plenum the CP central committee refuses to accept Kakhar Makhkamov's resignation as first secretary and Vaadad is criticised for contributing to the destabilisation of the situation in Tadjikistan.

February 25: Although the state of emergency remains in force, elections to the Supreme Soviet go ahead as scheduled.

April 12: The newly elected Supreme Soviet elects the first secretary of the CP, Kakhar Makhkamov, to the post of Chairman, i.e. President of the Republic.

August 25: Tadjikistan joins the list of republics declaring sovereignty and the precedence of their constitutions and laws over those of the Soviet Union.

November 30: The Supreme Soviet elects Kakhar Makhkamov, hitherto *de facto* President, to the new post of executive President of Tadjikistan.

1991

January 1: The curfew, which was imposed because of anti-government rioting and pogroms in February 1990 is lifted.

March 17: Tadjikistan holds the all-union referendum on the preservation of the Soviet Union. 96.2% of the population vote for the preservation of the Soviet Union and 3.1% vote against. The turnout is 94.4%.

April 23: President Mikhail Gorbachev signs, with nine of fifteen union republics including Tadjikistan, a pact aimed at achieving stable relations between the central and republican governments. He sets out a timetable for major political changes, starting with the signing of the new Union Treaty. No longer than six months after signature of the Treaty a new Union constitution would be promulgated, followed by elections to the Congress of People's Deputies.

August 19: Attempted *coup d'état* in Moscow.

August 28: Property of the Communist Party of the Soviet Union (CPSU), in the republic, is nationalised and some parties are banned from the Supreme Soviet's administrative bodies. The CP resolves to leave the CPSU. The republic drops "Soviet Socialist" from its name to become "Republic of Tadjikistan".

August 31: President Kakhar Makhkamov resigns after a vote of no confidence in the Supreme Soviet, on account of the *coup.*

September 9: The Supreme Council declares the country independent.

September 21: The Communist Party of Tadjikistan renames itself the Socialist Party of Tadjikistan.

September 22: Acting President Kadreddin Aslonov, appointed after the resignation of Kakhar Makhkamov, issues a decree banning the activities of the Socialist Party of Tadjikistan and nationalises its property.

September 23: The Supreme Council convenes a special session to overturn the ban on communists and acting President Aslonov resigns. The Supreme Council elects unanimously as its Chairman and therefore President of the Republic, the former CP first secretary, Rakhman Nabiyev. A state of emergency is introduced in the republic lasting until 1 January.

October 2: At the second vote in the Supreme Soviet, the ban on activities of the CP is reimposed. The government will control CP property until the latter's role in the August coup attempt can be determined.

October 6: Rakhman Nabiyev resigns as Chair of the Supreme Soviet and Akbarsho Iskandrov serves as an acting chairman until the presidential elections on 24 November.

November 24: Presidential elections are held. Rakhman Nabiyev is elected President with 58% of the vote and a turnout of 84.6% according to preliminary results. His nearest rival is a film producer, Davlar Koudonazarov, gains a quarter of the votes, despite being backed by both opposition parties: the Democratic Party and the Islamic Renaissance Party. Koudonazarov's allegation that the voting is manipulated is supported by the observer from the USSR Supreme Soviet.

December 8: Belarus, the Russian Federative Republic and Ukraine sign the Minsk agreement, establishing a Commonwealth of Independent States (CIS).

December 12: Tadjikistan signs the Alma Ata Agreement, thus joining the CIS.

December 21: The CIS formally replaces the Soviet Union, grouping eleven republics with the exception of Georgia. The Russian Federative Republic takes over many of the former Union functions, including its seat in the UN Security Council.

1992

March 6: The Supreme Council approves a land reform law, giving all citizens the right to a lifetime ownership of land and to lease and inherit land.

May 11: Demonstrations throughout April and the first part of May organised by activists opposed to President Rakhman Nabiyev's régime culminate in the formation of a coalition government, in which eight of the 24 ministerial posts go to opposition members, while Nabiyev remains President. A transitional legislative body, the 80-seat *Majlis*, consisting of Supreme Council deputies and representatives of political parties, is established and will sit until fresh elections on 6 December.

May 20: The local Soviets of the Khodjent and Kulyab regions refuse to recognise the new coalition government and to contribute to the republic's resources.

August 30: Prime Minister Akbar Mirzoyev resigns.

September 2: The Presidium of the Supreme Council passes a resolution on removing President Rakhman Nabiyev from power.

September 4, 5, 7: Because of the absence of deputies from Khodjent, there is no quorum to confirm the resolution passed on 2 September.

September 7: Due to his inability to restore stability in Tadjikistan, President Nabiyev is forced to resign.

September 24: Constitutionally, presidential powers pass to the Chair of the Supreme Council, Akbarsho Iskandrov, who appoints Abdumalik Abdullojanov as acting Prime Minister.

November 18: President Iskandrov's Islamic coalition government resigns because of the continuing conflict.

November 19: The deputies of the Supreme Council elect Imamoli Rakhmanov, a former communist, as President.

November 20: Abdumalik Abdullojanov is elected Prime Minister.

November 25: Leaders of a number of armed groups reach an agreement in the Supreme Council to end the fighting.

November 26: The Parliament marks this day as annual Day of Peace.

November 27: Parliament appeals for an end to the civil war, defends a temporary ban on strikes and rallies, and calls for the voluntary surrender of weapons. The Parliament abolishes the Presidency and creates by resolution a Parliamentary Republic.

December 1-3: The Supreme Council approves Rakhmanov's new government.

1993

January 7: After the declaration of emergency and the introduction of a curfew, relative calm returns to Dushanbe.

February 2: President Rakhmanov upgrades the State Committee for Foreign Economic Relations into a fully fledged Ministry for Foreign Economic Relations headed by Izzatullo Hayoyev.

May 25: President Rakhmanov and the Russian President Yeltsin sign a friendship, co-operation and mutual assistance treaty.

June 21: The Supreme Court bans four opposition parties; the DP, Lale Badakshon, the Islamic Renaissance Party of Tadjikistan and the Rastokhez (Rebirth) People's Front because of forming illegal militias, fomenting civil war and killing or kidnapping legislators.

July: In its first session since the civil war, the Supreme Council declares all decrees made under the Iskandrov administration illegal.

August 25: The Supreme Court imposes the death sentence on a senior member of the Islamic Renaissance Party, Ajik Aliyev, for attempting to overthrow the government.

September 24: Tadjikistan signs a framework designed gradually to build a common economic space on the basis of market relations with the CIS member states.

December 19: Abdumalik Abdullojanov resigns as Prime Minister and under a presidential decree of 22 December he is appointed First Deputy Prime Minister and Tadjik ambassador to Russia.

December 22: Deputy Prime Minister Abdujalil Samadov is appointed as Prime Minister.

1994

January 8: Tadjikistan introduces the Russian rouble as its currency replacing the Soviet rouble. The move is seen as ceding considerable sovereignty on economic issues to Russia.

February 2: A major government reorganisation reducing the number of Deputy Prime Ministers and Cabinet members is approved by the Presidium of the Supreme Council. The reorganisation includes the creation of a Security Ministry, replacing the National Security Committee.

March 11: Mayonsho Nazarshoyev, a Deputy Prime Minister, is murdered in an attempt to sabotage peace talks scheduled to be held in Moscow on 16 March between the government and opposition rebels.

April 11: The formation of the People's Party of Tadjikistan, the successor to the Socialist Party, chaired by Supreme Soviet First Deputy Chair Abdulmajikd Dostiyev, is announced.

April 13: The government reassumes control over the country's three main newspapers.

April 19: Representatives of the government and the democratic and Islamic opposition reach an agreement to co-operate in the return of refugees and will seek national reconciliation through political means alone. A draft constitution is published envisaging the re-establishment of the Presidency and is put for approval by referendum.

July 18: The Supreme Council approves the appointment of Inoyatova Munira Abdulloyevna as Deputy Prime Minister and Minister for Education.

July 20: The Supreme Council approves the draft constitution, which will be submitted to popular referendum on 25 September. The draft is opposed by the People's Party, criticising the introduction of a presidential government. The representatives of Gorny-Badakshan attack the draft's failure to propose full autonomy for their region and representatives of some ethnic minorities claim discrimination against non-Tadjiks in the country.

September 7: The Supreme Council postpones the presidential elections and the simultaneous constitutional referendum, originally scheduled for 25 September, until 6 November.

September 16: The leader of the banned pro-Western opposition Democratic Party, Shodmon Yusuf, announces its participation in the elections and referendum. The Islamic opposition will not take part and calls for "truly free elections".

November 6: President Rakhmanov wins a convincing victory in the presidential elections although there are boycotts by opposition groups following allegations of vote-rigging. Final results show that Rakhmanov obtains 58.32% of the vote, with 35% for his rival, Abdullojanov. (Turnout: 90%) The new constitution is adopted by a majority of votes.

November 15: Abdumalik Abdullojanov's supporters announce the formation of the Party of Popular Unity and Justice with Abdullojanov as its head.

December 2: President Rakhmanov orders a wide-ranging Cabinet reshuffle in early December and Jamshed Karimov is appointed as Prime Minister.

December 4: The ruling People's Party renounces its commitment to a one-party state.

1995

February 26: Parliamentary elections, for 181 seats, are held. Turnout 84%. The Democratic and Islamic opposition party's boycott the elections and 19 seats remain vacant.

March 6: The banned Islamic opposition party, the Islamic Renaissance Party, extends unilaterally the ceasefire agreed in September 1994.

March 12: Run-off elections for the remaining 19 parliamentary seats still vacant after the February elections. After this election 2 seats remain unfilled. About 60 seats of the new Parliament are occupied by the Communists.

May 10: The Tadjik rouble replaces the Russian rouble.

June 5: Dismissal of the chairman of the DP results in split of the party. The DP has been banned since its establishment in 1992, because of its involvement with the Islamic Renaissance Party in a guerilla war against the communist-led government.

August 14: Major-General Saidamin Gafurov is appointed as Interior Minister.

1996

January: Pro-Islamic rebel forces demand the immediate resignation of the government.

February 8: President Rakhmanov names Yahya Azimov as the new Prime Minister.

Constitution of Tadjikistan[1]

Adopted by the Supreme Council, 20 July 1994

---

1. The Constitution of the Republic of Tadjikistan is not included in this volume as it is presently not available in English.

Turkmenistan

Chronology

1990

January 19: The new Supreme Soviet is constituted. The first secretary of the Turkmen Communist Party (CP), Saparmurad Niyazov, is elected Chairman of the Supreme Soviet and becomes *ex officio* President of Turkmenistan.

August 22: Turkmenistan joins the list of republics declaring sovereignty and the precedence of their constitutions and laws over those of the Soviet Union. The Turkmen declaration is notable for pronouncing the republic a nuclear and chemical weapons-free zone.

October 27: The unopposed Chairman of the Supreme Soviet, Saparmurad Niyazov (CP) gains 98.3% of the votes in the first direct election for the new post of President.

1991

March 17: Turkmenistan holds the all-union referendum on the preservation of the Soviet Union. 97.9% of the population vote for the preservation of the Soviet Union and 1.7% vote against. The turnout is 97.7%.

April 23: President Mikhail Gorbachev signs, with nine of fifteen union republics including Turkmenistan, a pact aimed at achieving stable relations between the central and republican governments. It set out a timetable for major political changes, starting with the signing of the new Union Treaty. No longer than six months after signature of the Treaty a new Union constitution would be promulgated, followed by elections to the Congress of People's Deputies.

August 19: Attempted *coup d'état* in Moscow.

October 26: In a referendum, 94.6% of the population vote for the independence of Turkmenistan and 93.5% say that they support the policies of the President and the Supreme Soviet.

October 27: The Supreme Soviet declares the country independent.

December 8: Belarus, the Russian Federative Republic and Ukraine sign the Minsk agreement, establishing a Commonwealth of Independent States (CIS).

December 12: Turkmenistan signs the Alma Ata Agreement, thus joining the CIS.

December 21: The CIS formally replaces the Soviet Union, grouping eleven republics with the exception of Georgia. The Russian Federative Republic takes over many of the former Union functions, including its seat in the UN Security Council.

1992

May 18: The Supreme Soviet adopts unanimously the new constitution which increases the power of the President, making him both head of state and head of government, and abolishes the post of vice-president. The President is empowered to issue laws, except those altering the Constitution or the criminal code and to appoint judges and the heads of local administrations, which will enjoy less power than the former local Soviets. The new parliament, the Majlis, consists of 50 deputies elected by the district constituencies for a five-year term. The supreme representative body, the People's Council, consists of 50 separately elected members, the Majlis deputies, the chairs of the Supreme Court and the Supreme Economic Court, members of the government, the Procurator-General and the heads of local administration. The People's Council is headed by the President.

May 19: The Supreme Soviet becomes the Majlis.

June 21: With 99.5% of the votes, Saparmurad Niyazov is elected as President.

November 24-December 7: Elections to the 50-member People's Council are held. Turnout 99.5%.

1993

November 1: Turkmenistan introduces a new currency, the *manat,* which replaces the Turkmen rouble.

December 23: In order to ease ethnic tensions, President Niyazov and the Russian President Boris Yeltsin sign an agreement allowing Turkmenistan's Russians to hold jointly Turkmen and Russian citizenship.

1994

January 15: In a national referendum President Saparmurad Niyazov gains 99.9% of the votes in favour of an extension of his presidential term for another five years, exempting him from presidential elections due in 1997.

March 10: Abad Sebedovna Irzayeva is appointed Deputy Prime Minister.

September 9: Expressing concern at weakening sovereignty, the Prime Minister does not sign an agreement to strengthen economic links between the CIS member states.

November 8: President Niyazov dismisses Deputy Prime Minister Joraguly Babagulyyev. A decree names Matkarim Rajapov as his successor.

December 8: Matkarim Rajapov replaces the former Deputy Prime Minister.

December 11: Elections to the new 50-member Majlis are held (turnout: 99.8%). All candidates are returned unopposed, most of them belong to the one permitted political party, the ruling Turkmen Democratic Party (the former Communist Party). No opposition party is registered to contest the elections.

December 26: The Majlis holds its inaugural session and re-elects Sakhat Muradov as Chairman.

1995

February 19: New official holiday: State Flag Day. (coinciding with the President's birthday)

1996

April 29: President Saparmurad Niyazov names Ata Nobadov as Minister of Agriculture.

Constitution of Turkmenistan[1]

Adopted by the Supreme Soviet and promulgated by the President, 18 May 1992

We, the people of Turkmenistan,
basing ourselves on our inalienable right of self-determination,
proceeding from our responsibility for the present and the future of our Fatherland,
expressing our loyalty to the heritage of our forefathers to live in unity, peace, and harmony,
having as our purpose to protect the national values and interests and to strengthen the sovereignty of the Turkmen people,
guaranteeing the rights and liberties of each citizen and striving to ensure civil peace and national harmony and to establish the principles of the people's power and of a state based on law,
adopt the present Constitution – the Fundamental Law of Turkmenistan.

Section 1 – The fundamentals of the constitutional system

Article 1
Turkmenistan shall be a democratic, law-based, and secular state in which state rule shall be implemented in the form of a presidential republic.
Turkmenistan shall have ultimate and full power on its territory, and shall independently conduct its domestic and foreign policy. The state sovereignty and territory of Turkmenistan shall be single and indivisible.
The state shall defend the independence and territorial integrity of Turkmenistan and the constitutional system, and shall ensure legality and law and order.

Article 2
The people shall be the bearers of sovereignty and the sole source of power in Turkmenistan. The people of Turkmenistan shall exercise their power directly or through representative bodies.
No part of the people nor any organisation, structure, or individual person shall have the right to appropriate power in the state.

---

1. European Commission for Democracy through Law

Article 3

The human being shall be the highest value of society and the state in Turkmenistan.

The state shall be responsible to the citizen and shall ensure the creation of conditions for the free development of personality, and shall protect the life, honour, dignity and freedom, personal inviolability, and the natural and inalienable rights of the citizen.

The citizen shall be responsible to the state for the fulfilment of duties placed upon him by the Constitution and laws.

Article 4

The state shall be based on the principle of the separation of powers – the legislative, the executive, and the judiciary – which shall exercise their authority independently and interactively, checking and balancing one another.

Article 5

The state and all of its bodies and officials shall be linked together by law and the constitutional system.

The Constitution of Turkmenistan shall be the supreme Law of the state; the norms and provisions stipulated therein shall have direct effect. Laws and other legal acts that contradict the Constitution shall not have legal force.

Legal acts of state bodies shall be published for general dissemination or shall be made public in another manner, with the exception of those containing state or other secrets protected by law. Legal acts affecting the rights and freedoms of citizens that are not generally disseminated shall be invalid from the moment of their adoption.

Article 6

Turkmenistan shall recognise the priority of the generally accepted standards of international law, shall be an equal subject of the world community, and shall adhere in its foreign policy to the principles of peaceful coexistence, rejection of the use of force, and non-interference in the internal affairs of other states.

Article 7

Turkmenistan shall have its own citizenship. Citizenship shall be acquired, retained, and forfeited in accordance with the law.

No one may be deprived of his citizenship or the right to change his citizenship. A citizen of Turkmenistan may not be turned over to another state or deported from Turkmenistan or have his right to return to his motherland restricted.

Citizens of Turkmenistan shall be guaranteed the protection and patronage of the state, both in the territory of Turkmenistan and beyond its borders.

Article 8

Foreign citizens and stateless persons shall enjoy the rights and freedoms of citizens of Turkmenistan unless otherwise prescribed by law.

Turkmenistan shall grant the right of asylum to foreign citizens persecuted in their countries for their political, national, or religious convictions.

Article 9
Property shall be inviolable. Turkmenistan shall confirm the right of private ownership of means of production, land, and other material and intellectual assets. These may likewise belong to associations of citizens and the state. Objects that are the exclusive property of the state shall be established by law. The state shall guarantee equal protection and equal conditions for the development of all types and forms of property.
The confiscation of property shall not be permitted, with the exception of property acquired through means prohibited by law.
The forced alienation of property with compensation shall be permitted only in cases prescribed by law.

Article 10
The state shall be responsible for preserving the national historical and cultural legacy and the natural environment and for ensuring equality between social and nationality groups, and shall encourage scientific and artistic creativity and the dissemination of the results thereof and shall promote the development of international relations in the realm of science, culture, upbringing, education, sport, and tourism.

Article 11
The state shall guarantee the freedom of religions and confessions and their equality before the law. Religious organisations shall be separate from the state and may not fulfil state functions. The state educational system shall be separate from religious organisations and shall be of a secular nature.
Everyone shall have the right independently to define his attitude towards religions, to profess any religion or not to profess any either individually or jointly with others, to profess and disseminate beliefs associated with his attitude to religion, and to participate in the practice of religious cults, rituals, and rites.

Article 12
In order to protect its state sovereignty, Turkmenistan shall have its own armed forces.

Article 13
The state language of Turkmenistan shall be the Turkmen language.
All citizens of Turkmenistan shall be guaranteed the right to use their native language.

Article 14
The symbols of Turkmenistan as a sovereign state shall be its state flag, coat of arms, and anthem.
The flag, coat of arms, and anthem shall be established and protected by law.

Article 15
The capital of Turkmenistan shall be the city of Ashkhabad.

411

Section 2 – Fundamental human and civil rights, freedoms, and duties

Article 16

Human rights shall be inviolable and inalienable.

No-one shall have the right to deprive a person of any rights or freedoms whatsoever or to restrict his rights, except in accordance with the Constitution and the law.

The listing of specific human rights and freedoms in the Constitution and the laws may not be used for the negation or derogation of other rights and freedoms.

Article 17

Turkmenistan shall guarantee the equality of the rights and freedoms of citizens, as well as the equality of citizens before the law irrespective of nationality, origin, property status or official position, place of residence, language, attitude towards religion, political beliefs, or party membership.

Article 18

Men and women shall have equal civil rights in Turkmenistan. The violation of equal rights based on gender shall entail liability under the law.

Article 19

The exercise of rights and freedoms must not violate the rights and freedoms of other persons or the requirements of morality or social order or cause damage to national security.

Article 20

Every person shall have the right to life. No-one may be deprived of life. Capital punishment can be indicated only by the verdict of a court in the form of an exceptional means of punishment for the most serious crime.

Article 21

A citizen may not have his rights restricted or be denied the rights belonging to him, or condemned or subjected to punishment, other than in clear accordance with the law and upon the decision of a court.

No-one may be subjected to torture, cruel or inhuman treatment or punishment, or treatment or punishment that is degrading to his dignity, nor may he be subjected to medical or other experiments without his permission. A citizen may be arrested only upon the decision of a court or the sanction of a procurator, given the existence of grounds clearly indicated by law. In cases that brook no delay and that are clearly indicated by law, the state bodies empowered to do so shall have the right to detain citizens temporarily.

Article 22

Every citizen shall have the right to the support of the state in receiving well-appointed living space and in individual housing construction. Housing shall be inviolable. No-one shall have the right to enter into a residence or otherwise violate the sanctity of the home against the will of the persons residing therein or without legal grounds. The protection of the residence from unlawful encroachment shall be a civil right.

No-one may be deprived of housing except on grounds established by law.

Article 23

Every citizen shall have the right to protection from arbitrary interference in his personal life, as well as from infringement of the secrecy of his correspondence and telephone and other communications and of his honour and reputation.

Article 24

Everyone shall have the right to free movement and to choose his place of residence within Turkmenistan.

Restrictions on movement through specific territories, or those relative to specific persons, may be established only on the basis of law.

Article 25

Women and men, upon attaining the age of marriage, shall have the right to marry and create a family upon mutual consent. Spouses shall have equal rights in family relations.

Parents or legal guardians shall have the right and obligation to raise their children, care for their health and development and education, prepare them for labour, and to instil culture and respect for laws and historical and national traditions in them. Adult children shall be obliged to care for their parents and to render them assistance.

Article 26

Citizens of Turkmenistan shall have the right to freedom of thought and to the free expression thereof, and also to obtain information, if it is not a government, service, or commercial secret.

Article 27

The freedom of assembly, meetings, and demonstrations in the manner established by legislation shall be guaranteed.

Article 28

Citizens shall have the right to create political parties and other public associations operating within the framework of the Constitution and the laws.

The creation and activity of political parties and public organisations that have the goal of forcible change in the constitutional structure, allow violence in their activity, act against the constitutional rights and freedoms of citizens, propagandise war or racial, national, social, or religious hostility, or that encroach on the health and morality of the people, and also the creation of militarised associations and political parties on a national or religious basis shall be forbidden.

Article 29

Each citizen shall have the right to participate in managing the affairs of society and the state, both directly and through his or her freely elected representatives.

Article 30

Citizens shall have the right to elect and be elected to bodies of state government.

Only citizens of Turkmenistan in accordance with their capabilities and professional training shall have equal right of access to the civil service.

Article 31

All citizens shall have the right to work, to select at their own discretion a profession, type of employment, and place of work, and to healthy and safe working conditions. Forced labour shall be forbidden, except in cases established by law.

Persons who work for hire shall have the right to payment corresponding to the amount and quality of their work. This compensation shall not be less than the established minimum wage.

Article 32

Workers shall have the right to rest and leisure. For persons who work for hire, this right shall be reflected in the establishment of work weeks of limited duration, provision of paid annual vacation, and weekly days off.

The state shall create conditions that are conductive to relaxation at the place of residence and rational use of free time.

Article 33

Citizens shall have the right to health protection, including free use of a network of state health care institutions. Paid medical services shall be permitted on the basis and in the manner established by law.

Article 34

Citizens shall have the right to social security in their old age, in the case of illness, disability, loss of work capacity, loss of the breadwinner, and unemployment.

Families with many children, children who lost their parents, war participants, and other persons who have lost their health while defending state or public interests shall be provided additional support and privileges from public resources.

The procedures and conditions for implementing this right shall be governed by law.

Article 35

Each citizen shall have the right to education. General secondary education is obligatory, and everyone shall have the right to obtain this free at state educational institutions.

The state shall facilitate access for everyone in accordance with his/her abilities to professional, special secondary, and higher education.

Organisations and citizens shall have the right to create paid educational institutions on the basis and in the manner established by law.

Article 36

Citizens of Turkmenistan shall have the right to freedom of artistic, scientific, and technical creativity. Authors' rights and the legal interests of citizens in the area of scientific and technical creativity and artistic, literary, and cultural activity shall be protected by law.

The state shall facilitate development of national science, art, popular creativity, sport, and tourism.

Article 37

Exercise of rights and freedoms shall be inseparable from the performance by a citizen and a person of his or her obligations to the society and the state. Each person who lives or is located in the territory of Turkmenistan shall be obliged to adhere to its constitution and laws, and to respect national traditions.

Article 38

The defence of Turkmenistan shall be the sacred duty of every person. For male citizens of Turkmenistan there shall be established universal compulsory military service.

Article 39

Citizens of Turkmenistan shall be obliged to pay state taxes and other payments in the manner and amounts established by law.

Article 40

Citizens shall be guaranteed judicial defence of their honour and dignity, personal and political rights and freedoms of individuals and citizens, stipulated by the Constitution and by laws.

Actions of state bodies, public organisations, and officials that are performed in violation of the law, exceeding their authority, or infringing on the rights of and freedom of citizens may be appealed against to a court.

Article 41

Citizens shall have the right to compensation under judicial procedure for material and moral losses incurred as a result of the illegal acts of state bodies, other organisations, their employees, and also private parties.

Article 42

No-one shall be forced to give evidence against himself and close relatives. Evidence shall be recognised as invalid if it is obtained under the influence of physical or psychological pressure, and also by other illegal methods.

Article 43

A law that worsens the situation of a citizen shall not be retroactive. No-one shall be liable for an act that at the moment of its occurrence was not recognised as a violation of the law.

Article 44

Exercise of the rights and freedoms of citizens that are stipulated by this Constitution shall be suspended only under conditions of extraordinary or military situations in the manner and within the limits established by the Constitution and the law.

Section 3 – The system of state governmental bodies

Chapter 1 – General provisions

Article 45
The highest representatives body of popular power shall be the Khalk Maslakhaty (Peoples' Council) of Turkmenistan.

Article 46
Supreme executive and administrative power in Turkmenistan shall be exercised by the President, the Medzhlis, the Supreme Court, the Higher Economic Court, and the Cabinet of Ministers of Turkmenistan.

Article 47
Turkmenistan shall consist of administrative territorial elements: velayats, etraps, and shakers equivalent to entraps in which government administrative bodies shall be formed, and also shakers, villages, and obs, where local self-government bodies shall be established.

Chapter 2 – The Khalk Maslakhaty of Turkmenistan

Article 48
The Khalk Maslakhaty shall include:
the President;
the deputies of the Medzhlis;
khalk vekilleri, who are elected by the people, one from each entrap;
the Chairman of the Supreme Court, the Chairman of the Higher Economic Court, the Procurator General, members of the Cabinet of Ministers, heads of administration of velayats, archyns (mayors of municipal councils) of shakers and also villages that are the administrative centres of entraps.

Article 49
The term of office for the khalk vekilleri shall be five years. They shall perform their duties without compensation.

Article 50
The Khalk Maslakhaty shall consider and render decisions on the following matters:
    1.   on the expedience of making amendments and additions to the Constitution or adopting a new Constitution;
    2.   conducting national referendums;
    3.   development of recommendations on the basic aims of the economic, social, and political development of the country;
    4.   changes in state borders and administrative territorial divisions;
    5.   ratification and denunciation of treaties on inter-state unions and other formations;

6.   declaration of a state of war and peace;
7.   on other matters allocated to their management by the Constitution and laws.

Article 51

Decisions of the Khalk Maslakhaty shall be implemented by the President, the Medzhlis, and other state bodies in accordance with their authority as established by the Constitution and laws.

Article 52

The Khalk Maslakhaty shall be called as necessary, but not less frequently than once a year on the initiative of the President, the Medzhlis, or one-third of the established number of members of the Khalk Maslakhaty.

The President, the Medzhlis, or its Presidium, or not less than one-fourth of the established number of members of the Khalk Maslakhaty shall have the right to submit proposals for the consideration of the Khalk Maslakhaty.

Article 53

The work of the Khalk Maslakhaty shall be directed by the President or any member of the Khalk Maslakhaty elected by it.

The procedure for calling the Khalk Maslakhaty and for its work shall be determined by the Standing Rules approved by it.

Chapter 3 – The President of Turkmenistan

Article 54

The President of Turkmenistan shall be the head of state and the executor of power, the highest official in Turkmenistan, and shall act as a guarantor of national independence, territorial integrity, and adherence to the Constitution and international agreements.

Article 55

The President shall be a citizen of Turkmenistan, not younger than 40 years old, residing in Turkmenistan. The same person may not be President more than two terms in succession.

Article 56

The President shall be elected directly by the people of Turkmenistan for a five-year term and shall take office immediately after taking his oath at a session of the Khalk Maslakhaty.

The procedure for electing a President and his assumption of office shall be established by law.

Article 57 – The President of Turkmenistan shall:

1.   carry out the Constitution and the laws and ensure precise compliance with them;
2.   direct the implementation of foreign policy, represent Turkmenistan in relations with other states, appoint and recall ambassadors and other

diplomatic representatives of Turkmenistan in foreign states, and at interstate and international organisations, and accept letters of credence and letters of recall of diplomatic representatives of foreign states;

3. be the Commander-in-Chief of the Armed Forces, give orders concerning general or partial mobilisation and the utilisation of the Armed Forces with subsequent confirmation of these actions by the Khalk Maslakhaty, appoints the high command of the Armed Forces;

4. submit to the Khalk Maslakhaty annual reports on the state of the country and inform it about the most important issues of domestic and foreign policy;

5. submit the state budget and a report on its execution to the Medzhlis for its consideration and approval;

6. sign laws and have the right to return the law with his objections to the Medzhlis within two weeks for repeated discussion and voting. If the Medzhlis confirms the decision it previously took by a two-thirds majority, the President shall sign the law. The President shall not have the right of a delaying veto with regard to laws concerning changes and additions to the Constitution;

7. arrange for referendums on the decision of the Khalk Maslakhaty and have the right to call an extraordinary session of the Medzhlis;

8. decide questions of conferring citizenship in Turkmenistan and granting asylum;

9. confer decorations and other awards of Turkmenistan, and confer honorary, military and other special titles;

10. with the prior consent of the Medzhlis appoint and relieve from office the Chairman of the Supreme Court, the Chairman of the Higher Economic Court, and the General Procurator;

11. grant clemency and amnesty;

12. decide other matters assigned to his responsibility by the Constitutions and the laws.

Article 58
The President shall issue edicts, decrees and instructions that are binding in the entire territory of Turkmenistan.

Article 59
The President cannot be a deputy of the Medzhlis or receive monetary compensation, with the exception of honoraria for works of science, literature, and art.

Article 60
The President shall have the right of immunity.
The President may be relieved from office in the event that it is impossible for him to perform his duties as a result of illness. The Khalk Maslakhaty, on the basis of the conclusions of an independent medical commission established by it, shall make a decision on the early removal of the President from office by not less than a two-thirds majority vote of the established numbers of members of the Khalk Maslakhaty.

In the event of a violation by the President of the Constitution and laws, the Khalk Maslakhaty can express its lack of confidence in the President and submit the question of his removal to a popular vote. The question of no confidence in the President may be considered upon the request of not less than one-third of the established number of members of the Khalk Maslakhaty. A decision of no confidence in the President shall be adopted by not less than two-thirds of the established number of members of the Khalk Maslakhaty.

Article 61
The President shall not have the right to transfer performance of his powers to other bodies or officials with the exception of the powers stipulated in clauses 2, 9 and 11 of Article 57 of the Constitution, which may be transferred to the Chairman of the Medzhlis.
If the President for one reason or another cannot perform his duties, then his powers shall be transferred to the Chairman of the Medzhlis until the election of a new President. In this case the presidential election must be carried out no later than two months from the day his powers are transferred to the Chairman of the Medzhlis. The person performing the duties of the President cannot be voted for as a candidate for President.

Chapter 4 – The Medzhlis of Turkmenistan

Article 62
The Medzhlis (Parliament) shall be the legislative organ of Turkmenistan.

Article 63
The Medzhlis shall consist of 50 deputies elected from territorial districts with approximately equal numbers of voters for a term of five years.

Article 64
The Medzhlis may be dissolved prematurely:
by decision of a referendum;
by decree of the Medzhlis adopted by a majority of not less than two-thirds of the established number of deputies (self-dissolution);
by the President in the event that the executive bodies of the Medzhlis are not formed within a period of six months, or in the event no confidence in the Cabinet of Ministers is expressed twice in a period of eighteen months.

Article 65
The Medzhlis shall independently establish the correctness of election and powers of deputies, elect a Chairman and his deputy from among the deputies, and form committees and commissions.

Article 66
The Medzhlis can transfer the right to issue laws on specific matters to the President with obligatory subsequent confirmation of them by the Medzhlis. The Medzhlis cannot transfer legislative functions with regard to matters of:
1. the adoption and amendment of the Constitution;

2. criminal and administrative legislation;
3. legal procedure.

Article 67
The following shall be delegated to the Medzhlis:
1. adoption and amendment of the Constitution and laws and their interpretation;
2. scheduling elections of the President, the Medzhlis and members of the Khalk Maslakhaty;
3. forming the Central Commission on Elections and conducting refer-endums;
4. approving the programme of activity of the Cabinet of Ministers and expressing lack of confidence in it;
5. approving or rejecting candidates for the positions of Chairman of the Supreme Court, the Chairman of the Higher Economic Court, the General Procurator, and also recommendations concerning their removal;
6. adopting the budget of Turkmenistan and the report on its execution;
7. instituting state awards, conferring state awards on the President, conferring on him honorary titles, military titles, and distinctions;
8. determining the conformity of normative documents of government bodies with the Constitution and laws;
9. other matters allocated to the responsibility of the Medzhlis by the Constitution and laws.

Article 68
The right of legislative initiative in the Medzhlis shall belong to the President, deputies of the Medzhlis, and the Cabinet of Ministers.

Article 69
Deputies of the Medzhlis shall have the right to submit oral and written questions to the Cabinet of Ministers, ministers, and directors of other state bodies.

Article 70
A deputy can be relieved of his authority as a delegate only by the Medzhlis. A decision on this matter shall be made by a majority vote of not less than two-thirds of the established number of deputies in the Medzhlis.
A deputy cannot be brought to criminal liability, arrested, or be deprived of his freedom in any other way without the approval of the Medzhlis, or in the period between sessions, of the Presidium of the Medzhlis.

Article 71
The Medzhlis is a permanent body. Deputies cannot simultaneously occupy positions as members of the Cabinet of Ministers, heads of administration of velayats, shakers, and entraps, archyns, judges, procurators.

Article 72

The Chairman of the Medzhlis shall be elected by secret vote. He shall be accountable to the Medzhlis and can be removed by decision of the Medzhlis adopted by a majority of not less than two-thirds of the established number of deputies.

The Deputy Chairman of the Medzhlis shall be elected by open vote, and shall perform specific functions of the Chairman on his authorisation, replace the Chairman in the case of his absence or incapacity to exercise his authority.

Article 73

The Presidium of the Medzhlis shall organise the work of the Medzhlis and consider matters assigned to it by the Constitution and laws.

The Presidium shall consist of: the Chairman of the Medzhlis, his deputy, and representatives of the committees and commissions.

Article 74

The procedure for activity of the Medzhlis, its bodies and deputies, their functions and powers that are not prescribed by the Constitution shall be established by law.

Chapter 5 – The Cabinet of Ministers

Article 75

The Cabinet of Ministers shall be the executive and administrative organ. The Cabinet of Ministers shall be headed by the President.

Article 76

The Cabinet of Ministers shall include: the deputy chairmen of the Cabinet of Ministers and ministers.

The Cabinet of Ministers shall be formed by the President within a month after he takes office and shall lay down its powers before the newly elected President.

Article 77

Sessions of the Cabinet of Ministers shall be conducted by the President or upon his authorisation by one of the deputy chairmen of the Cabinet of Ministers.

The Cabinet of Ministers within the limits of its responsibility shall issue binding decrees and instructions.

Article 78

The Cabinet of Ministers shall:

1. organise the implementation of laws, the decrees of the President, and the decisions of the Khalk Maslakhaty;

2. carry out measures to ensure and defend the rights and freedoms of citizens, protect property, and preserve public order and national security;

3. develop and submit to the Khalk Maslakhaty proposals on the basic aims of domestic and foreign policy activity of the state and programmes for the economic and social development of the country;

4.   carry out state management of economic and social development and ensure the rational use and protection of natural resources;

5.   take measures to strengthen the monetary and credit system;

6.   form committees, main administrations and other departments attached to the Cabinet of Ministers as needed;

7.   implement foreign economic policy and ensure the development of cultural ties with foreign states;

8.   direct the activity of government institutions, state enterprises and organisations; have the right to rescind the acts of ministries and agencies;

9.   perform other duties assigned to it by laws and other normative documents.

Article 79
The powers of the Cabinet of Ministers, the manner in which it operates, and its relations with other state bodies shall be determined by law.

Chapter 6 – Local executive power

Article 80
Local executive power shall be exercised by: the velayat khyakimi in the velayats, the shakher khyakimi in the shakers, and the entrap khyakimi archyns in the entraps.

Article 81
Khyakimi shall be local representatives of the head of state and shall be appointed and relieved from duty by the President and his subordinates.

Article 82
Khyakimi shall direct the activity of local administrative bodies, ensure implementation of the Constitution, laws, and acts of the President and the Cabinet of Ministers. Within the limits of their competence the khyakimi adopt decrees that are mandatory in the territory under their administration.

Article 83
The archyns shall ensure the implementation of decisions of the Gengeshi and the decrees of governmental authorities, manage municipal facilities, execute the local budget, and also deal with other matters of local significance.

Article 84
The scope of the functions and powers of the khyakimi and archyns and the procedures for their activity and interaction with other government authorities shall be established by law.

Section 4 – Local self-government

Article 85
The system of local self-government shall be made up by the Gengeshi and bodies of territorial public self-government.

The Gengeshi shall be representative bodies of popular power in the territory of shakers, villages and obs. They shall be elected directly by the citizens for a term of five years.

Article 86
The following are the responsibility of the Gengeshi:
1. determining the basic lines of economic, social, and cultural development of their authorities;
2. approving the local budget and reporting on its execution;
3. instituting local taxes and fees and the procedure for collecting them;
4. specifying measures for the rational utilisation of natural resources and protection of the environment;
5. other matters assigned to the Gengeshi by legislation.

Within the limits of their responsibility the Gengeshi shall make decisions that are mandatory in their territory.

Article 87
The Gengeshi shall elect the Archyn, who shall direct the work of the Gengeshi and be accountable to it, from among their members.

Article 88
Members of the Gengeshi shall perform their duties without compensation. The procedures for the activity of the Gengeshi and other bodies of public self-government shall be prescribed by law.

Section 5 – The election system, referendum

Article 89
Elections of the President, deputies of the Medzhlis, khalk vekilleri, and other persons elected by the people shall be universal and equal: citizens of Turkmenistan who have attained the age of 18 years shall have the right to vote, each voter having one vote.
Mentally ill citizens who have been adjudged incompetent by a court shall not participate in elections, nor shall persons imprisoned by virtue of a court sentence. Persons in preventive detention in accordance with procedure established by criminal-procedural legislation shall not take part in voting.
Any direct or indirect limitation of the voting rights of citizens in other cases shall not be permitted and shall be punishable by law.

Article 90
Citizens of Turkmenistan who have reached the age of 25 by the date of the elections may be elected as deputies of the Medzhlis, and khalk vekilleri.
The age qualification for members of the Gengeshi, archyns and other persons elected to state positions shall be prescribed by law.

Article 91
Elections shall be direct; deputies and other persons shall be elected by citizens directly.

Article 92
Voting at elections shall be secret, polling of voters during the course of voting is not permitted.

Article 93
The right to nominate candidates shall be held by the political parties, public organisations, and groups of citizens in accordance with the election law.

Article 94
To decide the most important matters of state and public life national and local referendums may be conducted.
The question of rescinding an act adopted by referendum shall be resolved only through a national referendum.

Article 95
The right to schedule a national referendum shall belong to the Khalk Maslakhaty upon the proposal of not less than one-fourth of its members, or by proposal of not less than 250 000 citizens having the right to vote.

Article 96
The right to schedule local referendums shall belong to the Gengeshi on their own initiative or by proposal of not less than one-fourth of the voters living in the territory concerned.

Article 97
Referendums shall be conducted by means of universal, equal, direct and secret balloting.
Citizens of Turkmenistan having the right to vote shall participate in referendums.

Article 98
The procedure for conducting elections and national and local referendums shall be prescribed by law. Elections and referendums shall not be conducted during a state of emergency.

Section 6 – Judicial authority

Article 99
Judicial authority in Turkmenistan shall belong only to the courts.
Judicial authority shall be intended to defend the rights and freedom of citizens and, maintenance by law of state and public interests.

Article 100
Judicial authority shall be exercised by the Supreme Court, the Higher Economic Court, military, and other courts stipulated by law, in the form of civil, economic, administrative and criminal judicial procedure.
The creation of extraordinary courts and other structures endowed with the powers of a court shall not be permitted.

Article 101
Judges shall be independent and subordinate only to the law and shall be guided by their inner convictions. Interference in the activity of judges from any side whatsoever shall not be permitted and shall be punishable by law. The inviolability of judges shall be guaranteed by law.

Article 102
Judges of all courts shall be appointed by the President for a term of five years. The procedure for appointment and removal of judges shall be determined by law. Until the expiration of the established term judges can be removed from their position without their consent only by court order and for grounds indicated in the law.

Article 103
Judges cannot occupy any other paid position, except for teaching and scientific research; for the period of their tenure judges shall not participate in political parties or public organisations that pursue political objectives.

Article 104
Cases in courts shall be considered collegially and, in cases stipulated by law, by individual judges.

Article 105
The proceedings in all courts shall be open. Closed hearings shall be permitted only in cases stipulated by law, with adherence to all rules of judicial procedure.

Article 106
Judicial procedure shall be conducted in the state language. Persons participating in the case who do not speak the language of the judicial procedure shall be ensured the right to acquaint themselves with the materials of the case and to participate in judicial action, and also the right to testify in court in their native language.

Article 107
Justice shall be administered on the basis of contention and the equality of the parties.
The parties shall have the right to appeal against decisions, sentences, and other judicial decrees of all courts of Turkmenistan.

Article 108
The right to professional juridical assistance shall be recognised at any stage of the judicial process.
Juridical assistance to citizens and organisations shall be rendered by lawyers and other persons and organisations.

Article 109
The competence, manner of formation, and activity of courts shall be determined by law.

Section 7 – The Procurator's Office

Article 110

Oversight of exact and uniform compliance in the territory of Turkmenistan with laws and acts of the President by bodies of state government, administration of the armed forces, and local self- government, by participants in economic and commercial activity, by organisations, institutions, public associations, officials, and citizens shall be assigned to the General Procurator of Turkmenistan and his subordinate procurators.

The Procurator shall participate in consideration of cases in courts on the basis and in the manner established by law.

Article 111

The Procurator's Office shall exercise oversight over the legality of operational investigative activity and the investigation of criminal cases and materials.

Article 112

The unified and centralised system of the Procuracy shall be headed by the Procurator General, who shall be appointed by the President for five years.

Deputies of the Procurator General and procurators of velayats shall be appointed by the President. The procurators of shakers and entraps shall be appointed by the Procurator General.

Article 113

The Procurator General and his subordinate procurators shall be governed only by the law in carrying out their powers. In his activity the Procurator General is accountable to the President.

For the period of their appointment, procurators shall not participate in political parties and other public associations that pursue political objectives.

Section 8 – Final provisions

Article 114

The laws and other acts of state organs of Turkmenistan shall be published on the basis of and in accordance with the Constitution.

In the case of a discrepancy between the Constitution and a law the Constitution is valid.

Article 115

The provisions of the Constitution on the republic's form of government cannot be changed.

Article 116

The law on amending the Constitution shall be considered adopted if not less than two-thirds of the established number of deputies of the Medzhlis vote for it.

Adopted by the Supreme Soviet and promulgated by the President on 18 May 1992 in the city of Ashkhabad.

President of Turkmenistan   S. Niyazov

Ukraine

Chronology

1989

September 8-10: The People's Movement of Ukraine, which is campaigning for political liberation and Ukrainian autonomy, holds its constituent congress.

1990

June 4: The Supreme Soviet elects Vladimir Ivashenko as its Chairman, i.e. *de facto* President of Ukraine.

July 16: The Supreme Soviet adopts, by 355 votes to 4, with 1 abstention, a declaration proclaiming "supremacy, independence and indivisibility of the republic's power on its territory".

July 23: The Supreme Soviet elects Leonid Kravchuk as its Chairman, after accepting Vladimir Ivashenko's resignation.

November 14: The Supreme Soviet elects Vitold Fokin as Prime Minister, after the resignation of Vitalii Masol in October.

1991

January 20: In a referendum 93.26% of the residents of Crimea vote in favour of restoring Crimea as an autonomous republic, independent of Ukraine. Turnout 81%.

February 12: The Supreme Soviet votes to restore Crimea as an Autonomous Soviet Socialist republic (ASSR) within Ukraine.

March 17: In an all-union referendum 70.2% vote in favour of the preservation of the USSR. Turnout 83.5%.

April 23: President Mikhail Gorbachev signs, with nine of the fifteen union republics including Ukraine, a pact aimed at achieving stable relations between the central government and the governments of the republics. It sets out a timetable for major political changes, starting with the signing of the new Union Treaty. No longer than six months after signature of the Treaty a new Union constitution would be promulgated, followed by elections to the Congress of People's Deputies.

June 30: The Supreme Soviet approves the creation of the post of a directly elected President.

August 19: Attempted *coup d'état* in Moscow.

August 24: The Supreme Council declares Ukraine independent.

August 31: The Chairman of the Supreme Council bans the activity of the Ukrainian Communist Party (UCP).

September 4: The Crimean Supreme Council declares independence, but as a part of Ukraine.

September 13: The Supreme Council passes a law on single Ukrainian citizenship.

December 1: A referendum is held on the independence of the republic, which results in a 90.32% endorsement with a turnout of 84%. Simultaneously in the presidential elections, Leonid Kravchuk gains 61.59% of the votes defeating the six other candidates.

December 8: Ukraine, the Russian Federative Republic and Belarus sign the Minsk Agreement, establishing a Commonwealth of Independent States (CIS).

December 10: The Supreme Council ratifies the CIS declaration.

December 21: The CIS formally replaces the Soviet Union, grouping eleven republics with the exception of Georgia. The Russian Federative Republic takes over many of the former Union functions, including its seat in the UN Security Council.

1992

January 10: The government issues coupons to be used temporary as legal tender, instead of the Russian rouble.

February 20: The Parliament approves a bill to alter the administrative system and the President holds talks with the opposition on the possibility of forming a coalition government.

May 5: The Crimean Parliament declares Crimean independence.

May 6: The Crimean Parliament adopts a constitution citing Crimea as "within" Ukraine.

May 13: The Ukrainian Parliament votes, by 340 votes to 6, to annul the independence declaration and the Crimean constitution.

May 20: The Crimean Parliament repeals the independence declaration.

May 21: The Russian Federation Supreme Soviet votes to annul the 1954 decree ceding the Crimea from Russia to Ukraine.

May 25: The Ministry of Foreign Affairs states that the status of Crimea is an internal Ukrainian matter, which cannot be subjected to external interference.

June 2: The Parliament issues a statement rejecting the Russian Supreme Soviet annulment of the 1954 decree.

June 30: The Parliament passes, by 264 votes to 4, the amendments to the Ukrainian law on the status of Crimea as proposed by joint sittings of the Ukrainian and Crimean parliamentary Presidiums.

September 16: The Council of Europe grants Ukraine its Special Guest Status.

September 30: Prime Minister Vitold Fokin resigns on account of the socio-economic and political situation in the republic.

October 1: The Parliament passes a motion of no confidence in the government, on account of the country's economic situation, leading to the resignation of the government.

October 13: The Parliament elects, by 316 votes to 68, Leonid Kuchma as the new Prime Minister.

October 27: Kuchma presents a new government to the Parliament.

November 12: The coupon currency, *karbovanets,* officially replaces the rouble.

1993

March 6-7: 318 regional delegations and 8 deputies of the Parliament participate in a conference to found a new Communist Party.

May 20: Prime Minister Leonid Kuchma resigns on account of constant confrontation and opposition with the Parliament, making his job impossible.

May 21: The Parliament refuses to accept Kuchma's resignation.

July 9: The Russian Supreme Soviet passes a resolution declaring Russian sovereignty over Sebastopol. President Kravchuk describes the resolution as an interference in Ukraine's internal affairs.

July 10: President Yeltsin declares that he is ashamed of the Russian Supreme Soviet resolution.

July 20: The UN Security Council expresses concern at the Russian resolution.

September 21: The Parliament votes to accept the resignation of Prime Minister Kuchma and passes a motion of no confidence in the government.

September 27: President Kravchuk assumes direct control over the government.

October 30: A new constitution is adopted, specifying the Parliament as the highest legislative body and a government, in which the executive powers are vested, guided by a directly elected President.

November 18: The Parliament approves a new electoral law, providing for the election of 450 deputies by absolute majority; a second round will be held, in constituencies where no candidate gained the absolute majority in the first round, between the two candidates who received the most votes in the first round. Repeat elections take place only if the turnout is less than 50%.

1994

January 20: The Parliament approves constitutional amendments, allowing the President to overrule any act of the Crimean authorities which are in conflict with Ukrainian law.

January 31: Yuri Meshkov becomes President of the Republic of Crimea, winning 72.9% of the votes cast with a turnout of 75.1%.

March 27: Parliamentary elections result in the election of only 49 deputies, 401 seats remain vacant. Till now the Communist Party gains 86 seats and the rest is divided among left-wing parties and independents. Simultaneously referendums are held in largely Russian-populated regions on closer ties between Ukraine and Russia. Turnout 74.7%.

April 3 and 10: Second rounds of parliamentary elections are held. 289 members are elected and 112 constituencies require a third round of elections. Turnout 56.7%. Observers of the CSCE and the UN criticise the Central Electoral Commission.

April 14: Kuchma declares his candidature for the presidential elections, after being nominated by the Ukrainian Union of Industrialists and Nationalists (UUIN).

April 30: In spite of an earlier declaration, Kravchuk registers as a candidate for the presidential elections.

May 20: The Crimean Parliament approves the restoration of the Crimean constitution, first introduced in May 1992.

June 16: The Parliament approves, by 199 votes to 24, the appointment of Vitalii Masol as Prime Minister.

June 26: In the presidential elections, President Kravchuk gains 37.68% of the votes and former Prime Minister Kuchma 31.25%. The remaining five candidates gain a total of 31.07%. Turnout 70.37%.

July 10: A second round of presidential elections between Kravchuk and Kuchma results in a victory for Kuchma, gaining 52% of the votes cast, with a turnout of 71.74%.

July 19: Leonid Kuchma is sworn in as President of Ukraine.

August 7: The third round of parliamentary elections is held in 112 unrepresented constituencies, resulting in the election of 59 deputies; 53 seats remain unfilled.

November 10: An attempt by the Parliament to lift the ban on the Communist Party fails. 189 deputies are in favour of legalisation, which is 9 votes short of the required majority.

November 16: The Parliament passes a law which invalidates automatically Crimean legislation deemed to conflict with Ukrainian law.

November 20: Run-off parliamentary elections are held for the remaining 53 seats, resulting in the election of 10 deputies; 43 seats remain vacant.

1995

February 28: Social Democratic Party of Ukraine (SDPU) is officially registered. It is an alliance between the Ukraine Party of Justice, the Party of Human Rights and the Social Democratic Party.

March 1: Conservative Prime Minister, Vitalii Masol, resigns and Yevhenii Marchuk, a pro-reformist, is appointed as Prime Minister by President Kuchma.

March 17: The Supreme Court annuls the constitution of the Republic of Crimea. This constitution has been regarded as a marking step towards a separation from Ukraine. The Supreme Court approves the dissolution of the Crimean Parliament.

April 1: The President assumes by decree direct control over the Republic of Crimea. The relationship with Russia deteriorates since the ethnic majority of Crimea is Russian.

April 4: The Parliament passes a motion of no confidence, by 292 votes to 4, against the government of Prime Minister Marchuk. The President instructs the Prime Minister to form a new government.

May 18: The Parliament presents an interim constitutional law, awarding significant additional power to the President pending the adoption of a new constitution.

May 30: The Parliament fails to ratify the interim constitutional law.

May 31: The President tries to force a referendum on the interim law by decree.

June 1: The Parliament declares this act unconstitutional.

June 15: A "Constitutional Treaty" is signed on the division of powers between the parliament and the President, awarding the President enhanced powers to issue decrees and appoint ministers. It also stipulates that the constitution is to be replaced within one year.

June 25: Pro-Russian groups are defeated in local elections in Crimea.

August 28: Presidential rule, proclaimed on 1 April in Crimea, is lifted.

November 9: Ukraine acquires its membership of the Council of Europe.

December 10: Repeat parliamentary elections are held in the 43 constituencies where the result of the 1994 legislative elections have been declared invalid because the turnout had been below 50%. Results: only 18 constituencies are declared valid, 25 seats of the 450-member parliament remain vacant.

1996

March 4: The Minister of Environmental Protection and Nuclear Safety, Yurii Kostenko, warns against the danger of explosion of the nuclear reactor at Chernobyl.

March 8: Disclosure of the occurrence of a "serious incident" at a reactor at Chernobyl.

March 11: The Constitutional Commission approves the draft Constitution.

March 15: The Russian State Duma passes a resolution in order to "deepen the integration of the peoples previously united in the USSR". This resolution revokes the 1991 agreement which established the CIS, and the Supreme Soviet's resolution of 12 December 1991 which abrogates the treaty on the formation of the USSR. The Duma also adopts a resolution upholding the legal validity of the results of the 17 March 1991 referendum on the future of the USSR.

March 21: President Leonid Kuchma denounces the resolution adopted by the Russian State Duma on 15 March.

May 27: President Kuchma dismisses Prime Minister Yevhenii Marchuk.

May 28: The President appoints Pavlo Lazarenko, who is linked to the "Unity" faction, as Prime Minister.

June 28: The Supreme Council adopts the new Constitution, replacing the "Constitutional Treaty". It endorses a strong presidential system and renames the 450-member parliament of *Verkhovna Rada to Narodna Rada.*

July 5: The government of Prime Minister Pavlo Lazarenko resigns, but continues in an interim capacity until the formation of a new government. President Kuchma formally reappoints Lazarenko as Prime Minister.

July 10: The Supreme Council endorses the reappointment of Lazarenko.

July 16: Prime Minister Lazarenko escapes an assassination attempt.

September 2: The *hyrvna* replaces the coupon as official currency.

December 5: Deputy Prime Minister Mykhalo Zubets is elected Chairman at the constituent congress of the Agrarian Party.

December 5: The Federation Council states that the Ukrainian port Sebastopol should be returned to Russia.

December 6: The members of the Crimean and Ukrainian parliaments reject the statement of the Russian Federation Council.

Constitution of Ukraine[1]

Adopted by the Supreme Council, 28 June 1996

Draft prepared by agreement among representatives of the President of Ukraine, the Verkhovna Rada of Ukraine, the Supreme Court of Ukraine and the High Court of Arbitration of Ukraine, dated February 24, 1996.[2]

We, the Ukrainian people – citizens of Ukraine of all nationalities –
expressing our sovereign will,
standing on a centuries-old history of Ukrainian state-building and on the basis of the right to self-determination achieved by the Ukrainian nation,
caring about the protection of human rights and freedoms and appropriate conditions of life,
being concerned to strengthen civil harmony in society,
endeavouring to develop and strengthen a democratic, social, law-governed state,
being conscious of the responsibility before the present and future generations,
taking guidance from the Act on the Proclamation of the Independence of Ukraine, dated 24 August 1991, that was approved by a nation-wide vote on 1 December 1991,
adopt this Constitution – the Fundamental Law of Ukraine.

Section 1 – General principles

Article 1
Ukraine is a sovereign, unitary, democratic, social, law-governed state.

Article 2
The sovereignty of Ukraine extends over its entire territory.
The territory of Ukraine is integral, indivisible and inviolable.

Article 3
The human being, his or her life and health, honour and dignity, inviolability and security are recognised in Ukraine as the highest social value.

---

1. The translation of the draft constitution was prepared by the Ukrainian Legal Foundation on 12 March 1996. The translation may be freely used if appropriate credit is given.
2. Prepared by the Working Subcommission of the Constitutional Commission on the basis of a text prepared by the Working Group and approved by the Constitutional Commission on 23 November 1995).

Human rights and freedoms and their guarantees determine the essence and course of the activity of the state. The establishment and protection of human rights and freedoms is the main duty of the state.

Article 4
Ukraine has single citizenship. The grounds for acquiring and terminating Ukrainian citizenship are determined by law.

Article 5
Ukraine is a republic.
The people are the only source of power in Ukraine. The people exercise power directly and through the bodies of state power.

Article 6
State power in Ukraine is exercised on the basis of its division into legislative, executive and judicial branches.
Bodies of legislative, executive and judicial branches exercise their powers within the limits established by the Constitution.

Article 7
The state recognises and guarantees local self-government.

Article 8
The principle of the rule of law is operative in Ukraine.
The Constitution has the highest legal force. The norms of the Constitution are realised directly. Laws and other legal acts shall be adopted on the basis of and in conformity with the Constitution.

Article 9
International treaties, ratified in accordance with the Constitution, and which have gained legal force for Ukraine, form a part of its national law.
International treaties of Ukraine shall not contravene the Constitution.

Article 10
The state (official) language of Ukraine is Ukrainian.
In the areas of dense concentrations of citizens, who are part of one or several national minorities, the language acceptable for the majority of residents of that specific populated region may be used in addition to the state language in the activity of bodies of state power and of state organisations.

Article 11
The state promotes the consolidation and development of the Ukrainian nation, its historical consciousness, traditions and culture, and the development of ethnic, cultural, linguistic and religious distinctive features of all national minorities.
Ukraine cares about the satisfaction of the national, cultural and linguistic needs of Ukrainians living beyond its borders.

Article 12
Societal life in Ukraine is based on principles of political, economic and ideo-
logical diversity.
No ideology shall be recognised by the state as mandatory.
The state guarantees freedom of political activity not prohibited by the Con-
stitution or by law.
The state ensures the equal protection of all forms of property and econom-
ic management, as well as the social orientation of the economy.
Censorship of the mass media is prohibited.

Article 13
The foreign political activity of Ukraine is aimed at ensuring its national interests and security by means of maintaining peaceful and mutually beneficial
co-operation with members of the international community.

Article 14
The people have the right to resist anyone who attempts to subvert the State
of Ukraine or the constitutional order, to violate territorial integrity of Ukraine,
or to perform acts with the purpose of seizing state power, if the measures
provided by the Constitution cannot be applied.

Article 15
The state flag of Ukraine is a blue and yellow banner of two horizontal bands
of equal width.
The state coat-of-arms of Ukraine is the Trident of golden colour on a blue
shield.
The state anthem of Ukraine is the national anthem – "Shche ne vmerla
Ukraina". (Ukraine Has Not Yet Perished.)
The capital of Ukraine is the city of Kyiv.

Section 2 – Rights and freedoms of the person and the citizen

Article 16
All people are free and equal in their dignity and rights.
Rights and freedoms of a human being are inalienable and inviolable.

Article 17
Rights and freedoms of the person and the citizen, established by this Con-
stitution, are not exhaustive.
Constitutional rights and freedoms may not be abolished.

Article 18
Every person has the right to the free development of his or her personality,
as long as this does not violate the rights and freedoms of other individuals.

Article 19
Citizens have equal constitutional rights and freedoms and are equal before
the law.

There shall be no privileges or restrictions based on race, skin colour, political or other convictions, sex, ethnic and social origin, property, place of residence, language, religion or other circumstances.

Article 20
A citizen of Ukraine shall not be deprived of citizenship nor of the right to change Ukrainian citizenship.
A citizen of Ukraine shall not be expatriated from Ukraine or extradited to a foreign state.
Ukraine guarantees its citizens care and protection beyond its borders.

Article 21
Foreigners and persons without citizenship in Ukraine shall enjoy the same rights and freedoms, and also bear the same duties as citizens of Ukraine, except as provided by the Constitution, by law or international treaties of Ukraine.
Foreigners and persons without citizenship may be granted asylum.

Article 22
Every person has an inalienable right to life.
No-one shall be wilfully deprived of life. The duty of the state is to protect human life.
Everyone has the right to protect his or her life and the lives of other persons against unlawful encroachments.

Article 23
Everyone has the right to respect of his or her dignity.
No-one shall be subjected to medical or scientific experiments without his or her free consent.

Article 24
Every person has the right to freedom and personal inviolability.
No-one may be arrested or be held in custody, except in accordance with a well-founded verdict of court and only on the basis of reasons determined by law.
In the event of an urgent necessity to prevent or stop a crime, the authorised bodies may hold a person in custody as a temporary preventive measure, on a basis which shall be verified by a court within 48 hours. The detained person shall be immediately released, in the event that he or she has not been provided, within 48 hours from the moment of detention, with a well-founded court decision.
Everyone who is arrested or detained shall be promptly informed of the reasons for arrest or detention, shall have his or her rights explained, and shall be given the opportunity to defend himself or herself personally or through the aid of legal counsel.
Everyone who is detained has the right at any time to challenge his or her detention in court.

Article 25
Everyone is guaranteed the inviolability of his or her dwelling place.
Entry into a dwelling place or any other personal possession, for the purposes of search or examination, shall be prohibited except on the basis of a well-founded court decision.
In urgent cases related to the direct pursuit of persons suspected of committing a crime, and to the salvation of life and property, other forms of entry into a dwelling place or any other personal possession, their search and examination are possible through another procedure determined by law.

Article 26
Everyone is guaranteed privacy of mail, telephone communication, telegraph and other forms of communications. Exceptions may be determined by law for the purpose of preventing crimes or determining the truth in the course of investigation and consideration of criminal cases.

Article 27
No-one shall be subjected to wilful interference into his or her personal and family life.
The collection, preservation, use and dissemination of confidential information about a person without his or her consent is prohibited, except in cases determined by law and only in the interests of national security, economic well-being and human rights.
Every citizen has the right to examine information about himself or herself at the bodies of state power, institutions and organisations, bodies of local self-government, unless it is a state secret or other secret protected by law.
Everyone is guaranteed judicial protection of the right to correct untruthful information and to demand the removal of the information collected in an unlawful manner, as well as compensation for material and moral damages caused by the collection, preservation, use and dissemination of such information.

Article 28
Everyone who is lawfully on the territory of Ukraine is guaranteed freedom of movement, free choice of place of residence, and the right to leave the territory of Ukraine freely, except through limitations determined by law for protection of national security, public order, health and morality of the population, or the rights and freedoms of others.
A citizen of Ukraine shall not be deprived of the right to return to Ukraine at any time.

Article 29
Everyone is guaranteed the right to freedom of thought and speech, and to the free expression of his or her views and convictions.
Everyone has the right freely to collect, use and disseminate information in oral, written and any other form that he or she chooses.
The exercise of these freedoms can be restricted by law in the interests of national security, territorial integrity or public order with the purpose of the

prevention of disturbances or crimes, to protect the health and morality of the population, to protect the reputation or rights of other persons, to prevent the divulging of information obtained confidentially, or to support the authority and impartiality of justice.

Article 30

Everyone has the right to freedom of conscience and religion. This right shall include the freedom to profess or not to profess any religion, to perform without constraint religious rites and ceremonial observances, either alone or communally, and to conduct religious activity.

The realisation of this right may be limited by law only in the interests of the protection of social order, health and morals of the population or for the protection of rights and freedoms of other people.

No religion may be recognised as compulsory by the state.

No-one can be released from his or her duties before the state or can refuse to observe the law on the grounds of religious convictions. In the event that the performance of military service is contrary to the religious convictions of a citizen, this obligation shall be replaced with alternative (non-military) service.

Article 31

Everyone has the right to freedom of association in order to exercise and to protect his or her rights and freedoms and to satisfy his or her political, economic, social, cultural and other interests, with the exception of limits prescribed by law in the interests of national and social security, the protection of the health and morals of the population or the protection of rights and freedoms of other people.

Political parties in Ukraine promote the expression of the political will of citizens and participate in elections. Only citizens of Ukraine may be members of political parties.

No-one may be forced to join any association whatsoever.

All public associations are equal before the law.

Article 32

The formation and operation of parties and public associations, that have as programmatic goals and pursue actions aimed at the liquidation of the independence of Ukraine, the change of the constitutional order by means of violence, the violation of the sovereignty and territorial integrity of Ukraine, the subversion of its security, the unlawful seizure of state power, religious enmity, the encroachment on human rights and freedoms, the health and morals of the population shall be prohibited.

Parties and public associations may not have paramilitary formations.

The formation and operation of organisational structures of political parties within the bodies of state power and bodies of local self-government, in military formations, as well as in state enterprises, institutions, educational establishments and other state organisations, shall not be permissible.

Public associations can be banned and dissolved only by order of the court.

Article 33
Citizens have the right to participate in the conduct of state affairs, in Ukrainian-wide and local referendums, to freely elect and be elected to the bodies of state power and local self-government.
Citizens shall enjoy the equal right of access to state service and to service in bodies of local self-government.

Article 34
Citizens have the right to assemble peacefully without arms and to hold rallies, meetings, marches and demonstrations, in accordance with notice given to bodies of executive power and local self-government.
The limitation of this right may be determined by law only in the interests of the security of the state or citizens to prevent disturbances and crimes, for the protection of the health and morals of the population or for the protection of rights and freedoms of other people.

Article 35
Everyone has the right to submit individual or collective written appeals to bodies of state power, bodies of local self-government and their officials, who are obliged to consider them and provide a reasoned reply.

Article 36
The right of private ownership is guaranteed.
Everyone has the right to possess, use and manage his or her parcel of land, other property, and has the right to the results of his or her intellectual work.
In order to secure the interests of national importance, the law determines a comprehensive list of objects which may not be owned privately.
To meet their needs, citizens have the right to use objects of state and communal property in accordance with law.
The right of private ownership to land is acquired in accordance with the order determined by law.
No-one shall be illegally deprived of his or her property.
Expropriations of objects of private property are allowable only as exceptions on the grounds of social necessity and on the condition of prior and full reimbursement of their value. Expropriation of objects of private property with subsequent full reimbursement is permissible only under conditions of martial law or the state of emergency.
Confiscation of property may take place in cases, amounts and in accordance with the order determined by law, only in connection with the commission of an offence.
The use of property shall not bring any harm to the rights, freedoms and dignity of citizens, the interests of society, or cause the deterioration of the ecological situation and natural qualities of land.

Article 37
Everyone has the right to entrepreneurial activity which is not prohibited by law.
Entrepreneurial activity by Deputies, Senators and officials of the bodies of state power and local self-government is prohibited.

The state ensures the protection of competition in entrepreneurial activity. The abuse of monopolistic market positions, illegitimate restriction of competition or unfair competition is not permitted. The kinds and limits of monopolies shall be determined by law.

The state shall protect the rights of consumers, exercise control over the quality and safety of products, all kinds of services, and shall support the activities of public consumer associations.

Article 38
Everyone has the right to labour that includes the possibility to earn a living by work that is freely chosen or freely agreed to.

The state creates conditions for citizens to realise this right fully, guarantees equal opportunities in the choice of professions and kinds of work, and implements programmes of professional and technical education, training and retraining according to the needs of society.

The use of forced labour is prohibited. Military or alternative service, as well as work or services carried out by a person in compliance with a verdict of a court or in accordance with the laws on the state of emergency or martial law shall not be considered to be forced labour.

Everyone has the right to proper, safe and healthy work conditions, and to remuneration for work that is not less than the minimum wage determined by law.

The use of women and minors for labour at jobs which are dangerous to their health is prohibited.

Citizens are guaranteed protection from unlawful dismissal.

Article 39
Those who are employed have the right to strike for the protection of their economic and social interests.

The order of exercising this right shall be determined by law, taking into account the necessity to ensure national security, the protection of health, and the rights and freedoms of other persons.

No-one shall be forced to participate or not to participate in a strike.

Article 40
Everyone who is employed has the right to rest.

The maximum duration of working hours, the minimum duration of rest and of paid annual vacation, non-working days and holidays, as well as other basic conditions of exercising this right, shall be determined by law.

Article 41
Citizens have the right to social protection in their old age, in cases of full or partial loss of their ability to work, the loss of their principal wage-earner, unemployment due to circumstances beyond their control, and in other cases provided by law.

This right is guaranteed by general and mandatory state social insurance made by payment of insurance premiums by enterprises, establishments and other organisations, budgetary and other sources of social welfare.

Pensions and other social payments and aid which that are the principal source of existence should provide a standard of living not lower than the minimum living standards established by the state.

Article 42
Everyone has the right to housing.
Citizens who are in need of social protection are provided with housing by the state and bodies of local self-government free of charge or at an affordable price in accordance with the law.
No-one shall be forcibly deprived of housing without lawful grounds and in no other way than in accordance with a court decision.

Article 43
Everyone has the right to a standard of living sufficient for himself or herself and his or her family, including sufficient nutrition, clothing and housing.

Article 44
Everyone has the right to the protection of health, medical aid and medical insurance.
The state creates conditions for effective medical service which is accessible to all citizens. State and communal health care institutions provide medical aid free of charge. The state promotes the development of private medical institutions.
The state cares for the development of physical culture and sports, and ensures sanitary and epidemiological welfare.

Article 45
Everyone has the right to an environment which is safe for life and health, and to the recovery of damages inflicted through violation of this right.
The law guarantees everyone the right of free access to information about the environment, the quality of food and consumer products, as well as the right to disseminate such information.

Article 46
Marriage is based on the free consent of a woman and a man. Each of the spouses shall enjoy equal rights and duties in family relations.
The family, childhood, motherhood and fatherhood shall be under protection of the state.

Article 47
Children shall be equal in their rights irrespective of their origin, and without regard to they are born in or out of wedlock.
Any form of violence to, or exploitation of, a child shall be prosecuted by law. Maintaining and raising orphans and children who are deprived of parental care shall be imposed upon the state. The state encourages and supports charitable activity in relation to children.

Article 48

Everyone has the right to education.

Basic secondary education is compulsory.

The state ensures accessible and free primary, secondary and professional education, in state and communal educational establishments. Citizens have the right to receive free higher education at state and communal educational establishments on a competitive basis.

The law guarantees citizens who belong to national minorities the right to receive instruction in their native language and to study their native language at state and communal educational establishments or through national cultural societies.

Article 49

Everyone has the right to enjoy the results of his or her intellectual work and nobody may exploit the results without his or her permission with the exception of cases determined by law.

Cultural heritage shall be protected by law.

The state shall take measures to return to Ukraine the cultural treasures of the nation that are located outside its borders.

Article 50

All human rights and freedoms shall be protected by the courts.

Everyone has the guaranteed right to appeal to the court against decisions, actions or inactions of the bodies of state power, bodies of local self-government or public officials.

Everyone shall have the right to appeal for the protection of his or her rights to the Authorised Human Rights Representative of the National Assembly of Ukraine.

Everyone shall have the right to appeal for the protection of his or her rights and freedoms to judicial and other institutions of the United Nations and the Council of Europe.

Everyone shall have the right to protect his rights and freedoms from violations by any means which are not prohibited by law.

Article 51

Everyone has the right to compensation from the state or local self-government for material or moral damages inflicted through unlawful decisions, actions or inaction of the bodies of state power and bodies of local self-government or their officials in the course of the exercise of their powers.

Article 52

Everyone is guaranteed the right to know his or her rights and duties.

Laws and other regulatory acts which determine the rights and duties of citizens should be brought to the notice of the population through proper means.

Article 53

The law shall not be retroactive, except in cases where it mitigates or repeals the responsibility of the person.

No-one shall bear responsibility for actions which, at the time they were committed, were not defined by law as an offence.

Article 54
Everyone has the right to legal assistance. In cases prescribed by law, such assistance shall be provided free of charge. Everyone shall be free to choose the defender of his or her rights.

Article 55
No-one is obliged to execute rulings or orders that are manifestly criminal. Issuing or executing a manifestly criminal ruling or order shall entail legal responsibility.

Article 56
The legal responsibility of a person has an individual character.
No-one shall be prosecuted twice for committing one and the same offence.

Article 57
A person shall be considered innocent of committing an offence until his or her guilt is proved in accordance with the law and is established by a guilty verdict of a court that has taken legal effect.
No-one is obliged to prove his or her innocence.
An accusation may not be founded on illegally obtained evidence, or on assumptions. All doubts in regard to the proof of the guilt of a person shall be resolved in his or her favour.
No-one shall be subjected to criminal punishment except by the verdict of a court.
In the event that a court verdict is revoked as unlawful, the state shall compensate for material and moral damages caused by the groundless conviction.

Article 58
A person shall not bear responsibility for the refusal to testify or explain anything relating to himself or herself, members of his or her family or close relatives whose circle is determined by law.
Persons who are suspected, accused or charged have the right to a defence.

Article 59
The convicted person enjoys all rights of a person and a citizen with the exception of restrictions determined by law and established by the verdict of a court.

Article 60
Constitutional human rights and freedoms may not be restricted, except in cases foreseen by the Constitution and laws adopted in accordance with it in order to protect the rights and freedoms of other persons, national security, and the protection of the health and morality of the population.

Such restrictions shall be minimal and shall correspond to the principles of the democratic state.

In conditions of martial law or a state of emergency, certain restrictions of rights and freedoms may be established with the specification of the period that such restrictions operate. Rights and freedoms envisaged by Articles 22, 23, 35, 42, 46, 47, 50, 51, 52, 53, 54, 55, 56, 57 or 58 of the Constitution may not be restricted.

Article 61

The defence of the Motherland, the independence and territorial integrity of Ukraine, and respect of its state symbols are the duty of citizens.

Citizens shall perform military service in accordance with the law.

Article 62

Everyone is obliged not to harm nature, or the cultural heritage and to compensate for any damage he or she has inflicted.

Article 63

Everyone is obliged to pay taxes and fees in accordance with the procedure and in the amounts determined by law.

Article 64

Everyone is obliged to observe the Constitution and laws of Ukraine faithfully, and not to contravene the rights and freedoms, honour and dignity of other persons.

Ignorance of the laws shall not exempt anyone from legal responsibility.

Section 3 – Elections and referendum

Article 65

The people express their will through elections, referendums and other forms of direct democracy.

Article 66

Citizens who reach the age of 18 years on the day of the elections or referendums have the right to vote at elections and referendums.

Citizens who have been declared incompetent by the court shall not have the right to vote.

Article 67

Elections to the bodies of state power and local self-government are free and occur periodically on the basis of general, equal and direct election law through secret voting.

Electors are guaranteed the right to express their will freely.

Article 68

An all-Ukrainian referendum shall be called by the National Assembly of Ukraine or the President of Ukraine on their own initiative in accordance with the Constitution.

An all-Ukrainian referendum on the people's initiative shall be called by the President of Ukraine upon the request of three million citizens who have the right to vote, on condition that the signatures in favour of calling the referendum have been collected in no less than two-thirds of the oblasts with no less than one hundred thousand signatures in each.

Article 69
Issues of altering the territory of Ukraine shall be resolved exclusively by an all-Ukrainian referendum.

Article 70
A referendum on draft laws in regard to matters of taxation, the budget or on amnesties is not permissible.

Section 4 – The National Assembly of Ukraine

Article 71
Legislative power in Ukraine is exercised by the Parliament, the National Assembly of Ukraine.

Article 72
The National Assembly consists of two Chambers that function on a permanent basis: the Chamber of Deputies and the Senate.

Article 73
The Chamber of Deputies consists of 370 deputies who are elected for a term of four years on the basis of universal, equal and direct suffrage by secret ballot.
A citizen is eligible to be a Deputy if he or she is not younger than 18 years of age on the day of elections, has the right to vote and has resided on the territory of Ukraine for the last five years.

Article 74
The Senate is formed on the basis of equal representation of three Senators from each oblast and the City of Kiev and two from the City of Sevastopol.
Senators are elected for a term of four years through direct elections in multi-member constituencies established in the Crimean Autonomy, each oblast, and the cities of Kiev and Sevastopol.
A citizen is eligible to be a Senator if he or she is not younger than 30 years on the day of elections, has the right to vote, and has resided in the appropriate territory for not less than five years.

Article 75
Regular elections of Deputies and Senators shall be held within the period of not earlier than 60 and no later than 45 days prior to the termination of the powers of the appropriate Chamber.
Extraordinary elections of Deputies shall be held within 60 days from the day of early termination of the powers of the Chamber of Deputies.

The day of elections of Deputies and Senators is determined by the President of Ukraine.
The order of the conduct of elections shall be prescribed by law.

Article 76
Deputies and Senators are not bound by imperative mandate.
No one can be a Deputy and a Senator at the same time. Deputies and Senators may not have another representative mandate.
Cases of the incompatibility of the mandate of Deputies and Senators with other kinds activity are prescribed by law.

Article 77
Deputies and Senators execute their functions on a permanent basis. The amount of monetary remuneration for Deputies and Senators shall be established by the previous Chamber of Deputies.
Deputies and Senators are equal in their status.

Article 78
Prior to taking office Deputies and Senators take the following oath before the National Assembly:

"I swear allegiance to Ukraine. I take the responsibility to dedicate all my deeds in defence of the sovereignty and independence of Ukraine, to care for the well-being of the motherland and the welfare of the Ukrainian nation. I swear to obey the Constitution and laws of Ukraine, to fulfil my obligations in the interests of all the compatriots."

Refusal to take the oath results in the loss of the mandate of the Deputy or Senator.
Deputies and Senators take office from moment of taking of the oath.

Article 79
Deputies and Senators are guaranteed parliamentary immunity.
Deputies and Senators are not legally responsible for the results of voting or of statements made in Chambers and the bodies of Chambers with the exception of responsibility for insult or slander.
Deputies and Senators cannot be detained or arrested without the consent of the appropriate Chamber prior to the verdict of a court, except if they have been detained whilst committing a crime.

Article 80
The powers of Deputies and Senators terminate simultaneously with the termination of the powers of the Chamber to which they have been elected.
The powers of a Deputy or a Senator are terminated pre-term in cases when:
1. he or she resigns on the basis of his or her personal application;
2. a court passes a guilty verdict, against him or her, that gains legal force;
3. a court declared him or her to be incompetent or absent without notice;

4.   he or she loses Ukrainian citizenship or departs for permanent residence outside of Ukraine;
5.   death.

In cases where the requirement of not performing incompatible activities with the mandate of a Deputy or a Senator is not observed, his or her powers shall be terminated pre-term pursuant to the decision of the appropriate Chamber. The decision of a Chamber about the pre-term termination of the powers of a Deputy or a Senator shall be adopted by the majority of the membership of the appropriate Chamber determined in the Constitution, and can be appealed against in court.

Article 81

The National Assembly works on a sessional basis. Sessions shall be opened and closed at joint sittings of both Chambers.

The National Assembly is legitimate upon the condition of the election of not less than two-thirds of the membership of each Chamber.

The first session of the National Assembly shall be opened by the eldest deputy.

Joint sittings of the National Assembly are chaired by the Chairman of the Chamber of Deputies or in the Chairman's absence by the Chairman of the Senate.

Voting at joint sittings of the Chamber is separate.

The order of work of the Chambers is determined by their Rules of Procedure. Joint sittings of Chambers are held pursuant to the Rules of Procedure of the Chamber of Deputies.

Article 82

Regular sessions of the National Assembly shall start annually on the first Tuesday of February and on the first Tuesday of September each year.

Special sessions of the National Assembly with the delineation of their agenda are convoked by the Chairman of the Chamber of Deputies on the joint request of not less than one-third of the membership of each of the Chambers or upon the request of the President of Ukraine.

In the event of the introduction of martial law or of a state of emergency in Ukraine, the National Assembly shall be called within a period of two days without its formal convocation.

In the event of expiration of powers of the National Assembly or any of the Chambers during the time of martial law or state of emergency their authority shall be prolonged until the day of the first sitting of the first session of the National Assembly elected after the termination of martial law or of the state of emergency.

Article 83

The sittings of the Chambers of the National Assembly shall be held in public. The decision of not less than two-thirds of the Deputies or Senators present at the meeting of each Chamber is required to hold a closed meeting. The voting at meeting of the Chambers is personal.

Article 84

The powers of the National Assembly include the following:

1. to introduce amendments to the Constitution of Ukraine in accordance with the limits and procedure envisaged by Section 13 of the Constitution;
2. to call an all-Ukrainian referendum on issues determined by Article 69 of the Constitution;
3. to adopt the state budget, control the execution of the state budget, and confirm the report on the execution of the state budget;
4. to adopt laws;
5. to appoint or elect and to discharge from office persons in cases envisaged by the Constitution;
6. to exercise parliamentary control in the forms and within the limits established by the Constitution;
7. to ratify and reject international treaties of Ukraine;
8. to hear of annual and special messages of the President of Ukraine about the internal and external situation of Ukraine;
9. to remove the President of Ukraine from office in accordance with the procedure established in the Article 109 of the Constitution;
10. to call the elections of the President of Ukraine in accordance with the terms established by the Constitution;
11. to announce, upon the submission of the President of Ukraine, war and conclusion of peace, to approve the decision of the President of Ukraine on the use of the armed forces of Ukraine and other military formations in the event of military aggression against Ukraine.

Issues envisaged by paragraphs 7, 8, 10, and 11 of this Article are considered and resolved at joint meetings of Chambers of the National Assembly.

The National Assembly also exercises other powers which, in accordance with the Constitution, are ascribed to the competence of the Chamber of Deputies and the Senate.

Each Chamber may consider any issues which are assigned to the competence of the National Assembly, except those which belong to the exclusive authority of another Chamber.

Article 85

The powers of the Chamber of Deputies include the following:

1. to ratify the appointment of the Prime Minister of Ukraine on the proposal of the President of Ukraine;
2. to consider and adopt a decision on the Programme of activity of the Cabinet of Ministers of Ukraine;
3. to oversee the activity of the Cabinet of Ministers of Ukraine in accordance with the Constitution;
4. to approve the most important national programmes of economic, scientific and technical, social and national cultural development, and environmental protection;
5. to approve decisions in regard to the granting of loans and economic assistance by Ukraine to foreign states and the receipt of loans by Ukraine from foreign countries, banks and international financial organisations, as well as overseeing their use;
6. to approve the general structure, strength of the armed forces of

Ukraine, the border troops of Ukraine, the National Guards of Ukraine, and other military formations created in accordance with the law;

7. to appoint and to discharge from office the Chairman of the Chamber of Accounting and half of its members;

8. to appoint and to discharge from office the Authorised Human Rights Representative of the National Assembly of Ukraine; to receive his or her annual report on the protection of human rights and freedoms in Ukraine;

9. to appoint and to discharge from office, upon the proposal of the President of Ukraine, the Chairman Director of the National Bank of Ukraine.

Article 86

Deputies have the right to inquire about the implementation of the programme of activity of the Cabinet of Ministers and other national programmes approved by the Chamber of Deputies.

After discussion of the response to the inquiry by the Cabinet of Ministers, the Chamber of Deputies may, on the proposal of not less than 100 Deputies, consider the issue of responsibility of the Cabinet of Ministers and adopt a resolution of no confidence by vote of the majority of its membership as determined by the Constitution.

The adoption of a resolution of no confidence by the Chamber of Deputies shall result in the resignation of the Cabinet of Ministers.

The issue of responsibility of the Cabinet of Ministers cannot be raised during the period of one year after the adoption of the programme of activity of the Cabinet of Ministers or twice during a regular session of the National Assembly.

Article 87

The powers of the Senate include the following:

1. to appoint one-half of the membership of the Constitutional Court of Ukraine;

2. to appoint and to discharge from office judges of the Supreme Court of Ukraine upon the submission of the President of Ukraine;

3. to ratify the appointment by the President of Ukraine of the heads of diplomatic missions of Ukraine to other states and to international organisations;

4. to appoint and to discharge from office the Deputy Chairman of the Chamber of Accounting and one-half of its members;

5. to ratify the appointment of the Procurator-General by the President of Ukraine;

6. to ratify the appointment of the Chairman of the Anti-monopoly Committee by the President of Ukraine;

7. to appoint, upon the submission of the President of Ukraine, the membership of the Central Electoral Commission on Elections to the National Assembly of Ukraine and of the President of Ukraine;

8. to establish, upon the submission of the President of Ukraine, the Defence Council of Ukraine;

9. to ratify the decision on provision of military assistance to other states, on the deployment of units of the armed forces of Ukraine to other countries, and on permission for the entry of units of armed forces of other states into the territory of Ukraine;

10. to adopt, within two days from the moment of the request, the decrees of the President of Ukraine on the introduction of marshal law or a state of emergency in Ukraine or in some part of its territory, on general or partial mobilisation, and on the declaration that certain localities are zones of ecological disaster;

11. to create and to abolish raions, to establish and to alter the boundaries of raions and towns, to reclassify settlements to the category of towns, and to name and rename settlements and raions.

Article 88

Each Chamber elects from its membership the Chairman of the Chamber and the Deputy Chairman of the Chamber.

The Chairmen of Chambers:

1. preside at sittings of the Chambers;
2. organise the preparation of issues for consideration at sittings of Chambers;
3. sign acts, adopted by a Chamber;
4. represent the Chambers in their relations with other bodies of state power in Ukraine;
5. perform other functions envisaged by the Constitution and the Rules of Procedure of the Chambers;

The Deputy Chairmen of Chambers perform the powers determined by the Rules of Procedure of the appropriate Chamber.

Article 89

The Chambers of the National Assembly approve the list of Committees of the Chambers and elect Chairmen of these Committees.

The Committees of the Chambers draft legislation and prepare and conduct preliminary consideration of issues within the jurisdiction of the National Assembly of Ukraine.

The Chambers of the National Assembly may establish, whenever they consider it to be necessary, temporary special commissions for preparation and preliminary consideration of issues within their jurisdiction.

Temporary investigation commissions are established, for examination of issues of interest to the whole of society, through a favourable vote of not less than one-third of the membership of the appropriate Chamber determined by the Constitution.

The conclusions and proposals of temporary investigation commissions are not mandatory for preliminary investigation and trial.

Article 90

The powers of each of the Chambers of the National Assembly are terminated on the day of the opening of the first sitting of the appropriate Chamber of the new convocation.

The Chamber of Deputies may be dismissed before the conclusion of their term by the President of Ukraine after consultations with the Prime Minister of Ukraine and Chairman of the Chamber of Deputies if the Chamber of Deputies has twice rejected, within sixty days after it first submission, the programme of activity of the Cabinet of Ministers of Ukraine.

The Chamber of Deputies elected in special elections conducted after dismissal of the previous composition of the Chamber by the President of Ukraine may not be dismissed for a year from the day of its election.

The Chamber of Deputies may not be dismissed during the last six months of the term of office of the President of Ukraine.

Article 91
The Chamber of Deputies and the Senate of the National Assembly adopt laws, resolutions and other acts by the majority of votes of the membership of the Chambers determined by the Constitution, except for cases envisaged by Articles 83, 94, 95, 109, 156, and 157 of the Constitution.

Article 92
The following are exclusively determined by the laws of Ukraine:

1.   the rights and freedoms of a human being and citizen, the guarantees of these rights and freedoms; and the principle duties of a citizen;
2.   citizenship, the legal status of citizens, the status of foreigners and persons without citizenship;
3.   the rights of national minorities;
4.   statutes of languages;
5.   the legal régime of property;
6.   the state budget, financial, monetary, price, credit, and investment regulations; the system of taxation; the types and amounts of taxes, collections and binding payments; currency, probes, kinds, value, types and minting of coins, order of issue and emission of banknotes, state securities, their kinds and types;
7.   units of weight, measure and time;
8.   principles and guarantees of entrepreneurship;
9.   the procedure for determining ecological standards;
10. the principle for the use of natural resources, the economic zone of the sea, the continental shelf, the exploration of outer space, the organisation and exploitation of power supply systems, and transport and communications;
11. the fundamentals of social protection, the principles of labour and employment regulation, marriage, family, childhood, motherhood, fatherhood, upbringing, education, culture and health care;
12. the principles of the regulation of demographic and migration processes;
13. the principles of the establishment and activity of political parties, other public associations, and the mass media;
14. the organisation and order of conduct of elections and referendums;
15. the organisation and order of activity of the National Assembly, the status of Deputies and Senators;
16. the principles of the organisation and activity of bodies of executive power and of state service, the principles of organisation of state statistics and information;
17. the judicial system, legal procedure, the status of judges, judicial expertise, the organisation and activity of the Office of the Procurator, investigation, the Notoriate, and bodies and institutions for the execution of punishments, and the principles of the organisation and activity of the bar;

18. territorial structure of Ukraine;
19. the principles of local self-government;
20. the establishment and order of functioning of free economic zones;
21. the principles of foreign relations, foreign economic activity and customs service;
22. the principles of national defence, the organisation of the Armed Forces and securing civil order;
23. the legal status of state borders;
24. the establishment and procedure for use and protection of state symbols;
25. the status of the Capital of Ukraine; special status of other cities;
26. legal status of martial law and state of emergency;
27. the establishment of state awards;
28. the establishment of military ranks, diplomatic ranks and other special ranks;
29. state holidays;
30. actions which constitute crimes, administrative or disciplinary offences, and responsibility for them;
31. amnesty.

Article 93
The right of legislative initiative in the National Assembly belongs to the President of Ukraine, Deputies and Senators.
Draft laws proposed by the President of Ukraine and defined by him as urgent shall be considered by the National Assembly in special order.

Article 94
In the event that contradictions arise between the Chambers of the National Assembly in regard to discussion of a draft law, the final decision is taken by the House of Deputies through a two-thirds majority of its members determined by the Constitution.

Article 95
A law shall be signed by the Chairman of the Chamber of Deputies of the National Assembly and sent without delay to the President of Ukraine.
The President of Ukraine, within fifteen days after receipt of the law, shall approve and officially promulgate it or shall return it with his remarks to the National Assembly for reconsideration.
In the event that the President of Ukraine, within the specified period of time, does not return the law for reconsideration, the law shall be regarded as approved by the President of Ukraine and must be signed and officially promulgated.
If the law returned for reconsideration is adopted by the National Assembly by a two-thirds majority of the members of each Chamber, determined by the Constitution, the President of Ukraine is required to sign and officially promulgate it within ten days.
A law shall come into effect after ten days from the moment of its official publication, if it is not otherwise provided by the law itself, but not prior to the date of its publication.

Article 96
The Law on the State Budget of Ukraine exclusively determines state expenditures, their amounts and purposes.
The law determines the limits of the budgetary deficit. The budgetary deficit can only be covered by issuing money through the decision of the National Assembly upon the proposal of the President of Ukraine.
In the event of the adoption of a state budget by the National Assembly in which expenditures exceed revenues, the sources and means of covering the deficit shall be stipulated in the law on the state budget. The law on the state budget cannot impose new taxes or other payments.

Article 97
The state budget of Ukraine is adopted annually by the National Assembly for the period from 1 January to 31 December, and in special circumstances for a different period.
The President of Ukraine submits the draft law on the state budget for the succeeding year to the House of Deputies of the National Assembly no later than on the fifteenth day of the fall session autumn. A report on the execution of the State Budget in the current year shall be submitted together with the draft budget.

Article 98
The President of Ukraine submits to the Chamber of Deputies the report on execution of the national budget for the previous year not later than on 31 March.
The submitted report shall be promulgated.

Article 99
The Chamber of Accounting, on behalf of the Chamber of Deputies, exercises control over the financial activity of the state and utilisation of state property.

Article 100
Parliamentary supervision of the observance of the constitutional rights of a person and citizen is performed by the Authorized Human Rights Representative of the National Assembly.

Section 5 – President of Ukraine

Article 101
The President of Ukraine is the head of state.
The President of Ukraine is the guarantor of state sovereignty, the territorial integrity of Ukraine, the observance of the Constitution and the securing of civil concord in society.
The President of Ukraine assists the co-ordination of the activity of bodies of state power and their interaction with bodies of local self-government.

Article 102
The President of Ukraine is elected by citizens for a term of five years on the basis of universal, equal and direct suffrage by secret ballot.

A citizen of Ukraine who is not younger than 35 years of age, has the right to vote, has resided in Ukraine for the last ten years prior to the day of elections, and has command of the state language is eligible to be elected the President of Ukraine.

The same person may not be the President for more than two consecutive terms.

The President of Ukraine may not have another representative mandate, occupy a position in bodies of state power and in associations of citizens, as well as perform any other paid or entrepreneurial activity or be a member of an administrative body or a board of supervisors of an enterprise aimed at making a profit.

Regular elections of the President of Ukraine shall be held not earlier than 45 days and not later than 30 days prior to the expiration of the term of office of the President of Ukraine. In the event of the pre-term termination of the powers of the President of Ukraine according to the Article 106 of the Constitution elections of the President of Ukraine shall be held within 90 days.

The procedure of the conduct of elections of the President of Ukraine is determined by law.

Article 103

A newly elected President of Ukraine assumes office from the moment of taking the oath at a ceremonial meeting of the National Assembly on the final date of the termination of the term of office of the previous President.

The Chairman of the Constitutional Court of Ukraine administers the oath:

"I, (name and surname) elected by the will of the people, entering upon this high office, solemnly swear allegiance to Ukraine. I pledge in all my undertakings to protect the state sovereignty and independence of Ukraine, to care for the well-being of the Motherland and the welfare of Ukrainian people, to protect rights and freedoms of citizens, to obey the Constitution and laws of Ukraine, to exercise my duties in the interests of all my compatriots, and to enhance the prestige of Ukraine in the world."

The President of Ukraine, elected by a special election, takes the oath within five days after the official announcement of the election results.

Article 104

The President of Ukraine enjoys the right of immunity.

Persons guilty of offending the honour and dignity of the President of Ukraine shall be brought to responsibility in accordance with law.

The title of President of Ukraine is protected by law and is reserved for the President for life.

Article 105

The President of Ukraine:

1.   ensures state independence, national security and legal succession of state;

2.   addresses the nation with messages, and the National Assembly with annual and special messages on the internal and external situation of Ukraine;

3.   represents the state in international relations, carries out general supervision of the external political activity of the state, conducts negotiations and concludes international treaties of Ukraine;

4.   takes decisions on the recognition of foreign states;
5.   with the consent of the Senate, appoints and discharges heads of diplomatic missions of Ukraine to other states and to international organisations; accepts credentials and letters of recall of diplomatic representatives of foreign states;
6.   calls an all-Ukrainian referendum regarding amendments to the Constitution in accordance with Article 157 of the Constitution; announces an All-Ukrainian referendum on the people's initiative;
7.   calls for the elections to the Chambers of the National Assembly within the terms stipulated in the Constitution;
8.   dismisses the Chamber of Deputies in cases stipulated by Article 90 of the Constitution;
9.   appoints the Prime Minister of Ukraine with the consent of the Chamber of Deputies and discharge him from office;
10.   upon the proposal of the Prime Minister of Ukraine, appoints members of the Cabinet of Ministers of Ukraine, the heads of other central bodies of executive power, as well as heads of state administrations and discharges them from office;
11.   appoints with the consent of the Senate the Procurator-General and discharges him from office;
12.   appoints, with the consent of the Senate, the Head of the Anti-monopoly Committee and discharges him from the office;
13.   creates, reorganises and dissolves ministries and other central bodies of executive power, within the limits of funding provided in the state budget for the maintenance of these bodies;
14.   revokes acts of the Cabinet of Ministers of Ukraine, central and local bodies of executive power and of the Government of the Crimean Autonomy;
15.   is the Commander-in-Chief of the Armed Forces of Ukraine; appoints and discharges the High Command of the Armed Forces of Ukraine;
16.   submits to the National Assembly proposals on declaration of war and makes decisions on the use of the armed forces in the event of armed aggression against Ukraine;
17.   in the event of a threat of aggression or danger to the state independence of Ukraine, takes the decision on total or partial military mobilisation and the introduction of martial law in Ukraine or in its separate territories;
18.   in case of necessity declares in Ukraine or in its separate territories the state of emergency; in case of necessity declares certain territories of Ukraine to be zones of ecological disaster;
19.   appoints one-half of the members of the Constitutional Court of Ukraine;
20.   establishes courts according to the procedure determined by law;
21.   confers high military ranks, diplomatic ranks and other special titles;
22.   awards national decorations, establishes presidential decorations and awards them;
23.   takes decisions about acceptance for citizenship of Ukraine and the termination of citizenship of Ukraine, and about the granting of asylum;
24.   exercises the right to grant pardons;
25.   for the execution of his powers establishes consultative, advisory and other subsidiary bodies and services within the limits of the funds stipulated in the state budget for maintenance of the bodies of executive power;

26. exercises other powers provided by the Constitution.

The President of Ukraine, on the basis and for implementation of the Constitution and laws of Ukraine, issues universals, decrees and directives that are mandatory for execution on the territory of Ukraine.

Acts of the President of Ukraine, issued within the limits of the authority provided by paragraphs 3, 4, 8, 10, 12, 13, 15, 16, 17, 18, and 21 of this Article shall be co-signed by the Prime Minister of Ukraine and the Minister responsible for its implementation.

Article 106

The President of Ukraine exercises authority until the assumption of office of a newly elected President.

The powers of the President of Ukraine shall cease before term in cases of:
1. resignation;
2. inability to exercise authority for the reasons of health;
3. removal by the procedure of impeachment;
4. death.

Article 107

The resignation of the President of Ukraine becomes valid from the moment of the announcement of the resignation by the President personally at a joint sitting of the Chambers of the National Assembly.

Article 108

The inability of the President of Ukraine to exercise his or her powers for the reasons of health shall be determined at a joint meeting of Chambers of the National Assembly and approved by the majority of votes of the members of each of the Chambers determined by the Constitution, upon the written submission of the Supreme Court of Ukraine on the grounds of an appeal of the Chamber of Deputies of Ukraine and a medical opinion.

Article 109

The President of Ukraine may be removed from office by the National Assembly through a special procedure (impeachment) in the event of the commission of state treason or another serious crime.

The issue of the removal of the President of Ukraine from office through the procedure of impeachment shall be initiated by not less than one-third of the members of the Chamber of Deputies provided by the Constitution.

To conduct the investigation, the Chamber of Deputies shall establish a special temporary investigation commission, which shall include a special procurator and special investigating officers. The conclusions and proposals of the investigation commission are considered at a sitting of the Chamber of Deputies which, upon proof of the presence of grounds, by majority of its membership determined by the Constitution, takes the decision to charge the President of Ukraine and refers the case to the Senate for consideration.

The Senate considers the charges against the President of Ukraine and takes a decision to submit the issue of removal of the President of Ukraine from office to the National Assembly or to dismiss the case.

The decision on removal of the President of Ukraine from office through the procedure of impeachment is adopted by the National Assembly by not less than two-thirds of the members of each of the Chambers determined by the Constitution, after the examination of the case by the Constitutional Court of Ukraine and the receipt of its conclusion about observance of the procedure of investigation and consideration of the case of impeachment envisaged by the Constitution, and after receiving the decision of the Supreme Court of Ukraine that charges brought constitute a serious crime.

A person, removed from office of the President of Ukraine, is subject to responsibility for the committed crime according to the general procedure.

Article 110
In the event of the early termination of the term of office of the President, in accordance with Articles 106, 107, 108 and 109 of the Constitution, the duties of the President of Ukraine, for the period until election of a new President of Ukraine and his assumption of office, are vested in the Prime Minister of Ukraine. The Prime Minister of Ukraine while executing the duties of the President of Ukraine shall not exercise the powers determined by paragraph 2, 6, 8, 10, 11, 12 or 13 of Article 105 of the Constitution.

Article 111
The Cabinet of Ministers of Ukraine is the central collegial body of executive power.

The Cabinet of Ministers is subordinate to the President of Ukraine and is accountable to the National Assembly within the limits determined in Articles 85 and 86 of the Constitution.

The Cabinet of Ministers conducts its activity in accordance with the Constitution and the laws of Ukraine and the acts of the President of Ukraine.

Article 112
The Cabinet of Ministers is composed of the Prime Minister, the Vice-Prime Minister and the Ministers.

The Prime Minister organises the activity of the Cabinet of Ministers, directs it to execute the programme of activity of the Cabinet of Ministers, adopted by the Chamber of Deputies of the National Assembly.

Article 113
The Cabinet of Ministers is established for the period of the term of office of the President of Ukraine.

The Prime Minister and other members of the Cabinet of Ministers have the right to announce their resignation to the President of Ukraine.

Rejection by the Chamber of Deputies of the programme of activity of the Cabinet of Ministers or adoption of the resolution of no confidence in accordance with Article 86 of the Constitution entails the resignation of the Cabinet of Ministers which shall be accepted by the President of Ukraine.

The Cabinet of Ministers, whose resignation is accepted by the President of Ukraine, shall continue to exercise its powers, by order of the President, until a new Cabinet of Ministers commences its functions.

Article 114

The Cabinet of Ministers of Ukraine:

1.   secures state sovereignty and the economic independence of Ukraine, implements internal and external policies of the state, and realises the Constitution, laws and acts of the President of Ukraine;

2.   takes measures to secure rights and freedoms of persons and citizens;

3.   secures the conduct of financial, monetary, pricing, credit, investment, and taxation policies as well as policies in regard of labour and employment, social protection, education, science and culture, protection of the environment, ecological safety and use of natural resources;

4.   prepares and implements national programmes of economic, scientific and technical, social and cultural development of Ukraine;

5.   organises the management of objects of state property and promotes the development of other forms of property;

6.   secures the preparation and implementation of the state budget;

7.   takes measures to ensure the defence and national security of Ukraine, civil order, prevention of crime;

8.   organises and secures the implementation of external economic activity of Ukraine as well as the operation of customs;

9.   directs and co-ordinates the activities of ministries, and other bodies of executive power;

10. exercises other powers, delineated in the Constitution, laws and acts of the President of Ukraine.

The Cabinet of Ministers passes resolutions and orders that are binding. The acts of the Cabinet of Ministers shall be signed by the Prime Minister.

Article 115

Ministries and other central bodies of executive power conduct management over corresponding spheres of administration.

The heads of these bodies are accountable to the President of Ukraine for the results of their activities.

Article 116

The executive power in oblasts, raions, and the cities of Kiev and Sevastopol is exercised by the heads of the appropriate state administrations.

In the exercise of their authority, local bodies of self-government are subordinated to bodies of executive power of a higher authority.

Article 117

The heads of state administrations on the appropriate territory ensure: adherence to the Constitution of Ukraine and the laws of Ukraine, the acts of the President of Ukraine, the Cabinet of Ministers and other bodies of executive power; adherence to the rights and freedoms of citizens; the implementation of programmes of social and economic as well as of cultural development and environmental protection; the exercise of powers vested in them in regard to management of state property; the co-ordination of the activity of local bodies of state power and interrelation with bodies of local self-government.

The heads of local state administration have no right to resolve issues which are assigned by the Constitution and the law as a power of bodies of local government.

Article 118
The organisation and procedure of the operation of the Cabinet of Ministers of Ukraine and other bodies of executive power are determined by law.

Section 7 – The Procuracy

Article 119
The Office of the Procurator of Ukraine constitutes a single system, vested with the following:
1.   oversight to ensure the observance of laws by bodies that conduct direct searches, inquires and pre-trial investigations;
2.   the investigation of criminal offences in cases determined by law;
3.   conduct of prosecutions on behalf of the state in court;
4.   oversight to ensure the observance of laws in the execution of judgements of the court in criminal cases as well as the application of the other compulsory measures related to the restraint of personal freedoms of citizens;
5.   the representation of the interests of the state or of a citizen in court in cases that are determined by law.

Article 120
The Office of the Procurator is headed by the Procurator-General, who is appointed to and discharged from office by the President of Ukraine. The appointment of the Procurator-General requires the consent of the Senate. The term of office of the Procurator-General shall be five years.

Article 121
The organisation and procedure of the Office of Procurator are determined by law.

Section 8 – The system of justice

Article 122
Justice in Ukraine is exercised solely by courts. The delegation of the functions of courts, as well as the appropriation of these functions by other bodies and officials, is not permitted.
Judicial decisions are made by courts on behalf of Ukraine.

Article 123
The judicial system in Ukraine is formed in accordance with the territorial principle and the principle of specialisation.
The highest judicial body is the Supreme Court of Ukraine.
The highest judicial bodies of specialised courts are the respective high courts.
The establishment of extraordinary and special courts, except in cases of the introduction of martial law, is prohibited.
The powers, procedure and operation of courts and bodies of judicial self-government, as well as the conditions of taking the office of a judge are determined by law.

Article 124

Judges may not be replaced and they hold their office for life, except for judges appointed for the first time.

Judges of the Supreme Court of Ukraine are elected by the Senate upon the proposal of the President of Ukraine. Judges of other courts are appointed to office by the President of Ukraine upon the proposal of the Minister of Justice in accordance with the procedure determined by law.

The first appointment of a judge to office shall be for the term of five years.

Judges may not be members of political parties, perform any entrepreneurial or other paid activity, except for academic and teaching activity.

Article 125

The powers of a judge shall be terminated before the expiration of the term of appointment in the event of:

1.   his or her announcement of discharge or resignation;
2.   his or her incapability to perform his or her functions for the reasons of health;
3.   upon reaching the age of 70 years;
4.   his or her violation of the requirements of incompatibility;
5.   the violation of the oath.

The decision on the early termination of the powers of a judge, in cases envisaged by paragraphs 2, 4 and 5 of this Article, as well as in the case when he or she has committed a crime, shall be taken in accordance with a special procedure envisaged by law.

Article 126

Judicial proceedings shall be conducted on the basis of the equal status of all participants at a trial, an adversarial relation between the parties, open courts, and the binding character of court decisions.

Article 127

In carrying out judicial proceedings, judges are independent and are subject only to the law.

Any form of influence upon judges is prohibited.

Persons guilty of disrespect to the court are brought to account as determined by law.

Article 128

Judges are guaranteed immunity.

A judge may not be brought to criminal account, if detained or arrested without the consent of the Senate, except for detention while he or she was committing a crime.

Article 129

The state ensures the necessary funding and proper conditions for the operation of courts and the activity of judges. Expenditure for maintenance of courts shall be separately stipulated in the state budget.

The execution of court decisions is vested in the bodies of executive power.

Section 9 – Territorial structure of Ukraine

Article 130
The territorial structure of Ukraine is based on the grounds of the unity and integrity of state territory, the combination of centralisation, and decentralisation in the exercise of state power, the balance of social and economic development of regions taking into account their historical, economic, geographic and demographic specificities, and ethnic and cultural traditions.

Article 131
The system of administrative and territorial structure of Ukraine is composed of the Crimean Autonomy, oblasts, raions, cities, municipalities and villages. The cities of Kiev and Sevastopol have a special status determined by law.

Section 10 – The Crimean Autonomy

Article 132
The Crimean Autonomy is an integral part of Ukraine and, within the authority determined by this Constitution and the Statute of the Crimean Autonomy, decides the issues falling within its jurisdiction.
The Statute of the Crimean Autonomy shall be approved by the National Assembly of Ukraine in accordance with the order determined for the adoption of the laws of Ukraine.

Article 133
Normative legal acts of the Crimean Autonomy shall not contradict the Constitution and the laws of Ukraine.

Article 134
The Representative Body of the Crimean Autonomy shall be the Verkhovna Rada of the Crimean Autonomy.
The Verkhovna Rada of the Crimean Autonomy shall, within its jurisdiction, take decisions and adopt resolutions which are binding in the Crimean Autonomy.
The Government of the Crimean Autonomy shall be the Council of Ministers of the Crimean Autonomy. The Head of the Council of Ministers of the Crimean Autonomy shall be appointed by the Verkhovna Rada of the Crimean Autonomy upon agreement of the President of Ukraine.
The authority, order of formation and procedure of the Verkhovna Rada of the Crimean Autonomy and of the Council of Ministers of the Crimean Autonomy shall be determined by this Constitution and the Statute of the Crimean Autonomy.
Justice is administered in the Crimean Autonomy by the courts which are part of the unified judicial system of Ukraine.

Article 135
The Crimean Autonomy shall, within the limits determined by law, create, approve and implement its budget, impose taxes and duties of the Crimean Autonomy.

The Crimean Autonomy shall administer costs received from taxes and duties it imposes, as well as contributions from general national taxes, the amount of which is determined by the law of Ukraine.

Article 136
In the event that the decisions and resolutions of the Verkhovna Rada of the Crimean Autonomy contradict the Constitution of Ukraine, the President of Ukraine may suspend their effectiveness while simultaneously applying to the Constitutional Court of Ukraine.

Article 137
The Representative Office of the President of Ukraine, whose legal status shall be determined by law, shall operate in the Crimean Autonomy.

Section 11 – Local self-government

Article 138
Territorial communities – the residents of villages, municipalities and cities have the right of local self-government, to independently resolve issues of local character within the limits established by the Constitution and laws of Ukraine.
Local self-government shall be exercised by communities both directly and through the bodies of local self-government: village, municipality and city councils and their executive bodies.
Raion and oblast Councils are the bodies of local self-government, that represent the common interests of the citizenry of villages, municipalities and cities.

Article 139
The chairmen of village, municipality or city councils and representatives elected by residents of villages, municipalities or cities shall be the members of the respective village, municipality and city council.
The Chairman of a village, municipality or city shall preside at the respective council and head its executive body.
The raion council shall be formed by the village, municipality and city councils of the raion, while the oblast council shall be formed by the raion and city (cities of oblast importance) councils of the oblast.
The Chairmen of raion and oblast councils shall be elected by the respective councils and shall preside over its executive body.

Article 140
The material and financial basis for local self-government is personal and real property, revenues to local budgets, other funds, land, natural resources that form the communal property of territorial communities of villages, municipalities and cities as well as objects of joint property that are governed by raion and oblast councils.
The state shall provide financial support for local self-government.

Article 141

The communities of a village, municipality or city, either directly or through the bodies of local self-government, within limits established by the law, resolve issues of the municipal economy and housing, public transport, social aid, education, culture, health care, environment, public order, trade and services, the support of entrepreneurship, municipal property, and create, approve and implement budgets of the respective administrative territorial units, impose local taxes and duties as well as other matters of local character.

Bodies of executive power may delegate certain powers to bodies of local self-government by law or agreement. The state shall finance the execution of state powers and, should the necessity arise, transfer ownership of state properties to bodies of local self-government.

In the exercise of the authority delegated to them, bodies of local self-government implement joint programmes of social and economic development and shall resolve other issues of regional character determined by legislation.

Article 142

Bodies of local self-government shall, within the limits of their authority, adopt resolutions which are binding in the respective territory.

In the event that resolutions of bodies of local self-government violate the Constitution, laws or other acts of legislation of Ukraine, they shall be suspended by the representative of the President of Ukraine in the Crimean Autonomy or the heads of respective state administrations with a simultaneous address to a court to declare them to be ineffective.

Article 143

The rights of local self-government shall be protected by the courts.

Article 144

Other issues concerning the organisation, formation, operation and responsibilities of the bodies of local self-government shall be determined by law.

Section 12 – The Constitutional Court

Article 145

The Constitutional Court is the sole body of constitutional jurisdiction in Ukraine.

The Constitutional Court determines whether laws and other legal acts conform to the Constitution (the constitutional character) and provides the official interpretation of the Constitution and the laws.

Article 146

The Constitutional Court is composed of fourteen judges.

The President of Ukraine and the Senate each appoint seven judges to the Constitutional Court.

The Judges of the Constitutional Court are appointed for a term of ten years without the right of re-appointment.

A citizen of Ukraine may be appointed as a judge of the Constitutional Court who on the day of appointment has reached the age of 40 years, has higher legal education and experience of practical, academic or pedagogical activity as a legal professional of not less than ten years.

The Head of the Constitutional Court is elected by a secret ballot vote by the members of the court for a term of five years at a special sitting of the Constitutional Court.

Article 147

In the course of exercising their authority, judges of the Constitutional Court are independent and obey only the Constitution of Ukraine.

A judge of the Constitutional Court may not be a member of a political party, a Deputy or a Senator, hold another representative mandate, occupy any office in bodies of state power in institutions and organisations, in public associations, bodies of local self-government, or perform other paid or entrepreneurial activity, except for academic and educational activity.

Article 148

Judges of the Constitutional Court are guaranteed immunity.

A judge of the Constitutional Court may not be brought to criminal responsibility, detained or arrested without the consent of the Constitutional Court, except if the judge is detained while committing a crime.

Article 149

The powers of a judge of the Constitutional Court are terminated before the expiration of the term in the cases of :
1.   the judge's announcement of discharge or resignation;
2.   incapability to perform his or her powers by reasons of health;
3.   reaching the age of 70 years;
4.   violation of the requirements of incompatibility determined by Article 142 of the Constitution;
5.   violation of the oath;
6.   death.

The decision on pre-term cessation of office of a judge of the Constitutional Court, in cases provided by paragraphs 2, 4 and 5 of this Article as well as in the case that the judge has committed a crime, shall be taken in the order of special procedure provided by law.

Article 150

The Constitutional Court has the following powers:
1.   the official interpretation of the Constitution and the laws;
2.   the resolution of issues in regard to conformity with the Constitution (Constitutionality) of:
   * laws and other legal acts of the National Assembly;
   * normative legal acts of the Crimean Autonomy;
   * acts of the President of Ukraine;
   * acts of the Cabinet of Ministers.

These issues are considered upon submission of the President of Ukraine, not less than 75 Deputies or 25 Senators, the Supreme Court of Ukraine, the Authorised Human Rights Representative of the National Assembly, the Procurator-General of Ukraine, or the Verkhovna Rada of the Crimean Autonomy.

The decisions of the Constitutional Court, on matters determined by this article, are binding throughout the territory of Ukraine, and are final and not subject to appeal.

Article 151

Upon submission of the President of Ukraine or of the Cabinet of Ministers, the Constitutional Court determines whether international treaties of Ukraine submitted for ratification conform with the Constitution.

Upon submission of the Senate, the Constitutional Court determines whether the Constitutional procedure of investigation and consideration of the case for removal of the President of Ukraine in the order of impeachment was observed.

Article 152

The Constitutional Court may declare laws and other legal acts unconstitutional in whole or in regard to a certain part, if they do not conform to the Constitution or if there was a violation in the procedure determined by the Constitution of their consideration, adoption or coming into force.

Laws and other legal acts, or their particular provisions, declared to be unconstitutional by the Constitutional Court, lose their force and effects from the date that the decision about their unconstitutionality was adopted.

Material and moral damages caused to physical and legal persons through unconstitutional acts or actions are compensated by the state.

Article 153

The order of organisation and operation of the Constitutional Court and the procedure for the consideration of cases is determined by law.

Section 13 – Introduction of amendments to the Constitution

Article 154

Amendments to the Constitution may be submitted by a draft law to the National Assembly by the President of Ukraine or jointly by one-third of the Deputies and one-third of the Senators.

Article 155

The Constitution may not be amended to abolish or limit the rights and freedoms of a person or citizen or negatively effect the independence and territorial integrity of Ukraine.

The Constitution may not be amended during a state of emergency or martial law.

Article 156

The draft law on amendments to the Constitution, except for Sections 1, 3, 13, that is adopted by a majority of the members of each Chamber of the

National Assembly as determined by the Constitution, is considered to be adopted if at the next regular session of the National Assembly not less than three-quarters of the members of each Chamber as determined by the Constitution vote in favour of the law.

Article 157

Amendments to Section 1 of the Constitution ,"General Provisions", Section 3 "Elections and referendum" and Section 13 "Introduction of Amendments to the Constitution" may be made by draft law submitted to the National Assembly by the President of Ukraine subject to the condition that it is approved by three-quarters of the composition of each Chamber determined by the Constitution and submitted for adoption by an all-Ukrainian referendum appointed by the President of Ukraine.

A draft law on amendments to Sections 1, 3, 13 of the Constitution regarding the same issue may only be resubmitted to the National Assembly of the next convocation.

Article 158

A draft law on amendments to the Constitution concerning the issue previously considered by the National Assembly without adoption of the law may be submitted not earlier than one year from the date that the decision concerning the previous draft law was taken.

Within the term of its authority, the National Assembly may not amend the same provisions of the Constitution twice.

Article 159

A draft law on changes and amendments to the Constitution is considered by the National Assembly upon presence of the decision of the Constitutional Court of Ukraine about the conformity of the draft law with the requirements of Articles 155 and 158 of the Constitution.

Section 14 – Final provisions

Article 160

The Constitution of Ukraine enters into force from the day of its adoption.

Article 161

The day of adoption of the Constitution of Ukraine is a national holiday the Day of the Constitution of Ukraine.

Article 162

On the day on which the Constitution of Ukraine enters into force, the Constitution of Ukraine of 20 April 1978 with subsequent changes and amendments and the Constitutional Accord between the President of Ukraine and the Verkhovna Rada of Ukraine "On Principles of the Organisation and Operation of State Power and Local Self-Government in Ukraine in the Period till

Adoption of a new Constitution of Ukraine" of 8 June 1995 cease to have force and effect.

Section 15 – Transitional provisions

1.   Laws and other normative acts, adopted prior to the entering of this Constitution into force, are valid in so far as they do not contravene the Constitution.

2.   After adoption of the agreed text of the Constitution by the parties to the Constitutional Accord, the Verkhovna Rada of Ukraine exercises the powers of both Chambers of the National Assembly of Ukraine from the date that this Constitution enters into force. From the day of the first sitting of the Senate and until the day of the first sitting of the newly elected Chamber of Deputies of the National Assembly of Ukraine, the Verkhovna Rada of Ukraine exercises powers of this Chamber determined by the Constitution.

Other bodies of state power, elected or appointed prior to adoption of the Constitution, exercise the powers determined by it throughout the term to which they were elected or appointed.

The Senate shall be elected within six months from the date that this Constitution enters into force.

The House of Deputies is to be elected in March 1998.

3.   The Cabinet of Ministers of Ukraine shall be formed in accordance with this Constitution within six months after it enters into force.

4.   Until the formation of the judicial system of Ukraine in accordance with Article 123 of this Constitution, the Supreme Court and the High Court of Arbitration exercise their powers according to Law of Ukraine of 5 June 1981 "On the Judicial System" and Law of Ukraine of 4 June 1991 "On the Court of Arbitration".

Judges of all the courts of Ukraine, elected or appointed prior to the date this Constitution enters into force, continue to exercise their powers in accordance with the current legislation until the completion of the term for which they were elected or appointed.

Judges, whose term of office expires on the date that this Constitution comes into effect, continue to exercise their powers for a period of six months.

5.   For six months after this Constitution enters into force, the current procedure of arrest, custody and detention of persons suspected of committing crimes, as well as the procedures for search and examination of a dwelling place and other possessions of a person shall be preserved.

6.   After this Constitution enters into force, the heads of state administrations acquire the status of heads of state administration in accordance with Article 116 of this Constitution and after the election of heads of respective councils, they resign from the office of head of these councils.

7.   After this Constitution enters into force, village, municipality, city councils and their heads perform the powers determined by it until the election of a new composition of the councils in 1998.

Raion and oblast councils, elected prior to this Constitution entering into force, perform the powers determined by it until the formation of a new composition of these councils according to Article 139 of this Constitution.

Uzbekistan

Chronology

1989

March 6: Mirzoalim Ibragimov replaces Pulat Khabibullayev as Chairman of the Presidium of the Supreme Soviet.

June 23: Islam Karimov replaces Rafik Nishanov as first secretary of the Uzbek Communist Party (UCP).

September: The Unity People's Movement publishes its founding charter, in which Uzbekistan's sovereignty and the Uzbek language are promoted.

October 20: The Supreme Soviet adopts legislation providing for a gradual elevation of Uzbek to the status of state language.

October 21: The Supreme Soviet elects Irakhmat Mirkasymov as Prime Minister.

1990

March 24: The Supreme Soviet elects Islam Karimov as Chairman of the Presidium of the Supreme Soviet, i.e. *de facto* head of state, and Shakurulla Mirsaidov as Prime Minister.

June 20: The Supreme Soviet adopts a declaration on Uzbekistan's sovereignty "within a renewed Soviet Federation".

November 1: The Supreme Soviet abolishes the government and installs a new government which is attached to President Islam Karimov. The Prime Minister now carries the title of Vice-President.

1991

March 17: In an all-union referendum 93.7% vote in favour of the preservation of the USSR. Turnout 95.4%

April 23: President Mikhail Gorbachev signs, with nine of the fifteen union republics including Uzbekistan, a pact aimed at achieving stable relations between the central government and the governments of the republics. It sets out a timetable for major political changes, starting with the signing of the new Union Treaty. No longer than six months after signature of the Treaty a new Union constitution would be promulgated, followed by elections to the Congress of People's Deputies.

August 19: Attempted *coup d'état* in Moscow.

August 24: The President resigns from the politburo of the Communist Party of the Soviet Union (CPSU).

August 28: The Republican Party breaks away from the UCP, which is renamed the People's Democratic Party (PDP).

August 31: The Supreme Council declares the country independent and changes its name to "Republic of Uzbekistan".

December 8: The Russian Federative Republic, Belarus and Ukraine sign the Minsk Agreement, establishing a Commonwealth of Independent States (CIS).

December 12: Uzbekistan signs the Alma Ata Agreement, thus joining the CIS.

December 21: The CIS formally replaces the Soviet Union, grouping eleven republics with the exception of Georgia. The Russian Federative Republic takes over many of the former Union functions, including its seat in the UN Security Council.

December 29: President Islam Karimov wins the presidential elections by gaining 86% of the votes cast. Simultaneously a referendum is held, in which 98.2% vote in favour of independence.

1992

July 2: The Supreme Council approves a draft constitution.

September 7: Former Prime Minister and Vice-President Shakurulla Mirsaidov resigns as Deputy Chair of the Supreme Council and as People's Deputy on account of the increased repression of the opposition in the last months.

December 8: The Uzbek Supreme Council adopts a new constitution. It declares Uzbekistan to be a democratic, presidential republic with a multi-party system. The *Oliy Majlis* is the new 250-member unicameral Parliament, elected by absolute majority. Repeat elections will be held if the turnout is below 50%.

December 9: The Supreme Council decides, by 383 votes to 7, to ban the nationalist parties *Birlik* (unity) and its ally *Erk* (will) for anti-government activities.

1993

January 14: The US State Department and the Russian Parliament's Human Rights Committee express their concern about human rights violations, regarding the disappearance of members of opposition parties and the allegations of the involvement of the Uzbek government.

January 19: The Supreme Court extends the ban on the Birlik Party for a further three months, on the grounds of "the intent to organise" illegal public demonstrations.

1994

June 12: A new party is founded: the Independence Path, led by Shadi Karimov a former member of the banned opposition party Birlik and its ally Erk.

July 1: The national currency, *sum,* is introduced.

October 15: The Russian rouble is officially banned.

December 25: The first elections to the *Oliy Majlis* since independence are held, candidates contesting are affiliated to two parties: the former communist People's Democratic Party (PDP) and its ally the Progress of the Fatherland Party (FP). The results are not conclusive.

1995

January 8: Second round of elections are held in the constituencies where no absolute majority of votes was attained. Results are not conclusive.

January 22: Final round of elections are held in 39 constituencies. The PDP officially gains 69 of the 250 seats, the FP gains 14 seats and the remaining 167 seats are taken by local candidates, of which 124 are PDP members; turnout 93.6%. OSCE representatives question the freedom and fairness of the elections.

February 18: The new opposition party, the Adolat (justice) Social Democratic Party of Uzbekistan is founded.

March 26: In a referendum 99.6 % of the voters back the extension of Karimov's Presidential term by three years, with a turnout of 99.3%, thus postponing the presidential elections to 2000.

May 25: The pro-government Khalq Birligi (People's Unity) Party is established.

June 3: The intellectual National Revival Democratic Party (NRDP) is founded.

December 21: Otkir Sultunov replaces Abdulhashim Mutalov as the new Prime Minister. He now becomes Deputy Prime Minister.

1996

March 6: Abdulhashim Mutalov loses his job as Deputy Prime Minister.

March 15: The Russian State Duma passes a resolution in order to "deepen the integration of the peoples previously united in the USSR". This resolution revokes the 1991 agreement which established the CIS, and the Supreme Soviet's resolution of 12 December 1991 which abrogates the treaty on the formation of the USSR. The Duma also adopts a resolution upholding the legal validity of the results of the 17 March 1991 referendum on the future of the USSR.

March 16: The Parliament condemns the resolution adopted by the Russian State Duma on 15 March.

June 21: President Karimov resigns as chair of the PDP.

Constitution of the Republic of Uzbekistan

*Adopted by the Supreme Council of the Republic of Uzbekistan,
8 December 1992*

Preamble

The people of Uzbekistan,
solemnly declaring their adherence to human rights and principles of state sovereignty,
aware of their ultimate responsibility to the present and future generations,
relying on historical experience in the development of Uzbek statehood,
affirming their commitment to the ideals of democracy and social justice,
recognising priority of the generally accepted norms of the international law,
aspiring to a worthy life for the citizens of the Republic,
setting forth the task of creating a humane and democratic rule of law,
aiming to ensure civil peace and national accord,
represented by their plenipotentiary deputies adopt the present Constitution of the Republic of Uzbekistan.

Part 1 – Fundamental principles

Chapter 1 – State Sovereignty

Article 1
Uzbekistan is a sovereign democratic republic. Both names of the state – the Republic of Uzbekistan and Uzbekistan – shall be equivalent.

Article 2
The state shall express the will of the people and serve their interests. State bodies and officials shall be accountable to society and the citizens.

Article 3
The Republic of Uzbekistan shall determine its national-state and administrative-territorial structure, its structure of state authority and administration, and shall pursue independent home and foreign policies.
The State frontier and the territory of Uzbekistan shall be inviolable and indivisible.

Article 4
The state language of the Republic of Uzbekistan shall be Uzbek.
The Republic of Uzbekistan shall ensure a respectful attitude toward the languages, customs and traditions of all nationalities and ethnic groups living on its territory, and create the conditions necessary for their development.

Article 5
The Republic of Uzbekistan shall have its state symbols – the flag, the emblem, and the anthem – sanctioned by law.

Article 6
The capital of the Republic of Uzbekistan shall be the city of Tashkent.

Chapter 2 – Democracy

Article 7
The people are the sole source of state power. State power in the Republic of Uzbekistan shall be exercised in the interests of the people and solely by the bodies empowered therefor by the Constitution of the Republic of Uzbekistan and the laws passed on its basis. Any seizure of powers belonging to state authority, suspension or termination of activity of the bodies of state authority contrary to the procedure prescribed by the Constitution, as well as the formation of any new or parallel bodies of state authority shall be regarded as unconstitutional and punishable by law.

Article 8
All citizens of the Republic of Uzbekistan, regardless of their nationality, constitute the people of Uzbekistan.

Article 9
Major matters of public and state life shall be submitted for a nation-wide discussion and put to a direct vote of the people (a referendum). The procedure for holding referendums shall be specified by law.

Article 10
The Oliy Majlis (Supreme Assembly) and President of the Republic, elected by the people, shall have the exclusive right to act on behalf of the people.
No section of society, political party, public association, movement or individual shall have the right to act on behalf of the people of Uzbekistan.

Article 11
The principle of the separation of power between the legislative, executive and judicial authorities shall underlie the system of state authority in the Republic of Uzbekistan.

Article 12
In the Republic of Uzbekistan, public life shall develop on the basis of a diversity of political institutions, ideologies and opinions.
No ideology shall be granted the status of state ideology.

Article 13
Democracy in the Republic of Uzbekistan shall rest on the principles common to all mankind, according to which the ultimate value is the human being, his life, freedom, honour, dignity and other inalienable rights.
Democratic rights and freedoms shall be protected by the Constitution and the laws.

Article 14
The State shall function on the principles of social justice and legality in the interests of the people and society.

Chapter 3 – Supremacy of the Constitution and the law

Article 15
The Constitution and the laws of the Republic of Uzbekistan shall have absolute supremacy in the Republic of Uzbekistan.
The state, its bodies, officials, public associations and citizens shall act in accordance with the Constitution and the laws.

Article 16
None of the provisions of the present Constitution shall be interpreted in a way detrimental to the rights and interests of the Republic of Uzbekistan.
None of the laws or normative legal acts shall run counter to the norms and principles established by the Constitution.

Chapter 4 – Foreign policy

Article 17
The Republic of Uzbekistan shall have full rights in international relations. Its foreign policy shall be based on the principles of sovereign equality of the states, non-use of force or threat of its use, inviolability of frontiers, peaceful settlement of disputes, non-interference in the internal affairs of other states, and other universally recognised norms of international law.
The Republic may form alliances, join or withdraw from unions and other inter-state organisations proceeding from the ultimate interests of the state and the people, their well-being and security.

Part 2 – Basic human and civil rights, freedoms and duties

Chapter 5 – General provisions

Article 18
All citizens of the Republic of Uzbekistan shall have equal rights and freedoms, and shall be equal before the law, without discrimination by sex, race, nationality, language, religion, social origin, convictions, individual and social status.
Any privileges may be granted solely by the law and shall conform to the principles of social justice.

Article 19
Both citizens of the Republic of Uzbekistan and the state shall be bound by mutual rights and mutual responsibility. Citizens' rights and freedoms, established by the Constitution and the laws, shall be inalienable. No-one shall have the power to deny a citizen his rights and freedoms, or to infringe on them except by the sentence of a court.

Article 20
The exercise of rights and freedoms by a citizen shall not encroach on the lawful interests, rights and freedoms of other citizens, the state or society.

Chapter 6 – Citizenship

Article 21
In the Republic of Uzbekistan, uniform citizenship shall be established throughout its territory.
Citizenship in the Republic of Uzbekistan shall be equal for all regardless of the grounds of its acquisition.
Every citizen of the Republic of Karakalpakstan shall be a citizen of the Republic of Uzbekistan.
The grounds and procedure for acquiring and forfeiting citizenship shall be defined by law.

Article 22
The Republic of Uzbekistan shall guarantee legal protection to all its citizens both on the territory of the republic and abroad.

Article 23
Foreign citizens and stateless persons, during their stay on the territory of the Republic of Uzbekistan, shall be guaranteed rights and freedoms in accordance with the norms of international law.
They shall perform the duties established by the Constitution, laws, and international agreements signed by the Republic of Uzbekistan.

Chapter 7 – Personal rights and freedoms

Article 24
The right to exist is the inalienable right of every human being. Attempts on anyone's life shall be regarded as the gravest crime.

Article 25
Everyone shall have the right to freedom and inviolability of the person.
No-one may be arrested or taken into custody except on lawful grounds.

Article 26
No-one may be adjudged guilty of a crime except by the sentence of a court and in conformity with the law. Such a person shall be guaranteed the right to legal defence during open court proceedings.

No-one may be subject to torture, violence or any other cruel or humiliating treatment.
No-one may be subject to any medical or scientific experiments without his consent.

Article 27
Everyone shall be entitled to protection against encroachments on his honour, dignity, and interference in his private life, and shall be guaranteed inviolability of the home.
No-one may enter a home, carry out a search or an examination, or violate the privacy of correspondence and telephone conversations, except on lawful grounds and in accordance with the procedure prescribed by law.

Article 28
Any citizen of the Republic of Uzbekistan shall have the right to freedom of movement on the territory of the Republic, as well as free entry to and exit from it, except in the events specified by law.

Article 29
Everyone shall be guaranteed freedom of thought, speech and convictions. Everyone shall have the right to seek, obtain and disseminate any information, except that which is directed against the existing constitutional system and in some other instances specified by law.
Freedom of opinion and its expression may be restricted by law if any state or other secret is involved.

Article 30
All state bodies, public associations and officials in the Republic of Uzbekistan shall allow any citizen access to documents, resolutions and other materials, relating to their rights and interests.

Article 31
Freedom of conscience is guaranteed to all. Everyone shall have the right to profess or not to profess any religion. Any compulsory imposition of religion shall be impermissible.

Chapter 8 – Political rights

Article 32
All citizens of the Republic of Uzbekistan shall have the right to participate in the management and administration of public and state affairs, both directly and through representation. They may exercise this right by way of self-government, referendums and democratic formation of state bodies.

Article 33
All citizens shall have the right to engage in public life by holding rallies, meetings and demonstrations in accordance with the legislation of the Republic of

Uzbekistan. The bodies of authority shall have the right to suspend or ban such undertakings exclusively on the grounds of security.

Article 34

All citizens of the Republic of Uzbekistan shall have the right to form trade unions, political parties and any other public associations, and to participate in mass movements.

No-one may infringe on the rights, freedoms and dignity of the individuals constituting the minority opposition in political parties, public associations and mass movements, as well as in representative bodies of authority.

Article 35

Everyone shall have the right, both individually and collectively, to submit applications and proposals, and to lodge complaints with competent state bodies, institutions and public representatives.

Such applications, proposals and complaints shall be considered in accordance with the procedure and within the time-limit specified by law.

Chapter 9 – Economic and social rights

Article 36

Everyone shall have the right to own property.

The privacy of bank deposits and the right to inheritance shall be guaranteed by law.

Article 37

Everyone shall have the right to work, including the right to choose their occupation. Every citizen shall be entitled to fair conditions of labour and protection against unemployment in accordance with the procedure prescribed by law.

Any forced labour shall be prohibited, except as punishment under the sentence of a court, or in some other instances specified by law.

Article 38

Citizens working on hire shall be entitled to a paid rest. The number of working hours and the duration of paid leave shall be specified by law.

Article 39

Everyone shall have the right to social security in old age, in the event of disability and loss of the breadwinner as well as in some other cases specified by law.

Pensions, allowances and other kinds of welfare may not be lower than the officially fixed minimum subsistence wage.

Article 40

Everyone shall have the right to receive skilled medical care.

Article 41
Everyone shall have the right to education. The state shall guarantee free secondary education. Schooling shall be under state supervision.

Article 42
Everyone shall be guaranteed the freedom of scientific research and engineering work, as well as the right to enjoy cultural benefits. The state shall promote the cultural, scientific and technical development of society.

Chapter 10 – Guarantees of human rights and freedoms

Article 43
The state shall safeguard the rights and freedoms of citizens proclaimed by the Constitution and laws.

Article 44
Everyone shall be entitled to legally defend his rights and freedoms, and shall have the right to appeal any unlawful action of state bodies, officials and public association.

Article 45
The rights of minors, the disabled, and the elderly shall be protected by the state.

Article 46
Women and men shall have equal rights.

Chapter 11 – Duties of citizens

Article 47
All citizens shall perform the duties established by the Constitution.

Article 48
All citizens shall be obliged to observe the Constitution and laws, and to respect the rights freedoms, honour and dignity of others.

Article 49
It is the duty of every citizen to protect the historical, spiritual and cultural heritage of the people of Uzbekistan.
Cultural monuments shall be protected by the state.

Article 50
All citizens shall protect the environment.

Article 51
All citizens shall be obliged to pay taxes and local fees established by law.

Article 52

Defence of the Republic of Uzbekistan is the duty of every citizen of the Republic of Uzbekistan. Citizens will be obliged to perform military or alternative service in accordance with the procedure prescribed by law.

Part 3 – Society and the individual

Chapter 12 – The economic foundation of society

Article 53

The economy of Uzbekistan, evolving towards market relations, is based on various forms of ownership. The state shall guarantee freedom of economic activity, entrepreneurship and labour with due regard for the priority of consumers' rights, as well as equality and legal protection of all forms of ownership.

Private property, along with the other types of property, shall be inviolable and protected by the state. An owner may be deprived of his property solely in cases and in accordance with the procedure prescribed by law.

Article 54

An owner shall possess, use and dispose of his property. The use of any property must not be harmful to the ecological environment, nor shall it infringe on the rights and legally protected interests of citizens, juridical entities or the state.

Article 55

The land, its minerals, fauna and flora, as well as other natural resources shall constitute the national wealth, and shall be rationally used and protected by the state.

Chapter 13 – Public associations

Article 56

Trade unions, political parties, and scientific societies, as well as women's, veterans' and youth leagues, professional associations, mass movements and other organisations registered in accordance with the procedure prescribed by law, shall have the status of public associations in the Republic of Uzbekistan.

Article 57

The formation and functioning of political parties and public associations aiming to do the following shall be prohibited: changing the existing constitutional system by force, coming out against the sovereignty, territorial integrity and security of the Republic, as well as the constitutional rights and freedoms of its religious hostility, and encroaching on the health and morality of the people, as well as of any armed associations and political parties based on the national or religious principles.

All secret societies and associations shall be banned.

Article 58
The state shall safeguard the rights and lawful interests of public associations and provide them with equal legal possibilities for participating in public life. Interference by state bodies and officials in the activity of public associations, as well as interference by public associations in the activity of state bodies and officials, is impermissible.

Article 59
Trade unions shall express and protect the socio-economic rights and interests of the working people. Membership in trade unions is optional.

Article 60
Political parties shall express the political will of various sections and groups of the population, and through their democratically elected representatives shall participate in the formation of state authority. Political parties shall submit public reports on their financial sources to the Oliy Majlis or their plenipotentiary body in a prescribed manner.

Article 61
Religious organisations and associations shall be separated from the state and be equal before law. The state shall not interfere with the activity of religious associations.

Article 62
Public associations may be dissolved or banned, or subject to restricted activity solely by the sentence of a court.

Chapter 14 – Family

Article 63
The family is the primary unit of society and shall have the right to state and societal protection.
Marriage shall be based on the willing consent and equality of both parties.

Article 64
Parents shall be obliged to support and care for their children until the latter are of age.
The state and society shall support, care for and educate orphaned children, as well as children deprived of parental guardianship, and encourage charity in their favour.

Article 65
All children shall be equal before the law regardless of their origin and the civic status of their parents.
Motherhood and childhood shall be protected by the state.

Article 66
Able-bodied children who are of age shall be obliged to care for their parents.

Chapter 15 – Mass media

Article 67

The mass media shall be free and act in accordance with the law. They shall bear responsibility for trustworthiness of information in a prescribed manner. Censorship is impermissible.

Part 4 – *Administrative and territorial structure and state system*

Chapter 16 – Administrative and territorial structure of the Republic of Uzbekistan

Article 68

The Republic of Uzbekistan shall consist of regions, districts, cities, towns, settlements, kishlaks and all villages in Uzbekistan and the Republic of Karakalpakstan.

Article 69

Any alteration of the boundaries of the Republic of Karakalpakstan, regions, the city of Tashkent, as well as the formation and annulment of regions, cities, towns and districts shall be sanctioned by the Oliy Majlis of the Republic of Uzbekistan.

Chapter 17 – Republic of Karakalpakstan

Article 70

The sovereign Republic of Karakalpakstan is part of the Republic of Uzbekistan.
The sovereignty of the Republic of Karakalpakstan shall be protected by the Republic of Uzbekistan.

Article 71

The Republic of Karakalpakstan shall have its own Constitution.
The Constitution of the Republic of Karakalpakstan must be in accordance with the Constitution of the Republic of Uzbekistan.

Article 72

The laws of the Republic of Uzbekistan shall be binding on the territory of the Republic of Karakalpakstan.

Article 73

The territory and boundaries of the Republic of Karakalpakstan may not be altered without the consent of Karakalpakstan. The Republic of Karakalpakstan shall be independent in determining its administrative and territorial structure.

Article 74

The Republic of Karakalpakstan shall have the right to secede from the Republic of Uzbekistan on the basis of a nation-wide referendum held by the people of Karakalpakstan.

Article 75
The relationship between the Republic of Uzbekistan and the Republic of Karakalpakstan, within the framework of the Constitution of the Republic of Uzbekistan, shall be regulated by treaties and agreements concluded by the Republic of Uzbekistan and the Republic of Karakalpakstan.
Any disputes between the Republic of Uzbekistan and the Republic of Karakalpakstan shall be settled by the way of reconciliation.

Part 5 – Organisation of State Authority
Chapter 18 – Oliy Majlis of the Republic of Uzbekistan

Article 76
The highest state representative body is the Oliy Majlis (the Supreme Assembly) of the Republic of Uzbekistan. This body exercises legislative power.

Article 77
The Oliy Majlis of the Republic of Uzbekistan shall consist of 150 deputies, elected by territorial constituencies on a multi-party basis for a term of five years.
All citizens of the Republic of Uzbekistan who have reached the age of 25 by election day shall be eligible for election to the Oliy Majlis of the Republic of Uzbekistan.
Requirements to candidates shall be determined by law.

Article 78
The exclusive powers of the Oliy Majlis of the Republic of Uzbekistan shall include:
    1. the adoption and amending of the Constitution of the Republic of Uzbekistan;
    2. enactment and amending of the Constitution of the Republic of Uzbekistan;
    3. determination of the guidelines of home and foreign policies of the Republic of Uzbekistan and approval of long-term projects;
    4. determination of the structure and powers of the legislative, executive and judicial branches of the Republic of Uzbekistan;
    5. admission of new states into the Republic of Uzbekistan and approval of their decisions to secede from the Republic of Uzbekistan;
    6. legislative regulation of customs, as well as of the currency and credit systems;
    7. legislative regulation of the administrative and territorial structure, and alteration of frontiers of the Republic of Uzbekistan;
    8. approval of the budget of the Republic of Uzbekistan submitted by the Cabinet of Ministers, and control over its execution; determination of taxes and other compulsory payments;
    9. scheduling elections to the Oliy Majlis of the Republic of Uzbekistan and local representative bodies, and formation of the Central Election Committee;
    10. setting the date of elections for the President of the Republic of Uzbekistan on completion of his term of office;

11. election of the Chairman and Vice-Chairman of the Oliy Majlis of the Republic of Uzbekistan;

12. election of the Constitutional Court of the Republic of Uzbekistan;

13. election of the Supreme Court of the Republic of Uzbekistan;

14. election of the Higher Arbitration Court of the Republic of Uzbekistan;

15. appointment and dismissal of the Chairman of the State Committee for the Protection of Nature of the Republic of Uzbekistan upon the nomination of the President of the Republic of Uzbekistan;

16. ratification of the decrees of the President of the Republic of Uzbekistan on the appointment and removal of the Prime Minister, the First Deputy Prime Minister, the Deputy Prime Ministers and the members of the Cabinet of Ministers;

17. ratification of the decrees of the President of the Republic of Uzbekistan on the appointment and removal of the Procurator-General of the Republic of Uzbekistan and his Deputies;

18. appointment and removal of the Chairman of the Board of the Central Bank of the Republic of Uzbekistan upon the nomination of the President of the Republic of Uzbekistan;

19. ratification of the decrees of the President of the Republic of Uzbekistan on the formation and abolition of ministries, state committees and other bodies of state administration;

20. ratification of the decrees of the President of the Republic of Uzbekistan on general and partial mobilisation, and on the declaration, prolongation and discontinuance of a state of emergency;

21. ratification and denouncement of international treaties and agreements;

22. institution of state awards and honorary titles;

23. formation, annulment and renaming of districts, towns, cities and regions and alteration of their boundaries;

24. execution of other powers defined by the present Constitution.

Article 79
A session of the Oliy Majlis shall be legally qualified if it is attended by at least two-thrids of the total number of the deputies.

Article 80
The President of the Republic of Uzbekistan, the Prime Minister, and the members of the Cabinet of Ministers, the Chairmen of the Constitutional Court, the Supreme Court and the Higher Arbitration Court, the Procurator-General of the Republic and the Chairman of the Board of the Central Bank shall have the right to attend the sessions of the Oliy Majlis.

Article 81
Upon completion of its term, the Oliy Majlis of the Republic of Uzbekistan shall retain its powers until the newly-elected Oliy Majlis is convened.
The first session of the newly-elected Oliy Majlis of the Republic of Uzbekistan shall be convened by the Central Electoral Committee within two months of the elections.

Article 82
The right to initiate legislation in the Oliy Majlis of the Republic of Uzbekistan is vested in the President of the Republic of Uzbekistan, the Republic of Karakalpakstan through the highest body of state authority, the deputies of the Oliy Majlis of the Republic of Uzbekistan, the Cabinet of Ministers of the Republic of Uzbekistan, the Constitutional Court, the Supreme Court, the Higher Arbitration Court and the Procurator-General of the Republic of Uzbekistan.

Article 83
The Oliy Majlis of the Republic of Uzbekistan shall pass laws, decisions and other acts. Any law shall be adopted when it is passed by a majority of the total voting power of the deputies of the Oliy Majlis.
Promulgation of the laws and other normative acts shall be a compulsory condition for their enforcement.

Article 84
The Chairman and the Vice-Chairmen of the Oliy Majlis shall be elected from among the deputies of the Oliy Majlis of the Republic of Uzbekistan by secret ballot.
The Chairman and the Vice-Chairmen of the Oliy Majlis shall present annual reports to the Oliy Majlis.
One of the Vice-Chairmen of the Oliy Majlis, a deputy of the Oliy Majlis of the Republic of Uzbekistan, shall represent Karakalpakstan.
The Chairman and the Vice-Chairmen of the Oliy Majlis of the Republic of Uzbekistan shall be elected for the same term as the Oliy Majlis.
No-one may be elected Chairman of the Oliy Majlis of the Republic of Uzbekistan for more than two consecutive terms.
The Chairman of the Oliy Majlis of the Republic of Uzbekistan may be recalled before completion of his term of office by the decision of the Oliy Majlis of the Republic of Uzbekistan approved by more than two-thirds of the deputies of the Oliy Majlis of the Republic of Uzbekistan by secret ballot.

Article 85
The Chairman of the Oliy Majlis of the Republic of Uzbekistan shall:
    1.   exercise the general direction over a preliminary review of matters to be submitted to the Oliy Majlis;
    2.   convene the sessions of the Oliy Majlis and draft their agenda together with the Chairmen of the committees and commissions;
    3.   preside at the sessions of the Oliy Majlis;
    4.   co-ordinate the work of the committees and commissions of the Oliy Majlis;
    5.   organise control over the execution of the laws and the decisions passed by the Oliy Majlis;
    6.   direct interparliamentary relations and the work of the groups connected with international parliamentary organisations;
    7.   nominate candidates for the posts of the Vice-Chairmen of the Oliy Majlis and the Chairmen of the committees and commissions of the Oliy Majlis;

8. alter the composition of the committees and commissions and submit them for confirmation to the Oliy Majlis on the proposal of the Chairmen of the committees and commissions;

9. direct the work of the organs of the press of the Oliy Majlis;

10. approve the rules and the editorial staff of the organs of the press of the Oliy Majlis and their expense budgets;

11. appoint and dismiss the editors of the organs of the press of the Oliy Majlis;

12. approve the estimated allowances of the deputies and the administrative expenses of the Oliy Majlis;

13. sign the resolutions passed by the Oliy Majlis of the Republic of Uzbekistan.

The Chairman of the Oliy Majlis of the Republic of Uzbekistan shall issue ordinances.

Article 86

The Oliy Majlis shall elect committees and commissions to draft laws, conduct preliminary review of matters to be submitted to the Oliy Majlis, and control the execution of the laws and other decisions passed by the Oliy Majlis of the Republic of Uzbekistan.

In the event of necessity, the Oliy Majlis shall form deputies, auditing and other commissions which shall function on a permanent or temporary basis.

Article 87

The expenses of the deputies connected with their work for the Oliy Majlis shall be reimbursed in prescribed manner. The deputies working for the Oliy Majlis on a permanent basis may not hold any other paid posts, nor engage in commercial activity during their term of office.

Article 88

Deputies of the Oliy Majlis shall have the right of immunity. They may not be prosecuted, arrested or incur a court-imposed administrative penalty without the sanction of the Oliy Majlis.

Chapter 19 – The President of the Republic of Uzbekistan

Article 89

The President of the Republic of Uzbekistan is head of state and executive authority in the Republic of Uzbekistan. The President of the Republic of Uzbekistan simultaneously serves as Chairman of the Cabinet of Ministers.

Article 90

Any citizen of the Republic of Uzbekistan who has reached the age of 35, is in full command of the state language and has permanently resided in Uzbekistan for at least 10 years, immediately preceding the elections, shall be eligible for the post of President of the Republic of Uzbekistan. A person may not be elected to the office of President of the Republic of Uzbekistan for more than two consecutive terms.

The President of the Republic of Uzbekistan shall be elected for a term of five years. He shall be elected by citizens of the Republic of Uzbekistan on the basis of universal, equal and direct suffrage by secret ballot. The procedure for electing President shall be specified by the electoral law of the Republic of Uzbekistan.

Article 91
During his term of office, the President may not hold any other paid post, serve as a deputy of a representative body or engage in commercial activity. The President shall enjoy personal immunity and protection under the law.

Article 92
The President shall be regarded as having assumed office upon taking the following oath at a session of the Oliy Majlis:
"I do solemnly swear to faithfully serve the people of Uzbekistan, to strictly comply with the Constitution and the laws of the Republic, to guarantee the rights and freedoms of its citizens, and to conscientiously perform the duties of the President of the Republic of Uzbekistan".

Article 93
The President of the Republic of Uzbekistan shall:
1. guarantee the rights and freedoms of citizens and observance of the Constitution and the laws of the Republic of Uzbekistan;
2. protect the sovereignty, security and territorial integrity of the Republic of Uzbekistan, and implement the decisions regarding its national-state structure;
3. represent the Republic of Uzbekistan in domestic matters and in international relations;
4. conduct negotiations, sign treaties and agreements on behalf of the Republic of Uzbekistan, and ensure the observance of the treaties and agreements signed by the Republic and the fulfilment of its commitments;
5. receive letters of credence and recall from diplomats and other representatives accredited to him;
6. appoint and recall diplomats and other representatives of the Republic of Uzbekistan to foreign states;
7. present annual reports to the Oliy Majlis on the domestic and international situation;
8. form the administration and lead it, ensure interaction between the highest levels of state authority and administration, set up and dissolve ministries, state committees and other bodies of administration of the Republic of Uzbekistan, with subsequent confirmation by the Oliy Majlis;
9. appoint and dismiss the Prime Minister, his First Deputy, the Deputy Prime Minister, the Deputy Prime Ministers, the members of the Cabinet of Ministers of the Republic of Uzbekistan, the Procurator-General of the Republic of Uzbekistan and his Deputies; with subsequent confirmation by the Oliy Majlis;
10. present to the Oliy Majlis of the Republic of Uzbekistan his nominees for the posts of Chairman and members of the Constitutional Court, the Supreme Court, and the Higher Economic Court, as well as the Chairman of the Board of the Central Bank of the Republic of Uzbekistan, and the

Chairman of the State Committee for the Protection of Nature of the Republic of Uzbekistan;

11. appoint and dismiss judges of regional, district, city and arbitration courts;

12. appoint and dismiss khokims (heads of administrations) of regions and the city of Tashkent with subsequent confirmation by relevant Soviets of People's Deputies; the President shall have the right to dismiss any khokim of a district or a city, should the latter violate the Constitution or the laws, or perform an act discrediting the honour and dignity of a khokim;

13. suspend and repeal any acts passed by the bodies of state administration or khokims;

14. sign the laws of the Republic of Uzbekistan. The President may refer any law, with his own amendments, to the Oliy Majlis for additional consideration and vote. Should the Oliy Majlis confirm its earlier decision by a majority of two-thirds of its total voting power, the President shall sign the law;

15. have the right to proclaim a state of emergency throughout the Republic of Uzbekistan or in a particular locality in cases of emergency (such as a real outside threat, mass disturbances, major catastrophes, natural calamities or epidemics), in the interests of people's security. The President shall submit his decision to the Oliy Majlis of the Republic of Uzbekistan for confirmation within three days. The terms and the procedure for the imposition of the state of emergency shall be specified by law;

16. serve as the Supreme Commander-in-Chief of the Armed Forces of the Republic and is empowered to appoint and dismiss the high command of the Armed Forces and confer top military ranks;

17. proclaim a state of war in the event of an armed attack on the Republic of Uzbekistan or when it is necessary to meet international obligations relating to mutual defence against aggression, and submit the decision to the Oliy Majlis of the Republic of Uzbekistan for confirmation;

18. award orders, medals and certificates of honour of the Republic of Uzbekistan, and confer qualification and honorary titles of the Republic of Uzbekistan;

19. rule on matters of citizenship of the Republic of Uzbekistan and on granting political asylum;

20. issue acts of amnesty and grant pardon to citizens convicted by the courts of the Republic of Uzbekistan;

21. form the national security and state control services, appoint and dismiss their heads, and exercise other powers vested in him.
The President shall not have the right to transfer his powers to a state body or official.

Article 94
The President of the Republic of Uzbekistan shall issue decrees, enactments and ordinances binding on the entire territory of the Republic on the basis of and for enforcement of the Constitution and the laws of the Republic of Uzbekistan.

Article 95
Should any insurmountable differences arise between the deputies of the Oliy Majlis, jeopardising its normal functioning, or should it repeatedly make

decisions in opposition to the Constitution, the Oliy Majlis may be dissolved by a decision of the President, sanctioned by the Constitutional Court. In the event of the dissolution of the Oliy Majlis, elections shall be held within three months. The Oliy Majlis may not be dissolved during a state of emergency.

Article 96

Should the President of the Republic of Uzbekistan fail to perform his duties due to poor health, confirmed by a certificate of a State Medical Commission formed by the Oliy Majlis, an emergency session of the Oliy Majlis shall be held within ten days. This session shall elect an acting President of the Republic of Uzbekistan from among its deputies for a term of not more than three months. In this case, the general elections of the President of the Republic of Uzbekistan shall be held within three months.

Article 97

Upon completion of his term of office, the President shall be a lifetime member of the Constitutional Court.

Chapter 20 – Cabinet of Ministers

Article 98

The Cabinet of Ministers shall be formed by the President of the Republic of Uzbekistan and approved by the Oliy Majlis.

The head of government of the Republic of Karakalpakstan shall be an *ex officio* member of the Cabinet of Ministers.

The Cabinet of Ministers shall provide guidance for the economic, social and cultural development of the Republic of Uzbekistan. It should also be responsible for the execution of the laws and other decisions of the Oliy Majlis, as well as of the decrees and other enactments issued by the President of the Republic of Uzbekistan.

The Cabinet of Ministers shall issue enactments and ordinances in accordance with the current legislation. This shall be binding on all bodies of administration, enterprises, institutions, organisations, officials and citizens throughout the Republic of Uzbekistan.

The Cabinet of Ministers shall tender its resignation to the newly elected Oliy Majlis.

The procedure for the work of the Cabinet of Ministers and its powers shall be defined by law.

Chapter 21 – Fundamental principles of local bodies of state authority

Article 99

The Soviets of People's Deputies led by khokims are the representative bodies of authority in regions, districts, cities and towns, except in towns subordinate to district centres, and city districts. They shall act upon all matters within their authority, in accordance with the interests of the state and citizens.

Article 100
The local authorities shall:
ensure the observance of laws, maintain law and order, and ensure the security of citizens;
direct the economic, social and cultural development within their territories;
propose and implement the local budget, determine the local taxes and fees, and propose non-budget funds;
direct the municipal economy;
protect the environment;
ensure the registration of civil status acts;
pass normative acts and exercise other powers in conformity with the Constitution and the legislation of the Republic of Uzbekistan.

Article 101
The local authorities shall enforce the laws of the Republic of Uzbekistan, the decrees of the President and the decisions of the higher bodies of state authority. They shall also direct the work of the subordinate Soviets of People's Deputies and participate in the discussion of national and local matters. The decisions of the higher bodies on matters within their authority shall be binding on the subordinate bodies.
The term of office of the Soviets of People's Deputies and khokims is five years.

Article 102
The khokims of regions, districts, cities and towns shall serve as heads of both representative and executive authorities of their respective territories.
The khokim of the region and city of Tashkent shall be appointed and dismissed by the President with subsequent confirmation by the appropriate Soviet of People's Deputies.
The khokims of districts, cities and towns shall be appointed and dismissed by the khokim of the appropriate region, with subsequent confirmation by the appropriate Soviet of People's Deputies.
The khokims of city districts shall be appointed and dismissed by the khokim of the city, with subsequent confirmation by the city Soviet of People's Deputies.
The khokims of towns subordinate to district centres shall be appointed and dismissed by the khokim of the district with subsequent confirmation by the district Soviet of People's Deputies.

Article 103
The khokims of regions, districts, cities and towns shall exercise their powers in accordance with the principle of one-person management, and shall bear personal responsibility for the decisions and the work of the bodies they lead. Organisation of the work and the powers of khokims and local Soviets of People's Deputies, as well as the procedure for elections to the local Soviets of People's Deputies shall be specified by law.

Article 104
The khokim shall make decisions within his vested powers which are binding on all enterprises, institutions, organisations, associations, officials, and citizens on the relevant territory.

Article 105
Residents of settlements, *kishlaks* and *auls* (villages), as well as of residential neighbourhoods (*makhallyas*) in cities, towns, settlements and villages shall decide all local matters at general meetings. These local self-governing bodies shall elect a Chairman (*aksakal*) and his advisers for a term of two and a half years.
The procedure for elections, organisation of the work and the powers of self-governing bodies shall be specified by law.

Chapter 22 – Judicial authority in the Republic of Uzbekistan

Article 106
The judicial authority in the Republic of Uzbekistan shall function independently from the legislative and executive branches, political parties and public organisations.

Article 107
The judicial system in the Republic of Uzbekistan shall consist of the Constitutional Court of the Republic, the Supreme Court, the Higher Economic Court of the Republic of Uzbekistan, along with the Supreme Court, and the Arbitration Court of the Republic of Karakalpakstan. These courts shall be elected for a term of five years. The judicial branch also includes regional, district, town, city, Tashkent city courts and arbitration courts appointed for a term of five years.
The organisation and procedure for the operation of the courts shall be specified by law.
The formation of extraordinary courts shall be inadmissible.

Article 108
The Constitutional Court of the Republic of Uzbekistan shall hear cases relating to the constitutionality of acts passed by the legislative and executive branches.
The Constitutional Court shall be elected from political and legal scholars and shall consist of a Chairman, Vice-Chairman and judges including a representative of the Republic of Karakalpakstan.
No member of the Constitutional Court, including the Chairman, shall have the right to serve simultaneously as a deputy. The Chairman and the members of the Constitutional Court may not belong to any political parties or movements, nor hold any other paid posts.
The judges of the Constitutional Court shall have the right of immunity.
The judges of the Constitutional Court shall be independent in their work and subject solely to the Constitution of the Republic of Uzbekistan.

Article 109
The Constitutional Court of the Republic of Uzbekistan shall:
    1.   judge the constitutionality of the laws of the Republic of Uzbekistan and other acts passed by the Oliy Majlis of the Republic of Uzbekistan, the decrees issued by the President of the Republic of Uzbekistan, the enactments

of the government and the ordinances of local authorities, as well as obligations of the Republic of Uzbekistan under interstate treaties and other documents;

2. ensure the conformity of the constitutionality of the Constitution and laws of the Republic of Karakalpakstan to the Constitution and laws of the Republic of Uzbekistan;

3. interpret the Constitution and the laws of the Republic of Uzbekistan;

4. hear other cases coming within its authority under the Constitution and the laws of the Republic of Uzbekistan.

The judgements of the Constitutional Court shall take effect upon publication. They shall be final and shall not be subject to appeal.

The organisation and procedure of the Constitutional Court shall be specified by law.

Article 110

The Supreme Court of the Republic of Uzbekistan shall be the highest judicial body of civil, criminal and administrative law.

The rulings of the Supreme Court shall be final and binding throughout the Republic of Uzbekistan.

The Supreme Court of the Republic of Uzbekistan shall have the right to supervise the administration of justice by the Supreme Court of the Republic of Karakalpakstan, as well as by regional, city, town and district courts.

Article 111

Any economic and management disputes that may arise between entrepreneurs, enterprises, institutions and organisations based on different forms of ownership shall be settled by the Higher Arbitration Court and other arbitration courts within their authority.

Article 112

Judges shall be independent and subject solely to the law. Any interference in the work of judges in administering the law shall be inadmissible and punishable by law.

The immunity of judges shall be guaranteed by law.

The Chairmen and the members of the Supreme Court and the Higher Arbitration Court may not be deputies of the Oliy Majlis of the Republic of Uzbekistan.

Judges, including district ones, may not belong to any political parties or movements, nor hold any other paid posts.

Before the completion of his term of office, a judge may be removed from his post only on grounds specified by law.

Article 113

Legal proceedings in all courts shall be open to the public. Hearings in camera shall be only allowed in cases prescribed by law.

Article 114

All court verdicts shall be binding on state bodies, public associations, enterprises, institutions, organisations, officials and citizens.

Article 115
All legal proceedings in the Republic of Uzbekistan shall be conducted in Uzbek, Karakalpak, or in the language spoken by the majority of the people in the locality. Any person participating in court proceedings who does not know the language in which they are being conducted shall have the following right to be fully acquainted with the materials in the case, to have the services of an interpreter during the proceedings, and to address the court in his native language.

Article 116
Any defendant shall be guaranteed legal assistance at any stage of the investigation and judicial proceedings. Legal assistance to citizens, enterprises, institutions and organisations shall be given by the College of Barristers. The organisation and procedure of the College of Barristers shall be specified by law.

Chapter 23 – Electoral system

Article 117
All citizens of the Republic of Uzbekistan are guaranteed the equal right to vote. Every citizen shall have only one vote. Any citizen shall be eligible for election to public office.
The President and representative bodies of authority in the Republic of Uzbekistan shall be elected on the basis of universal, equal and direct suffrage by secret ballot. All citizens of the Republic of Uzbekistan over the age of 18 shall be eligible to vote.
Citizens who have been legally certified as insane, as well as persons in prison may neither vote nor be eligible for election. Any other direct or indirect infringement on citizens' voting rights is inadmissible.
A citizen of the Republic of Uzbekistan may not simultaneously be elected to more than two representative bodies.
The electoral procedure shall be specified by law.

Chapter 24 – Procurator's Office

Article 118
The Procurator-General of the Republic of Uzbekistan and the procurator subordinate to him shall supervise the strict and uniform observance of the laws on the territory of the Republic of Uzbekistan.

Article 119
The Procurator-General of the Republic of Uzbekistan shall direct the centralised system of agencies of the procurator's office.
The Procurator of the Republic of Karakalpakstan shall be appointed by the highest representative body of the Republic of Karakalpakstan and subject to confirmation by the Procurator-General of the Republic of Uzbekistan.
The procurators of regions, districts, cities and towns shall be appointed by the Procurator-General of the Republic of Uzbekistan.
The term of office shall be five years for the Procurator-General of the Republic of Uzbekistan, the Procurator of the Republic of Karakalpakstan and procurators of regions, districts, cities and towns.

Article 120

The agencies of the Procurator's Office of the Republic of Uzbekistan shall exercise their power independently of any state bodies, public association and officials, and shall be subject solely to the law.

While in office procurators shall suspend their membership of political parties and any other public associations pursuing political goals.

Organisation, powers and procedure for the agencies of the Procurator's Office shall be specified by law.

Article 121

On the territory of the Republic of Uzbekistan it is prohibited to set up and run any private co-operative or other non-governmental agencies or their branches, independently conducting any operational work, investigations, inquiries or any other functions connected with combating crime.

The law enforcement agencies may enlist the assistance of public associations and citizens to safeguard law and order, as well as the rights and freedoms of citizens.

Chapter 25 – Finance and crediting

Article 122

The Republic of Uzbekistan shall have independent financial, monetary and credit systems.

The state budget of Uzbekistan shall consist of the national budget, the budget of the Republic of Karakalpakstan and local budgets.

Article 123

The Republic of Uzbekistan shall have a single taxation system. The right to determine taxes shall belong to the Oliy Majlis of the Republic of Uzbekistan.

Article 124

The banking system of the Republic of Uzbekistan shall be directed by the Central Bank of the Republic.

Chapter 26 – Defence and Security

Article 125

The armed forces of the Republic of Uzbekistan shall be formed to defend the state sovereignty and territorial integrity of the Republic of Uzbekistan, as well as the peaceful life and security of its citizens.

The structure and organisation of the armed forces shall be specified by law.

Article 126

The Republic of Uzbekistan shall maintain the armed forces at a level of reasonable adequacy to ensure its security.

Part 6 – Procedure for amending the Constitution

Article 127

The Constitution of the Republic of Uzbekistan shall be amended by laws, passed by at least two-thirds of the deputies of the Oliy Majlis of the Republic.

Article 128

The Oliy Majlis of the Republic of Uzbekistan may pass a law altering or amending the Constitution within six months of submission of the relevant proposal, with due regard for its nation-wide discussion. Should the Oliy Majlis of the Republic of Uzbekistan reject an amendment to the Constitution, a repeated proposal may not be submitted for one year.

Bibliographical suggestions

General

Berton-Hogge R., Crosnier M.A. (eds.), "Ex-URSS: les Etats du divorce - édition 1993", *Notes et études documentaires,* No. 4982, 17, p. 198, 1993.

Berton-Hogge R., Crosnier M.A. (eds.), "Ukraine, Biélorussie, Russie: trois Etats en construction - Ex-URSS, édition 1995" (série d'articles), *Notes et études documentaires,* No. 5022, 17, 1995.

Berton-Hogge R., Crosnier M.A. (eds.), "Arménie, Azerbaïdjan, Géorgie: l'an V des indépendances - La Russie: 1995-1996 - Ex-URSS, édition 1996" (série d'articles), *Notes et études documentaires,* No. 5040-41, 15-16, 1996.

Brown A., *The Gorbachev factor,* Oxford University Publishers, Oxford, 1996.

Carothers T., "Democracy without illusions", *Foreign Affairs,* Vol. 76, No. 1, p. 85-99, January-February 1997.

Chinn J., Kaiser R., *Russians as the new minority: ethnicity and nationalism in the Soviet successor states,* Westview Publishers, Boulder, U.S.A., 1996.

Dawisha K., Parrott B., *Russia and the new states of Eurasia: the political upheaval,* Cambridge University Publishers, Cambridge, 1995.

Eastern Europe and the Commonwealth of Independent States 1997, Europa Publications, London, 1996.

European Commission for Democracy through Law, Annual *report of activities for 1994,* Council of Europe, Strasbourg.

European Commission for Democracy through Law, *Annual report of activities for 1995,* Council of Europe, Strasbourg.

European Commission for Democracy through Law, Annual *report of activities for 1996,* Council of Europe, Strasbourg.

European Commission for Democracy through Law, *Bulletin on constitutional case-law,* Council of Europe, Strasbourg (quarterly).

Fowkes B., *The disintegration of the Soviet Union: a study in the rise and triumph of nationalism,* Macmillan, London, 1997.

Mark D.E., "Eurasia letter: Russia and the new Transcaucasus", *Foreign Policy, Winter* 1996-1997, No. 105, pp. 141-159, 1997.

Mullerson R., *International law, rights and politics: developments in Eastern Europe and the CIS,* Routledge, London, 1994.

Soberg Shugart M., "Presidents and parliaments: executive-legislative relations in post-communist Europe", *Transition,* Vol. 2 (13-12-1996), No. 25, pp. 6-11, 1996.

Vereshcetin V.S., "New constitutions and the old problem of relationship between international law and national law", *European Journal of International Law,* Vol. 7 (1996), No. 1, pp. 29-41, 1996.

Specific country studies

Armenia

Fuller E., "Armenia's constitutional debate", *RFE/RL research report,* Vol. 3, No. 21, p. 6, 27 May 1994.

Belarus

European Commission for Democracy through Law, *Opinion on the amendments and addenda to the Constitution of the Republic of Belarus as proposed by: a. The President of the Republic, b. The agrarian and communist groups of parliamentarians,* 18 November 1996.

Markus U., "Belarus: a new Parliament, despite the President", *Transition,* Vol. 2, No. 1, p. 62, 12 January 1996.

Sanford G., "Belarus on the road to nationhood", *Survival,* Vol. 38, No. 1, p. 131, Spring 1996.

Georgia

The Constitution of Georgia, *Review of Central and East European Law,* Vol. 22, No. 1, p. 89, 1996.

The new Constitution of Georgia, *Review of Central and East European Law,* Vol. 22, No. 1, p. 9, 1996.

Intskirveli G.Z., The Constitution of independent Georgia, *Review of Central and East European Law,* Vol. 22, No. 1, p. 1, 1996.

Pinelli C., "Functions of a Constitutional Court, and elections of judges", Report for the European Commission for Democracy through Law, 26 November 1996.

Schmid U., "Georgia after the fall", *Swiss review of world affairs,* No. 7, p. 7, 1993.

Kazakhstan

Dave B., "Kazakhstan: a new parliament consolidates presidential authority", *Transition,* Vol. 2, No. 6, p. 33, 22 March 1996.

Trutanow I., "Le Kazakhstan, un membre très actif de la CEI", *Le Courrier des pays de l'Est,* No. 397-398, p. 129, 1995.

Kyrghyzstan

Giroux A., "Les Etats d'Asie centrale face à l'indépendance: Ouzbékistan, Republique Kirghize, Tadjikistan, Turkménistan", *Le Courrier des pays de l'Est,* No. 388, p. 3, 1994.

Moldova

Jungwiert K., M.A. Nowicki, "Rapport sur la législation de la République de Moldova", *Revue universelle des droits de l'homme,* Vol. 6, No. 9-10, p. 376, 22 décembre 1994.

Jungwiert K., Nowicki M.A., "Report on the legislation on the Republic of Moldova", *Human rights law journal,* Vol. 15, No. 8-10, p. 383, 30 November 1994.

Ionescu D., Munteanu I., "Moldova: likely presidential rivals gear up for elections", *Transition,* Vol. 2, No. 2, p. 50, 26 January 1996.

Mongolia

La Constitution de la Mongolie, *Informations constitutionnelles et parlementaires,* Année 43, Sér. 3, No. 165, p. 75, 1993.

Reinhardt M., "Verfassungsrechtliche Auswirkungen der Perestroika in der ausseren Mongolei", *Recht in Ost und West,* Jahrg. 37, Heft 1, p. 6, 1993.

Russia

Beliaev S.A., "The evolution in constitutional debates in Russia in 1992-1993: a comparative review", *Review of Central and East European Law,* Vol. 20, No. 3, p. 305, 1994.

Berg van den G.P., "Human rights in the legislation and the draft constitution of the Russian Federation", *Review of Central and East European Law,* Vol. 18, No. 3 (1992), p. 197-251, 1992.

Bernhardt E. *et al.,* "Rapport sur la conformité de l'ordre juridique de la Fédération de Russie avec les normes du Conseil de l'Europe", *Revue universelle des droits de l'homme,* Vol. 6, No. 9-10, p. 325, 1994.

Berton-Hogge R. (ed.), "Russie 1993-1996: une fragile démocratisation", *Problèmes politiques et sociaux,* No. 772, p. 79, 13 septembre 1996.

Bordato E., *La nuova costituzione russa,* Edizioni Osiride, Rovereto, 1994.

Busygina I.M., "Das Institut der Vertreter des Präsidenten in Russland: Probleme des Werdegangs und Entwicklungsperspektiven", *Osteuropa,* Jahrg. 46, Heft 6, p. 664, 1996.

Clem R.S., Craumer P.R., "The geography of the Russian 1995 parliamentary election: continuity, change, and correlates", *Post-Soviet geography,* Vol. 36, No. 10, p. 587, 1995.

Coulloudon V., "La Russie entre deux élections?", *Politique internationale,* No. 70, p. 19, 1995-96.

Fraisseix P., "La Constitution russe du 12 décembre 1993: vers un nouvel état de droit?", *Revue du droit public et de la science politique en France et à l'étranger,* T. 110, No. 6, p. 1769, 1994.

Gockeritz W., "Präsidentenwahlen in der Russischen Föderation (Teil 1)", *Recht in Ost und West,* Jahrg. 40, Heft 5, p. 168, 1996.

Hahn J.W., ed., *Democratization in Russia: the development of legislative institutions,* Sharpe, New York, 1996.

Hartwig M., "Verfassungsgerichtsbarkeit in Russland: der dritte Anlauf", *Europäische Grundrechte Zeitschrift,* Jahrg. 23, Heft 7-8, p. 177-191, 219-233, 30 April 1996.

Henderson J., "All power to the President", *Russia and the successor states briefing service,* Vol. 2, No. 6, p. 3, 1994.

Henderson J., "Election time in Russia", *European public law,* Vol. 2, Issue 1, p. 63, 1996.

Henderson J., "The Russian constitutional court", *European public law,* Vol. 1, Issue 4, p. 508, 1995.

Kieniewicz J., "La Rusia de los destinos inciertos", *Política exterior,* Vol. 10, No. 53, p. 41, 1996.

Korkeakivi A., "A modern day czar?: presidential power and human rights in the Russian Federation", *Journal of constitutional law in Eastern and Central Europe,* Vol. 2, No. 1, p. 76, 1995.

Koudryavtsev Y., "The national rules: Russian Federation", Report for the European Commission for Democracy through Law, 27 September 1996.

Lesage M., "La Constitution russe du 12 décembre 1993 et les six premiers mois du système politique", *Revue du droit public et de la science politique en France et à l'étranger,* T. 110, No. 6, p. 1735, 1994.

Lesage M., "L'organisation du pouvoir sous Boris Eltsine", *Le Courrier des pays de l'Est,* No. 404, p. 5, 1995.

Mendras M., "Elections présidentielle et crise de succession", *Pouvoirs,* No. 80, p. 133, 1997.

Mendras M., "Lettre de Russie: le suffrage universel dans la tourmente", *Pouvoirs,* No. 77, p. 219, 1996.

Orttung R.W., "Russian elections: battling over electoral laws", *Transition,* Vol. 1, No. 15, p. 32, 25 August 1995.

"Russia's struggle: can they make a democracy?", *The Economist,* Vol. 329, No. 7831, p. 21, 2 October 1993.

"Russian presidential election" (Collection of articles), *Transition,* Vol. 2, No. 11, pp. 5-22, 31 May 1996.

Schneider E., "Russlands Präsident Boris Jelzin", *Osteuropa,* Jahrg. 42, Heft 6, p. 501, 1992.

Schweisfurth T., "Die Verfassung Russland vom 12. Dezember 1993: Entstehungsgeschichte und Grundzuge", *Europäische Grundrechte Zeitschrift,* Jahrg. 21, Heft 19-20, pp. 473-491, 519-533, 23 November 1994.

Slater W., "Russia: the return of authoritarian government?", *RFE/RL research report,* Vol. 3, No. 1, p. 22, 7 January 1994.

Tolz V., "Russia's new parliament and Yeltsin: co-operation prospects", *RFE/RL research report,* Vol. 3, No. 5, p. 1, 4 February 1994.

Vitrouk N., "The role of the constitutional court in the economic field: the role of the constitutional court in the transition to a market economy", Report for the European Commission for Democracy through Law, 4 May 1993.

Westen K., "Die Verfassung der Russischen Föderation", *Osteuropa,* Jahrg. 44, Heft 9, p. 809, 1994.

Zorgbibe C., "Moscou: d'un coup d'Etat à l'autre", *Revue politique et parlementaire,* Année 95, No. 967, p. 9, 1993.

Tadjikistan

Brown B., "Tajikistan to restore presidency", *RFE/RL research report,* Vol. 3, No. 31, p. 11, 12 August 1994.

Giroux A., "Les Etats d'Asie centrale face à l'indépendance: Ouzbékistan, Republique Kirghize, Tadjikistan, Turkménistan", *Le Courrier des pays de l'Est,* No. 388, p. 3, 1994.

Pannier B., "Tajikistan: just a peace of paper", *Transition,* Vol. 2, No. 18, p. 42, 6 September 1996.

Turkmenistan

Panico C.J., "Turkmenistan unaffected by the winds of democratic change", *RFE/RL research report*, Vol. 2, No. 4, p. 6, 22 January 1993.

Ukraine

Bojcun M., "The Ukrainian parliamentary elections in March-April 1994", *Europe-Asia studies*, Vol. 47, No. 2, p. 229, 1995.

European Commission for Democracy through Law, *Opinion on the present constitutional situation in Ukraine following the adoption of the constitutional agreement between the Supreme Rada of Ukraine and the President of Ukraine*, 1 October 1995.

Markov I., "The role of the president in the Ukrainian political system", *RFE/RL research report*, Vol. 2, No. 48, p. 31, 3 December 1993.

Markus U., "Ukraine: rivals compromise on Constitution", *Transition*, Vol. 2, No. 15, p. 36, 26 July 1996.

"Nation-building in Ukraine" (Collection of articles), *Transition*, Vol. 2, No. 18, p. 6, 6 September 1996.

Semsucenko J., "Der Verfassungsentwurf der Ukraine", *Recht in Ost und West*, Jahrg. 36, Heft 10, p. 289, 15 Oktober 1992.

Uzbekistan

Dailey E., "Uzbekistan: the human rights implications of an abuser government's improving relations with the international community", *Helsinki monitor*, Vol. 7, No. 2, p. 40, 1996.

Saidov A., "Le système juridique de l'Ouzbekistan: histoire et droit contemporain", *Revue internationale de droit comparé*, Année 44, No. 3, p. 703, 1995.

Sales agents for publications of the Council of Europe
Agents de vente des publications du Conseil de l'Europe

AUSTRALIA/AUSTRALIE
Hunter publications, 58A, Gipps Street
AUS-3066 COLLINGWOOD, Victoria
Fax: (61) 33 9 419 7154

AUSTRIA/AUTRICHE
Gerold und Co., Graben 31
A-1011 WIEN 1
Fax: (43) 1512 47 31 29

BELGIUM/BELGIQUE
La Librairie européenne SA
50, avenue A. Jonnart
B-1200 BRUXELLES 20
Fax: (32) 27 35 08 60

Jean de Lannoy
202, avenue du Roi
B-1060 BRUXELLES
Fax: (32) 25 38 08 41

CANADA
Renouf Publishing Company Limited
5369 Chemin Canotek Road
CDN-OTTAWA, Ontario, K1J 9J3
Fax: (1) 613 745 76 60

DENMARK/DANEMARK
Munksgaard
PO Box 2148
DK-1016 KØBENHAVN K
Fax: (45) 33 12 93 87

FINLAND/FINLANDE
Akateeminen Kirjakauppa
Keskuskatu 1, PO Box 218
SF-00381 HELSINKI
Fax: (358) 9 121 44 50

GERMANY/ALLEMAGNE
UNO Verlag
Poppelsdorfer Allee 55
D-53115 BONN
Fax: (49) 228 21 74 92

GREECE/GRÈCE
Librairie Kauffmann
Mavrokordatou 9, GR-ATHINAI 106 78
Fax: (30) 13 23 03 20

HUNGARY/HONGRIE
Euro Info Service
Magyarország
Margitsziget (Európa Ház),
H-1138 BUDAPEST
Fax: (36) 1 111 62 16
E-mail: euroinfo@mail.matav.hu

IRELAND/IRLANDE
Government Stationery Office
4-5 Harcourt Road, IRL-DUBLIN 2
Fax: (353) 14 75 27 60

ISRAEL/ISRAËL
ROY International
17 Shimon Hatrssi St.
PO Box 13056
IL-61130 TEL AVIV
Fax: (972) 3 546 1423
E-mail: royil@netvision.net.il

ITALY/ITALIE
Libreria Commissionaria Sansoni
Via Duca di Calabria, 1/1
Casella Postale 552, I-50125 FIRENZE
Fax: (39) 55 64 12 57

MALTA/MALTE
L. Sapienza & Sons Ltd
26 Republic Street
PO Box 36
VALLETTA CMR 01
Fax: (356) 233 621

NETHERLANDS/PAYS-BAS
InOr-publikaties, PO Box 202
NL-7480 AE HAAKSBERGEN
Fax: (31) 53 572 92 96

NORWAY/NORVÈGE
Akademika, A/S Universitetsbokhandel
PO Box 84, Blindern
N-0314 OSLO
Fax: (47) 22 85 30 53

POLAND/POLOGNE
Główna Księgarnia Naukowa im. B. Prusa
Krakowskie Przedmiescie 7
PL-00-068 WARSZAWA
Fax: (48) 22 26 64 49

PORTUGAL
Livraria Portugal
Rua do Carmo, 70
P-1200 LISBOA
Fax: (351) 13 47 02 64

SPAIN/ESPAGNE
Mundi-Prensa Libros SA
Castelló 37, E-28001 MADRID
Fax: (34) 15 75 39 98

Llibreria de la Generalitat
Rambla dels Estudis, 118
E-08002 BARCELONA
Fax: (34) 343 12 18 54

SWITZERLAND/SUISSE
Buchhandlung Heinimann & Co.
Kirchgasse 17, CH-8001 ZÜRICH
Fax: (41) 12 51 14 81

BERSY
Route du Manège 60, CP 4040
CH-1950 SION 4
Fax: (41) 27 203 73 32

UNITED KINGDOM/ROYAUME-UNI
HMSO, Agency Section
51 Nine Elms Lane
GB-LONDON SW8 5DR
Fax: (44) 171 873 82 00

**UNITED STATES and CANADA/
ÉTATS-UNIS et CANADA**
Manhattan Publishing Company
468 Albany Post Road
PO Box 850
CROTON-ON-HUDSON, NY 10520, USA
Fax: (1) 914 271 58 56

STRASBOURG
Librairie Kléber
Palais de l'Europe
F-67075 STRASBOURG Cedex
Fax: +33 (0)3 88 52 91 21

Council of Europe Publishing/Editions du Conseil de l'Europe
Council of Europe/Conseil de l'Europe
F-67075 Strasbourg Cedex
Tel. +33 (0)3 88 41 25 81 – Fax +33 (0)3 88 41 39 10 – E-mail: ce.publishing@seddoc.coe.fr

DISCARDED